VORWORT

Focus on Success PLUS 13 ist für Lernende an Fachoberschulen, Berufsoberschulen und Beruflichen Gymnasien konzipiert. Das Lehrwerk setzt einen erfolgreichen Abschluss der Jahrgangsstufe 12 (Fachhochschulreife/B2) voraus und führt gezielt zur allgemeinen sowie zur fachgebundenen Hochschulreife (B2+/C1).

Focus on Success PLUS 13 setzt die Vorgaben der KMK-Bildungsstandards für moderne Fremdsprachen sowie der neuen Generation kompetenzorientierter Lehrpläne für das Fach Englisch in Unterrichtseinheiten um und gewährleistet so die systematische Entwicklung der Kommunikativen Kompetenzen, der Interkulturellen Kompetenz, der Text- und Medienkompetenz sowie der Methodischen Kompetenz im Sinne eines vernetzten Lernens.

Das Lehrwerk besteht aus vier großen thematischen Einheiten (Units), bestehend aus jeweils vier Kapiteln. Durch die in jedem Kapitel angebotenen realitätsnahen Handlungssituationen zum Erwerb der vielschichtig vernetzten Kompetenzen und die zahlreichen prüfungsrelevanten Aufgabenstellungen ermöglicht **Focus on Success PLUS 13** einen lehrplangerechten Unterricht und bereitet umfassend auf die Abschlussprüfung vor.

Mit einem vielfältigen Angebot an authentischen Materialien werden die Lernenden dazu befähigt, gehörte, gesehene und gelesene Texte sowohl zu verstehen als auch selbst mündliche und schriftliche Äußerungen und Texte zu produzieren. Texte zu aktuellen Themen fördern das Leseverstehen, ansprechende Audio- und Videomaterialien trainieren das Hör-/Hörsehverstehen, vielfältige Bilder, Cartoons, Statistiken, Grafiken, Zitate etc. bieten Denkanstöße für Schreibanlässe mit realitätsnahem Situations- und Adressatenbezug. Die lebensnahen Diskussionsthemen dienen der Förderung der Sprechfertigkeit und der Vorbereitung auf die mündliche Gruppenprüfung.

Jede der vier Units beginnt mit einem Einstieg ins Thema, der den Lernenden einen Zugang und einen Überblick verschafft:

- **Focus:** Hinführung zum Thema durch visuelle Denk- und Sprechanlässe.
- **Words in Context:** Intensive Wortschatzerarbeitung mittels vielfältiger und gezielter Übungen anhand eines Textes, der den wichtigsten Themenwortschatz enthält.

Innerhalb jeder Unit behandeln vier Kapitel (A–D) verschiedene Aspekte des Hauptthemas, jeweils mit folgendem Aufbau:

- **Exploring the topic:** Im Kontext einer realistischen Situation befassen sich die Schüler/innen mit einem Text und seinem Informationsgehalt.
- **Testing Your Reading Skills:** Hier wird anhand prüfungsrelevanter Aufgaben zum Text das Leseverständnis trainiert.
- **Developing Your Language Skills:** Die Schüler/innen setzen sich mit lexikalischen und stilistischen Aspekten der im Text verwendeten Sprache auseinander. Zudem trainieren sie im thematischen Zusammenhang des Kapitels ihr Hör-/Sehverstehen.
- **Testing Your Writing and Speaking Skills:** Hier werden systematisch prüfungsrelevante sprachproduktive Kompetenzen trainiert.

Der Anhang, auf den in den Units verwiesen wird, enthält folgende Teile:

- **Files for group discussion**
- **Skills files:** Leitfaden zur Schulung/Förderung der Fähigkeiten Lesen, Schreiben, Hören und Sprechen.
- **Unit word list:** Während den Vokabelanmerkungen unter den Texten rein informative Funktion zukommt, enthält die Unit word list den Wortschatz, den die Schüler/innen lernen sollen, damit sie ihn in möglichst großem Umfang rezeptiv und zunehmend auch produktiv verwenden können. Daher empfiehlt es sich, mit dieser Liste zu lernen.
- **A–Z word list**

Nicht zu vergessen: Die **Umschlagklappen.** Sie enthalten griffbereit englischsprachige Landkarten sowie nützliche Wendungen fürs Diskutieren und Schreiben.

Das Team von Focus on Success PLUS 13 wünscht Ihnen mit diesem Lehrwerk viel Erfolg!

CONTENTS

CONTENTS

THE POWER OF LANGUAGE 1

FOCUS

The quiet world

Jeffrey McDaniel

In an effort to get people to look
into each other's eyes more,
and also to appease the mutes,
the government has decided
to allot each person exactly one hundred
and sixty-seven words, per day.

When the phone rings, I put it to my ear
without saying hello. In the restaurant
I point at chicken noodle soup.
I am adjusting well to the new way.

Late at night, I call my long distance lover,
proudly say *I only used fifty-nine today.*
I saved the rest for you.

When she doesn't respond,
I know she's used up all her words,
so I slowly whisper *I love you*
thirty-two and a third times.
After that, we just sit on the line
and listen to each other breathe.

Read the poem above. Then discuss the following questions with a partner.

1 How would you cope if you were only allowed to use 167 words per day?
2 Why do you think the government came to its decision?
3 a When do you think this poem was published? Find out if you were right.
  b Does the publication date surprise you? Explain your answer.
4 This unit is entitled "The power of language". How do you think the poem reflects the topic of this unit?

Language and communication

02

01

"One cannot not communicate" (Paul Watzlawik, Austrian philosopher and psychologist). The moment we share some space with another human being, we send out messages and the other person receives and deciphers them.

Language – the use of words and phrases – is, of course, one powerful means of communication, but it is not the only one. Silence is another one. Your silence in the face of a communication partner who expects you to take notice of what he or she says and to address his or her views may be understood as indifference or even hostility. If, however, the other person is busy focusing on something important in their life, your silence may come across as consideration, respect, empathy or love.

In addition to words and silence, there are further means of communication. Body language, posture, gestures, facial expressions or, in written communication, handwriting or typeface, layout, decorative drawings, pictures or, these days, emoticons – everything adds to the message that we convey in words and phrases.

Communication is successful if what you want to say is received in the same way in which you intend it to be understood. If you use a common language, like your mother tongue, or even a foreign language acquired later in life, communication is likely to be successful; but it is not a guarantee. Words and phrases have different meanings in different cultures: The question "Would you mind opening the window?" can be *just* a question, but it may also be meant as a request or a command. Communication is an incredibly complex process, which is often fuzzy, vague and ambiguous. Thus it can lead to misunderstandings.

People in jobs where successful communication is essential must have a good command of their first language as well as of at least one other language, first and foremost English. English is often called the "lingua franca" of our days and rightly so, since, due to historical reasons, it can be used practically everywhere in the world. But there are large parts of the world where a command of Spanish, Arabic or Chinese would make communication even more successful. Apart from language knowledge, people who communicate across countries need to have cultural awareness, i.e. an awareness of the fact that both the language and behaviour you are used to can cause problems elsewhere. For this reason the global players in business and industry usually provide intercultural training for their more senior employees so that they can work abroad or in international teams at home more effectively and, in the end, more profitably.

People who are aware of the way language and communication work are very likely to be good and effective communicators; but they are also potentially dangerous. Language and communication can serve a political purpose and be used to deliberately hurt, manipulate or brainwash people. Since time immemorial, great orators from Cicero to Barack Obama have used every possible rhetorical device to create a powerful effect and so convince their audiences, for good or bad, to strengthen social cohesion and to foster solidarity, or to marginalize and ostracize groups of people. With the development of mass media, advertisers and marketers joined the politicians in the art of persuasion. And the era of social media has created influencers telling people what they should like or buy, as well as hate mail writers and troll factories spreading fake news that is able to destroy individual lives, families, economies and even political systems. In this climate, the politically correct use of language, for instance the avoidance of racist or sexist language, has become an issue.

The complexity of communication may cause problems of understanding and manipulation, but it is also the basis of a rich culture: poetry, drama, film scripts, speeches, stand-up comedy – all these works of art would not exist without the vagueness and ambiguity of human communication, or at least they would be far less enjoyable.

(645 words)

Working with words

1 Fill the gaps in the following sentences with a word that belongs to the same word family as the one from the text given in brackets.

1. When people gain a large following on social media they become very ▬. (INFLUENCER)
2. In some messaging apps, the pictures or videos that get sent disappear once the ▬ has seen them. (RECEIVE)
3. Social media can offer ▬ youngsters the opportunity to raise issues they are interested in. (MARGINALIZE)
4. The ▬ power of influencers will increase over the next few years, so that social media stars will become the new celebrities. (PERSUASION)

2 Translate the following sentences into English, using expressions from the given lines in the text.

1. Die Botschaften, die gute Redner aussenden, sind oft einfach. *(lines 11 and 33)*
2. Große Reden dienen dem Zweck, die Zuhörer von einem bestimmten Standpunkt zu überzeugen, indem sie sie eher emotional als rational ansprechen. *(lines 6 and 32)*
3. Jemand, der das Reden gut beherrscht, ist der ehemalige US-Präsident Barack Obama. *(line 31)*
4. In ihrer Rede hat die Präsidentin die Europäische Union dazu aufgefordert, den sozialen Zusammenhalt in den Mitgliedsländern zu stärken. *(lines 34 and 35)*
5. Das Selbstvertrauen des Redners wirkte wie Arroganz. *(line 8)*

3 Which word or expression (A, B, C or D) fits into the numbered gaps in the text below?

Gap 1	**A** common language	**B** mother tongue	**C** foreign language	**D** first language
Gap 2	**A** postures	**B** gestures	**C** expressions	**D** handwriting
Gap 3	**A** send	**B** receive	**C** decipher	**D** address
Gap 4	**A** language knowledge	**B** cultural awareness	**C** intercultural training	**D** rhetorical device

English is the ▬[1] of business people in the former British colonies of India and South Africa. And yet, when Indian and South African business executives meet, misunderstandings may occur. There are certain ▬[2] that a South African might make that could cause problems because an Indian might not be able to ▬[3] them. So, employers should think of giving their executives some ▬[4] before they send them abroad.

4 **a** Which words can be used together with the keywords from the text? There is always only one word or expression (A,B,C or D) that does not collocate.

1. indifference:	**A** show	**B** to (sb./sth.)	**C** a matter of	**D** point of
2. hostility:	**A** arouse	**B** for (sb./sth.)	**C** outright	**D** face
3. respect:	**A** mutual	**B** earn	**C** hold	**D** for (sb./sth.)
4. empathy:	**A** suffer	**B** emotional	**C** with (sb./sth.)	**D** lack of

b Form five sentences, one for each keyword, using one of the correct collocations. The sentences should be about a public figure that you all know.

1

A GLOBAL LANGUAGE(S)

Exploring the topic

SITUATION

Many of you have been learning English for several years now, and so you all know how important this one particular language is on the world stage. But professional career advisors, for instance, see the need for those who want to be successful in our globalized world to learn at least two other foreign languages. You decide to research the topic of global language and write about it in a blog about foreign-language learning, as you want to share your personal conclusions drawn from your existing and newly gained knowledge.

1 Get together in small groups and discuss the following questions. The maps on these two pages may help you.

- **What is a global language?**
- **How did other languages before English become global languages?**
- **How did English become today's global language?**
- **Is the dominance of English a good thing for the world?**
- **What are the chances of English remaining the dominant world language?**

Make notes on your discussion.

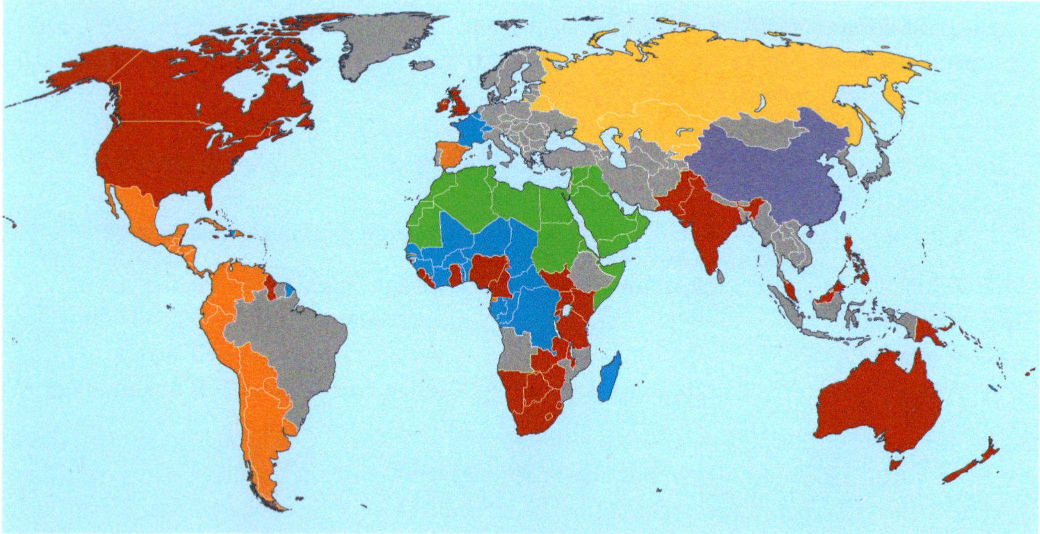

Some official languages of the world:

English, Spanish, Arabic, French, Russian, Mandarin Chinese

For countries having two of the languages above as official languages, the one with the most speakers is shown.

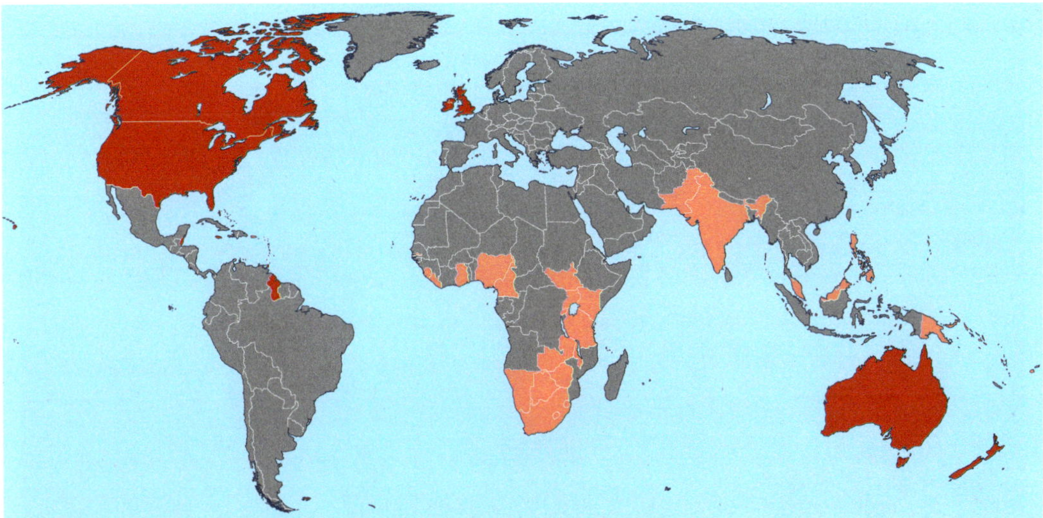

English is the first language of the majority of the population.

English is the official language or one of the official languages.

2 **Read the following text and compare the information given there with the notes you made during your discussion in task 1. Find passages in the text that confirm or contradict your notes.**

GLOBAL ENGLISH

A The development of English as a global language is one of the most remarkable phenomena of the late 20th and early 21st centuries. For the first time in the history of human society, a single language has become sufficiently universal that it can be used as a global lingua franca for communication between speakers of many languages. […]

B Although Global English is largely a product of economic globalization and very recent developments in communications technology (and indeed has helped accelerate both), the wider roots of English as a world language lie much further in the past. Some point to the first English colonies in Wales and Ireland in the 12th century, or to the late 17th century when English-speaking settlements were established in North America and the slave trade brought cheap labour from Africa. But it was largely the British colonial expansion in the 19th century which helped establish the large communities in which English now serves as a second language – in West and East Africa, South and South-East Asia.

C New varieties of English – often referred to as New Englishes – quickly emerged from contact with local languages. Indeed, by the end of the nineteenth century there was concern that these New Englishes were diverging so much from native-speaker varieties that English would become a group of mutually unintelligible languages – in the same way as Spanish, French and Italian evolved from Latin. […]

The Linguistic Nature of Global English

D […] The use of English continues to diverge in many new, largely uncharted, ways. One major domain of Global English lies within

38 uncharted: *unbekannt*
39 domain: *Gebiet, Bereich*

the many dispersed specialist communities – from air traffic control to microbiology to international finance. […] And improved communications are encouraging new forms of social networking which allow individuals to stay in touch simultaneously with friends, family and work colleagues with different language backgrounds.

E The evidence points to a growing tolerance of multiple standards in English and growing flexibility and fluidity in the use of English by global citizens. In this context, what are the mechanisms for maintaining the effectiveness of English as an international language?

F First, there is a principle of mutual intelligibility. […] Speakers of Global English can happily carry over linguistic features from their first languages provided they do not endanger intelligibility. At the same time, native-speaker features which cause problems for learners and which are not essential for international intelligibility can be safely disregarded. In other words, it is not necessary to sound like a native speaker in order to be understood around the world, and speakers of Global English do not have to give up their existing identities. For example, research has shown that a "correct" articulation of "th" may be the mark of a native speaker, but is unimportant in Global English. On the other hand, the distinction between short and long vowels (e.g. the difference between "sit" and "seat") remains crucial to intelligibility.

G Second, there are pragmatic strategies used by any skilled cross-cultural communicator which need to be adopted even by native speakers if they wish to be understood in lingua franca contexts. For example, using highly idiomatic language should be avoided, as should appeals to very specific cultural knowledge. Many native speakers, unfortunately, tend to speak more colloquially and informally when they want to make things clearer. However, in lingua franca contexts more formal language may actually be more comprehensible. […]

The Wave of Global English to Come

H […] English will cease to be a foreign language for many, perhaps most, of the world's citizens as it becomes repositioned as a "basic skill", to be learned by primary school children alongside other 21st century skills in Information Technology. […] We have entered a period in world history, unprecedented and probably unrepeatable, when children throughout formal education – from early primary school to college and university – are all learning beginner or intermediate level English. […] But looking further ahead, this wave of learners may subside almost as quickly as it came. If the project to make English a second language for the world's primary school children is successful, a new generation of English-knowing children will grow up who will not need English lessons in the future. As this generation of children move through the education system, secondary school children will be expected to start learning curriculum subjects such as maths and science through the medium of English. Indeed, this is already happening in many countries.

The Politics of Global English

I […] Undoubtedly, there has been an economic advantage for English speakers during recent decades. Individual native speakers have found themselves with a skill much in demand overseas. Multinationals based in English-speaking countries have found it easier to outsource manufacturing and services to parts of the world with cheap labour. But Global English has not arisen because of a conspiracy between English-speaking governments or multinationals. Learning English is now seen as being of economic benefit to individuals and national economies in every part of the world.

J In fact, the continuing spread of English may no longer be in the economic and political interests of English-speaking countries. Universities across the world are now able to attract international students who might otherwise have gone to English-speaking countries by teaching their courses through the medium of English. And in future, monolingual English-speaking graduates will find it difficult to compete, even in their own countries, with job applicants from other countries who speak several languages – including English – fluently, who are more internationally mobile and more experienced in intercultural communication.

K For many centuries, Latin served as a lingua franca between educated elites in Europe. Global English may be the new global Latin but just as the use of Latin gradually faded away, so Global English may not prove to be a permanent phenomenon. It took centuries for Global English to develop and, like Latin, it may take centuries for its influence to decline. The global linguistic future is already looking more complex. Language learners in some parts of the world are already queuing for classes in Chinese, Spanish and Arabic.

(988 words)

Source: David Graddol, the website of the Open University, 28.07.2005

73 pragmatic strategies: *nützliche Strategien*
89 become repositioned as: *(hier) neu definiert werden als*

3 **Think about what you have learned from the maps and the text and draw a personal conclusion for your future as a language learner. Make some notes that you can use in your blog later.**

Testing your reading skills

1 Short-answer questions

Answer the following questions. You may use words from the text. The letter at the end of each question indicates the paragraph in which you will find the answer.

1	Which recent processes have helped turn English into a global language and have, as a result, also gained momentum? (2 aspects)	B
2	What may be hard to preserve if the different "Englishes" become even more different?	E
3	What should native speakers of English stop doing in order to be better understood by foreigners? *(2 aspects)*	G
4	What have speakers of English gained from their knowledge of the language?	I
5	Judging from what happened to Latin, what may Global English not turn out to be?	K

2 Mediation Englisch – Deutsch

Beantworten Sie folgende Fragen auf Deutsch. Der Buchstabe am Ende der jeweiligen Frage gibt an, in welchem Absatz die Antwort zu finden ist.

1	Welche Gefahr für die englische Sprache sahen die Menschen im 19. Jahrhundert heraufziehen?	C
2	Wie könnte sich die Tatsache, dass so viele Schülerinnen und Schüler in der Grundschule schon Englisch lernen, auf das Fach in höheren Klassenstufen auswirken?	H
3	Welche negativen Konsequenzen könnte die weitere Verbreitung von Englisch als Weltsprache in den englischsprachigen Ländern selbst haben für ■ die Universitäten? ■ die jungen Menschen?	J

3 Multiple matching

In which paragraph (A–K) do you find the following aspect or element? Two aspects/elements are not in the text at all.

1	ways in which the global success of English may not always benefit English-speaking countries and individuals
2	the historical reasons why so many people in the world speak English as their mother tongue
3	reasons why English is so popular with young learners worldwide
4	the effect of the global spread of English on the English language itself
5	the reason why political leaders have promoted the spread of the English language
6	the fact that English may not continue to be the global language in the long run
7	features of English that are or are not essential for a non-native to master

Developing your language skills

1 Giving a short presentation

Get together in groups of four and choose one country (check the map on page 11) where English is not the native but an official language. Research the history of English in the country and put a presentation together on how English came to be the official language there. Also, try to find out what people in the country think of English as their official language.

2 Improving your listening skills

03

When the British Library in London staged an exhibition on the English language in 2010, Prof. David Crystal gave an introductory speech. David Crystal has written many books on the English language, including its history. In this excerpt from his speech he talks about the story of global English.
While listening, follow the words of the gapped summary below and fill the gaps with the correct words from David Crystal's lecture. (One word per gap.)

The biggest explosion of the number of people speaking English around the world happened within the last 50 years. The fact that a ■[1] of the world's population speak English right now gives the impression that English is today's lingua franca. However, lingua franca is the wrong term, as it suggests all these English speakers use one single ■[2] of the language.

As you look around the world you find many "Englishes" – American, Nigerian, Dutch, German, etc. As people make English their language they ■[3] it. That's why these Englishes differ in their use of grammatical structures and words and in their pronunciation from the original British English. An example is ■[4] English. Unlike in "good" British English, here the ing-form of verbs like *think* or *remember* in the present tense are common – and this usage is spreading around the world. It has found its way into American advertising, for instance. So it is not so simple any more to say that this kind of English is ■[5].

Nobody knows where the English language is going in the future, but one thing is certain: As global English ■[6] around the world, it is diversifying more and more. Thus people ask themselves the following question: Will English split up into varieties so different from each other that they may become ■[7] to other speakers of English in the world?

The same thing happened 1000 years ago to vulgar Latin which split into the Romance languages of Spanish, Italian, Portuguese, etc. Like those Romance languages, English is now not a single language, but a ■[8] of languages, consisting, for instance, of Singlish, which is spoken in ■[9] and is a mixture of mainly English and Chinese.

As this exhibition shows, the distant future of English is unclear. Nobody can predict what its status will be in 1000 years' time. The status of English as a global language was achieved through the political power of the British ■[10], the global power of the USA, the scientific and economic power of those leading the Industrial Revolution, as well as the ■[11] power of English in the 20th century. Yet if the power of the speakers of English ■[12], another people's language will dominate one day – Spanish, Chinese, Arabic or some other language.

In the foreseeable future, however, English is likely to keep its status, because it is still seen as essential to ■[13] ■[14], not least by the Chinese.

3 Improving your vocabulary

Below, there is a text on language learning written by a German student. It is grammatically correct but would not get a really good mark for language use, because the language is rather simple and repetitive and sometimes it sounds a bit "German". Improve the style by changing the highlighted passages with the help of phrases from the text "Global English" (page 11). The letters on the right show you in which section/paragraph of the text you need to search for the phrase. You may have to adapt the words in the text to fit the sentence structure.

A precise, effective, varied and idiomatic use of words is the most important feature of good, advanced writing.

I don't see why I should learn French or Spanish or any other language in addition to English,
today's lingua franca. Speaking English is a skill many employers want you to have [1] because 1 I
they want their employees to be prepared to go abroad [2]. 2 J
Of course, I do admire people who speak more than one language without problems [3]. 3 J
I have a lot of respect for their decision to learn several languages. But I think it could
really be that they [4] just do it for themselves, because they like it, and not because it is 4 G
very important [5] to be successful in our world. 5 F
My English is not bad, but it is not too good either. I don't see this as a problem, as people
usually think it is okay if I make [6] mistakes, as long as I remain understandable [7]. Therefore, 6 E
if I think about what my future will be like [8], I am not worried. 7 F
And anyway, I do speak another language, apart from German and English. It's called 8 H
Franconian.

4 Writing an entry in a blog

Go through the notes you made earlier on your future as a language learner and turn them into an entry in your blog titled "The role of languages in my future life".
With task 3 in mind, go through your text again and try to improve it before posting it.

Testing your writing and speaking skills

1 Mediation Deutsch – Englisch

In einem Seminar im Studiengang International Business Management wird die Bedeutung der guten sprachlichen Verständigung bei internationalen Geschäften thematisiert. Dabei taucht die Frage auf, wie es anderen Sprachen als der englischen auf dem internationalen Markt geht. Sie haben die Aufgabe, die Stellung der deutschen Sprache in der Welt zu recherchieren, und Sie lesen dazu das folgende Interview mit dem Linguisten Ulrich Ammon.

Verfassen Sie unter Verwendung der Information aus dem Interview ein kurzes informatives Papier in ca. 150 Wörtern, das Sie im Seminar vorlegen können. Gehen Sie dabei auf die folgenden Aspekte ein:

- **die Position des Deutschen im Vergleich zu anderen Weltsprachen**
- **Gründe für das gestiegene Interesse an der deutschen Sprache**
- **ein Beispiel dafür, dass in Deutschland das Bewusstsein dafür fehlt, dass Deutsch als internationale Verständigungssprache gepflegt werden sollte**

Deutsche Sprache ist deutlich attraktiver geworden

Welt am Sonntag: Sie beschäftigen sich mit der Stellung der deutschen Sprache in der Welt. Wo steht sie denn?

Ammon: Wenn man die Zahlen der Muttersprachler vergleicht, so liegt Deutsch im weltweiten Vergleich auf Platz zehn. Interessanter ist aber die Zahl derjenigen, die Deutsch als Fremdsprache erlernen. Da liegt Deutsch auf Rang vier hinter Englisch, Französisch und Chinesisch, dicht gefolgt vom Spanischen. Man kann sagen, dass Deutsch in den letzten fünf bis zehn Jahren wieder deutlich attraktiver geworden ist.

Welt am Sonntag: Woran liegt das?

Ammon: Wenn ein Land wirtschaftlich stark ist, dann gibt es ein großes Interesse, die Sprache zu lernen. […]

Welt am Sonntag: Welche Bedeutung hat eine Sprache denn für wirtschaftliche Beziehungen, wenn ohnehin alle Geschäfte auf Englisch abgewickelt werden?

Ammon: Gewiss, Verhandlungen werden auf Englisch geführt. Aber sowohl erste Kontakte als auch nachhaltige Geschäftsbeziehungen erfordern noch immer tiefer gehende Sprachkenntnisse. […] Leider sind die Zusammenhänge von Sprache und internationalen Beziehungen nur unzureichend erforscht […]. Und so erkennt auch die Politik nicht, warum es wichtig wäre, wenn Deutsch in größerem Umfang gelernt würde.

Ulrich Ammon

Welt am Sonntag: Erklären Sie es uns.

Ammon: Es liegt auf der Hand, dass der, der die Sprache gut kann, sich viel leichter integriert. Wir fragen uns oft, warum qualifizierte Leute aus Indien lieber in angelsächsische Länder auswandern als nach Deutschland. Bei den Erklärungsversuchen bleibt die Sprache als Motiv meistens unterbelichtet, dabei ist sie von zentraler Bedeutung. […]

Welt am Sonntag: Aber der deutsche Staat gibt doch viel Geld für Bildungseinrichtungen wie das Goethe-Institut oder die Deutsche Welle aus, die auch die Aufgabe haben, die deutsche Sprache in die Welt hinauszutragen.

Ammon: Das ist richtig. Da wird auch viel geleistet. […] Aber insgesamt könnte man seitens des Auswärtigen Amts der eigenen Sprache […] mehr Gewicht geben als bisher. Und was die Deutsche Welle angeht, so ist deren Hauptaufgabe, über Deutschland zu informieren. Deutschsprecher im Ausland beklagen sich immer wieder darüber, dass nur ein Drittel der Sendezeit in Deutsch ausgestrahlt wird. Und das oft zu ungünstigen Zeiten. […]

Welt am Sonntag: Könnten nicht auch die im Ausland lebenden Deutschen ihren Teil dazu beitragen? Der Verein der Deutschen Sprache beklagt regelmäßig, dass die Deutschen ihre Sprache zu wenig achten und pflegen. […]

Ammon: […] Man muss bei diesem Thema immer aufpassen, dass man nicht in den Nationalismus abgleitet. Es geht nicht darum, andere Länder unterzubuttern. Aber man muss auch nicht übertreiben mit der Rücksichtnahme. Kürzlich las ich in einer Regionalzeitung von einem Besuch einer englischen Schülergruppe in einer Schule am Niederrhein. Diese englischen Schüler lernten alle Deutsch, ihr Besuch sollte dazu dienen, die Sprache zu vertiefen. In der Zeitung wurde dann ein deutscher Lehrer zitiert, der voller Stolz berichtete, die Gäste hätten ihr Deutsch gar nicht gebraucht, weil sich alle auf Englisch unterhalten konnten. Da wurde offensichtlich etwas missverstanden.

Source: Andreas Fasel, Die Welt, *25.01.2015*

2 Group discussion

Situation: According to statistics, German students are not as good at English as is commonly believed. Therefore the Federal Ministry of Education has invited a selection of students from different parts of Germany to conduct a series of discussions in English on the following topic:

What should and can be done to improve German students' standard of English?

You are a group of Bavarian students preparing for a discussion of this topic in Berlin. The suggestions to be discussed can be found on page 142.

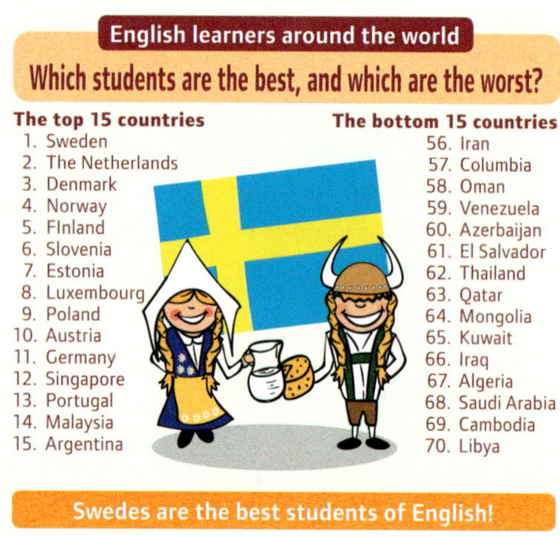

Preparation phase: Think about how much English and what kind of English a German needs to master in order to keep up with the rest of the world.

Presentation phase: Present your suggestion and your arguments in favour of it to the group.

Interaction phase: Discuss all the different measures that are suggested. Agree on one which you think would work best and is most feasible.

Optional *(if you have time left at the end of the discussion):* Discuss which modern language (e.g. French, Spanish, Russian, Arabic, Chinese) should be taught as a second foreign language to students aiming for a university-entrance qualification *(Abitur).*

Exploring the topic

SITUATION

You are studying at a university in Europe which has students from all around Europe and which stages regular workshops on intercultural learning in English. You decide to learn more about the issue of intercultural learning in order to be able to submit an essay as an application for such a workshop and, after being admitted, you write the summary of a short talk you have to give at the workshop.

1 Discuss the following questions with a partner.

1 Which of the following adjectives do you think would be used by foreigners to characterize
- the Germans?
- the British?
- the Americans?

arrogant, organized, clean, patriotic, tactile, punctual, efficient, relaxed, individualistic, direct, humorous, polite, xenophobic, self-confident, disciplined, nationalistic, helpful, shy, nostalgic, industrious, open, boisterous, tolerant

2 Would you say that the "German" characteristics apply to you and the Germans you know?

3 What situations can you imagine where different national characteristics may cause problems in the world of business?

2 Many international companies offer cultural awareness training, especially to employees who are being sent to work in other countries or who work with international clients. They need to know about possible pitfalls in dealing with people from different cultural backgrounds, as misunderstandings can be costly. Cultural awareness trainers often work with so-called "critical incidents" – examples of cultural clashes.

Study the critical incidents on page 20 and, together with a partner, try to work out what the actual problems are.

CRITICAL INCIDENTS

A Sales representatives from Germany and Britain are in a difficult negotiation. Things are getting tense. Franz Bauer sits upright and is disturbed as Jim Banks relaxes in his chair. Franz Bauer feels that Jim is not taking the negotiation seriously. Jim feels that Herr Bauer is getting more and more aggressive.

B A US manager reports problems with Japanese staff. "I asked them how the project was going and, of course, not much has been done: I was suspicious when they didn't even look me in the eyes," he said.

C A German manager working in the US subsidiary of an insurance company was pleased to find that he had an excellent secretary. After yet another piece of work had been completed long before the deadline he went up to her, tapped her on the shoulder and said, "Pat, thanks again. It really is such a help that you are here." She complained to his boss.

D Julio, an Argentinian student who is keen to improve his English is attending a course in Business English at a German university. He often stays behind class to ask Jim Ford, the lecturer, a native speaker from Britain, some questions. When Julio approaches, Mr Ford looks uneasy and moves away. Julio wonders whether Mr Ford doesn't like him.

E Magda Sapinska [...] has been sent to Hamburg to work with the German partner company. The German office is very impressed with her performance and would like her to stay on for another six months. Helmut Stauss, the German manager of the Hamburg office asks her to ring Warsaw to see what they think. The telephone conversation is in Polish. Although Helmut Stauss can't speak Polish, it quickly seems clear to him that Magda Sapinska is having a row with the Warsaw Office. When she puts the phone down he says to her, "Magda, sorry to have got you into this mess – I hope we haven't made you unpopular in Warsaw." Magda is puzzled and says, "What are you talking about? Everything's fine – Warsaw has given us the okay."

F Researchers looking into intercultural communication asked an Italian and a Japanese businessman to find out particular information from each other. They interviewed them separately after the conversation. The Italian said, "He seemed like a nice guy, but he never really said anything"; the Japanese said, "He was very friendly but he never gave me the chance to speak."

G A German manager working in Thailand is unhappy that his secretary regularly arrives at work at least 30 minutes, sometimes as much as an hour, late for work. He knows that the traffic in Bangkok is bad, but this is getting ridiculous – one morning when she arrives he explodes in front of the others in the busy office, and then takes her aside and tells her that if she cannot get to work on time she may risk losing her job. She hands in her resignation.

H A group of German academics were meeting for a Friday afternoon seminar. A paper was presented and then there was a heated discussion. A US guest professor was disturbed by the atmosphere and had the impression that the professors didn't like each other at all. She was surprised that after the discussion had ended they left the room in a good mood wishing each other a good weekend.

I A German businessman in Saudi Arabia is keen to get an important deal agreed on. He has a tight schedule and can't afford to waste any time. Frustration is increasing as he has to wait for ages to get an appointment with his Saudi partner, meetings never start on time and when they do begin there are frequent interruptions, with people coming in to get papers signed. The Saudi partner even answers phone calls while the German is in the room.

Source: Robert Gibson, Intercultural Business Communication, *Cornelsen, Berlin 2000*

EXPLANATIONS

1	A problem of how different cultures see body distance. Private space is valued highly in the Northern hemisphere; in the Southern hemisphere people get quite close and touch each other when they talk.
2	A problem of "shame". Being told off in front of others means losing face in East Asian cultures.
3	A problem of focus in a discussion. Well-educated Germans tend to be topic- and task-oriented, and if the topic is controversial, they argue in a non-personal way. In Anglo-American cultures discussions usually have a personal element to them.
4	A problem of eye contact. In the Western world eye contact is interpreted as openness and honesty; in the Eastern world it is read as disrespect.
5	A problem of body language and how it is interpreted. Germanic cultures associate concentration and seriousness with an upright position. In Anglo-American cultures a relaxed position signals an attempt to deflate a potentially critical situation.
6	A problem of interpreting the non-verbal features of communication, like pronunciation, intonation and gesturing. To some people, Slavic languages can sound hard and unfriendly. So if they don't understand what is being said, they may misinterpret a conversation as an argument.
7	A problem of politically correct behaviour, especially in the USA. Since women have become more aware of the way they are treated by men at work, they have become more sensitive. Touching a female colleague or employee may be interpreted as sexual harassment.
8	A problem of different time concepts. The Western world is predominantly monochronic: Things are done one at a time. The Arab world is predominantly polychronic: People are used to doing things simultaneously.
9	A problem of turn-taking in a conversation. In Western cultures you are expected to find your own way into a conversation; in Eastern cultures people expect to be invited into a conversation.

8 monochronic: *bestrebt, immer eine Sache nach der anderen möglichst effektiv zu erledigen*
8 polychronic: *fähig und gewöhnt, mehrere Dinge gleichzeitig zu erledigen*

3 Now match the incidents (A–I) on page 20 with their explanations (1–9) on page 21.

4 Read the text "Culture Shock: How to Speak Business Anywhere" on page 22 and find passages that confirm the critical incidents and their explanations from task 2.

Culture Shock: How to Speak Business Anywhere

Telephone shock

An abrupt response to a simple telephone greeting changed the trajectory of Gayle Cotton's career. When Cotton began her career working at the United Nations in Geneva in the early 90s, she answered a routine phone call with a polite, "Hello, how are you?" Surprisingly, the person on the other end of the call was annoyed. "He answered, 'That's none of your business. Now what I want to talk about is…'," recalled Cotton, now president of Circles Of Excellence Inc, which offers training and coaching programs to global clients from its offices in the US and Europe. It was nothing personal; the caller, a Swiss German, wanted to get down to business […]. In an increasingly globalised workplace, where team members might be spread across continents and clients spread even more widely, communicating proper cultural norms can be the difference between working well together and securing a deal – or watching things crumble.

Crossed wires, burned ground

Many professionals err in assuming it is enough to speak a common tongue when speaking with people from other cultures. In fact, spoken language is only 30% of communication, says Denis LeClerc, professor of cross-cultural communication at Thunderbird School of Global Management in Arizona, USA. How people say things, how they listen, body language and how they perceive authority all influence interactions. Not recognising those vital factors can result in crossed wires and serious miscommunication. […] LeClerc says he finds people focus on do's and don'ts, such as not showing the soles of your shoes in Muslim country and how to shake hands. Those behaviours, he says, are easy enough to teach. But communicating seamlessly across cultures requires a "chameleon" approach, he said. That requires being ok with changing who you are and how you think from a cultural standpoint – and also being comfortable with being a little uncomfortable.

Here is what you should know to effectively communicate across certain cultures. Keep in mind that cultural traits should never be taken as absolutes. […] While a particular communication style may be fairly common in a certain culture, individual people, businesses and industries also have their own styles.

Asian countries: indirect and hierarchical

Respect and honour are prevailing themes that influence typical Asian communication style. This quickly becomes apparent in speaking patterns. There is a strong emphasis on listening, and many Asian business people, following what they are taught growing up, will wait for a sentence to end before responding, then also wait for a couple of beats of silence before talking. […] Business people from Asian countries tend to be stronger negotiators compared with managers from Western cultures, said Cotton. That's because they wait to speak – which often throws off the people on the other side of the table – and they reveal very little with facial expressions and body language. […]

Asian cultures also are the least direct cultures in the world, said [Erin] Meyer, author of *The Culture Map*. […] Open criticism, negative feedback and the word "no" are almost always avoided, because they all are considered highly disrespectful. "Maybe is a no," Cotton said. Asian cultures tend to be very hierarchical. Authority is highly respected and meetings that straddle hierarchy are not encouraged. For instance, vice presidents meet with vice presidents or their equivalent, but rarely a senior executive. […]

Latin countries: small talk and relationships

In Latin countries, including Italy and Spain, family is priority – and business is also very relationship-focused. Meaningful small talk is a necessity and something people engage in freely and enjoy, asking in earnest about families and weekend activities. […] Latin countries also have a great respect for authority figures and defer to them. One Swedish person working in Mexico […] realised he needed to change his communication approach after he voiced disagreement in meetings – intending to contribute to the conversation – and the group would go silent. […]

United States: direct outcomes, direct talk

Independence and personal initiative characterise US communication style, Cotton said, because US work culture is very outcome-oriented. People of varying status are given the authority to make decisions, and they are expected to speak up. […] US communication style also prioritises clarity, Meyer said. […] Feedback is given in a very distinct way in the US, too, […] A negative is often heavily sandwiched between multiple positives. Meyer tells a story of a French employee, recently transplanted to the US. Her boss informed her that her performance needed to change. But because he delivered the negative feedback by expounding first on what he appreciated about her work – and she was generally unaccustomed to receiving positive feedback – she floated out of the meeting […].

United Kingdom: soft criticisms

Even though English is a common language, there are clear distinctions in communication style between the UK and the US. In general, communication in the UK is more hierarchical, conservative and indirect. In particular, the prevailing UK communication style involves a lot of "downgraders", words or phrases that introduce criticism in order to soften it, Meyer said. She recalls a German whose British boss suggested he "think about doing this differently". The employee thought about it, and decided not to do it. "He was surprised later when his boss chewed him out for insubordination," she said. In many Asian cultures, criticism or suggestions are generally not voiced outright. In the UK they are expressed, but obliquely when compared with American, German and Scandinavian cultures. For example, "that is an original point of view" or "could you consider some other options?" all are cloaked British negatives […].

Germany, Scandinavia and the Netherlands: precise and pointed

Germanic, Scandinavian and Dutch communication styles can be traced to the languages themselves, which are very precise and direct, Cotton said. […] These cultures also tend to be very objective. When topics are presented, they want facts and research as backup. […] The Law of Jante, which is little known outside of Scandinavia, offers 10 rules to live by such as "you're not to think you're anything special". The law, which emphasises the collective over the individual, is pervasive in Scandinavia, according to Meyer. As a result, the region is likely the most egalitarian place in the world, she said. In fact, Meyer says, it's often difficult for an outsider to pick out the boss when watching people in a meeting in Scandinavian countries. (1052 words)

Source: Karina Martinez-Carter, the website of the BBC, 07. 01. 2014

03 trajectory: *Laufbahn*
61 beat: *(hier) Moment*
78 to straddle hierarchy: *(hier) Hierarchien außer Acht lassen*
108 to transplant sb.: *jdn. versetzen*
111 to expound on sth.: *etw. ganz genau erläutern*
128 to chew sb. out (AE): *jdn. zurechtweisen*
136 cloaked: *versteckt*
136 negatives: *(hier) Kritik*

4 **Reflect on which of the national ways of doing things you were aware of before you started on this topic and which ones were new to you. Also, reflect on the question of whether this knowledge might be of use to you one day. Note down your thoughts and ideas.**

Testing your reading skills

1 Multiple matching

Match the names with the descriptions. Some will fit more than one description. There are, however, two descriptions that do not fit anybody.

Names	Gayle Cotton	Denis LeClerc	Erin Meyer

DESCRIPTIONS	
1	pursued an academic career
2	talks about a culture where everyone regardless of status is expected to say something
3	believes some languages are more precise than others and that this affects communication style
4	supports her views with the experiences of individual businesspeople
5	teaches a foreign language at an elementary school
6	completely changed her line of work
7	warns that language knowledge is of limited value for people working abroad
8	gives intercultural coaching for free in developing countries

2 Gapped summary

Copy the summary of lines 1–52 of the text and fill the gaps with appropriate words from the corresponding passages of the text (one word per gap). Do not make any changes. Please also provide the number of the line in which you found the word or expression.

Gayle Cotton discovered that cultural coaching might be a growing market, when her friendliness on the phone led to a rather ___[1] (line ___) reproach on the part of the caller. In the world of global business, awareness of cultural differences can be instrumental in negotiating and concluding a good ___[2] (line ___). According to Denis LeClerc, it is not enough to speak a foreign client's language. There are other ___[3] (line ___) at play, such as the dos and don'ts of everyday conduct, if misunderstandings are to be avoided. But cross-cultural coaches need to ___[4] ___[5] (line ___) more important issues than those. In order to interact ___[6] (line ___) with other cultures, business people have to accept that they are bound to encounter situations where they will feel ___[7] (line ___). Even if they have learned about the most common ___[8] (line ___) of a certain culture, they will still have to understand the ___[9] (line ___) ways in which their business partners communicate.

3 Mediation Englisch – Deutsch

Beantworten Sie folgende Fragen zum Rest des Textes (Zeilen 53–155) auf Deutsch.

1	Was verschafft asiatischen Geschäftsleuten potenziell einen Vorteil in Geschäftsverhandlungen?
2	Warum wurde es bei den Terminen des schwedischen Geschäftsmanns in Mexiko oft plötzlich still?
3	In welcher Stimmung befand sich die französische Angestellte nach dem Gespräch mit ihrem Chef, und warum lag sie da falsch?
4	Was hatte der deutsche Angestellte an dem Satz „think about doing [things] differently" (line 125) seines britischen Chefs missverstanden?
5	Woher kommt es, laut Erin Meyer, dass bei einer geschäftlichen Besprechung in Skandinavien oft schwer zu erkennen ist, wer der Boss ist?

Developing your language skills

1 Improving your viewing skills

02

You are going to watch four young people talk about the conduct of people in their countries and what their business partners should expect. While viewing, answer the following multiple-choice questions. There is always only one correct answer.

1 The young Nigerian woman …
  - **a** tells us that Nigerians are proud to be African.
  - **b** warns us not to mix up Nigeria and Africa.
  - **c** makes fun of the world's ignorance about Africa.

2 She points out that Nigerians who wear colourful clothing …
  - **a** are traditionalist and considered a bit weird.
  - **b** are probably greeting visitors from abroad.
  - **c** might well be business people at work.

3 Nigerians speak loudly when …
  - **a** the topic is important to them.
  - **b** they try to hide the real emotions about a topic.
  - **c** they are angry with their conversation partner.

4 What creates a bad impression with a Nigerian business partner?
  - **a** wasting time
  - **b** talking too much
  - **c** not being punctual

5 The young Indian man describes Indians as …
  - **a** tough negotiators.
  - **b** good doctors.
  - **c** party animals.

6 He points out that Indians …
  - **a** don't speak when others speak.
  - **b** do many things at the same time.
  - **c** shake their heads to mean "yes".

7 The young man from Pakistan was asked "Are you listening to me?" because he …
  - **a** didn't answer a simple question.
  - **b** didn't look his conversation partner in the eyes.
  - **c** tried to show respect to an older man.

8 The young Russian woman explains that in her country clothes express …
  - **a** a sense of fashion.
  - **b** glamour.
  - **c** one's status.

9 She tells us that women should dress …
  - **a** smart but decently.
  - **b** expensively.
  - **c** in bright colours.

10 She warns business people not to …
  - **a** say no to dining with their opposite numbers.
  - **b** accept an invitation to the *banya* (sauna).
  - **c** underestimate Russian hospitality.

2 Doing project work

Get together in groups of four and search for "intercultural training" and the name of a German international company of your choice. Use the various materials you find to put a presentation together on:

- **the reason(s) why the company you chose offers such training,**
- **the target group of the training sessions,**
- **some of the contents of the training course.**

3 Writing complex sentences

Here is a text on cultural awareness written by a student. It is grammatically correct and displays good vocabulary knowledge, but the sentence structure is rather simple and monotonous. With the help of the instructions on the right, improve the highlighted passages.

A varied use of structures, some of them simpler, some of them complex, is a feature of good advanced writing.

I believe that the awareness of cultural differences is important for my career prospects. During my apprenticeship I twice had experience of intercultural misunderstandings. In my second year my international company sent me to their Oxford factory for three months. We were three apprentices from the firm there. In my third year they sent us to England again, to another office near Leeds. My first impression was that the management was so much more easy-going than the management at home. They talked to us as if we were on the same level. One day our boss Mr. Cargill told us that we "may want to get a bit of a move on". We didn't realise what he meant. He wanted to stress that we were behind schedule and had to hurry to finish our job in time. But to us it sounded like something we didn't have to take seriously.
We weren't the only ones who were confused by the British. There were senior managers from the German office there at the same time as us. They often complained about being really put off by their British colleagues in negotiations. Our people wanted to get down to business. Their British counterparts chatted away about all sorts of things at the beginning of each meeting.
I am going to study mechanical engineering. Many medium-sized German companies in this field are global players. And I expect to be sent abroad often in my working life and to be offered intercultural coaching for such placements abroad.

Stress the word "believe".

Make one sentence out of the two. Use a passive construction instead of "my company sent me"

Avoid the repetitions of "In my … year" and "sent".

Avoid the repetition.

Make one sentence out of the two.

Combine into one sentence.

Combine the two sentences with the help of "while".

Find a better linking word than "and".

4 Writing a short composition

Go through the notes you took earlier (task 4 on page 23). Turn the notes into a 200-word composition with the title:

Where and when cultural knowledge and awareness may be essential for me one day.

Keep task 3 in mind as you write, in order to make longer and more complex sentences.

Testing your writing skills

1 Material-based writing

You now need to write the essay you are supposed to submit in order to prove that your English is good enough to participate in a workshop on intercultural learning at your university. The topic is:

Can cultural competence be taught in school?

Write at least 300 words on this question, using your own ideas and the information given in the materials below.

MATERIAL 1

Students nowadays are more likely to have travelled abroad by the age of 16 and have easy access to a world of information through the internet. […] The history trip to Berlin, the French exchange, the cultural visit to Andalucía, pen pal writing schemes and foreign language assistants who bring a little bit of abroad into our classrooms are just a few of the many examples of contextualised learning* that we provide our students. At my school we have three foreign language assistants and hold four foreign exchanges each year – in addition to a range of cultural trips abroad. […] The awkward dinner conversations of foreign exchange students with their German host families, the sudden realisation that Dubai is such a long way away on so many different levels. These are character building experiences that bring out the best and worst in all of us and from which we learn so much.

Source: José Picardo, The Guardian, *25. 09. 2012*

MATERIAL 2

* kontextualisiertes Lernen

MATERIAL 3

Das Eisbergmodell der Kultur

Der Eisberg über dem Meeresspiegel zeigt sich als sichtbar, jedoch unter dem Wasser unsichtbar. […] Das Eisbergmodell verdeutlicht, dass einige Bereiche leicht sichtbar und hörbar sind, wie Sprache, Bräuche, Kleidung, Essen. Der überwiegende Teil bleibt „unter der Wasseroberfläche" verborgen. Das sind unsere Normen, Werte, Glaube, Philosophie. Dazu gehören schmerzliche und glückliche Erfahrungen.

Source: Beate Antonie Tröster, the website of Interkulturelle Dimensionen, 08. 12. 2017

2 Mediation Deutsch – Englisch

Sie nehmen im „Zentrum für interkulturelles Lernen" an der Universität nun an dem Workshop teil, für den Sie sich mit Ihrem Aufsatz beworben hatten. Die Teilnehmer sollen einander in Vorträgen darüber informieren, was in ihren eigenen Ländern als typisches sprachliches Verhalten gilt, das im Ausland Probleme hervorrufen könnte. Dazu ist von jedem eine Kurzfassung einzureichen, die an alle verteilt wird. Für die Kurzfassung zu dem von Ihnen zu haltenden Vortrag verwenden Sie die Information aus dem folgenden Text.
Fassen Sie die wesentliche Information in ca. 150 Wörtern auf Englisch zusammen. Gehen Sie auf die folgenden Punkte ein:

- **typisch „deutsches" Verhalten**
- **was dem Deutschen schwer fällt**
- **zu welchen Problemen es dadurch beim Zusammentreffen von Deutschen mit Menschen aus anderen Kulturkreisen kommen kann**

Kulturunterschiede und Sprache – ein spannendes Team

Wir Deutschen haben es mitunter besonders schwer: Die deutsche Kultur ist dafür bekannt, dass wir sehr direkt und ehrlich kommunizieren – anders als in den meisten anderen Kulturkreisen. Das heißt, dass wir meist sagen, was wir denken und die Dinge so meinen, wie wir sagen. In den meisten asiatischen Ländern wird eher indirekt kommuniziert, das heißt, dass häufig „durch die Blume" kommuniziert wird oder die eigentliche Botschaft „zwischen den Zeilen" zu lesen ist, was für Deutsche mitunter eine richtige Herausforderung darstellen kann.

Es gibt beispielsweise Länder, in denen es als unhöflich gilt, eine Frage mit einem klaren Nein zu beantworten, was vor allem in Asien der Fall ist. Hierzu gibt es sogar eine Theorie: Schuld an der Nein-Phobie sei angeblich die Lehre Konfuzius, nach der das Fremde geachtet werden soll und nachdem es unhöflich ist, einem Fremden mit einem Nein zu begegnen. Alternativen sind zum Beispiel ein schweigendes Lächeln oder ein verschmitztes „Maybe". Die japanische Sprache verfügt nicht mal über ein Pendant zum deutschen „Nein", Japaner wechseln stattdessen lieber unerwartet das Thema oder ändern die Tonlage beim Sprechen. Da Kommunikation jedoch nicht nur verbal sondern sogar größtenteils non-verbal erfolgt, gibt es unzählige Möglichkeiten, seine Meinung dennoch kundzutun, die es zu verstehen gilt.

Ein weiteres gutes Beispiel für Quellen häufiger Missverständnisse sind Floskeln, die zum Beispiel zum Verabschieden verwendet werden sowie höflichkeitsorientierte bejahende Aussagen ohne signifikante inhaltliche Bedeutung. In Südamerika muss man sich zum Beispiel nicht wundern, wenn einen der Busfahrer beim Aussteigen mit „Hasta luego" (wörtlich ins Deutsche übersetzt „bis dann" oder „bis später") verabschiedet, obwohl man sich vermutlich nie wieder sieht. […]

Andere Länder, andere Sitten

Spätestens seit dem Facebook Zeitalter machen wir uns außerdem Gedanken über die Übersetzung des Begriffes „Freund" aus dem (amerikanischem) Englisch ins Deutsche. Während ein Freund für die meisten Deutschen eine Person ist, die wir seit längerem kennen und der wir recht nahe stehen, bezeichnet der Begriff „Friend" oder auch das spanische „Amigo" ein lockeres Verhältnis und kann auch für weniger nahestehende Personen aus dem persönlichen Umfeld oder neuere Bekanntschaften verwendet werden, ohne das er gleich ein intimeres persönliches Verhältnis, Zuneigung oder viele gemeinsame Erlebnisse voraussetzt. Im Ausland oder im Kontakt mit US-Amerikanern ist es also vorteilhaft, solche Bezeichnungen nicht zu viel Bedeutung zuzumessen.

Source: the website of bildungsdoc, 01.06.2017

Exploring the topic

SITUATION

You find out that as part of your study course at university, you will spend some time at a British or US college. The International Relations Office of your university has published a guide for students, which – among other things – points out the importance of "political correctness" at British and American colleges. You decide to find out more about this concept and to share your findings with your fellow students through a video blog.

1 **Get together in small groups and research the background of these stories from recent years and the consequences that followed on from them:**

- **Harvey Weinstein and/or Kevin Spacey**
- **Eugen Gomringer's poem "Avenidas"**
- **John William Waterhouse's painting "Hylas and the Nymphs"**
- **Jennifer Lawrence at a photo-call for the film *Red Sparrow***
- **Marlies Krämer's court case against her bank**
- **Echo award for German rappers Kollegah and Farid Bang**

Look at the definition of political correctness below and decide what these stories have got to do with it.

POLITICAL CORRECTNESS: language, behaviour and attitudes that are carefully chosen so that they do not offend or insult anyone – used especially when you think someone is too careful in what they say or how they behave. *(Longman Dictionary of Contemporary English)*

Put your findings together in a structured and concrete way.

2 **Read the following text and find examples of political correctness described in it. Compare and contrast them to the stories you researched in task 1.**

Is free speech in British universities under threat?

A Until less than a year ago, only pigeons took much notice of the statue that sits in an alcove on the High Street facade two floors above the entrance to the Rhodes building of Oriel College, Oxford. A 4ft-high slab of limestone erected in 1911, it depicts Cecil Rhodes, the arch imperialist, and one-time student of Oriel. Then a campaign was started called Rhodes Must Fall aimed at removing what the protesters see as an offensive symbol of colonialism. Rhodes, after all, was a white supremacist who was instrumental in the exploitation of southern Africa. […]

The protest is the latest of a series of flash-points and incidents at British universities over the past year that have centred on issues of freedom of expression and protection from offence. […]

B The National Union of Students is committed to the creation of safe spaces and the idea has been adopted by many student unions across the country. Its deputy president, Richard Brooks, recently said: "Student unions are often the only place where students can be themselves, a place where they can think about

02 alcove: *Nische*
05 slab of limestone: *Kalksteinplatte*
21 student union: an association of students at a college, concerned with students' rights, living conditions, etc.

the statue of Cecil Rhodes on Oriel College

things and challenge ideas and thoughts in a safe environment."

But it's also a development that is filtering out into lecture halls and campuses at large. In recent years "trigger warnings" have been adopted by many universities in America to alert students to syllabus material that might be distressing. Faculty staff at Oberlin College, a liberal arts college in Ohio, were advised to remove "triggering" material if it didn't contribute to course goals. [...]

C A survey published last week by *Spiked*, the online political magazine with a libertarian agenda, found curbs on freedom of expression were in place in 90% of British universities – up from 80% the previous year – and that almost two-fifths of student unions had "no-platform" policies, reserving the right to ban any speakers deemed offensive to students. [...]

The University of Leeds and Leeds University's student union earn a "red card" in *Spiked's* free speech university rankings, because the university explicitly places restrictions on racist and offensive speech, and the union in the past three years has banned Page 3, Blurred Lines and sexist greeting cards.

The Leeds University Union building stands in pride of place on campus. Catering to some 33,000 students, it is large and well resourced and bustling with activity. The president of the union is an amiable young Dane called Toke Dahler. Unlike many other student representatives who support the principle of no platform, Dahler is happy to speak on the record about his enthusiasm for the policy.

[...] "We have more student societies than ever before, more external speakers, more student-led events, and to me it's not that surprising, because why would a student group want to invite a fascist on campus?" [...]

D Last November a curious scene took place at Goldsmiths (College) that captured something of the contradictions that surround the debate on acceptable speech. It happened during a talk given by the human-rights activist Maryam Namazie. The Iranian-born Namazie is spokesperson for the Council of Ex-Muslims and campaigns for secularism, feminism, freedom of expression and against Islamist extremism. As such she is a controversial figure. [...]

E There is a video of what took place on YouTube. Namazie is heckled and subject to a prolonged campaign of disruption by a group of students from the Isoc. They shout out, get up and sit down, walk around the room, laugh when she refers to Bangladeshi bloggers being hacked to death, and at one stage shut down her overhead projector when it displays a [...] cartoon. An atmosphere of agitation and tension pervades the room, and in spite of the presence of a security guard, the sight of a number of men trying to silence a lone woman seems uncomfortably close to physical intimidation. [...]

F All of this might seem like a storm in an unwashed tea cup – just more student politics getting worked up over nothing. But that would be to miss a new paradigm which the Goldsmiths incident illustrates. Universities are not just becoming less tolerant of a range of viewpoints and more indulgent of those who demand that such views be silenced. The language of equality, justice and "safe spaces" has been adopted by groups who intend to promote their own views at the expense of others. […]

G A […] veteran of student life in the 1970s, and now a classics professor at Cambridge, is Mary Beard. I asked her about the change in attitudes and what her own position was when she was a student. "I think I would have resisted the notion that ideas put over in free debate were 'threatening'. I remember feeling challenged, cross, outraged, provoked, inspired, but threatened, no." She doesn't believe that "appalling censorship" has broken out across Britain's campuses, but she thinks it important that students are taken out of their comfort zone. […]

"I have always thought it is my job to challenge students, confront them with views they find unfamiliar, uncomfortable, even shocking, and to take them intellectually out of the 'safe space' and to encourage them to argue with those with whom they fundamentally disagree, or whose views they might find offensive." […]

Mary Beard, Professor of Classics, Cambridge University

H It would be an exaggeration to suggest that free speech and open debate are in crisis at British universities. There is a perfectly legitimate debate underway at Oriel and perhaps the outcome will be the removal of Rhodes's limestone effigy, which would not be a defeat for free speech.

But history, like literature, is messy and complex and should not be reduced to a bland consensus designed to avoid offence. In education a safe space is the communal incarnation of a closed mind.

(947 words)

Source: Andrew Anthony, The Guardian, *24.01.2016*

38 libertarian: a person who strongly believes that people should have the freedom to do and think as they like
51 Page 3: (until 2015) the third page of the *Sun,* a tabloid newspaper, which contained a photo of a topless model
51 Blurred Lines: song (2013) by Robin Thicke, which was considered offensive due to its sexual lyrics
54 pride of place: the most important location
74 secularism: *Säkularismus (die Trennung von Religion und Staat)*
80 Isoc = Islamic Society: (in UK) organization of Muslim students
94 paradigm: *Denkart*
97 indulgent: *duldsam*
129 effigy: *Abbild*
135 incarnation: *Inkarnation, Verkörperung, Inbegriff*

3 **Think about what you have learned from your research for task 1 and from the text and decide where you stand on political correctness. Which demands of which groups in society do you support, and which ones do you not support? Make some notes for your video blog later.**

Testing your reading skills

1 Multiple-choice questions

Choose the most suitable option.

1 The Rhodes Must Fall campaign is mentioned as an example of …

- a how students reject British nostalgia for the past.
- b racial discrimination against African students at Oriel College.
- c how students have started to challenge things they find offensive.
- d the lack of interest of the university in its students' well-being.

2 According to Richard Brooks, some students feel the need for safe spaces because they …

- a want somewhere where they can exchange ideas without feeling threatened.
- b need a professor-free environment to think and talk.
- c don't want to deal with ideas that they disagree with.
- d are overwhelmed by crowded seminar rooms and lecture theatres.

3 The online magazine *Spiked* …

- a honoured the Leeds students for their outstanding academic performance.
- b has a clear mission: defending the principle of free speech.
- c criticized the Leeds student union for inviting controversial speakers.
- d collects and publishes statistical data on British universities.

4 The atmosphere at Namazie's lecture at Goldsmiths College is described as …

- a threatening.
- b reflective.
- c unreasonable.
- d festive.

5 Professor Mary Beard …

- a tried to avoid discussing provocative ideas as a student.
- b fears for the future of British universities.
- c wants students to examine opinions that are controversial or provocative.
- d blames today's students for being too laid back and lazy.

6 In the last paragraph, the writer …

- a welcomes the likely removal of the Rhodes statue at Oriel college.
- b insists that education is not about making students feel comfortable.
- c warns students off the arts subjects because they are controversial.
- d criticizes censorship at British universities as getting out of control.

2 Mediation Englisch – Deutsch

Beantworten Sie folgende Fragen auf Deutsch (Abschnitte A–C).

1 Welche Inhalte dürfen Lehrende am Oberlin College (Zeile 33) nicht entfernen, selbst wenn sie problematisch sind?

2 Erläutern Sie, was mit den "'no-platform' policies" (Zeilen 42 – 43) vieler britischer Studentenvertretungen gemeint ist.

3 Was erfahren wir über das Gebäude der Studentenvertretung an der Universität (Zeilen 53 – 56)?

Developing your language skills

1 Improving your listening skills

04

Listen to a conversation between radio host Rachel Martin and her guest Suzanne Nossel of the free-speech advocacy group PEN America. Their talk focuses on the First Amendment* to the United States Constitution, which guarantees the freedom of speech.
Listen out for eight aspects in their talk and recreate the order in which they occur. The starting point (1) is already marked. Copy the table and put numbers 2–8 into the correct boxes. There are two aspects that do not come up in the conversation at all. Mark their boxes with an X.

* Zusatzartikel

	changes over time in attitude to what can and cannot be said
	the need for universities to show what their principles and values are
	a university administration ignoring the students' wishes
1	an activist who loves to cause controversy
	a clever way in which a Florida university marginalized a right-wing speaker
	a student proud to be Black and free to speak
	people suing universitres for violating their right to free speech and winning
	the importance of free speech for every political movement in US history
	a wise decision by the University of California concerning a speaker
	the question of whose rights are actually protected by the First Amendment

2 Using connectives

Here is a text on political correctness written by a student. It is not bad, but some connectives are not used correctly. Improve the highlighted passages. An asterisk (*) means that there is something missing.

A good piece of writing uses connective words and phrases to help the reader follow the train of thought.

According to Marlies Krämer's court case, there is still not enough awareness * that women do not feel addressed when they read or hear "Liebe Kunden".
I can understand Ms Krämer. If the principal of my school started his speeches with "Liebe Schüler", I would feel excluded. It's lucky that saying "Liebe Schülerinnen und Schüler" it is quite common nowadays. Due to my teacher, this is not the case in our curricula, where a footnote says that the female form is included in the word "Schüler". I don't approve of this bad habit of writers of documents. Research has proven that women do feel excluded from the male forms of nouns regarding to people. It is well-known that job ads using only the male forms in the past received fewer applications by women, even * the job could clearly be done by a man or a woman. Following this, nowadays the majority of job ads address both genders. If school principals and personnel managers can use the male and female forms, for sure administrators are able to do so, too! In my point of view, the ruling of the German court against Ms Krämer is bad, not because of it is "politically incorrect", but because it does not take into account that language use is not neutral and always reflects the state of society.

3 Preparing and recording a video blog

Go through the notes you took earlier (see task 3 on page 31) about what you think of political correctness and turn them into a script for your video blog. With task 2 in mind, go through your script again and, if necessary, improve it before recording the blog.

Testing your writing and speaking skills

1 Mediation Deutsch–Englisch

Sie haben Ihr Jahr an einer britischen Hochschule absolviert und sind seitdem im Austausch mit einem Studienkollegen aus London. Er hat Sie u. a. gefragt, wie in Deutschland über das Leben an britischen Unis berichtet wird und Sie antworten ihm mit der Information aus unten stehendem Text. Verfassen Sie den Teil Ihrer Antwort, der sich mit dem o. g. Thema befasst (150 Wörter). Gehen Sie dabei auf die folgenden Aspekte ein:

- **der Grund, weshalb Professoren an den Unis Alarm schlagen**
- **ein Erlebnis der Feministin Greers und eines des Journalisten O'Neils als Beispiele**
- **Position der Studentenvertreter**
- **zukünftiges Problem, vor dem gewarnt wird**

Bedrohte Meinungsfreiheit: Politisch ganz korrekt

Die „neue politische Korrektheit" an Britanniens Universitäten läuft aus dem Ruder. Kurz vor Weihnachten schlug eine Gruppe von Professoren in der Zeitung „Telegraph" Alarm und sprach von einer „zutiefst besorgniserregenden Entwicklung". Eine Kultur, die den freien Austausch von Ideen beschränke, fördere die Selbstzensur und mache Menschen Angst, ihre Meinung zu äußern: „Dies droht das Wesen der Demokratie zu zerstören."

Es trifft nicht nur Redner, die man auf der konservativen Seite verorten würde. Unlängst wurde Germaine Greer zum Opfer, eine Art britische Alice Schwarzer, die allerdings nicht die neuerdings gebotene Sensibilität für Transsexuelle aufbringt. Weil sie vor Jahren geschrieben hatte, dass man durch eine Operation nicht zur Frau werde, ging ihrem Auftritt in der Cardiff-Universität ein digitaler „Shitstorm" voraus. Eine Online-Petition, die von 3 000 Studenten unterschrieben wurde, forderte ein Redeverbot auf dem Campus. Das gleiche wiederholte sich in Oxford. Dutzende Studenten beschimpften sie von der Galerie [...]

Der Journalist Brendan O'Neill spricht von einer „no platform policy", einer Strategie also, mit der die Studentenführer das Auftreten von Leuten, die nicht dem vorherrschenden „Gruppendenken" entsprächen, systematisch verhinderten. O'Neill hat dies am eigenen Leib erfahren. [...] Er war [...] niedergebrüllt worden: in Cambridge, als er argumentierte, dass Jungenkultur nicht notwendigerweise Vergewaltiger produziert, in Cork, als er sich gegen die Homoehe aussprach, in London, wo er der industriellen Entwicklung Afrikas den Vorrang vor dem afrikanischen Kampf gegen den Klimawandel gab. [...]

Die Studenten fordern einen [...] Schutz- oder Sicherheitsraum, aber so, wie er definiert wird, läuft er dem Grundelixier der britischen Demokratie zuwider: der freien Rede. Der „Independent" stellte kürzlich ein Glossar der neuen politischen Korrektheit zusammen und erklärte den Begriff so: [...] frei von Diskriminierung, Belästigung und Hassreden gegen unterprivilegierte Gruppen wie Frauen, Schwule, Lesben, Bisexuelle, Transsexuelle und ethnische Minderheiten ... Menschen können aus diesem Schutzraum entfernt werden, wenn ihre anstößigen Sichtweisen denselben bedrohen." In Cambridge pochten Studenten auf ihr „Recht auf Behaglichkeit". [...]

In den Vereinigten Staaten, wo die neue politische Korrektheit ihren Ausgang genommen hat, wird schon über die „Verhätschelung der amerikanischen Psyche" [...] diskutiert. O'Neill sieht auch auf Großbritannien etwas zukommen. [...] Besorgt blickt der Journalist in die Zukunft, wenn diese Studenten, die sich vor jeder Kontroverse schützten, das Land führen und komplexe politische Entscheidungen werden treffen müssen.

Source: Jochen Buchsteiner, FAZ, *13. 01. 2016*

2 Group discussion

Situation: AIESEC is the largest international association of university students. The AIESEC group at your university is considering inviting a motivational speaker who could encourage students to think out of the box while also being socially responsible. You have been elected to the selection committee. Each of you has found an inspirational speaker from a website called "Rent a Speaker".

Preparation phase: Think about the speaker you have found. What area of expertise might he or she be able to talk about? Why might he or she be attractive as a speaker? Do you see any reasons why he or she should not be invited?

Presentation phase: Present your speaker and your thoughts on him or her to the others.

Interaction phase: Discuss all the suggested speakers and decide who to invite.

Optional *(if you have time left at the end of the discussion):* Discuss how to advertise this event so as to attract as large an audience as possible.

1 NIELS CARLSON
Niels is a passionate computer programmer and hacker. He has just turned 18 but has already gained the skills needed to solve complex computer problems and hack the internet. In his talks he usually goes deeply into hacking techniques and the Darknet, using spectacular examples from his own experience. He explains why hacking makes for a safer, better society.

2 PAULA PAVLOVA
Paula was a student of Fine Arts before starting a marketing career, gaining experience in online marketing and e-commerce. With the media agency that she founded two years ago she pioneered software solutions for increasing marketing possibilities on social media platforms. In her talks she focuses on her attraction to ancient Far Eastern systems of philosophy and meditation practices, which she believes to be the basis of self-knowledge and vital for the realization of important personal goals.

3 GEORGE NIGHEY
George has worked in the digital business for over 20 years. Presently he is working for a leading bonus card system which gives people the most exciting shopping experience possible. In his talks George, who sees himself as a digital missionary, promotes the true value that lies in listening, getting connected and in helping each other.

4 LAURA THEODORAKIS
Laura studied politics and digital media development before she started working in journalism. Now she is a professional TV presenter and video editor and she also hosts her own podcast. Her pet topics are good storytelling, how to explain things well, and good food. In her talks she reflects on the rapid changes within the media environment, how disruptive technologies can lead to innovation and how organizations can handle all these innovations.

5 STEFANIE MAIER
She is the media manager of a major football club. The digital project she initiated now connects the European fan community. Her goal is to deliver the right content at the right time to millions of fans worldwide. In her talks she usually touches on ways of finding out what club fans want, how to meet the diverse demands of a global community and how to optimize the digital experience of fans.

1 D LANGUAGE AND POLITICS

Exploring the topic

SITUATION

"Fake news" is a big topic these days, even in the classroom. Your teacher has asked your class to choose a novel that deals with the topic. You have heard about a British dystopian (= opposite of utopian) novel from the past which apparently reads like a prediction of some of the things that are happening now. The novel is called *1984*. It was written by George Orwell and the novel was published in 1949. You decide to find out about the book to see if it might be of interest today. You then write a proposition for or against reading the novel and post it to your classmates.

1 **In small groups, research the history of fake news and collect some recent cases. Together, examine why people create fake news.**

2 **Read the following excerpt from the novel *1984* and find parallels to and differences from the situation that we are experiencing today.**

1984

The novel is set in a world consisting of three super states: Oceania, Eurasia and Eastasia. Winston Smith is a low-ranking member of the ruling Party in London, in the nation of Oceania. Everywhere he looks he sees the face of the Party's seemingly omniscient leader, a figure known only as Big Brother. The Party controls everything in Oceania, even the people's history and language. Currently, the Party is forcing the implementation of an invented language called Newspeak, which attempts to prevent political rebellion by changing the way people talk. Even thinking rebellious thoughts is illegal. Winston works in the Ministry of Truth. The following chapter describes his work.

A With the deep, unconscious sigh which not even the nearness of the telescreen could prevent him from uttering when his day's work started, Winston pulled the speakwrite towards him, blew the dust from its mouthpiece, and put on his spectacles. Then he unrolled and clipped together four small cylinders of paper which had already flopped out of the pneumatic tube on the right-hand side of his desk.

B In the walls of the cubicle there were three orifices. To the right of the speakwrite, a small pneumatic tube for written messages, to the left, a larger one for newspapers; and in the side wall, **1**, a large oblong slit protected by a wire grating. This last was for the disposal of waste paper. Similar slits existed in thousands or tens of thousands throughout the building, not only in every room but at short intervals in every corridor. For some reason they were nicknamed memory holes. When one knew that any document was due for destruction, or even when one saw a scrap of waste paper lying about, it was an automatic action to lift the flap of the nearest memory hole and drop it in, whereupon it would be whirled away on a current of warm air to the enormous furnaces which were hidden somewhere in the recesses of the building.

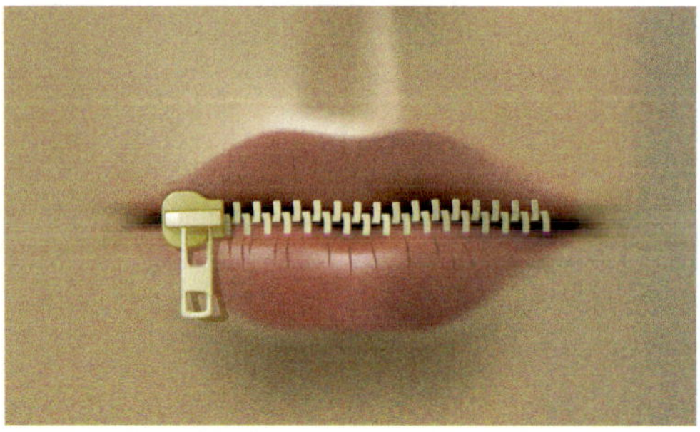

2 speakwrite: (invented word) a machine that you speak into that writes your words on a screen
8 wire grating: *Drahtgitter*

Examples of Newspeak taken from the novel *1984*

unperson → person who has been executed and whose life is erased so that there is no evidence that he or she ever existed.

crimethink → a verb and a noun that refers to thoughts that are different to the official government standpoint

joycamp → hard labour camp

oldthink → ideas inspired by events or memories of times before the Revolution

C Winston examined the four slips of paper which he had unrolled. Each contained a message of only one or two lines, in the abbreviated jargon – not actually Newspeak, but consisting largely of Newspeak words – which was used in the Ministry for internal purposes. […]

D Winston dialled "back numbers" on the telescreen and called for the appropriate issues of *The Times*, **2** . The messages he had received referred to articles or news items which for one reason or another it was thought necessary to alter, or, as the official phrase had it, to rectify. For example, it appeared from *The Times* of the seventeenth of March that Big Brother, in his speech of the previous day, had predicted that the South Indian front would remain quiet but that a Eurasian offensive would shortly be launched in North Africa. As it happened, the Eurasian Higher Command had launched its offensive in South India and left North Africa alone. It was therefore necessary to rewrite a paragraph of Big Brother's speech, in such a way as to make him predict the thing that had actually happened. Or again, *The Times* of the nineteenth of December had published the official forecasts of the output of various classes of consumption goods in the fourth quarter of 1983, which was also the sixth quarter of the Ninth Three-Year Plan. Today's issue contained a statement of the actual output, from which it appeared that the forecasts were in every instance grossly wrong. Winston's job was to rectify the original figures by making them agree with the later ones. As for the third message, it referred to a very simple error **3** . As short a time ago as February, the Ministry of Plenty had issued a promise (a "categorical pledge" were the official words) that there would be no reduction of the chocolate ration during 1984. Actually, **4** , the chocolate ration was to be reduced from thirty grammes to twenty at the end of the present week. All that was needed was to substitute for the original promise a warning that it would probably be necessary to reduce the ration at some time in April.

E As soon as Winston had dealt with each of the messages, he clipped his speakwritten corrections to the appropriate copy of *The Times* and pushed them into the pneumatic tube. Then, with a movement which was as nearly as possible unconscious, he crumpled up the original message and any notes that he himself had made, and dropped them into the memory hole to be devoured by the flames.

F What happened in the unseen labyrinth to which the pneumatic tubes led, he did not know in detail, but he did know in general terms. As soon as all the corrections which happened to be necessary in any particular number of *The Times* had been assembled and collated, that number would be reprinted, **5** and the corrected copy placed on the files in its stead. This process of continuous alteration was applied not only to newspapers, but to books, periodicals, pamphlets, posters, leaflets, films, sound-tracks, cartoons, photographs – to every kind of literature or documentation which might conceivably hold any political or ideological significance. Day by day and almost minute by minute the past was brought up to date. In this way every prediction made by the Party could be shown by documentary evidence to have been correct, nor was any item of news, or any expression of opinion **6** ever allowed to remain on record. […]

From the film *1984* (1956)

G A number of *The Times* which might, because of changes in political alignment, or mistaken prophecies uttered by Big Brother, have been rewritten a dozen times still stood on the files bearing its original date, **7** . Books, also, were recalled and rewritten again and again, and were invariably reissued without any admission that any alteration had been made. Even the written instructions which Winston received, and which he invariably got rid of as soon as he had dealt with them, never stated or implied that an act of forgery was to be committed: always the reference was to slips, errors, misprints, or misquotations which it was necessary to put right in the interests of accuracy.

H But actually, he thought as he re-adjusted the Ministry of Plenty's figures, it was not even forgery. It was merely the substitution of one piece of nonsense for another. Most of the material that you were dealing with had no connection with anything in the real world, not even the kind of connection that is contained in a direct lie. Statistics were just as much a fantasy in their original version as in their rectified version. A great deal of the time you were expected to make them up out of your head. For example, the Ministry of Plenty's forecast had estimated the output of boots for the quarter at one-hundred-and-forty-five million pairs. The actual output was given as sixty-two millions. Winston, however, in rewriting the forecast, marked the figure down to fifty-seven millions, so as to allow for the usual claim that the quota had been overfulfilled. In any case, sixty-two millions was no nearer the truth than fifty-seven millions, or than one-hundred-and-forty-five millions. Very likely no boots had been produced at all. Likelier still, nobody knew how many had been produced, **8** . All one knew was that every quarter astronomical numbers of boots were produced on paper, while perhaps half the population of Oceania went barefoot. And so it was with every class of recorded fact, great or small. Everything faded away into a shadow-world in which, finally, even the date of the year had become uncertain.

(1206 words)
Source: George Orwell, 1984, *1949*

3 **Make some notes on your impression of the book and on your reasons for wanting or not wanting to read more of it.**

Testing your reading skills

1 Mediation Englisch – Deutsch

Beantworten Sie folgende Fragen auf Deutsch.

1 Was sagt uns der erste Satz des Textes über Winstons Verhältnis zu seiner Arbeit und über die Bedingungen, unter denen er arbeitet?

2 Erläutern Sie, weshalb die Bezeichnung „memory hole" (Zeile 50) eigentlich unpassend ist.

3 Winston's Tätigkeit wird folgendermaßen beschrieben: „Day by day and almost minute by minute the past was brought up to date." (Zeilen 58–60). Was sind die Konsequenzen seiner Arbeit?

4 Das „Ministry of Plenty" (Zeilen 37, 81, 86):
- **a** Wofür ist es zuständig?
- **b** Was suggeriert der Name des Ministeriums?
- **c** Was sagt uns der Erzähler mit dem Beispiel der Stiefelproduktion über dieses Ministerium?

2 Gapped summary

Copy the summary of lines 6–31 of the text and fill the gaps with appropriate words from the corresponding passages of the text (one word per gap). Do not make any changes. Please also provide the number of the line in which you found the word.

On this particular day at work we see Winston Smith start work in his ▬[1] (line ▬). He reads the short instructions given to him in the language used for ▬[2] (line ▬) documents. His job is to change a certain article in *The Times* of 17 March. The article is about the start of an ▬[3] (line ▬) by an enemy state. Since Big Brother had wrongly ▬[4] (line ▬) in a public address where it was supposed to take place, Winston has to rewrite the speech. The original *Times* article is just one of the documents that would later be disposed of in one of the ▬[5] (line ▬) deep in the building.

3 Multiple matching

The following parts of sentences were deleted from the text and replaced by a small grey gap with a number. Match them to the gaps in the text (1–8) where they belong. There are two phrases that do not belong in any of the gaps.

A which slid out of the pneumatic tube after only a few minutes' delay
B as Winston was aware
C and no other copy existed to contradict it
D which for one reason or another were to be retained in the anthologies
E within easy reach of Winston's arm
F once the deed was done
G which conflicted with the needs of the moment
H the original copy destroyed
I much less cared
J which could be set right in a couple of minutes

Developing your language skills

1 Improving your research skills

In a brief class discussion, nominate two "researchers" to find out about how Winston Smith's story continues.

Task for the researchers in preparation for one of the next lessons: Read a plot summary of *1984* and pick out the main elements of the story. Describe the plot to the others, but leave out the ending.

2 Writing a proposition

Listen to the presentation of the plot of *1984* by the "researchers" and go through the notes you took earlier while reading the excerpt from *1984* again. Then write a 200-word proposition for or against reading the book and post it on your common platform.

3 Improving your listening skills

05

The programme you are going to hear is about Russian propaganda on social media. While listening, compare the following list of statements with what is being said in the programme. All together there are six correct statements in the list. Note down which statements are correct.

Russian propaganda …

- **a** dominates most social media platforms.
- **b** is disguised so that you don't perceive it to be propaganda.

The Blacktivist page …

- **c** was established by Ms Blunt's friends.
- **d** was linked to the "Black Lives Matter" movement.
- **e** targeted people worried about racism in the police.

Propaganda in general …

- **f** works by confirming what people already believe.
- **g** confronts people with what they don't want to see.
- **h** splits society into groups that hate each other.
- **i** makes democratic countries more authoritarian.

Twitter account @TEN_GOP …

- **j** sent out tweets from supporters of the Republican Party.
- **k** claimed that voting in California had been manipulated.
- **l** was known by the Trump's family to be a fake news site.

Facebook …

- **m** said that it will be more open about who advertises with them.
- **n** issued advertisements in self-defence.

Testing your writing skills

1 Mediation Deutsch – Englisch

In einem Medienseminar im Studiengang Kulturwissenschaft an Ihrer Universität wird das Thema *Fake News* recherchiert. Ihre Aufgabe ist es, historische (d.h. vor den Skandalen um Brexit und US-Wahlen liegende) Fälle von Falschmeldungen in den Medien zu sammeln.
Verfassen Sie unter Verwendung der Information aus dem folgenden Text ein kurzes informatives Papier mit ca. 150 Wörtern, das Sie im Seminar vorlegen können. Gehen Sie dabei auf die folgenden Aspekte ein:

- **zwei Beispiele für historische Falschmeldungen und deren Folgen**
- **das Qualitäts- und Selbstverständnis des traditionellen Journalismus**

FAKE NEWS, LÜGEN, ZEITUNGSENTEN:
ALTE PHÄNOMENE, NEUE BEDROHUNG

Fake News sind kein neues Phänomen: Schon immer wurde mit Gerüchten und falschen Behauptungen Politik gemacht. So ist die Geschichte des Antisemitismus auch eine Geschichte der Fake News: [...] Hier zieht sich eine blutige Spur vom Mittelalter bis zum Nationalsozialismus. In der antisemitischen Wochenzeitung „Der Stürmer“ fanden sich alle nur erdenklichen obszönen Falschmeldungen über Juden. Der Herausgeber Julius Streicher wurde dafür im Nürnberger Prozess gegen die Hauptkriegsverbrecher zum Tode verurteilt. Schon mit der Erfindung des Drucks mit beweglichen Lettern durch Johannes Gutenberg um das Jahr 1440 wurde es möglich, auch Falschmeldungen schnell weit zu verbreiten.

Im jahrhundertelangen Kampf gegen solche Lügen wurde aber auch das Handwerkszeug entwickelt, um richtige Fakten von falschen zu unterscheiden, seien es die Fußnoten in wissenschaftlichen Texten, mit denen Zitatquellen offen gelegt werden, oder das „Zwei-Quellen-Prinzip“ im Journalismus. Danach kann ein Tatbestand erst als dann gesichert erachtet werden, wenn er von zwei unterschiedlichen Quellen berichtet wurde.

Mit der Demokratisierung der Gesellschaften entwickelte sich der Journalismus zunehmend zur „Vierten Gewalt“, die die drei staatlichen Gewalten Exekutive, Legislative und Judikative überwacht. Am eindrucksvollsten gelang dies den beiden Reportern Bob Woodward und Carl Bernstein, die mit ihren monatelangen Recherchen für die „Washington Post“ maßgeblich dazu beitrugen, dass die Watergate-Affäre aufgedeckt wurde und US-Präsident Richard Nixon im August 1974 zurücktreten musste.

War die Aufdeckung der Watergate-Affäre eine Sternstunde des Journalismus, kam es 1983 zu einem Tiefpunkt: Das Magazin Stern präsentierte auf einer internationalen Pressekonferenz die vermeintlichen Tagebücher Adolf Hitlers. In der Ausgabe dazu hieß es: „Die Geschichte des Dritten Reichs muss teilweise umgeschrieben werden.“ Zwei Wochen später war klar: Die Tagebücher waren Fälschungen und der Stern blamiert.

Dramatischer als solche Einzelfälle ist das gleichzeitige Versagen mehrerer Medien: In den Jahren 2002/03 folgten fast sämtliche führenden US-Medien der Argumentation der Regierung von George W. Bush, wonach der Irak Massenvernichtungswaffen besitze und Saddam Hussein an der Planung der Anschläge vom 1. September 2001 beteiligt gewesen sei. Berühmt wurde der Satz des Washington Post-Kolumnisten Richard Cohen, wonach „nur ein Narr, oder vielleicht ein Franzose“ die vorliegenden Beweise anzweifeln konnte. Heute wissen wir: Die Angaben waren alle falsch. Es gab keine Beweise. Es gab keine irakischen Massenvernichtungswaffen.

Source: Martin Muno, the website of Deutsche Welle, 01.01.2017

2 Material-based writing

The next task in your media studies course is to write a 300-word essay on the following topic:

Many people don't trust traditional news media any more. Explain why and say what should be done about it.

Make use of the following materials:

MATERIAL 1

Which media sources do you get your news from? 2012–2017

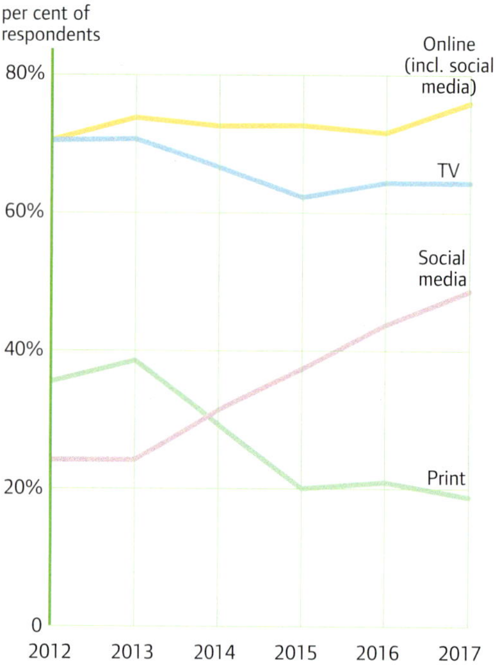

Source: Nic Newman, "Digital News Sources", Reuters Institute for the Study of Journalism, 2017

MATERIAL 2

a sign at a Kagida demonstration in Kassel on 22 Dec 2014 (GEZ: ehemaliger Name für den ARD ZDF Deutschlandradio Beitragsservice)

MATERIAL 3

From a review of the book Mainstream *by media scientist Uwe Krüger:*

Da ist zum einen die fortschreitende Prekarisierung* des journalistischen Berufs. Überall werden Stellen gestrichen, freie AutorInnen immer weniger eingesetzt, was den Konformitätsdruck erhöhe. Zum anderen seien aber auch die Anforderungen an Journalisten gestiegen. So müssten etwa Auslandskorrespondenten von Krisenherden in immer schnelleren Takten berichten. Die notwendige Zeit für Recherche und die selbsttätige Inaugenscheinnahme sei oftmals nicht vorhanden. Statt vor Ort Besuche vorzunehmen schaue man lieber das lokale Fernsehprogramm. Journalisten würden zu „Lieferanten", müssten sich durch massenhafte Agenturmeldungen und Pressemittellungen kämpfen und formulierten sie nur noch ein wenig um. „Es wird schon stimmen", heiße es: eine Mischung aus Gottvertrauen und Arroganz. Politische Zusammenhänge würden gerne personalisiert und zugespitzt und damit oft genug boulevardisiert. Und schließlich litten Print-Medien unter teilweise drastischen Rückgängen der Werbeeinnahmen, was durch höhere Verkaufspreise nur bedingt kompensiert werden könne.

Source: Lothar Struck, the website of literaturkritik, 19.04.2016

* Prekarisierung: Zunahme unsicherer Beschäftigungsverhältnisse

EMPOWERING PEOPLE

2

FOCUS

1 **Look at the pictures below and discuss what kind of development in society they illustrate.**

1

2

3

2 **One reason why societies change is that various groups within society achieve empowerment and change the existing order. Before looking at some examples in detail, examine the concept of empowerment by working through all six questions below in small groups.**

1	Describe	What does empowerment mean?
2	Compare	Which phrases mean the same as or the opposite of empowerment?
3	Analyse	What do you need for empowerment? What are its characteristics?
4	Associate	What do you associate with the concept of empowerment?
5	Argue	Why is empowerment usually a good thing? How might it be dangerous?
6	Apply	What can empowerment be used for?

3 **How can the concept of empowerment be connected with the topics illustrated in photos 1 and 2 from task 1.**

2 WORDS IN CONTEXT

Empowering people

06 03

Empowerment is about how marginalized individuals and communities gain control of their circumstances, achieve their own goals and claim their rights. As people empower themselves, they also change the power structures within society, which then adapt to the new circumstances or are replaced completely. As such, societies are always in transition.

Present-day societies are undergoing enormous transformations due to massive demographic, political and environmental changes. While globalization may have made the world a smaller place, it has also widened the gap between rich and poor, thereby contributing to economic and political divisions within societies. Western societies are also drifting apart culturally, due to the movement towards less homogenous societies and the increasing acceptance of different sexual, cultural and religious identities. While diversity can be celebrated as a significant cultural achievement, nevertheless there is opposition to it from people in communities that have been left behind economically. Often socially conservative and less educated, these people feel threatened by mass immigration, economic displacement and cultural liberalization. They cling to traditional values and ethnic identities and reject the views of what they perceive to be the metropolitan elite.

In addition, one dangerous development in recent decades has been the decline of the middle class, which fears drifting into poverty. This has resulted in the destabilization of democracy and the rise of populist politics. Parties offering simple solutions to complex problems are gaining momentum. As a result, the future of the democratic mainstream parties seems to be at stake.

Democratic values seem less embedded in people's thinking nowadays than one might hope. There has been a global retreat from democratic principles, with many countries embracing authoritarian regimes. Some speak of 2017 as a turning point when democracy faced a serious crisis in Western societies, which had until then been its most ardent supporters. At the same time, the independent mainstream media is losing ground to social media while being attacked by extremists on both sides. According to studies by non-governmental organizations, the right to choose leaders in free and fair elections, freedom of the press and the rule of law are under assault and in retreat globally.

Democracies will have to find ways to persuade their citizens to believe once more in democratic values and prove that they can solve pressing problems such as climate change, migration, shifting demographics, the distribution of wealth and the technological revolution.

In the struggle for an open-minded, democratic way of life, women and young people in particular will play a significant role. In the wake of right-wing populism, misogynist views are on the rise in an increasing number of countries, endangering the movement towards gender equality worldwide. Even where women supposedly enjoy equal rights, they still struggle with the glass ceiling in the job market. However, there is hope that gender bias may be on the wane. The global #MeToo debate has helped to bring sexual harassment and male dominance in the workplace into the limelight and has strengthened women's causes in many arenas.

Generation Z, the first generation born in the 21st century, experienced the economic hardships caused by the financial crisis of 2009 and has grown up acutely aware of the dangers of environmental degradation. As digital natives who are at home with the internet and digital devices, they have the skills to develop the entrepreneurial competence needed at a global level. Having experienced how consumerist society is in the process of destroying the environment, Generation Z is rethinking consumer behaviour and developing a sharing culture – as opposed to their parents' culture of owning. Unable to afford to own cars or apartments, Generation Z has developed into a responsible and compassionate generation in comparison to its predecessors. With the internet at their fingertips, young people are more self-confident in promoting their own voices and fighting for the right to be heard.

(635 words)

Working with words

1 **Complete these sentences using the words or phrases in the boxes, in the correct form. Each word or phrase can be used three times.**

at home	drift	grow	undergo

a The train station will ___ major repairs this summer.	**b** I've got a stay-___ dad. It's because he freelances.	**c** Last year the company ___ a significant restructuring.
d In recent years the population ___ away from the old industrial areas.	**e** I just ___ into teaching, really. Nothing else really interested me.	**f** Even today, many people don't feel ___ with new technology.
g After graduation my college friends and I ___ apart.	**h** What do you want to be when you ___ up?	**i** He's continuing ___ as a musician.
j My team always loses away matches but usually wins ___.	**k** Fears ___ that the government may increase taxes again.	**l** She ___ surgery last week, so she cannot come to the meeting.

2 **a** Find adjectives highlighted in the text which match the following definitions taken from a monolingual English dictionary.

1 large or important enough to have an effect or to be noticed
2 intensely devoted and enthusiastic
3 not connected with or influenced by a particular group
4 willing to consider and accept other people's ideas and opinions
5 sensible and able to make good judgements so that you can be trusted
6 feeling sympathy for people who are suffering
7 certain that you can do things well

b Write four sentences about four famous people using at least one of the adjectives in each sentence. Explain why you think the chosen adjective fits this person.

3 **Translate the following sentences into English, using expressions from the given lines in the text.**

1 Bildung muss frei von geschlechtsspezifischen Vorurteilen sein. *(line 33)*
2 Es darf keinerlei Toleranz gegenüber frauenfeindlichen Ansichten in der Politik geben. *(line 30)*
3 Auch homogene Gesellschaften müssen mit Problemen fertig werden. *(line 9)*
4 Populismus scheint an Boden zu gewinnen. *(lines 17 and 30)*
5 Journalisten müssen alle Fakten zur Hand haben, ehe sie Politiker interviewen. *(line 43)*
6 Unternehmerische Kompetenz ist erforderlich, um in neuen Märkten Fuß zu fassen. *(line 39)*
7 Die Skandale in der Filmindustrie wurden von mutiger Frauen ans Licht der Öffentlichkeit gebracht. *(line 34)*

2 A A NEW GENERATION ON THE RISE

Exploring the topic

SITUATION

A new generation, to which you belong, is on the rise: Generation Z. As part of a youth group, you have been asked by your local town council to come up with ideas for bridging the gap between the generations. To prepare yourself for a discussion at the town hall, you collect information about the different generations.

1 **The term "generation" can be defined as a group of individuals born and living around the same time. There's a general consensus about the names, time frames and characteristics of the various generations in the USA. Match the following characteristics with the generations' names and time periods.**

1 GI Generation

2 Generation X

3 Silent Generation

4 Baby Boomers

5 Millennials

6 Generation Z

7 born roughly 1925–1942

8 born roughly 1901–1924

9 born roughly 1980–2000

10 born roughly 1943–1964

11 born after 2001

12 born roughly 1965–1979

13
- born when birth numbers went down
- lived through the AIDS epidemic and the fall of the Berlin Wall
- also called the MTV Generation
- independent-minded, tolerant, cautious of authority, unimpressed by institutions

14
- children during World War II
- stuck to the rules, conformed with social norms, loyal and hard-working
- created the nuclear family (working dad, housewife mother and two kids)

15
- experienced rise of the Internet and September 11 (2001)
- team workers, assertive with strong views
- envision the world as a 24/7 place
- strong affinity to technology

16
- born with the Internet
- digital natives who grew up with computers and digital toys
- prone to lack of concentration but good multi-taskers

17
- teenagers during Great Depression of 1929
- fought in World War II
- liked swing and jazz music
- community-minded, strong sense of personal civic duty and loyalty (they vote, they often worked for one company)

18
- born during an economic and baby boom following World War II
- against the Vietnam War and stood up for civil rights
- self-oriented, changed society, women pursued careers

2 **The following sentences describe Generation Z. Talk about the characteristics with a partner. Do you agree with them?**

- **Generation Z can quickly and efficiently shift between work and play.**
- **If Generation Z doesn't feel appreciated, they'll move on.**
- **Generation Z desires more individualized work environments.**
- **Generation Z knows the true value of independence, and knowledge is no exception here.**
- **Generation Z's attention spans are significantly lower than those of other generations.**
- **Generation Z expects to live and work in a world characterized by diversity.**
- **Nearly 92% of Gen Z has a digital footprint.**

3 **Read the article below about a generation trying to find its place in today's America.**

THE GUNS DEBATE IS A CULTURE WAR. AND YOUNG PEOPLE WILL WIN IT

This is a fight between a young, diverse, feminist generation and an old, white, male minority desperate to hang on to power.

A Young activists raised on social media and memes were bound to come up with the best protest signs. At the March for Our Lives, and the national school walkout earlier this month, teenagers held posters blasting politicians and declaring, "I should be writing my college essay, not my will." Some were hilarious, many were sad, and all were designed to go viral.

B The one that I can't get out of my mind, though, was held by a teenage Pakistani immigrant in New York's Union Square: "Girls' clothing in school is more regulated than guns in America." The 18 year-old high school senior who carried the poster, Sana Haider, tells me she wanted to find "the perfect sign that stood out" and one that reflected her feminist values. She just went to her first protest, the Women's March, last year.

C We know that the gun debate is a culture war. But Haider and her sign reminded me that it's more than an abstract debate over ideology or constitutional principles. It's a fight between a young, diverse, feminist generation representing an emerging majority and an old, white, male minority desperate to hang on to power. And guns are their security blanket of choice.

March for Our Lives demonstration in Washington, DC, opposing gun violence and mass shootings in American schools.

D Just 3% of Americans own half of the guns in America. And that 3% isn't just anyone. According to a Harvard study flagged by *Scientific American* this month, the person most likely to stockpile guns in this country is an older, white man from a rural conservative area. And an alarming body of research shows that they're motivated by racial anxiety and a fear of emasculation.

E A 2017 Baylor University study, for example, found that men's attachment to guns often stemmed from economic woes and fear of losing traditional "breadwinner" status. The researchers wrote that "engaging in fantasies about being an NRA 'good guy' who uses his gun to protect his family and community from the 'bad guys' was one way for men to reclaim that threatened

03 March for Our Lives: student-led demonstration on 24 March 2018 in support of tighter gun control
23 Women's March: worldwide protest on 21 January 2017 for women's rights
52 NRA = National Rifle Association: a US organization that advocates for gun rights

masculinity." And in 2015, researchers from the University of Chicago reported that racial resentment was a strong predictor of opposition to gun control; and that the more racist respondents were, the more steadfast that opposition was.

F There's a long history of white male support for gun rights being connected to anger and fear over gains for women and people of color. That's part of the reason that many of the most irate responses to recent young activists have skewed racist or misogynist. It should not surprise us that when a Republican politician in Maine attacked student activist Emma Gonzalez, he called her a "skinhead lesbian"; or that a senior columnist at the rightwing publication *Townhall* used Twitter to mock the appearance of protesting teenage girls. Just as it's no surprise when so many mass shooters are white men with histories of domestic violence, and why so many of their victims are women.

G But while issues of race and gender confound and alarm those on the right, young activists are doing nuanced thinking to bolster their work on gun violence. This generation is calling out the hypocrisy of conservatives who abhor government interference unless it's over women's bodies, talking about how arming teachers would endanger students of color, and recognizing how white students are getting the support that young Black Lives Matter activists never did. Perhaps the brightest star of this weekend's march was 11-year-old Naomi Wadler, who dedicated her speech to black girls and women who were victims of gun violence who in the past "have just been numbers".

H The new America is made up of communication-savvy, digital natives. They're not cowed easily, and they see through the arguments that may have stumped their forebears. That's why Parkland students didn't hesitate to boo when NRA spokeswoman Dana Loesch tried to appeal to women's rights concerns – arguing guns could protect potential rape victims – at a CNN town hall. They saw through her rhetorical posturing immediately, and reacted accordingly.

I A generation ago, before social media and digital activism, it wouldn't have been mainstream common knowledge that the NRA failed to support Marissa Alexander, a black woman who used a gun to defend herself from domestic violence. Or that they similarly ignored Bresha Meadows, a teenage girl of color who shot her abusive father. But today's young activists can see these failures and hypocrisies clearly and quickly – adults don't fool them, nor do well-funded lobbying groups. As Emma Gonzalez said in her viral speech, they're calling bullshit.

J A lot of us adults watching the march and the walkout felt hope for the first time in a long time, and not just because of the incredible signs. We saw a generation who is succeeding where we failed, an emerging new force that thinks differently and who is willing to take the power they democratically deserve. I, for one, am ready to take my cues from this smart new America for whom creating change comes so easily. As Haider said to me when I asked why she protested, "Why wouldn't I? It's insane not to."

From the mouths of babes.

(840 words)

Source: Jessica Valenti, The Guardian, *27.03.2018*

66 skew: (here) become
95 Parkland students: students who survived a school shooting in Parkland, Florida, on 14 February 2018
99 CNN town hall: programme about current events on CNN which involves audience participation

4 **The author describes the debate on gun control as "a culture war". Which groups are "fighting" each other, according to the author?**

5 **Make notes on the characteristics of the young generation, as described in the text.**

Testing your reading skills

1 Multiple-choice questions (paragraphs A–F)

Choose the most suitable option.

1 In Paragraph A the writer says that because the young protestors are digital natives, they …

- **a** do not limit their message to just one topic.
- **b** excel at using their creativity to make their protest heard.
- **c** blame politics for having failed them.
- **d** are able to create posters on their computers.

2 "And guns are their security blanket of choice" (lines 31–32) means that elderly white men own guns …

- **a** in order to defend their traditional status.
- **b** in order to protect their community.
- **c** in order to feel more secure at home.
- **d** in order to set them apart from their neighbours.

3 Which of the following is not true according to paragraphs D and E?

- **a** Gun owners can predominantly be found in the countryside.
- **b** Gun owners tend to have chauvinist views.
- **c** Gun owners usually hold conservative social values.
- **d** Gun owners are more often prone to attacks than other groups.

4 The angry reactions to the latest activities in favour of gun control have often been …

- **a** ridiculed by college students.
- **b** inspired by hatred for women.
- **c** made by violent husbands.
- **d** fueled by irrational ideas.

2 Mediation Englisch – Deutsch (paragraphs G–J)

Beantworten Sie folgende Fragen auf Deutsch.

1	Erläutern Sie die von den jungen Aktivisten erkannte Widersprüchlichkeit der Haltung bestimmter Konservativer.
2	Welche weiteren Kritikpunkte neben der in Frage 1 erwähnten Widersprüchlichkeit werden von den jungen Aktivisten in Paragraph G genannt? *(2 Aspekte)*
3	Warum reagierten die jungen Menschen auf die NRA Sprecherin Dana Loesch mit Buh-Rufen?

Developing your language skills

1 Improving your vocabulary

With a partner, match the sentences (1–6) with those that have the same meaning (a–f) and decide which one of the two is stylistically better. Find reasons why you think your choice is better. Words and phrases used in the sentences can be found in paragraphs C–E.

1 It is not just an abstract debate over right or wrong.	**a** These people are mainly motivated by racial anxiety and a fear of emasculation.
2 Some people very much want to keep their old-fashioned values. It is these people who very probably want to fight for the status quo.	**b** People who are very racist are the most stubborn when it comes to opposing gun control.
3 These people are mainly doing this because they are afraid of persons of other races and they are also afraid of losing their male power.	**c** It is more than just people abstractly discussing if something is right or if it is wrong.
4 The gun owners' fear of losing power stems from observing an upcoming, self-confident generation.	**d** Many of the NRA's supporters come from rural areas.
5 Many of the NRA's supporters live in the countryside.	**e** The people who are desperate to hang on to traditional values are the ones most likely to fight for the status quo.
6 The more racist people are, the more steadfast they are when it comes to opposing gun control.	**f** Due to the fact that they observe an emerging, self-confident generation, gun owners are afraid of losing their power.

2 Improving your listening skills

07

The attitude towards car ownership is also changing among members of the emerging generation. Learn more about what will probably change in the future and how automobile companies are trying to meet this change by listening to the following podcast.

1 What is meant when Bettendorf says "Gen Z is a game changer"?
2 Explain in your own words what the three areas are which American automakers are working on in order to stay up to date with the changing market?
3 Fill in the following text to sum up what Shaheen and Bettendorf say towards the end of the programme.

Although young people are increasingly changing the way they travel by car, ___[1] ___[2] are still an important player in this new market. Since young people use their ___[3] through ride-sharing apps, the companies can collect information on their ___[4], for example where they go and how they get there. Through their use of car-sharing apps young people are, in the view of the car manufacturers, already on the way to ___[5] a car. On the other hand, living in huge cities doesn't require car ownership any more, which could result in a ___[6] for car manufacturers.

4 After having listened to the programme, discuss the option of not owning a car in the future with your partner. What advantages would this have for the infrastructure of cities, for the people living in big cities and for you personally?

Testing your writing and speaking skills

1 Mediation Deutsch – Englisch

In Ihrer Recherche zur Generation Z fragen Sie sich, wie sich diese Generation von der vorherigen Generation bezüglich der Einstellung zur Arbeitswelt unterscheidet. Folgender Artikel hilft Ihnen bei der Analyse. Fassen Sie diesen in ca. 150 Wörtern unter Bezugnahme auf folgende Aspekte zusammen:

- **Generation Z und ihre Einstellung zur Arbeitswelt bezüglich Selbstverständnis von Beruf, Privatleben und Arbeitszeit**
- **Erläuterung des Begriffs „flexible feste Strukturen"**
- **Generation Z und ihre Beziehung zum Arbeitgeber**

WAS GENERATION Z VOM BERUFSLEBEN ERWARTET

Die Jugendlichen von heute ticken anders. […] Die Generation Z, das sind grob gesagt die nach 1995 geborenen Jugendlichen. Der Arbeitsweltexperte Christian Scholz von der Universität des Saarlandes forscht seit Jahren über sie. […]

Der Professor für Betriebswirtschaftslehre befragt seine Studenten, lässt sie Tagebuch schreiben oder ihr Leben als Z-ler szenisch umsetzen. Dabei hat er beobachtet: „Denkrichtung und Merkmale dieser Jugendlichen sind vollkommen anders als die der Generation Y." Scholz zufolge herrscht in der Generation Z ein ganz neues Selbstverständnis in Bezug auf die Arbeitswelt.

Die Vermischung von Beruf und Privatleben findet kaum noch Anklang. Zu genau haben die Jugendlichen von heute beobachtet, wie die Generation Y oftmals die Arbeit mit nach Hause nimmt und nicht vom Laptop wegkommt. „Die Z-ler wollen geregelte Arbeitszeiten, unbefristete Verträge und klar definierte Strukturen im Job haben", so der Arbeitsweltexperte: „Wenn Feierabend ist, dann lesen sie auch keine Arbeitsmails."

Der Jugendforscher Klaus Hurrelmann hält Vorhersagen darüber, wie diese neue Generation der Berufstätigen das Arbeitsleben verändern wird, noch für „voreilig und spekulativ". Doch auch er erkennt, dass die Z-ler nicht mehr an eine faire Fusion von Job und Privatleben glauben. „Meine Prognose ist, dass es hinausläuft auf flexible feste Strukturen", sagt der Professor of Public Health and Education an der Hertie School of Governance. „Die Generation Z möchte eine feste Grundlage haben, beispielsweise feste Arbeitszeitkontingente." Diese wollen die Jugendlichen dann aber eigenverantwortlich erfüllen.

[…] Auch Arbeitsmarktforscher Scholz bekräftigt, dass sich die Generation Z neben einem klar definierten Arbeitsanfang und -ende auch mal einen Homeoffice-Tag wünscht: Aber nur wenn sie will – nicht verordnet vom Unternehmen. Loyalität zum Arbeitgeber gibt es in der Generation Z kaum noch. Denn andersherum ist das genauso, sagt Scholz. Das Denken sei: Wenn mir etwas nicht passt, bin ich morgen weg. „Da prallen Welten aufeinander."

Doch Scholz warnt: Während die Z-ler schon auf den Arbeitsmarkt strömen, haben sich die Unternehmen darauf noch nicht eingestellt. „In der Personalwirtschaft liegt der Fokus derzeit noch ausschließlich auf der Generation Y", kritisiert er. „Es wird große Probleme geben." Denn rosige Karriereversprechungen nützen bei den realistischen Z-lern in Bewerbungsgesprächen nichts. […]

Die Generation der künftigen Arbeitnehmer setzt zudem auf Lebensqualität und Gesundheit. „Anti-Stress-Kurse für die Generation Y sind für typische Z-ler zum Lachen, das machen sie schon automatisch", erklärt Scholz. Ihr Privatleben ist ihnen noch wichtiger, noch bewusster und abgegrenzter als der Vorgängergeneration. Jugendforscher Hurrelmann sagt: „Das hat nichts mit Faulheit zu tun, sondern damit, dass Arbeit im digitalen Zeitalter überall und jederzeit möglich ist." Wenn man nicht aufpasse, bestehe das Leben nur noch aus Arbeit.

[…] Jungendforscher Hurrelmann identifiziert ein neues Stärke-Schwäche-Profil für die Arbeitnehmer von morgen. „Wir bekommen eine hochsensible junge Generation, die alles blitzschnell aufnimmt und erfasst und enorm multitaskingfähig ist", sagt er, „dann aber auch nicht mehr so konzentriert ist, sich schnell ablenken lässt und ein kurzes Durchhaltevermögen besitzt." Darauf müssen sich die Unternehmen schon heute einstellen.

Source: David Bedürftig, Die Welt, *06. 03. 2016*

2 Group discussion

Situation: In view of the current discussion on the demographic development and the problems facing an ageing society, you have joined a group in your town to find projects to improve understanding between the various generations. Choose one of the projects on page 143, then discuss how they might contribute towards the development of society and how they could tackle some of the problems we are already facing today.

Presentation phase: Present your project to the others and point out its strengths.

Interaction phase: Decide on at least two of these projects to be implemented in your town, taking the feasibility of the project and its impact on the generations to come into account.

Optional *(if you have time at the end of the discussion):* Which aspects would you additionally see as important for a workshop on "Working together in a multi-generational team"?

Exploring the topic

SITUATION

Inspired by current discussions in the media, you have become interested in how countries are trying to achieve equality between men and women in the labour market and in society in general. That is why you decide to attend an international students' symposium. As each of the participants has to hand in a short report on equality in today's world, you start doing some more research on the topic.

1 **What experience do you have of unjust pay between men and women?**

2 **Look at the two visuals. What do they tell you?**

initiiert vom:
Business and Professional Women Germany e.V.

The global gender gap index 2017

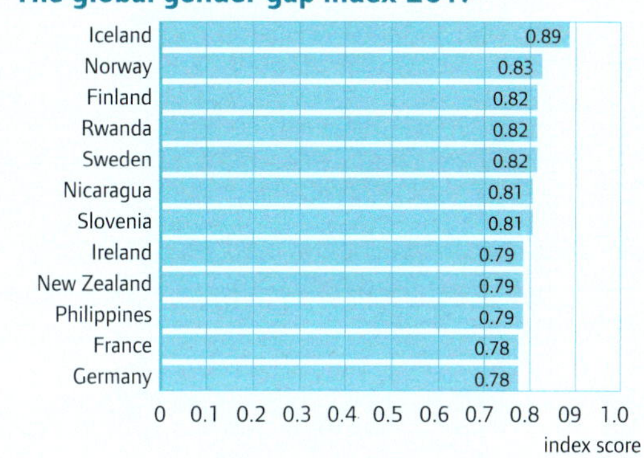

Source: World Economic Forum 2017; © Statista

3 **Read the following article "Equality won't happen by itself: how Iceland got tough on gender pay gap", which explains how Iceland has become one of the first countries worldwide to legally enforce equal pay. Collect important information from the text in a flow chart like the one below.**

Equal pay = ▬

Case study: Iceland
- reasons why it is the world's most gender-equal country: ▬ ▬ ▬ ▬
- 1961: ▬
- but ▬

↔

Why legally enforced equal pay?
- legislative measures ▬

↓

How does the law work in practice?
- employers must prove ▬
- companies with more than ▬ employees are affected
- time-limit to get ▬
- failure to comply results in ▬

Still to do
- gender-based ▬
- overcome gaps between ▬

↔

↓

Positive outcome for firms
- ▬
- ▬
- ▬
- improved decision-making
- ▬
- all-round ▬

EQUALITY WON'T HAPPEN BY ITSELF: HOW ICELAND GOT TOUGH ON GENDER PAY GAP

Despite its image as a paradise of fairness, women still earn less than men. Now Iceland has become the first country in the world to enforce equal pay.

A On the face of it, Iceland is a good place to be a woman. For nearly a decade, it has been rated the world's most gender-equal country. It was the first to directly elect a female president, nearly half its MPs and company directors are women, and first-class daycare and parental leave help ensure almost four in five women have jobs. So it came as a shock for Fríða Rós Valdimarsdóttir to learn, when she was managing a key team of 10 home carers at Reykjavik council a few years ago, that male colleagues in other departments, with far fewer responsibilities than her, were being paid a great deal more. "It has been illegal for decades, for jobs that are worth the same, to pay people differently because of gender, but still it happens – it's simply been allowed," says Valdimarsdóttir, who is now the chair of the Icelandic Women's Rights Association, in her bright offices in the country's capital.

B Despite an equal pay act that dates back to 1961, Icelandic women still earn, on average, between 14% and 20% less than men. So Valdimarsdóttir and her association were one of many campaign groups to back a plan that finally resulted, last month, in the island becoming the first country in the world to legally enforce equal pay. Within four years from January 2018, any public or private body in Iceland employing more than 25 people that has not been independently certified as paying equal wages for work of equal value will face daily fines. "The legislation will take some time to bed in, of course," Valdimarsdóttir says. "There will be challenges. But it's possible, and we can do it. Mainly, I'm just so proud we actually made it happen."

C Rósa Guðrún Erlingsdóttir, head of the equality unit at Iceland's welfare ministry, says equality "won't come about by itself, from the bottom up alone. Our experience is that you need legislative measures to move things forward. People accept that; we saw it with mandatory quotas for women on company boards. If politicians want to wait until no one opposes it, it will never happen."

D Some in Iceland still do oppose it, albeit cautiously. The new law requires employers to show, through certification by an accredited auditor, that their pay management system complies with a national equal pay standard modelled on the international ISO environmental management standards familiar to all companies. The standard was published in 2012 and welcomed by Iceland's trade unions and employers, who helped design it. [...]

E The process – assessing the worth of very different jobs, classifying and ranking occupations, analysing salary structures, collating and recording data, making sure the new system meshes with collective labour agreements – is "quite complex", says Hannes Sigurðsson of the Business Iceland confederation. "You need to put resources into it. It's easier for big companies, with whole HR departments." As it stands, the legislation is staggered over four years. Large firms and institutions such as government ministries and the national hospital, with workforces of more than 250 people, have until the end of this year to become certified; those with fewer than 90 employees but more than 25 have until the end of 2021. The fine for those that do not comply is ISK 50,000 (£350) a day. And the public shame, it is hoped, will be worse.

F None of Business Iceland's members have openly criticised the new law, Sigurðsson says. "It's quite difficult to come out publicly against a measure that enhances gender equality. But I think it's clear there is opposition to the method. We would have preferred the process to be bottom-up." Others, however, are delighted. "This will not eliminate the gender pay gap overnight," says Maríanna Traustadóttir, an equality adviser at the Icelandic trade union confederation ASI. "But it is the best toolbox I have seen, and it will make a big difference. It will force employers to think differently." [...]

G Traustadóttir cites Reykjavik Energy, the parent company of Iceland's largest power provider, which was forced to fire one-third of its workforce in the aftermath of the financial crash, but seized on its subsequent restructuring as an opportunity to become a fully gender-equal employer. Within five years, by "putting the gender glasses on before taking every single decision", it had boosted the proportion of women in management positions from 29% to 49%. Over the same period, its adjusted gender pay gap shrank from 8.4% to 2.1% – and now stands at 0.2% in favour of women. The company's chief executive, Bjarni Bjarnason, says the net outcome has been "more open discussions, higher productivity, greater job satisfaction, improved decision-making, higher morale, and an all-round far better atmosphere".

H For many, the legislation reflects the fact that more than 40 years after 90% of Iceland's women famously went on strike for a day, the country "is not quite the gender-equality paradise it's often painted", says Annadís Gréta Rúdólfsdóttir, an assistant education professor. "That WEF index is fairly crude. It doesn't reflect the pay gap, or gender-based violence. We have our fair share of toxic masculinity. #MeToo was as shocking here as anywhere." Her colleague, Berglind Rós Magnúsdóttir, says a broader "re-engineering" of society is still needed. "This won't fix the huge gap between typically male and typically female sectors," she says. "Between engineering, for example, and nursing or teaching. Anything to do with care or education is paid less."

I But there is confidence the legislation is a major step in the right direction. "The pay gap was hidden behind a lack of transparency," says Magnea Marinósdóttir of the welfare ministry's equality unit, noting that the standard could be used to justify a pay difference as much as to eliminate it. "Employers can take into account experience, qualifications – it's just that it now has to be transparent, and justified," Marinósdóttir adds. "The standard is simply designed to eliminate factors that are irrelevant by law – such as gender. It could equally be used to eliminate discrimination by race or disability."

J Legislation, she is convinced, "can impact attitudes and behaviour. We've seen that time and again. We still live in a very gendered reality in Iceland. Even here, the patriarchal culture, a male sense of entitlement, is deep-rooted. This can be a real impetus for change." Erlingsdóttir says the Icelandic model could also be adopted elsewhere: Portugal is exploring doing so, raising the possibility that Iceland's equal pay standard could eventually become a European one.

(1099 words)

Source: John Henley, The Guardian, *20.02.2018*

49 accredited auditor: *zugelassene/r Wirtschaftsprüfer/in*
52 ISO: *Vereinigung, die internationale Normen in allen Bereichen erarbeitet*
61 mesh with sth.: *mit etwas verzahnt werden*
73 ISK: (Icelandic currency) krona
118 WEF index: listing made by the World Economic Forum of countries according to how equal the genders are

4 **What is your opinion of Iceland's method of achieving equal pay? Do you think this system could work in your country as well? Give reasons for your answer.**

5 **What problems could arise with the Icelandic method? How might they be solved?**

Testing your reading skills

1 Gapped summary (paragraphs A–E)

Copy the summary and fill the gaps with appropriate words from the corresponding passages of the text (one word per gap). Do not make any changes. Please also provide the number of the line in which you found the word or phrase.

Globally, Iceland has been for many years an excellent example of a ___[1] ___[2] (line ___), but the country has still struggled with the fact that women have actually been paid less than their male counterparts despite this having been ___[3] (line ___) for more than half a century. Instead of trying to solve this problem on a voluntary level, the government decided to use ___[4] ___[5] (line ___) to make sure that the country moved towards equality. Now companies have to prove that their payment policy ___[6] ___[7] (line ___) national standards. Since a process like this cannot be implemented overnight, companies have been given a timeframe in which to promote equal pay among their ___[8] (line ___). If they fail to do so, they will face a daily ___[9] (line ___) and probably even ___[10] ___[11] (line ___).

2 Multiple-choice questions (paragraphs F–G)

Choose the most suitable option.

1 Which of the following is not mentioned concerning the new law? The new law …

a	is not particularly liked by members of Business Iceland.
b	will be hard to implement.
c	will compel business leaders to take a new approach to gender equality.
d	won't solve the issue of gender equality immediately.

2 At Reykjavik Energy, gender equality …

a	resulted in the firing of one in every three workers.
b	had to be introduced in order to improve the atmosphere at work.
c	was introduced in order to deal with the economic crisis.
d	led to women taking up about half of all managerial positions.

3 Mediation Englisch – Deutsch (paragraphs H–J)

Beantworten Sie folgende Fragen auf Deutsch.

1	Laut Frau Rúdólfsdóttir gibt es trotz des neuen Gesetzes noch einiges in Island zu tun. Erläutern Sie im Textzusammenhang, was ihre Aussage zu Island „not quite the gender-equality paradise it's often painted" (Zeilen 115–116) bedeutet.
2	Was meint ihre Kollegin Frau Magnúsdóttir mit der Aussage, „a broader re-engineering of society is still needed" (Zeilen 123–125)?
3	Trotz allem war laut Frau Marinósdóttir der Weg über die Legislative der richtige. Wie begründet sie diese Aussage?

Developing your language skills

1 Using idiomatic expressions

The idiomatic use of language (in other words, how "English" your writing sounds) is one of the criteria on which you are graded. German speakers often write English sentences that are grammatically correct but which could actually have been written in a way that sounds more English.

A Rewrite these rather wordy English sentences by using words or expressions from paragraphs A to C in order to make them stylistically more English.

1 Iceland is very good at taking care of children while their parents are at work and allows fathers to stay at home for a period of time in order to enable the majority of women to work.
2 The new law makes sure that men who do not have as many things to take care of as their female colleagues are not paid more.
3 The person who is leader of the Icelandic Women's Rights Association is Ms Valdimarsdóttir.
4 The first law to guarantee the same wages for men and women was passed in 1961. Yet it wasn't until a month ago that Iceland became the first country which passed a law that made sure that there was equality of income for men and women.
5 This law means that every state institution and privately owned business will have to pay the same amount of money to people for doing the same work.
6 As the process will not start just by citizens and companies changing things, Iceland introduced new laws to improve gender equality.

B Using the phrases from the box, write sentences that sound more idiomatic. You may need to rewrite the sentences.

in the aftermath of • to enhance • albeit • to comply with

1 He accepted the job offer, but he was still hesitant.
2 His company has to follow European employment laws.
3 Having a lot of work experience will make your career prospects better.
4 In the difficult period that resulted from the worldwide financial crisis, the company faced serious problems.

2 Improving your viewing skills

04

A Before watching the report, try to guess what a report using the following words could be about.

cohabitation • camaraderie • conscription • female soldiers

B Watch the video and answer the following questions.

1 What was significant about the law from 2013 concerning female military service in Norway?
2 Give an example where women in the military are especially important.
3 What example is given as proof of Norway's long term politics of gender equality?

C Work in groups of three. Each group member reads one part of the report that accompanies the video. The other two group members answer the questions after listening to the report being read by the third member. You are not allowed to take notes. If necessary, the different parts can be read more than just once.

Part 1:

1. How does Norway make gender equality a reality in the context of military service?
2. What does Lieutenant Colonel Berglund like about the new conscription policy?
3. What process started 40 years ago in the Norwegian military?

Part 2:

1. What do Israel and Norway have in common?
2. What advantage of having women in the military is mentioned?
3. What does "It enables you to cut the umbilical cord" mean in the context of the text?

Part 3:

1. Explain the phrase "You don't shit in your own nest" in the context of the text.
2. What do the women say about their behaviour in mixed groups?
3. Could one say that de-genderization has been a complete success in Norway?

3 Improving your listening skills

08

NPR host Ari Shapiro talks to Valeria Jarrett and John Zimmer from Lyft, one of the fastest growing ride-hailing companies about how they are addressing gender equality in their company and how their company is part of a fundamental change taking place in the working world and in urbanization. You and your partner take notes on the respective issues listed in the table below. Then talk about your findings with your partner.

	PARTNER A	PARTNER B
1	What do we learn about Valerie Jarrett's position at Lyft and about her former employment in the introduction and conclusion given by the host of the news programme?	What do we learn about John Zimmer's role at Lyft in the introduction and conclusion given by the host of the news programme?
2	Which two things are mentioned by Zimmer to show what the company stands for?	Shapiro mentions two examples that show that Lyft might be taking a certain position on political matters. Which two examples does Shapiro mention?
3	Jarrett and Zinner give examples of how many women were in different positions in the company. Which facts accompany the figures below? ■ 37% ■ 10 ■ 42% ■ 30% ■ 1%	Why was Jarrett impressed when she visited her future employer? How does this compare to other companies and especially Silicon Valley companies? How does Shapiro interpret her comment?
4	What is the main benefit of driving for Lyft? Note down one example which illustrates this benefit.	Between which two types of workers does Zimmer distinguish? Lyft is also working on "portable benefits". What is meant by that?
5	(inference question) What do the mentioned portable benefits have to do with health care and being employed as a contractor?	(inference question) Listen to how Zimmer and Jarrett answer the question about privacy. How do they try to answer this question? Also listen to what Shapiro tells the audience at the very end of the programme.
6	What influence will ride-hailing companies have on urban infrastructure in the future?	What will listening to music, watching films and driving cars have in common in the future?

Testing your writing and speaking skills

1 Material-based writing

During your research on how equality might be achieved in the workplace, in schools or in society in general, you come across the notion of "affirmative action". This concept has been very popular since the 1980s and is an attempt to actively improve the educational and employment opportunities of members of minority groups and women by introducing different standards or by introducing quotas for disadvantaged people.

Your school wants you to write a short article about equality for the student newspaper. You choose the following title for your article:

Is affirmative action an effective means to achieve greater equality in society?

Write 300 words, using the material provided.

MATERIAL 1

Equality across the highest levels of business won't happen in our lifetime unless organisations are forced to retain and develop their talent, by quotas if necessary.

Source: Vicky Pryce (chief economic adviser at the Centre for Economics and Business Research), "Why we need quotas for women on boards", The Guardian, *23. 11. 2015*

MATERIAL 2

Schüler mit niedriger sozialer Herkunft haben im Schnitt deutlich schlechtere Schulnoten als Kinder aus Akademikerfamilien. 96 Prozent der Lehrer sagen einer Allensbach-Umfrage nach, dass das Elternhaus mit darüber bestimmt, wie erfolgreich Schüler sind. 83 Prozent glauben sogar, der Einfluss sei groß oder sehr groß. Wer die Lebensläufe von Arbeiterkindern betrachtet, sieht, dass sie oft erst später im Leben – in ihren 20ern oder 30ern – erfolgreich werden. Sie brauchen länger, um zu kompensieren, dass sie in ihrem Elternhaus vieles nicht gelernt haben, was in Akademikerfamilien normal ist.

Source: Jakob Simmank, "Gebt Arbeiterkindern endlich eine Chance", Die Zeit, *04. 10. 2017*

MATERIAL 3

"We got tired of explaining to everybody what 'affirmative action' means."

2 Mediation Deutsch – Englisch

Sie schreiben nun Ihren kurzen Bericht zum Thema gleichberechtigte Bezahlung in der Arbeitswelt anhand einen kürzlich in Ihrer Tageszeitung erschienen Artikel, indem Sie diesen in ca. 150 Wörtern zusammenfassen und sich auf die folgenden Aspekte konzentrieren:

- **Situation der Gleichberechtigung weltweit seit 2006**
- **Bereiche, die weltweit zur Erfassung der Geschlechterlücke herangezogen werden und deren Entwicklung**
- **allgemeine Situation in Deutschland in Bezug auf das Ranking und den Nachholbedarf**
- **Gründe, warum eine Gleichberechtigung v. a. auch wirtschaftlich sinnvoll ist**

GLEICHBERECHTIGUNG? VIELLEICHT IN 100 JAHREN

Die Daten wirken ernüchternd. Um die Gleichberechtigung zwischen Frau und Mann ist es weltweit trist bestellt. Erstmals seit dem Jahr 2006 ist die Ungerechtigkeit größer geworden. So schreibt es das Weltwirtschaftsforum (WEF) in einer neuen Studie zur „Gender Gap", der Geschlechterlücke. Wenn sich aktuelle Trends fortsetzen, dauert es global noch 100 Jahre bis zur Gleichberechtigung. Vor zwölf Monaten gingen die Forscher des WEF noch von 83 Jahren aus.

Diese Erkenntnisse leiten die Analysten aus einem Index ab. Diesen haben sie anhand der Kriterien Gesundheit, Bildung, ökonomische Teilhabe und politische Mitwirkung für 144 Länder entwickelt. Die Daten basieren unter anderem auf Statistiken der Weltgesundheitsorganisation und der Vereinten Nationen. Im Jahr 2017 habe es in allen vier Bereichen Rückschritte gegeben, heißt es. Gerade jene in Wirtschaft und Politik seien aber besorgniserregend, da sie am stärksten zur Geschlechterlücke beitragen würden. „Ein Jahrzehnt des langsamen, aber stetigen Fortschritts beim Verbessern der Gleichheit zwischen den Geschlechtern kam 2017 zum Erliegen", lautet das Fazit des WEF.

Insbesondere die durchschnittlichen Bruttolöhne zeigen die Trendwende, beim Versuch die Geschlechterlücke zu schließen. Vor einem Jahr verdienten Männer im weltweiten Durchschnitt noch etwa 9400 Dollar mehr als Frauen. Mittlerweile sind es knapp 10200 Dollar. [...] Deutschland bescheinigt das WEF eine positive Entwicklung in den vergangenen zwölf Monaten. Die Bundesrepublik verbesserte sich um einen Platz und steht nun auf Rang zwölf der Tabelle der gerechtesten Staaten zwischen Frankreich und Namibia. Gemessen am ersten Ranking 2006 ging es aber deutlich nach unten, damals stand die Bundesrepublik noch auf Platz fünf. Nachholbedarf gibt es vor allem in zwei Punkten. In Wirtschaft und Politik ist die Geschlechterlücke laut WEF längst nicht geschlossen. Mängel gibt es etwa bei Lohnunterschieden zwischen Mann und Frau bei ähnlicher Arbeit. Ebenso fehlt es an Frauen in Führungspositionen in Politik und Wirtschaft, auch wenn Konzerne zunehmend Frauen in Aufsichtsräte berufen. Bezüglich der wirtschaftlichen Gleichheit liegt Deutschland auf Platz 43 knapp hinter Kamerun und Jamaika. In den Bereichen Bildung und Gesundheit gibt es hingegen fast Bestwerte.

Die WEF-Expertin Saadia Zahidi betont: „Gleichberechtigung ist eine moralische und ökonomische Notwendigkeit." Die Autoren der Studie verweisen auf Modelle und empirische Erhebungen, die ökonomische Vorteile der Parität aufzeigen. Bei vollständiger Gerechtigkeit könne das Bruttoinlandsprodukt der USA um 1750 Milliarden Dollar gesteigert werden. Für Deutschland sei eine Erhöhung um 310 Milliarden Dollar, also 267 Milliarden Euro, möglich. Das wäre eine Steigerung des Bruttoinlandsprodukts um etwa zehn Prozent.

Source: Janis Beenen, Süddeutsche Zeitung, *02. 11. 2017*

Exploring the topic

SITUATION

You have been chosen by your school to take part in a pre-selection to the Forum of Young Global Leaders. As you will have to hand in at least one paper on the importance of the middle class for Western societies, you start preparing yourself by doing some research on the topic.

1 **Look at pictures 1 and 2. How would you describe the atmosphere they convey?**

2 **Try to find a connection between the first two pictures and picture 3.**

1

2

3

3 **Read the article on page 62 to find out what might be done to help declining places and their people.**

THE RIGHT WAY TO HELP DECLINING PLACES

Time for fresh thinking about the changing economics of geography

A Populism's wave has yet to crest. That is the sobering lesson of recent elections in Germany and Austria, where the success of anti-immigrant, anti-globalisation parties showed that a message of hostility to elites and outsiders resonates as strongly as ever among those fed up with the status quo.

B It is also the lesson from America, where Donald Trump is doubling down on gestures to his angry base, most recently by adopting a negotiating position on NAFTA that is more likely to wreck than remake the trade agreement. These remedies will not work. The demise of NAFTA will disproportionately hurt the blue-collar workers who back Mr Trump. Getting tough on immigrants will do nothing to improve economic conditions in eastern Germany, where 20% of voters backed the far-right Alternative for Germany. But the self-defeating nature of populist policies will not blunt their appeal. Mainstream parties must offer voters who feel left behind a better vision of the future, one that takes greater account of the geographical reality behind the politics of anger.

Location, location, vocation

C Economic theory suggests that regional inequalities should diminish as poorer (and cheaper) places attract investment and grow faster than richer ones. The 20th century bore that theory out: income gaps narrowed across American states and European regions. No longer. Affluent places are now pulling away from poorer ones. This geographical divergence has dramatic consequences. A child born in the bottom 20% in wealthy San Francisco has twice as much chance as a similar child in Detroit of ending up in the top 20% as an adult. Boys born in London's Chelsea can expect to live nearly nine years longer than those born in Blackpool. Opportunities are limited for those stuck in the wrong place, and the wider economy suffers. If all its citizens had lived in places of high productivity over the past 50 years, America's economy could have grown twice as fast as it did.

D Divergence is the result of big forces. In the modern economy, scale is increasingly important. The companies with the biggest hoards of data can train their machines most effectively; the social network that everyone else is on is most attractive to new users;

affluent Chelsea

run-down Blackpool

the stock exchange with the deepest pool of investors is best for raising capital. These returns to scale create fewer, superstar firms clustered in fewer, superstar places. Everywhere else is left behind.

E Even as regional disparities widen, people are becoming less mobile. The percentage of Americans who move across state lines each year has fallen by half since the 1990s. The typical American is more footloose than the average European, yet lives less than 30 kilometres from his parents. Demographic shifts help explain this, including the rise in two-earner households and the need to care for ageing family members.

F But the bigger culprit is poor policies. Soaring housing costs in prosperous cities keep newcomers out. In Europe a scarcity of social housing leads people to hang on to cheap flats. In America the spread of state-specific occupational licensing and government benefits punishes those who move. The pension of a teacher who stays in the same state could be twice as big as that of a teacher who moves mid-career.

G Perversely, policies to help the poor unintentionally exacerbate the plight of left-behind places. Unemployment and health benefits enable the least employable people to survive in struggling places when once they would have had no choice but to move. Welfare makes capitalism less brutal for individuals, but it perpetuates the problems where they live.

Welcome to the place age

H What to do? One answer is to help people move. Thriving places could do more to build the housing and infrastructure to accommodate newcomers. Accelerating the reciprocal recognition of credentials across state or national borders would help people move to where they can be most productive. But greater mobility also has a perverse side-effect. By draining moribund places of talented workers, it exacerbates their troubles. The local tax-base erodes as productive workers leave, even as welfare and pension obligations mount.

13 NAFTA: North American Free Trade Agreement: agreement on promoting free tade between Canada, the USA and Mexico
94 credentials: documents, qualifications

I To avoid these outcomes, politicians have long tried to bolster left-behind places with subsidies. But such "regional policies" have a patchy record, at best. South Carolina lured BMW to the state in 1992 and from it built a thriving automotive cluster. But the EU's structural funds raise output and reduce unemployment only so long as funding continues. California has 42 enterprise zones. None has raised employment. Better for politicians to focus on speeding up the diffusion of technology and business practices from high-performing places. A beefed-up competition policy could reduce industrial concentration, which saps the economy of dynamism while focusing the gains from growth in fewer firms and places. Fostering clusters by encouraging the creation of private investment funds targeted on particular regions might help.

J Bolder still would be to expand the mission of local colleges. In the 19th century America created lots of public technical universities. They were supposed to teach best practice to farmers and factory managers in small towns and rural areas. They could play that role again today for new technologies, much as Germany already has a network of applied-research institutions. Politicians might even learn from Amazon, whose search for a home for a second headquarters has set off a scramble among cities hoping to lure the giant retailer. Governments could award public research centres – in the mould of America's National Institutes of Health or Europe's CERN – to cities which prepare the best plans for policy reform and public investment. This would aid the diffusion of new ideas and create an incentive for struggling places to help themselves.

K Perhaps most of all, politicians need a different mindset. For progressives, alleviating poverty has demanded welfare; for libertarians, freeing up the economy. Both have focused on people. But the complex interaction of demography, welfare and globalisation means that is insufficient. Assuaging the anger of the left-behind means realising that places matter, too.

(988 words)
Source: the Economist, *09. 06. 2018*

121 to beef sth. up: *etwas aufpeppen*
155 progressives: people who are in favour of new ideas, modern methods and change
156 libertarians: people who believe in limiting the power of the state

4 **a** You and your partner focus on different parts of the text and try to find its most important messages:
Partner A concentrates on "Location, location, vocation" (C–G).
Partner B concentrates on "Welcome to the place age" (H–K).
Once you have finished your part, get together with a person with the same text part and visualize the content of "your" text (if possible with a digital visualization program).

b Now go back to your original partner who has prepared the other part of the text and explain your visualizations to each other. Then exchange your visualizations to have an outline of the full text.

Testing your reading skills

1 Mediation Englisch – Deutsch (paragraphs A–B)

Beantworten Sie folgende Fragen auf Deutsch. Der Buchstabe am Ende der jeweiligen Frage gibt an, in welchem Absatz die Antwort zu finden ist.

1	Worauf gehen die Wahlerfolge von Populisten in Deutschland und Österreich zurück?	A
2	Wie sieht der Autor Trumps Vorhaben NAFTA neu zu verhandeln, und wie wird sich dieses Neuverhandeln in den Augen des Autors auswirken?	B
3	Erläutern Sie im Textzusammenhang was mit „better vision" (Zeilen 24–25) gemeint ist.	B
4	Welche positive Folge hätte eine schnellere und einfachere Anerkennung von Zeugnissen überall im Land?	H
5	Welches Problem ergibt sich bei der staatlichen Subvention ausgewählter Regionen?	I

2 Multiple matching (paragraphs C–G)

Which headlines match paragraphs C to G? There are three more headlines than needed.

1	A sedentary nation
2	Subsidies work
3	Where you live matters
4	Local celebrities successful
5	Productivity lost
6	Well-meant but counterproductive
7	Size counts
8	Policies hinder progress

3 Multiple-choice question (paragraphs J–K)

Choose the most suitable option. Which of the following policies is not advocated?

a	Politicians should found new public institutions in areas which are willing to invest in the future.
b	Local colleges should again focus on training practical knowledge about farming.
c	American politicians should use Germany's universities of applied sciences as an example of how to invest in the future.
d	Politicians need to stop thinking just about the people who are left behind economically but also about the areas they live in.

Developing your language skills

1 Making comparisons

Paragraphs C and D of the text use many comparisons. Try to find the English equivalents of the given German phrases and use them in the gaps.

Writing about developments often requires the use of adjectives and adverbs, as you need to know how to compare things.

	GERMAN	ENGLISH
1	*schneller zu wachsen als*	Poor places should, according to theory, have the potential ___ rich places.
2	*haben Ihre Kinder eine doppelt so hohe Chance wie*	If you live in a prosperous area, ___ children from places that are in decline of becoming wealthy.
3	*leben viele Jahre länger als*	Even life expectancy is affected. People in rich areas can expect ___ people from poor areas.
4	*könnte doppelt so schnell wachsen*	The overall economy ___ if places were less divergent.
5	*wird immer wichtiger*	The size of companies ___ in our competitive global market.
6	*am effektivsten*	Machines can be programmed to run ___ when they are used by huge companies.
7	*der geeignetste für*	Which software company is ___ our needs?

2 Improving your listening skills

09

Society struggles not only to overcome differences between rich and poor areas, but also to overcome differences which are caused by racial bias. Listen to an interview with Alexis McGill Johnson who runs workshops for an institute dealing with the question as to how people from different races see (and then treat) each other. You are going to hear the audio twice.

1 In which order are the following questions answered by Ms McGill Johnson?
   - **a** Do most people think they are racially biased?
   - **b** What role does anticipation play?
   - **c** What is implicit bias?
   - **d** How much can a short seminar change participants' thinking?

2 Which of the following is true or false? If the given information is false, note down the correct information in your exercise book.
   - **a** Starbucks is doing a global training programme to improve its staff's awareness of racial bias.
   - **b** Our brain processes stereotypes automatically once they are embedded in our brain.
   - **c** We can easily learn to overcome implicit bias.
   - **d** With the help of our moral values we can overcome racial bias.
   - **e** The experiment McGill Johnson does with the host shows how our expectations affect mental processing.
   - **f** Starbuck's employees will have learned how to overcome their implicit bias once they finish the seminar.

Testing your writing skills

1 Material-based writing

Now it's time to write your paper for the Forum of Young Global Leaders. You decide on the following title for your paper:

For the sake of a successful region, the middle class needs to be treated more carefully.

Write at least 300 words on the topic, using your own ideas and the information given in the materials below.

MATERIAL 1

"I'm sorry, but to lower your taxes you're going to have to make more money."

MATERIAL 2

Die Mittelschicht schrumpft, sie verdient weniger, der Aufstieg in die soziale und ökonomische Mitte fällt schwerer – und die Kinder werden es nicht besser haben. Diese multiple Enttäuschung ist politisch hochbrisant. Sie stellt infrage, ob die Mittelschichtler und die Aufstiegswilligen weiter engagiert arbeiten, brav Steuern und Sozialabgaben zahlen und somit die Gesellschaft tragen. Umso verwirrender ist, dass die Politik darauf keine Antworten findet. Es gäbe eine ganze Menge Antworten: von mehr Chancen durch Bildung über eine Entlastung von Steuern und Sozialabgaben über bessere Löhne bis zu mehr Unterstützung für Familien. Doch die Politik bleibt stumm. Ihre Stummheit wird sich rächen. Nein, falsch: Dieser Prozess ist längst in vollem Gang.

Source: Alexander Hagelüken, "Die Mittelschicht schrumpft, die Politik schaut zu", Die Zeit, *21. 03. 2017*

MATERIAL 3

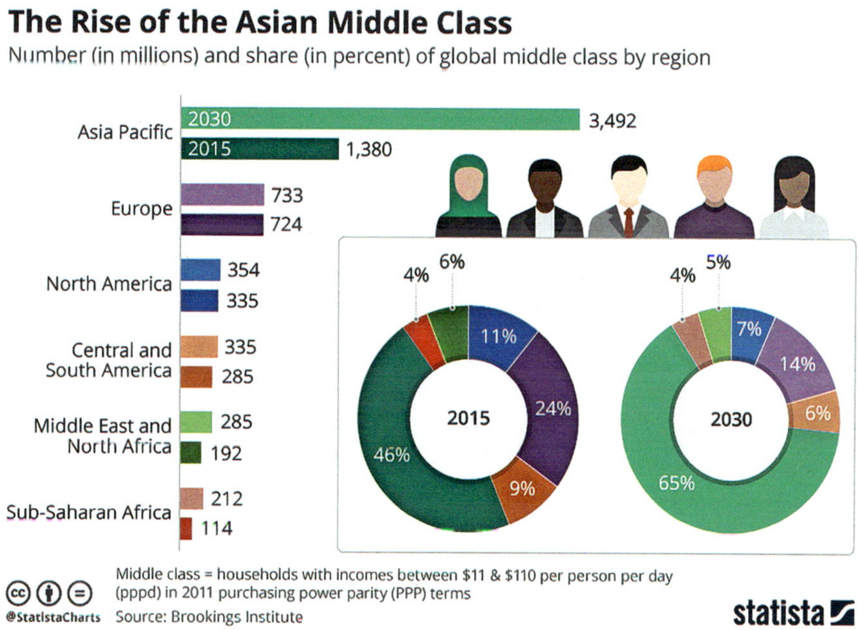

2 Mediation Deutsch – Englisch

Sie möchten Ihren Bericht um Informationen zu Deutschland erweitern. Sie finden folgenden Artikel, den Sie für Ihren Bericht in ca. 150 Wörtern kurz zusammenfassen unter Berücksichtigung folgender Aspekte:

- **Kennzeichen der Mittelschicht in Deutschland**
- **Bedeutung der Mittelschicht für die Gesellschaft in Bezug auf Zufriedenheit und Finanzierung der Gesellschaft**
- **Gründe und Folgen eines Schrumpfens der Mittelschicht (Aufstiegsmöglichkeiten, Zukunftsaussichten der nachrückenden Generation)**

Wohlstand in Deutschland:
Die Mittelschicht schrumpft, die Politik schaut zu

In den fünfziger Jahren rief der Soziologe Helmut Schelsky die Bundesrepublik zur „nivellierten Mittelstandsgesellschaft" aus. Das kennzeichnete eine Gesellschaft, in der die Unterschiede zwischen Kapitalisten und Arbeitern nicht mehr so groß waren wie in den 150 Jahren der Industrialisierung davor. Der Aufstieg war möglich, Arbeiter konnten als Facharbeiter einen Platz in der Mittelschicht ergattern. Von der Mietskaserne mit Klo auf dem Gang in das Reihenhaus am Stadtrand. Dazu gehörte auf jeden Fall die Vorstellung, dass man besser leben würde als die eigenen Eltern. Und den eigenen Kindern sollte es noch besser gehen.

Weil Aufstieg möglich war oder sogar wahrscheinlich, schuf dies eine nachhaltige Zufriedenheit mit dem Wirtschaftssystem der Bundesrepublik. Leistung lohnte sich ja. Die Arbeit im Betrieb genau wie das brave Bezahlen von Steuern und Sozialabgaben an ein anonymes Riesengemeinwesen, deren Gegenleistung eben nur indirekt zu spüren war. Die Mittelschicht war stets behaglich größer als in anderen europäischen Ländern, als in Großbritannien oder Italien. […]

Die Mittelschicht ist unter Druck geraten. Ihr Anteil an der Bevölkerung schrumpfte seit der Wiedervereinigung von 56 auf 48 Prozent, so die Forscher Bosch und Kalina. Damit ist sie nicht mehr die Mehrheit. […]

Und nicht nur die Mittelschicht schrumpft, sondern auch das, was die Mittelschicht verdient. Zwischen 1983 und 2000 war ihr mittleres Einkommen um etwa 20 Prozent gestiegen. […]

Auch der zweite Teil des Versprechens wackelt: Es ist schwieriger geworden, überhaupt in die Mittelschicht aufzusteigen. Manche Ausbildungsberufe wie Floristen, Friseure oder Verkäuferinnen sind heute so schlecht bezahlt, dass sie nicht mehr dazugehören. […]

Besonders frustrierend sind die Perspektiven für die Jüngeren. Jeder Dritte unter 35 hat einen Niedriglohnjob mit weniger als elf Euro die Stunde, aus dem der Mehrheit binnen fünf Jahren nicht der Aufstieg gelingt. In diesen Jobs verdienen sie 20 Prozent weniger als Gleichaltrige in den 80er Jahren. Damals gehörten noch 76 Prozent der 18- bis 30-Jährigen der Mittelschicht an. Inzwischen sind es nur noch 58 Prozent. Damit gerät der dritte Teil des Mitte-Versprechens ins Wanken, der die deutsche Gesellschaft seit der Nachkriegszeit zusammenhält. […]

Da sind zum einen unsichere, schlecht bezahlte Jobs. Da ist zum anderen die Explosion der Immobilienpreise, die eine großzügige Wohnung oder ein eigenes Haus im Grünen zumindest in den Ballungsräumen unerschwinglich macht.

Source: Alexander Hagelüken, "Die Mittelschicht schrumpft, die Politik schaut zu", Die Zeit, *21.03.2017*

D THE POWER OF FREEDOM

Exploring the topic

SITUATION

You are a member of this year's organizing committee of your school's EU-wide reading project called "The role of fiction in today's world". You are supposed to come up with this year's novel to be read by all students of your school and your partner school. The novel should deal in some way with empowerment or the lack of it.

1 **Using the following prompts, write a story in 25 minutes (general topic: "relationships").**

The delicious breath of rain was in the air.

Her husband's friend Richards was there, too, near her.

It was her sister who told her, in broken sentences.

There would be no one to live for during those coming years.

For heaven's sake, open the door.

2 **Your partner reads his or her story to you. What do you like about each other's stories?**

3 **Read the following short story by the American writer Kate Chopin (1850–1904).**

The Story of an Hour

Knowing that Mrs. Mallard was afflicted with a heart trouble, great care was taken to break to her as gently as possible the news of her husband's death.

It was her sister Josephine who told her, in broken sentences; veiled hints that revealed in half concealing. Her husband's friend Richards was there, too, near her. It was he who had been in the newspaper office when intelligence of the railroad disaster was received, with Brently Mallard's name leading the list of "killed". He had only taken the time to assure himself of its truth by a second telegram, and had hastened to forestall any less careful, less tender friend in bearing the sad message.

She did not hear the story as many women have heard the same, with a paralyzed inability to accept its significance. She wept at once, with sudden, wild abandonment, in her sister's arms. When the storm of grief had spent itself, she went away to her room alone. She would have no one follow her.

There stood, facing the open window, a comfortable, roomy armchair. Into this she sank, pressed down by a physical exhaustion that haunted her body and seemed to reach into her soul.

She could see in the open square before her house the tops of trees that were all aquiver with the new spring life. The delicious breath of rain was in the air. In the street below a peddler was crying his wares. The notes of a distant song which someone was singing reached her faintly, and countless sparrows were twittering in the eaves.

There were patches of blue sky showing here and there through the clouds that had met and piled one above the other in the west facing her window.
She sat with her head thrown back upon the cushion of the chair, quite motionless, except when a sob came up into her throat and shook her, as a child who has cried itself to sleep continues to sob in its dreams.

She was young, with a fair, calm face, whose lines bespoke repression and even a certain strength. But now there was a dull stare in her eyes, whose gaze was fixed away off yonder on one of those patches of blue sky. It was not a glance of reflection, but rather indicated a suspension of intelligent thought.
There was something coming to her and she was waiting for it, fearfully. What was it? She did not know; it was too subtle and elusive to name. But she felt it, creeping out of the sky, reaching toward her through the sounds, the scents, the color that filled the air.
Now her bosom rose and fell tumultuously. She was beginning to recognize this thing that was approaching to possess her, and she was striving to beat it back with her will – as powerless as her two white slender hands would have been.
When she abandoned herself, a little whispered word escaped her slightly parted lips. She said it over and over under her breath: "free, free, free!" The vacant stare and the look of terror that had followed it went from her eyes. They stayed keen and bright. Her pulses beat fast, and the coursing blood warmed and relaxed every inch of her body.
She did not stop to ask if it were or were not a monstrous joy that held her. A clear and exalted perception enabled her to dismiss the suggestion as trivial.
She knew that she would weep again when she saw the kind, tender hands folded in death; the face that had never looked save with love upon her, fixed and gray and dead. But she saw beyond that bitter moment a long procession of years to come that would belong to her absolutely. And she opened and spread her arms out to them in welcome. There would be no one to live for during those coming years; she would live for herself.
There would be no powerful will bending hers in that blind persistence with which men and women believe they have a right to impose a private will upon a fellow-creature. A kind intention or a cruel intention made the act seem no less a crime as she looked upon it in that brief moment of illumination.

And yet she had loved him – sometimes. Often she had not. What did it matter! What could love, the unsolved mystery, count for in the face of this possession of self-assertion which she suddenly recognized as the strongest impulse of her being!

"Free! Body and soul free!" she kept whispering.

Josephine was kneeling before the closed door with her lips to the keyhole, imploring for admission. "Louise, open the door! I beg; open the door – you will make yourself ill. What are you doing, Louise? For heaven's sake open the door."

"Go away. I am not making myself ill." No; she was drinking in a very elixir of life through that open window.

Her fancy was running riot along those days ahead of her. Spring days, and summer days, and all sorts of days that would be her own. She breathed a quick prayer that life might be long. It was only yesterday she had thought with a shudder that life might be long.

She arose at length and opened the door to her sister's importunities. There was a feverish triumph in her eyes, and she carried herself unwittingly like a goddess of Victory. She clasped her sister's waist, and together they descended the stairs. Richards stood waiting for them at the bottom.

Someone was opening the front door with a latchkey. It was Brently Mallard who entered, a little travel-stained, composedly carrying his grip-sack and umbrella. He had been far from the scene of the accident, and did not even know there had been one. He stood amazed at Josephine's piercing cry; at Richards's quick motion to screen him from the view of his wife.

But Richards was too late.

When the doctors came they said she had died of heart disease – of the joy that kills.

(1009 words)

4 **Compare your story to this story. What are the main differences?**

5 **Discuss the following questions about the short story:**

- **a** What is the message of this story?
- **b** What is your opinion of the message?
- **c** How do the descriptions in lines 15–20 underline Mrs. Mallard's change in life?
- **d** How would you interpret "the joy that kills" (line 69)?

Testing your reading skills

1 Gapped summary

Copy the summary of lines 1–39 and fill the gaps with appropriate words from the corresponding sections of the text (one word per gap). Do not make any changes or adjustments. Please also provide the number of the line in which you have found the word.

Having seen his friend's ___ 1 (line ___) on the casualty list, Richards rushes to the house of Mrs Mallard with the news of her husband's death. But it is Mrs Mallard's sister Josephine who in subtle ___ 2 (line ___) rather than in harsh detail breaks the terrible news to her. After overcoming her feelings of ___ 3 (line ___) on learning of her husband's fate, Mrs Mallard retires ___ 4 (line ___) to sit in her favourite armchair, where she rests, exhausted and ___ 5 (line ___). Her stillness is occasionally broken by the odd ___ 6 (line ___) that rises from deep within her. As she gazes up at the sky, slowly but surely she becomes aware of a feeling that she is ___ 7 (line ___) to fight off. After she finally gives in, she loses her ___ 8 (line ___) look and fearful countenance as she realizes that she is in fact now ___ 9 (line ___).

2 Mediation Englisch–Deutsch

Beantworten Sie folgende Fragen auf Deutsch.

1. Wie fühlte sich Frau Mallard von ihrem Mann behandelt?
2. Was erfahren wir über Frau Mallards Meinung zur ehelichen Beziehung im allgemeinen?

3 Multiple-choice questions

Choose the most suitable option.

1 Josephine wants Louise to open the door because …

- a she fears for her sister's health.
- b she wants to comfort her.
- c she thinks her sister has attempted suicide.
- d they need to go downstairs to talk with Richards.

2 On discovering her new-found freedom, Mrs Mallard …

- a plans ahead for sunny days.
- b feels as if her mind is playing tricks on her.
- c is sure that her ill health will go away.
- d looks forward to deciding how to spend her time herself.

3 When Brently comes through the door, …

- a he is surprised to hear his wife scream.
- b he is holding his luggage very close to his body.
- c he bears the marks from the railroad accident.
- d he wonders why Richards tries to stop his wife from seeing him.

Testing your writing and speaking skills

1 Material-based writing

You were chosen to write the introduction for this year's literature EU project leaflet. You have chosen the title "Reading is essential for the development of the individual and for the good of society". Use the given material to write at least 300 words.

MATERIAL 1

Young people's attitude towards reading in the UK

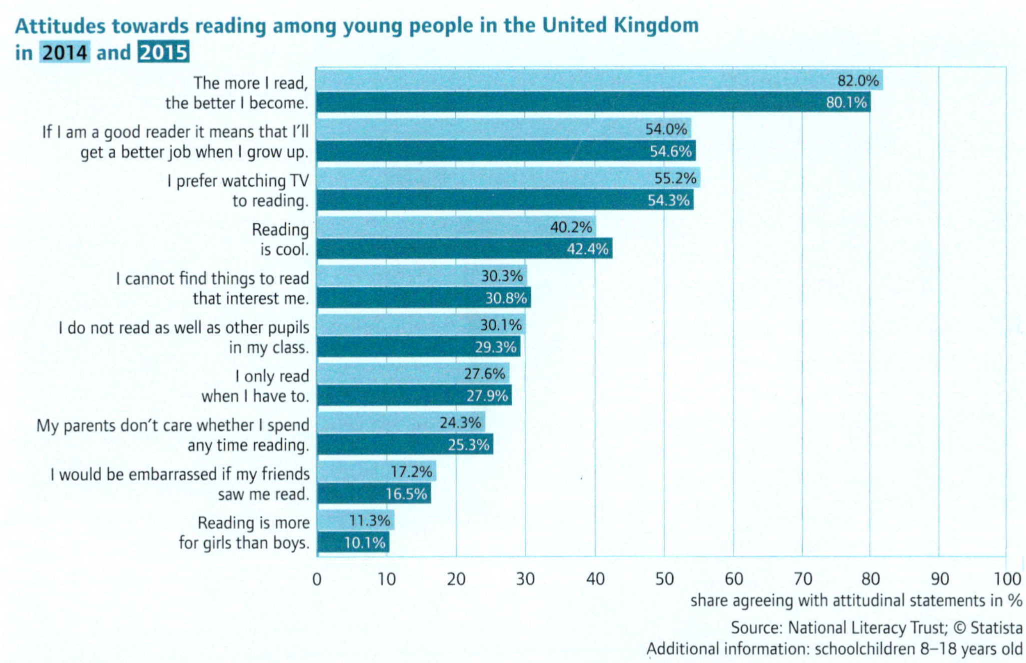

MATERIAL 2

Eine Analyse des Social Return on Investment zum britischen Bookstart-Projekt (dem Modell für das deutsche Lesestart-Programm) zeigt: Pro investiertem Britischen Pfund entsteht hochgerechnet ein volkswirtschaftlicher Nutzen in Höhe von £25, weil Folgekosten, die durch Defizite in den Lesefähigkeiten der Kinder ohne Bookstart entstanden wären, entfallen (Booktrust 2010).

Source: "Empfehlungen an die Politik", the website of Stiftunglesen

MATERIAL 3

Mir wurde als Kind viel vorgelesen: Jeden Abend vorm Zubettgehen gab es eine Gutenacht-Geschichte von meiner Mutter oder meinem Vater. Ich habe das geliebt und wollte so schnell wie möglich selbst Lesen lernen. Dass Bücher bei uns zu Hause immer präsent waren und eine große Rolle spielten, hat mein Leben sehr geprägt. Ich bin sicher, dass es für die Entwicklung eines Kindes einen gewaltigen Unterschied macht, ob es an das Abenteuer Lesen herangeführt wird oder nicht. Ob es lernt, mit Sprache umzugehen, fremde Gedankengänge nachzuvollziehen und seine Phantasie zu entwickeln, wenn beim Lesen Bilder im Kopf entstehen. Dass heutzutage so vielen Kindern überhaupt nicht mehr vorgelesen wird, finde ich sehr traurig und überaus bedenklich.

Source: Marietta Slomka, "Prominente Lesebotschafter", the website of Stiftunglesen

2 a Project

Situation: You now need to decide which novel should be read by all students at your school and your EU partner school. Therefore, you organize a first meeting where you find out more about five possible novels (cf. below).

Divide into small groups, with each group finding out more about one of the novels and its themes. Put all the information you can find onto posters.

Do a gallery walk and learn about the others' novels and their themes. Make sure everybody has the chance to learn about every novel.

b Group discussion

Situation: You have to decide which of the five novels is to be read by the students at your school and your EU partner school. The issues in the novel should have relevance for young people as they take their place in society and at the same time should show how fiction can play an important role in today's world. At the end of your meeting choose one of the novels.

Preparation phase: Find reasons why your novel (the one you initially prepared) should be read by all students at your school and your EU partner school. What could students from different cultural backgrounds learn from your novel? Why would your novel promote reading among young people?

Presentation phase: Give a short overview of the most important reasons why the committee should pick your novel.

Interaction: Agree on which of the presented novels should be read. Talk about what young people can learn from this novel.

THE ETHICS OF PROGRESS 3

FOCUS

organic vegetables

battery-cage hens

combat drone

cargo drone

Mark Zuckerberg testifying before the US Senate on the use of Facebook to promote fake news and hate speech

connecting across the globe through social media

Otto Hahn and Lise Meitner, who achieved nuclear fission (1938)

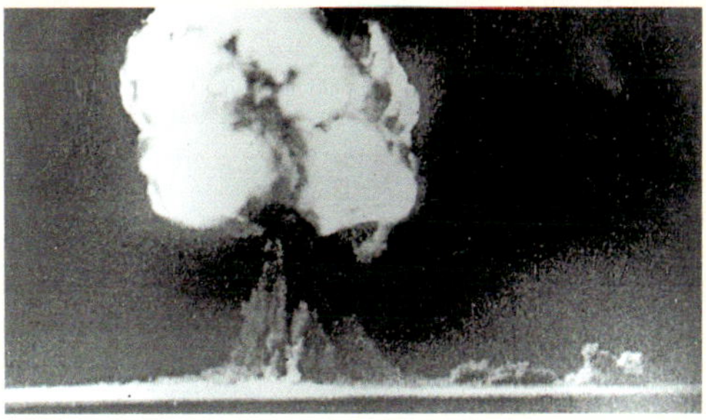

first atomic bomb explosion, New Mexico (1945)

1 **This unit is entitled "The ethics of progress". How do you think the pictures reflect the topic of this unit?**

The ethical responsibility of scientists

10

05

Scientific and technological progress has made great improvements in the quality of life for the majority of the world's population. At the same time, science and technology have often challenged the prevalent belief systems and values of society. The story of Galileo Galilei, who in the 17th century held the view that the earth revolves around the sun, is a case in point. The Catholic Church believed that his views belittled the position of the earth and humanity, who as God's creations were held to be at the centre of the universe. Eventually, he was forced to renounce his views.

If science is the attempt to understand the world around us, technology is the application of the knowledge gained through science. Humans are naturally curious and so have tried to comprehend the natural phenomena around them. However, humans are also rational and self-interested agents who pursue their own ends by using technology to make life easier and better, for instance, or by providing products and services for others in order to make a profit. Conflicts of interests and value gaps are a consequence of human nature. That is why even today, in "open" Western societies, scientists still find themselves at the centre of controversy. This is true for fields of study like biotechnology, nuclear or digital technology, as many innovations touch the ethical foundations of our societies.

One could argue that pursuing "pure science" furthers the cause of human knowledge and that scientists are not responsible for what others do with that knowledge. However, researchers always work within a particular context. Some work under oppressive regimes, knowing that their discoveries might be used to exercise power over people. Others work in weapons development, through which warfare of a kind unimaginable a century ago has been made possible. The latest biological, chemical or digital weapons in the hands of terrorists or dictators are indeed a worrying thought in our day and age. For although weapons deployment has become so technically precise that, according to military leaders, collateral damage to civilians can practically be ruled out, there still is the human factor at play and thus the possibility of grave error, or of grave misconduct. Ethical lapses in research can do significant harm. Fabricated data in a clinical trial may harm or even kill patients, and neglecting safety regulations, e.g. concerning radiation, bacteria or viruses, may jeopardize the health and safety of thousands. With the arrival of artificial intelligence, actions could be performed by robots without human involvement, which also raises ethical issues.

Moreover, all too often a development that is considered to be a potential good for humankind turns into its exact opposite. For instance, the development of chemicals supported farmers in their job of feeding the world by destroying pests, but used carelessly or too extensively these pesticides pose serious health risks to individuals, animals and plants. In the realm of reproductive medicine new technologies might be a blessing for couples who want but cannot conceive children, but they might also lend themselves to questionable but lucrative practices such as the production of designer babies. Digital technology has, on the one hand, the potential to connect, educate and liberate people, but, on the other hand, it has the potential to enslave, brainwash and endanger people.

This poses the question as to whether scientists and engineers can and should foresee the consequences of their research and discoveries. Perhaps the best advice to scientists is to ask them to assess the possible ethical ramifications of their work, and decide whether it will benefit or harm humanity in the long run. The ethics of science and technology has always been a matter of public discussion, and we can expect this debate to continue.

(625 words)

Working with words

1 **a** Each sentence below contains two gaps that can be filled with two expressions from one of the rows A–D. Choose the correct expressions and fill the gaps. You may have to adapt the expressions to make them fit into the sentence structure. There is one row you can't use for the sentences.

A	human nature	prevalent values	rational agents	scientific progress
B	exercise power	work in context	feed the world	pose a risk
C	foresee the consequences	gain knowledge	pursue an end	pose the question
D	grave error	human factor	collateral damage	lucrative practice

1 It's a ___ to assume that using highly sophisticated weapons greatly reduces the risk of ___.
2 While scientists might wish to ___ in their particular field, some become obsessed by their research to the point where they lose the ability to ___ of their actions.
3 In economics, consumers are regarded as ___, a view which is disputed by philosophers who have a very different concept of ___.

b Make up your own sentence with two expressions from the row that was not used.

2 **Fill the gaps in the following sentences with a word that belongs to the same word family as the one in capital letters taken from the text.**

1 Medical ___ postulates that the practitioner should act in the best interest of the patient. **ETHICAL**
2 At some ___ schools pupils can choose which lessons to attend. **PROGRESS**
3 Tourists are always advised to leave their ___ in the hotel safe. **VALUE**
4 For much of human history we have been convinced that progress can be achieved by the ___ of knowledge. **PURSUE**
5 In older cars, airbags are only ___ when the car is struck from the front. **DEPLOYMENT**

3 **With a partner, choose one of the scientists on the right. Collect everything that you know about them or find information about them. Then write a short text of about 150 words about them, using five highlighted expressions from the text opposite. You may choose another scientist if you wish.**

Stephen Hawking, physicist

Ibn al-Nafis, anatomist

Katherine Johnson, NASA mathematician

Emmy Noether, mathematician

Marie Curie, physicist and chemist

Charles Darwin, naturalist

A ENGINEERING AND ETHICS

Exploring the topic

SITUATION

The university of applied sciences at which you study has organized a series of open lectures by experts. The next lecture is called "The Ethics of Engineering", and the lecturer is a civil engineer from abroad. You want to write a response in English to the lecture on the website of your students' association, so you need to be prepared for the lecture and for the language the speaker is likely to use.

1 Thinking about scandals involving scientists

a Ethics plays a role in every aspect of life – science is no exception. Below, there are the details of four scandals involving scientists, which have been jumbled up. Copy the grid headings at the bottom and put the matching pieces of information into the grid.

1 The TDI diesel engines were programmed to activate emission controls only during testing.

2 A pesticide containing cyanide (Cyclone B) was used in extermination camps.

3 Engineers designed a processor that slowed down the phone as the battery aged.

4 One chemist was executed for knowingly selling the product to the SS.

5 The company issued an apology for not informing the clients that the reason was to prevent the phones from shutting down. Many customers lost trust in the company.

6 A computer expert revealed the surveillance and was prosecuted for theft and publication of government information.

7 Private people and public figures worldwide were covertly surveilled by the NSA.

8 Engineers developed devices to switch the cleaning mechanisms on and off in certain situations.

9 Several executives were arrested and several senior managers were suspended, leading to an image loss for the whole car industry.

10 Smartphones were slowed down so that clients thought they needed a new one.

11 Chemists developed a way of packaging the gas in a canister for easy transport and use.

12 Computer professionals developed a system that can infiltrate and manipulate selected computers.

2,11,4x
1,8,9x
10,3,5
7,12,6

THE OFFENCE	CONTRIBUTION OF THE SCIENTISTS	CONSEQUENCES

b Discuss with a partner whether the consequences of these scandals do justice to the offences committed.

2 Read the text on page 79 and find passages that can be related to the scandals you discussed in task 1. Some are more obvious than others.

AS ENGINEERS, WE MUST CONSIDER THE ETHICAL IMPLICATIONS OF OUR WORK

A One aspect of Edward Snowden's revelations in the *Guardian* about the NSA's surveillance activities has received less attention than it should. The algorithms that extract highly specific information from an otherwise impenetrable amount of data have been conceived and built by flesh and blood, engineers with highly sophisticated technical knowledge. Did they know the use to which their algorithms would be put? If not, should they have been mindful of the potential for misuse? Either way, should they be held partly responsible or were they just "doing their job"?

B One could ask similar questions about engineers who build technologies of violence. Although in the west, we use the euphemism "defence" – and weapons often do serve this purpose – arms are just as likely to be used for furthering less-than-honourable goals, whether [...] bombing rebellious populations or staging coups against democratically-elected governments. [...]

C When doctors or nurses use their knowledge of anatomy in order to torture or conduct medical experiments on helpless subjects, we are rightly outraged. Why doesn't society seem to apply the same standards to engineers? There is more than one answer to the question of course, but two points are especially pertinent: the common good we engineers see ourselves serving and our relationship to authority.

D Health is an unambiguously positive social good that gives the medical profession a strong moral purpose. The same can be said of justice for practitioners of the law. Lawyers and doctors are expected to act in a particular way and, sometimes, to become the custodians of the social good their respective professions embody. Whether they do or not is a different matter.

E Technology as a means of social progress is arguably the common good that engineers pursue. Modern engineering emerged in the 19th century, an age when technology was seen in almost unequivocally positive light. Engineers were to "[direct] the great sources of power in nature for the use and convenience of man", in the exultant words of the UK Institution of Engineers, written in 1828. The two World Wars, the gas chambers, the atomic bombs and agent Orange – the awfully destructive scope of technology – were yet to come.

2 algorithm: *Rechenvorgang nach einem bestimmten sich wiederholenden Schema*
8 euphemism: *beschönigende mildernde Umschreibung für ein unangenehmes Wort*
14 pertinent: *passend, relevant*
22 unequivocally: *eindeutig*

F Today, our profession seems to have preserved the sense that technology is almost by necessity a force for good. We are focused on the technical and managerial sides of technology – how to design algorithms; how to build machines – but not so much on the context of its deployment or its unintended consequences. […]

G Engineers need the resources of government and industry to do their work, far more than doctors do. Sometimes we are hired for a specific project, but more often, we sell our services wholesale as paid employees. We do not make weapons for a specific war or algorithms for a specific surveillance activity. As a result, engineers who build these devices usually operate at one remove from the consequences of their actions.

H […] Today, engineering in the English-speaking world largely sees itself as a tool of industry. There are many advantages to this of course, including more resources at our disposal to do our work. But one major drawback is that engineers, as a result, have far less intellectual and practical autonomy than they should.

I Our ethics have become mostly technical: how to design properly, how to not cut corners, how to serve our clients well. We work hard to prevent failure of the systems we build, but only in relation to what these systems are meant to do, rather than the way they might actually be utilised, or whether they should have been built at all. We are not amoral, far from it; it's just that we have steered ourselves into a place where our morality has a smaller scope.

J There have been encouraging attempts in the engineering profession aiming for a bigger, less reductionist vision of engineering: some mission statements have been written, codes of ethics redrafted and engineering curricula redesigned. However, we are still essentially producing what industry requires: engineers able to carry out technically complex projects, rather than professionals with an in-depth understanding of the social complexity of technology. In fact, we need both. We have very little appetite for engaging with social and political sciences that have something valuable (and sometimes unpleasant) to say about science and technology, including the roles, prejudices and vested interests of scientists and engineers. The cultural shift has simply not happened.

K Engineers have, in many ways, built the modern world and helped improve the lives of many. Of this, we are rightfully proud. What's more, only a very small minority of engineers is in the business of making weapons or privacy-invading algorithms. However, we are part and parcel of industrial modernity with all its might, advantages and flaws, and we therefore contribute to human suffering as well as flourishing.

L While there are no easy answers to the questions raised here, we can certainly do better. We can claim, and live up to, our role as social custodians of technology, conscious of its strengths and dangers, capable of navigating its technical, ecological, political and social dimensions alike – even if this might require more years of study for engineering University degrees.

M It will be a bright day for our profession when we start producing more engineers who […] have the will and the intellectual capacity to engage with bigger questions about the ethics, politics and social ramifications of their inventions.

(890 words)

Source: Abbas El-Zein, The Guardian, *05. 12. 2013*

45 reductionist: *vereinfacht*

3 **Choose one of the scandals from task 1. How could you use it to support or argue against the writer's view? Make some notes that you can use for your response to the lecture later.**

Testing your reading skills

1 Gapped summary

Copy the summary of the text and fill the gaps with appropriate words from the corresponding passages of the text (one word per gap). Do not make any changes. Please also provide the number of the line in which you found the word or expressions.

Using engineers involved in the development of ___[1] (line ___) systems and arms technology as examples, the writer asks whether such engineers, who possess very ___[2] (line ___) expertise in their particular area of technology, think about the possible consequences of their work. Unlike people working in the medical and legal professions, engineers are not required to adhere to a set of ___[3] (line ___) standards set by society. The once optimistic view of technology prevalent in the 19th century changed as its immense ___[4] (line ___) potential became clear in the 20th century. The problem with today's engineers is that they are ___[5] ___[6] (line ___) serving both government and industry. Their main concern is ___[7] ___[8] (line ___) do their job both well and cost-effectively. They often fail to focus on the wider ___[9] (line ___) in which their technology will be used. While the ___[10] (line ___) available to them are large, they often lack the ___[11] (line ___) to ask questions about the deployment of the technologies they develop. The writer does see ___[12] (line ___) efforts being made, e.g. mission statements, to provide future engineers with a wider understanding of what they do. But he hopes that one day universities will produce engineers who think of themselves as ___[13] (line ___) and not just producers of technology.

2 Short-answer questions (paragraphs A–C)

Answer the following questions. You may use words from the text.

1 The writer criticizes the media coverage of the NSA scandal. For what reason?

2 According to the writer, which word is used to make war technology sound less negative?

3 The writer points out two examples of misconduct in the medical profession that people find abhorrent. Name the two examples.

3 Multiple-choice questions

Choose the most suitable option in each case.

1 In paragraph G, the writer uses the expression "at one remove from" in order to say that engineers …

- a can't be harmed by their own technological products.
- b are less responsible for their own actions than doctors are.
- c can easily be dismissed when failing to comply with their employers' wishes.
- d are not directly confronted with the harm done by their products.

2 In paragraph K, the writer …

- a disputes the view that engineering has advanced peoples' lives.
- b emphasizes the fact that engineers are an integral part of our modern industrialized society.
- c expresses his pride in all the achievements of his fellow engineers.
- d makes excuses for the behaviour of a small number of engineers.

3 A

Developing your Language Skills

1 Improving your viewing skills

06

"Is everything that's possible permissible?" This was the question debated by science Nobel laureates with an audience of young people at a meeting in Lindau in 2014. Watch and listen to the summary of the lectures and debates at this meeting and take notes with the help of the prompts below.

Work with a partner and share the work by taking turns (partner A or partner B) in writing down the answers. Watch the video twice.

		ROALD HOFMAN	
1	A	the basic question every scientist needs to ask	
		UN DECLARATION OF HUMAN RIGHTS	
2	B	relevance for scientists	
3	A	consequence for scientific community	
		HIPPOCRATES	
4	B	his view on humanity's relationship to nature	
		DICKINSON RICHARDS	
5	A	"faiths" of the 18th century	
6	B	what he thinks of these faiths	
7	B	his view of humanity's relationship to nature	
		MAX WEBER	
8	A	point he makes about the objectivity of scientific research	
		WERNER FORSSMANN	
9	B	development he criticizes	
		FRANCIS BACON	
10	A	belief about scientific progress	
		CHRISTIAN DE DUVE	
11	B	his view on an ethical code of conduct for scientists	
12	A	genetic tendencies in human beings that once had an evolutionary purpose	
13	B	why they are a threat to humankind now	

2 Using collocations

Here is a text passage on a scandal concerning the German automobile industry. It is grammatically correct, but could be improved by using common collocations, like those used in the text. The letters in the right column refer to the paragraph in the text where you can find them.

Collocations are combinations of words particular to a language. In German we call a man who smokes a lot "ein starker Raucher", while in English this would be "a heavy smoker". Pay attention to such English collocations to make your own use of English more natural.

After doing tests[1], the engineers came up with a very smart[2] technology in order to hide the fact that the diesel engines emitted more dangerous particulates than allowed. They acted because they were under pressure from their seniors, but this doesn't mean that they can be let off. We have to give them part of the responsibility[3] for the scandal. How they should be punished is another thing[4].

The general public will never deeply understand[5] the technology involved in the scandal. The engineers are the ones who are able to find their way around this field and therefore bear responsibility.

[1] C
[2] A
[3] A
[4] D
[5] J
[6] L

3 Translating collocations

With the help of a dictionary, find the English version of the following German collocations. Part A contains verb and noun collocations. Part B contains verb and adverb collocations.

A
1. Schaden anrichten
2. Verantwortung übernehmen
3. Barrieren überwinden
4. den Lohn für etwas ernten
5. ins Chaos stürzen
6. eine Behauptung widerlegen

B
1. zu Unrecht beschuldigt werden
2. leicht übertrieben
3. absichtlich verletzen
4. genau beobachten
5. voll und ganz zustimmen/billigen
6. allen Ernstes behaupten

4 Writing a response to the lecture

As it turns out, the guest lecturer puts forward the same ideas and arguments that you read in the article. Use the notes you made earlier on the science scandals and the text and develop them into a 300-word response for the students' association website. You may find some of the collocations from tasks 2 and 3 above helpful.

Testing your writing and speaking skills

1 Mediation Deutsch–Englisch

Nach dem Gastvortrag an Ihrer Fachhochschule fragt Sie ein britischer Gasthörer in einer Email, ob an deutschen Hochschulen ähnliche Überlegungen angestellt werden, wie der Gastredner sie vorgetragen hat.

Verfassen Sie unter Verwendung der Information aus dem folgenden Text ein kurzes informatives Papier (ca. 150 Wörter), das Sie ihm mailen können. Gehen Sie dabei auf die folgenden Aspekte ein:

- **wer Christoph Wagner ist und welche Mission er hat**
- **was er konkret unterrichtet und wie er das tut**

Ethikkurse für Ingenieur-Studenten: Die Mission des Philosophen Wagner

Christoph Wagner lebt in Würzburg, der Enkel wegen, wie er sagt. Der Mann hat schlohweißes Haar, Falten, er ist 81. Ein Opi. Doch sobald er den Mund aufmacht und zu sprechen beginnt, flink im Kopf, messerscharf, verwandelt er sich, wirkt um Jahre verjüngt. […]

„Ich bedrohe die Menschheit noch 'ne Weile", sagt der promovierte Philosoph und grinst. Er meint: Nichts kann ihn davon abbringen, Studenten weiterhin mit seinem Lebensthema zu beglücken: der Ethik. […] Er will angehenden Ingenieuren „ethische Weisheit" in die Köpfe träufeln; das macht er als Gastdozent an gleich drei norddeutschen Fachhochschulen. Am Ziel sähe sich Wagner, wenn die zukünftigen Technik-Erfinder sich in jeder Phase ihres Handels bewusst machten, welche Entscheidung sie gerade treffen und welche Werte sie dieser zugrunde legen.

Wagner spricht über die ganz großen Themen der Technikgeschichte und die zugehörigen Personen. Albert Einstein, Robert Oppenheimer oder Wernher von Braun, die Väter von Atombombe und Raketenforschung, stehen für ein Dilemma. Die Folgen ihrer Forschung waren bahnbrechend – und menschenvernichtend zugleich. […]

Wie war es um die ethische Weisheit bei Einstein, Oppenheimer und Braun bestellt? Am Anfang stand die wertneutrale Wissenschaft: Es galt, erklärt Wagner, die ungeheure Kraft der Atome zu erforschen. Doch wer sollte über diese Kraft verfügen dürfen? Für Einstein war nach seiner Emigration klar, dass Nazi-Deutschland an der Atombombe forscht – eindeutig die Nation, in deren Hände die Waffe damals auf keinen Fall gelangen sollte. Deshalb schrieb er der US-Regierung einen Warnbrief. Seine Mahnung war die Initialzündung für deren Atomprogramm, das sogenannte Manhattan Project.

Einsteins Mitstreiter Oppenheimer stieg später aus dem Projekt aus. „Wir haben die Arbeit des Teufels getan, und wir kehren nun zu unseren wirklichen Aufgaben zurück", sagte er. Für Oppenheimer lautete die ethische Frage: Soll

ich eine Massenvernichtungswaffe entwickeln oder meinen Pazifismus leben? […]

Mühelos überträgt der alte Philosoph die Lehre auf aktuelle Fragen: Was mache ich als Ingenieur, wenn ich mit Risikotechniken umgehen muss wie dem Tiefseebohren nach Öl? Beispiel: Die Explosion der Plattform „Deepwater Horizon“ im Golf von Mexiko. Hätte eine genauere Prüfung der Bohrkonstruktion den Tod der Arbeiter und die beispiellose Umweltverschmutzung verhindern können? Das Mindeste sei, sagt Wagner, sich bei wichtigen Entscheidungen Besinnungspausen einzuräumen. […]

„Ethik heißt, wertebewusst zu leben“, sagt Wagner. Eine feste Größe im Stundenplan von Naturwissenschaftlern ist das Fach in Deutschland noch nicht. Aber eins steht fest: Christoph Wagner wird nicht aufhören zu drohen.

Source: Christoph Wöhrle, Der Spiegel, *03. 02. 2011*

2 Group discussion

Situation: You are all in your final year at uni and you help organize open lectures. You've invited the same engineer again to give his guest lecture on engineering and ethics to the younger students. It's now time to produce a poster for the event. Naturally, you want as many students as possible to attend the lecture, so the poster needs to be attractive. Design students have come up with a number of suggestions for an image that reflects the topic of the talk, and each of you concentrates on one particular suggestion. The suggestions can be found on page 144.

Preparation phase: Look at your suggestion and decide if
- it is appropriate to the guest speaker's message;
- it lends itself as a background image to the verbal information that needs to be included on the poster (day, time, name of lecturer, title of lecture, place);
- it is attractive for the students.

Presentation phase: Present your image and your arguments for it to the group.

Interaction phase: Discuss the images and decide on the best one.

Optional *(if you have time at the end of your discussion):* Discuss whether to open the guest lecture to the general public.

Exploring the topic

SITUATION

The working group Critical IT and Business Students at your university, of which you are a member, has decided to promote awareness among fellow students of critical but also constructive ideas about the IT business. For this reason, they've decided to invite a member of an international organization to address the student community at your university via video conferencing. Before you can discuss who to invite, you need to find out more about the issues at stake and about organizations that could provide your fellow students with a critical perspective.

1 Who might have said what, and why?

Match the descriptions with the people and discuss your matches with a partner.

	PEOPLE	
A	Renée DiResta	head of policy at Data for Democracy
B	Wael Ghonim	co-initiator of the Arab spring
C	Tristan Harris	founder of the *Time Well Spent* movement
D	Steve Jobs	founder of Apple Inc.
E	Roger McNamee	former venture capitalist
F	Cathy O'Neil	mathematician working for the Alternative Banking Group of the Occupy Wall Street movement
G	Marc Rotenberg	President of EPIC (Electronic Privacy Information Center), Washington

	DESCRIPTIONS
1	… helped spark a revolution through the Internet, but afterwards realized the Internet could not sustain a change in society.
2	… heads an organization that upholds the importance of personal data security in the face of digital data collection by companies.
3	… made sure that his own kids were not exposed too much to modern technology, although he himself was one of the leading entrepreneurs of Silicon Valley.
4	… has warned that social media is a form of addiction that takes total control of people's lives.
5	… was an early investor in social media platforms but now warns of the danger to society and democracy that social media poses.
6	… believes that social media can't be trusted to police themselves and should be monitored by third-party regulatory agencies.
7	… coined the term "weapons of math destruction" for algorithms and strongly advises against blind faith in data.

2 **Read the following text and find out more about Tristan Harris and Roger McNamee.**

"Our minds can be hijacked": the tech insiders who fear a smartphone dystopia

In a technology special for the Guardian, *reporter Paul Lewis talked to former Silicon Valley employees who have become critical of their trade. Here are excerpts from Lewis's interviews with two of the Silicon Valley "refuseniks", as he calls them.*

1. Tristan Harris, a 33-year-old former Google employee:

"All of us are jacked into this system," he says. " **1** ." Harris, who has been branded "the closest thing Silicon Valley has to a conscience", insists that billions of people have little choice over whether they use these now ubiquitous technologies, and are largely unaware of the invisible ways in which a small number of people in Silicon Valley are shaping their lives. A graduate of Stanford University, Harris studied under BJ Fogg, a behavioural psychologist revered in tech circles for mastering the ways technological design can be used to persuade people. Many of his students [...] have gone on to prosperous careers in Silicon Valley. Harris is the student who went rogue; a whistleblower of sorts, he is lifting the curtain on the vast powers accumulated by technology companies and the ways they are using that influence. " **2** ," he said at a recent TED talk in Vancouver. "I don't know a more urgent problem than this," Harris says. "It's changing our democracy, and it's changing our ability to have the conversations and relationships that we want with each other." Harris went public – giving talks, writing papers, meeting lawmakers and campaigning for reform after three years struggling to effect change inside Google's Mountain View headquarters.

It all began in 2013, when he was working as a product manager at Google, and circulated a thought-provoking memo, "A Call To Minimise Distraction & Respect Users' Attention", to 10 close colleagues. It struck a chord, spreading to some 5 000 Google employees, including senior executives who rewarded Harris with an impressive-sounding new job: he was to be Google's in-house design ethicist and product philosopher. Looking back, Harris sees that he was promoted into a marginal role. "I didn't have a social support structure at all," he says. Still, he adds: "I got to sit in a corner and think and read and understand."

He explored how LinkedIn exploits a need for social reciprocity to widen its network; how YouTube and Netflix autoplay videos and next episodes, depriving users of a choice about whether or not they want to keep watching; how Snapchat created its addictive

3 be jacked into sth.: *tief in etw. drinstecken*
12 behavioural psychologist: *Verhaltenspsychologe/in*
46 reciprocity: *Gegenseitigkeit*

Snap-streaks feature, encouraging near-constant communication between its mostly teenage users.

The techniques these companies use are not always generic: they can be algorithmically tailored to each person. An internal Facebook report leaked this year, for example, revealed that the company can identify when teens feel "insecure", "worthless" and "need a confidence boost". **3** . Tech companies can exploit such vulnerabilities to keep people hooked; manipulating, for example, when people receive "likes" for their posts, ensuring they arrive when an individual is likely to feel vulnerable, or in need of approval, or maybe just bored. **4** . "There's no ethics," he says. A company paying Facebook to use its levers of persuasion could be a car business targeting tailored advertisements to different types of users who want a new vehicle. Or it could be a Moscow-based troll farm seeking to turn voters in a swing county in Wisconsin.

Harris believes that tech companies never deliberately set out to make their products addictive. They were responding to the incentives of an advertising economy, experimenting with techniques that might capture people's attention, even stumbling across highly effective design by accident. A friend at Facebook told Harris that designers initially decided the notification icon, which alerts people to new activity such as "friend requests" or "likes", should be blue. [...]. "But no one used it," Harris says. "Then they switched it to red and of course everyone used it. [...] Red is a trigger colour. [...] That's why it is used as an alarm signal."

The most seductive design, Harris explains, exploits the same psychological susceptibility that makes gambling so compulsive: variable rewards. When we tap those apps with red icons, we don't know whether we'll discover an interesting email, an avalanche of "likes", or nothing at all. **5** . It's this that explains how the pull-to-refresh mechanism, whereby users swipe down, pause and wait to see what content appears, rapidly became one of the most addictive and ubiquitous design features in modern technology. [...]

2. Roger McNamee, a venture capitalist who benefited from hugely profitable investments in Google and Facebook:

[He] has grown disenchanted with both companies, arguing that their early missions have been distorted by the fortunes they have been able to earn through advertising. He identifies the advent of the smartphone as a turning point, raising the stakes in an arms race for people's attention. "Facebook and Google assert with merit that they are giving users what they want," McNamee says. "The same can be said about tobacco companies and drug dealers."

That would be a remarkable assertion for any early investor in Silicon Valley's most profitable behemoths. But McNamee, 61, is more than an arms-length money man. Once an adviser to Mark Zuckerberg, 10 years ago McNamee introduced the Facebook CEO to his friend, Sheryl Sandberg, then a Google executive who had overseen the company's advertising efforts. Sandberg, of course, became chief operating officer at Facebook, transforming the social network into another advertising heavyweight.

(838 words)

Source: Paul Lewis, The Guardian, *05. 10. 2017*

55 generic: *allgemeintypisch*
67 levers of persuasion: *Überzeugungskräfte*
72 swing county: *Bezirk in den USA, in dem nicht feststeht, welcher politische Kandidat die Mehrheit der Stimmen erhalten wird*
116 behemoth: *Riese*
117 an arms-length money man: *(hier) Wagniskapitalgeber*

3 **Which of the criticisms of social media that you encountered in task 1 and the text were already familiar to you, and which are new? What do you think of them? Make some notes, as they may come in handy in the group discussion later on.**

Testing your reading skills

1 Multiple matching

The text contains some numbered gaps where sentences were deleted. Match the sentences below to the gaps in the text (1–5). There are three sentences that do not match any of the gaps.

A	And the very same techniques can be sold to the highest bidder
B	A handful of people, working at a handful of technology companies, through their choices will steer what a billion people are thinking today
C	Since then the design has become one of the most widely emulated features in apps
D	All of our minds can be hijacked. Our choices are not as free as we think they are
E	He wanted to address the growing concern that technological manipulation was somehow harmful or immoral
F	Such granular information, Harris adds, is "a perfect model of what buttons you can push in a particular person"
G	It is the possibility of disappointment that makes it so compulsive
H	Not everyone working for Facebook knows exactly what they are doing.

2 Mediation Englisch – Deutsch

Beantworten Sie folgende Fragen auf Deutsch.

1 Tristan Harris und sein Lehrer BJ Fogg:

- **a** Was konnte Harris von Fogg lernen?
- **b** Was hat Harris anders gemacht als seine Mitstudenten?

2 Tristan Harris und sein Arbeitgeber Google:

- **a** Was hat seinen Arbeitgeber dazu bewogen, Harris die Position als „Hausphilosoph und Ethiker" zu geben?
- **b** Was hat ihm an der Position nicht gefallen?

3 Roger McNamee und Facebook:

Wie (außer durch finanzielles Engagement) beeinflusste er die Entwicklung von Facebook noch ganz entscheidend?

4 Tristan Harris und Roger McNamee:
Welche Meinungen über die großen Internetfirmen teilen beide?

- **a** in Bezug auf die Gründung der Firmen
- **b** in Bezug auf die Produkte und Dienstleistungen, die sie anbieten
- **c** in Bezug auf die Ursache der Probleme, für die sie heute kritisiert werden

Developing your language skills

1 Improving your listening skills

11

You are going to listen to an interview on US radio with Tim Wu, the author of a book called *The Attention Merchants: The Epic Scramble To Get Inside Our Heads.* While listening, answer the following multiple-choice questions. There is always only one correct answer.

1 Advertising on the internet became the problem it is today when
- **a** the first newspaper went online.
- **b** Google gave up its non-profit policy.
- **c** Wikipedia became a success.

2 In the 1990s, AOL helped
- **a** the computer overtake television as the medium of choice.
- **b** pair up internet services and advertising.
- **c** IT companies cheat on their customers.

3 The founders of Google were
- **a** clever business people.
- **b** involved in many arguments.
- **c** against an advertising business model.

4 For Wu, Google Maps and Google Directions are
- **a** moving in the wrong direction.
- **b** models of advertising success.
- **c** premium subscription services.

5 Google became attractive to advertisers because it presents them with
- **a** customers ready to be targeted.
- **b** masses of customers at the same time.
- **c** customers with lots of different interests.

2 Using participle constructions

For non-native speakers of English, using participles to shorten sentences is not always easy. The most common structures are shortened relative clauses and the use of the *-ing* form after *before* and *after*.

Advanced English is characterized by sentences shortened by participles. You should try and use participles to make your English sound better.

Examples:

The goods which were advertised on TV sold well.	*The goods advertised on TV sold well.*
One ad which showed toys was very popular.	*One ad showing toys was very popular.*
Before she went to school, she …	*Before going to school, she …*
After she saw the ad on TV, she …	*After seeing the ad on TV, she …*
When the manufacturers saw the way the markets were moving, they ...	*Seeing the way the markets were moving, the manufacturers ...*

Go through the text on pages 87–88 and find examples of participle constructions.

Testing your speaking and writing skills

1 a Project

Situation: Now that you have read about some issues concerning the IT business, you need to find organizations that you can approach for a guest speaker. Get together in groups. Each group researches the work of one the following organizations:

- Center for Humane Technology
- Corporate Critic
- Time Well Spent
- Common Sense Media
- EPIC

Discuss in your research group why your organization is important and may be of particular interest to your fellow students.

b Group discussion

Presentation phase: Form new groups, consisting of five experts, one for each organization. Present your organization and your arguments for it to the others in your expert group.

Interaction phase: Discuss which organization to approach for a speaker for your video conference address.

Optional *(if you have time at the end of the discussion):* Discuss which organization to approach next if your first choice does not work out.

2 Material-based writing

In order to prepare fellow students for the guest lecture, your group has decided to post a thought-provoking essay on the website of Critical IT and Business Students on the following topic:

Do online technologies change the way we live for better or worse?

Make use of the following materials and write about 300 words.

MATERIAL 1

"Did you get my Re: Marriage Proposal?."

MATERIAL 2

Beware of the following dangers of life online:

1. You only use one password.
2. You don't question what you read, hear and see.
3. You're too social and honest about yourself.
4. You shop and bank on public Wi-Fi.
5. You are online 24/7.

MATERIAL 3

Digitale Medien wie Internet oder Mobiltelefone erlauben nicht nur eine immer schnellere und unkompliziertere Kommunikation, sie fordern auch deren Beschleunigung. So bieten unsere elektronischen Begleiter Zugang zum Freundeskreis, zu Information und zu Produkten, sind Ratgeber, Spielplatz und Partnerbörse zugleich.

From: the website of Vögele Kultur Zentrum, 22. 10. 2015

Exploring the topic

SITUATION

You are a student of agricultural management. Each semester the student magazine asks some of its students for articles about a topic that concerns the subject they are studying and that is close to their hearts, and this semester they've asked you to write an article. You are concerned about industrial farming practices and decide to write about this. So, you collect information about the issue.

1 Competition

In groups of three, match the following parts of sentences to produce some basic information about agriculture in Europe. There are 12 sentences altogether. Their beginnings are signalled by a number (1–12) and their endings with letters (a–l). The group that is the first to read out the complete text correctly is the winner.

a the use of pesticides, genetically modified crops, antibiotics and growth hormones.	**7** Another segment of agriculture is arable farming,	**b** Europe is a powerhouse of the global agricultural industry.
c cattle, pigs, sheep and poultry.	**d** farming, fisheries and forestry.	**e** as can be seen in the case of the UK, where only 476,000 people work on farms.
12 One new development in farming is the production of biofuel,	**f** but it still remains to be seen whether this will become a lucrative industry.	**9** Organic farming is a sector of the agriculture industry
1 Due to its wide variety of natural resources and land types,	**11** Spain and Italy have the largest amount of land dedicated to organic produce and the largest number of organic food producers,	**4** One important segment of the farming industry is
2 Nevertheless, in many European countries the total number of people employed in agriculture has decreased,	**5** Livestock are domesticated animals	**g** with about 1.97 million hectares and more than 52,000 producers, respectively.
h has increased yields in all forms of agricultural cultivation.	**8** The development of chemicals, such as fertilizers and pesticides,	**3** The agricultural industry can be divided into three main sectors:
i that are reared and used to produce several different commodities.	**j** livestock.	**k** that is currently gaining in popularity.
l which is the production of crops such as cereals, vegetables and fruit.	**10** Organic farming forbids	**6** The main types of farm animals are

2 **Read the following text and find the main issues in industrial agriculture it mentions as well as the proposed solutions to these issues.**

WHY FACTORY FARMING IS NOT JUST CRUEL – BUT ALSO A THREAT TO ALL LIFE ON THE PLANET

A It's time the world woke up to the real impact of modern, industrial farming, says Philip Lymbery, author of *Farmageddon* and the *Deadzone*.

In an interview with the *Guardian*, Lymbery said that when he began campaigning on farm animals in 1990, it was still largely seen as a cruelty issue rather than something that went far beyond that. Since taking over as chief executive of CIWF in 2005, Lymbery has focused on "moving the issue out of being a technical niche to get people to understand industrial farming as a big, global problem".

"We need to go beyond an isolated approach," Lymbery says. "Not just looking at the technical problems around welfare, not just looking at the technical issues around the environment, not just looking at food security in isolation, but putting all of these issues together, then we can see the real problem that lies at the heart of our food system – industrial agriculture."

B Lymbery argues that factory farming is not – as some contend – an efficient, space-saving way to produce the world's food but rather a method in which the invisible costs are actually far higher than the savings.

"Factory farming is shrouded in mythology," he said. "One of the myths is that it's an efficient way of producing food when actually it is highly inefficient and wasteful. Another [myth] is that the protagonists will say that it can be good for the welfare of the animals. After all, if hens weren't happy, they wouldn't lay eggs. The third myth is that factory farming saves space. On the surface it looks plausible, because, by taking farm animals off the land and cramming them into cages and confinement you are putting an awful lot of animals into a small space. But what is overlooked in that equation is you are then having to dedicate vast acreages of relatively scarce arable land to growing the feed. The crops fed to industrially reared animals worldwide could feed an extra four billion [people] on the planet."

former rainforest in Brazil now growing soybeans to feed animals throughout the world

C As the global demand for cheap meat grows, the expansion of agricultural land is putting more and more pressure on our forests, rivers and oceans, contributing to deforestation, soil erosion, marine pollution zones and the global biodiversity crisis, he said.

trawling nets behind a ship to catch as much fish as possible

10 CIWF (Compassion in World Farming): animal welfare organization

"The UN has warned that if we continue as we are, the world's soils will have effectively gone within 60 years. And then what? We shouldn't look to the sea to bail us out because commercial fisheries are expected to be finished by 2048 … The rainforest homes of the likes of jaguars and the critically endangered Sumatran elephants are being razed to make way for intensive crop production and plantations that are feeding factory farm animals … the mixed farm habitats of once common farmland birds such as barn owls, turtle doves and skylarks are being stripped away, and … vast quantities of wild fish are being scooped up to feed industrially reared farmed fish and chickens and pigs, leaving the likes of penguins, puffins and other species starving."

D Antibiotic use is another red flag area. "There is now overwhelming evidence that the routine prophylactic use of antibiotics is leading to the rise of antibiotic resistant superbugs, and the World Health Organisation has issued warnings that if we don't do something to curb antibiotic use in both human and animal medicine we will face a post-antibiotic era where currently treatable diseases will once again kill." Although some countries, the UK and the US for example, are now trying to cut back, antibiotic use is totally unregulated in other parts of the world: in China the farmers can just prescribe and administer antibiotics for themselves.

E Lymbery believes that we already know the answer to this problem. Compassion advocates a reduction in meat-eating (Lymbery himself is vegan but is not "anti-meat"). In the long term regenerative farming – a broad term that includes all sorts of practices such as rotational grazing, tree planting, improving soils, reducing chemical inputs, silvopasture and increasing biodiversity – is, Lymbery believes, our only hope and a movement whose time has come. "Hilal Elver, the UN rapporteur for the right to food, has talked about the need to move away from industrial agriculture towards agro-ecological models. There is a groundswell – it's almost starting to be a zeitgeist as key thinkers in civil society start to join the dots and see that actually we do need a new style of agriculture which goes beyond industrial agriculture, which goes beyond simple sustainability, which brings us to a point of regeneration."

F On the whole national governments have shown little interest in radical farming reform. But there have been a few notable exceptions such as India, Rwanda and Kenya, and the international community and the corporate world is increasingly interested in financing and supporting these models. […] In the recent lead-up to the appointment of the head of the WHO, more than 200 scientists and campaigners signed a letter asking the appointee to promise to look at the "global health challenge" of factory farming which was widely circulated on social media and led to an editorial in the *New York Times*.

So how likely is it that we will get global action on food and farming? "I am sure that 20 years ago people calling for a solution to climate change were being asked exactly that question," says Lymbery. "I believe that nothing less will be needed if we are to secure the future for our children."

(906 words)

Source: Bibi van der Zee, The Guardian, *04. 10. 2017*

64, 68 barn owl, turtle dove, skylark, puffin: types of birds
92 silvopasture: practice of using woodland to rear farm animals
95 rapporteur: *Berichterstatter/in*

3 **What questions would you like to ask about the issues raised and their proposed solutions? Note them down, so that you can use them in your article.**

Testing your reading skills

1 Multiple-choice questions

Choose the most suitable option in each case.

1 Thirty years ago campaigners …

a	were largely opposed to the farming industry due to the issue of animal welfare.
b	were against technological developments in industrial farming.
c	were concerned about the isolation of particular farm animals from others.
d	recognized that industrial agriculture was a global problem.

2 Lymbery doesn't think that factory farming is efficient (line 30). His argument is that …

a	animal welfare is more important than the profits made.
b	factory farming is cost effective, but does not produce good meat.
c	even keeping animals crammed together requires too much space
d	the more animals that are bred, the less food there is for humanity.

3 "If hens weren't happy, they wouldn't lay eggs" (lines 34–35) is an argument used by …

a	Philip Lymbery himself.
b	opponents of animal rights activists.
c	supporters of industrial farming.
d	people who feel sorry for caged chickens.

4 In paragraph C Lymbery warns of the consequences of increased meat production. Which of the following consequences is not mentioned by him?

a	woods dying due to increased acidity in the water
b	more barren land that can easily be destroyed by the elements
c	a considerable decrease in the number of plants, animals, fish and insects in the world
d	life in the seas and oceans becoming endangered

5 In paragraph C commercial fishing is mentioned by Lymbery to show that …

a	the biodiversity crisis has reached all the oceans of the world.
b	we cannot rely on fish to feed us when other food sources become scarce.
c	nearly all of the oceans' fish are now fed to farm animals.
d	many fish species are suffering due to the polluting of the oceans.

6 Antibiotics are mostly used in animal farming in order to …

a	cure animals infected by diseases.
b	prevent animals from contracting diseases.
c	make animal meat safer for humans.
d	cover up the fact that animals suffer from malnutrition.

7 In view of the massive use of antibiotics by humans, Lymbery predicts …

a	that allergic reactions to antibiotics will become more common.
b	deaths from illnesses that are curable at present.
c	killer bacteria being developed by governments.
d	the deregulation of antibiotic use in China.

8 Which of the following is not a practice of regenerative farming (line 89), as mentioned in the text?

a	regularly changing the areas where animals are kept to graze
b	naturally enriching the earth that plants grow in
c	reversing deforestation
d	making more land available for animal grazing

9 In the final paragraph, Philip Lymbery …

a	explains that solutions to climate change and farming will be found.
b	feels that there is little hope for the next generation.
c	believes that our attitudes to the production of food will change.
d	thinks that it is likely that people will soon change their diets.

2 Mediation Englisch – Deutsch

Beantworten Sie folgende Fragen auf Deutsch.

1	Welchen Ausdruck verwendet Lymbery im Abschnitt E, um uns zu sagen, dass die kritische Öffentlichkeit jetzt immer stärker erkennt, wie in der Natur alles mit allem zusammenhängt? Finden Sie ihn und geben Sie einen entsprechenden deutschen Ausdruck dafür an.
2	Erläutern Sie, was Philip Lymberys „regenerative farming" von der „einfachen" nachhaltigen Landwirtschaft unterscheidet.

Developing your language skills

1 Improving your listening skills

12

Interested by what Philip Lymbery said in the text, you search for more information about him and find a radio interview he gave. Summarize the main points he made by copying and filling in the gird below with notes in German.

1	Was die Konferenz bewirken soll	▬
2	Was eigentlich die Aufgabe der Landwirtschaft ist	▬
3	Als was uns die industrielle Landwirtschaft verkauft wird	▬
4	Wieso der Fleischkonsum weltweit ansteigt	▬
5	Lymbery's Botschaft an die Zuhörerinnen und Zuhörer	▬
6	Wieso eine so einfache Botschaft wirksam ist	▬
7	Was außer Maßnahmen des Einzelnen noch geschehen muss	▬
8	Warum der Brexit eine positive Auswirkung haben könnte	▬

2 Using gerund constructions

Advanced English is characterized by gerund constructions. This contrasts with German, which makes use of noun phrases and infinitive constructions.

a Look at the examples taken from the text and translate them into German in order to see the difference in the ways the two languages express themselves. All these examples can be translated using noun phrases or infinitive constructions. Try both.

1 One of the myths is that it's an efficient way of producing food.
2 … dedicate vast acreages of relatively scarce arable land to growing the feed
3 … the corporate world is increasingly interested in financing and supporting these models.

b Translate the following sentences into English using gerund constructions.

1 Angesichts der Tatsache, dass die Viehzucht immens viele natürliche Ressourcen verbraucht, sollten wir wirklich damit aufhören, so viel Fleisch zu konsumieren.
2 Ich persönlich kann es mir nicht vorstellen, ganz ohne Fleisch auszukommen.
3 Ich bin es aber inzwischen gewöhnt, mehr Gemüse und Obst zu essen und nur ein- oder zweimal die Woche Fleisch.
4 Wenn es weiterhin so bleibt, dass Fleisch in vielen Supermarkten sehr billig angeboten wird, dann werden sich mir jedoch nicht viele Menschen anschließen.
5 Viele Leute wissen ja eigentlich, das sie auch aus gesundheitlichen Gründen weniger Fleisch essen sollten, aber sie schieben es immer wieder auf, diesen wichtigen Schritt zu einer besseren Lebensweise zu tun.

3 Writing an article for a student magazine

Using the information from the text and the radio interview as well as any other information you have, turn your findings into a 250-word article for the student magazine.

Testing your writing skills

1 Mediation Deutsch – Englisch

Sie schreiben eine Email an Ihren Freund / Ihre Freundin in Yorkshire, der/die eine etwas romantische Vorstellung vom Bauerndasein hat, über Ihre Entscheidung, Agrarmanagement zu studieren. Verfassen Sie für diese Email eine Passage zum Thema, was es bedeutet, Bauer zu sein. Verwenden Sie dazu die Information aus untenstehendem Text zu den Aspekten:

- **traditionelle Vorstellungen vom Leben des Bauern**
- **das Selbstverständnis der Bauern heute**
- **die Bedeutung der EU für die heutige Landwirtschaft**
- **ein kurzer Blick in die Zukunft der Landwirtschaft**

ZUKUNFT SUCHT BAUER

Wiesen und Felder sind das Werk von Bauern. Sie schufen damit überhaupt erst die Lebensräume für Pflanzen und Tiere, die als Kulturfolger die neu entstandenen ökologischen Nischen besiedelten und deren Vielfalt wir als so bereichernd empfinden, dass sie unter dem besonderen Schutz des Grundgesetzes stehen. [...]

Die Köpfe der Menschen sind voll von diesen idyllischen Bildern und den Vorstellungen, wie Landwirtschaft zu sein hat. Und die Bauern? Sie haben die Nase voll davon, ewig an der Vergangenheit gemessen zu werden, in der vieles anders aber eben längst nicht alles besser war.

Das Leben auf dem Land war harte Arbeit und bedeutete oft Armut, Krankheit und frühen Tod. Ganz zu schweigen von dem rückständigen Landei-Image, das sich hartnäckig hält [...]

Auch deshalb wollen Bauern heute keine Bauern mehr sein. Sie nennen sich lieber Landwirt, sind Milchviehhalter oder Schweinemäster und distanzieren sich mit diesen Berufsbezeichnungen von dem ganzen Ballast, den das Bauersein mit sich bringt.

Sie wollen sich nicht länger an dem orientieren, was einmal war. Sie wollen modern sein, ein Unternehmen managen und sich am globalen Markt behaupten. Sie sehen die Digitalisierung als Chance und ja, sie wollen auch einmal Urlaub machen. Bauer, das steht für das Gestern und ist inzwischen zu einem regelrechten Schimpfwort geworden.

Die kleinteilige, bäuerliche Landwirtschaft, in der Artenvielfalt ihren Raum fand, gibt es kaum noch. Die Betriebe sind größer geworden und können mit immer weniger Arbeitskräften bewirtschaftet werden. Angefangen hat diese Entwicklung Ende der 1950er Jahre, als die Europäische Union gegründet wurde und die Agrarpolitik die Landwirte mit hohen Subventionen anspornte, möglichst viele Nahrungsmittel zu produzieren.

Alles wurde diesem Ziel untergeordnet und jedes Hindernis aus dem Weg geräumt. Mit der Größe der Maschinen wuchs die Größe der Äcker. Auch die Ställe wurden größer. Der Einsatz von Kunstdünger und Pestiziden steigerte die Erträge. [...]

Die Grünen mahnen seit langem eine Agrarwende an, die wieder mehr Rücksicht auf die Natur nimmt. Auch die SPD fordert ein Umsteuern. Aber eine andere Ausrichtung der Landwirtschaft lässt sich nicht einfach von oben verordnen und schon gar nicht gegen den Widerstand der Landwirte.

(338 words)
Source: Claudia Ehrenstein, Die Welt, *14.08.2017*

2 Material-based writing

You decide to continue your studies and apply for an MA course in "Environmental Protection and Agricultural Food Production", which is taught in English. In order to apply you need to show that your English is of a high level by producing an essay on the following topic:

The destruction of the world's forests is inevitable as our need for land and food grows. Do you agree?

Write at least 300 words, making use of the materials below.

MATERIAL 1

Die Menschheit wächst, und sie hat Hunger. Wie werden Milliarden Menschen in Zukunft satt? Kakerlaken, Gen-Reis oder Designersteak – es gibt viele Wege. [...]
Die Uhr jedenfalls tickt: [...] Bis zum Jahr 2100 könnten laut UN über 10 Milliarden Menschen auf der Welt leben. [...]
Nach Meinung der Experten müssen [...] die weitere Ausbreitung landwirtschaftlicher Flächen gestoppt und die vorhandenen – derzeit sind das 1,5 Milliarden Hektar Ackerland und 3,4 Milliarden Hektar Weideland – effizienter genutzt werden. [...]
Auch das Potsdam-Institut für Klimafolgenforschung (PIK) warnt vor einer Ausweitung der Agrarflächen durch unkontrollierten Ausbau des Welthandels – denn der gehe zulasten der Natur.

Source: Alexandra Stahl, "Weltbevölkerung braucht Ressourcen von drei Erden", Die Welt, *11.01.2012*

MATERIAL 2

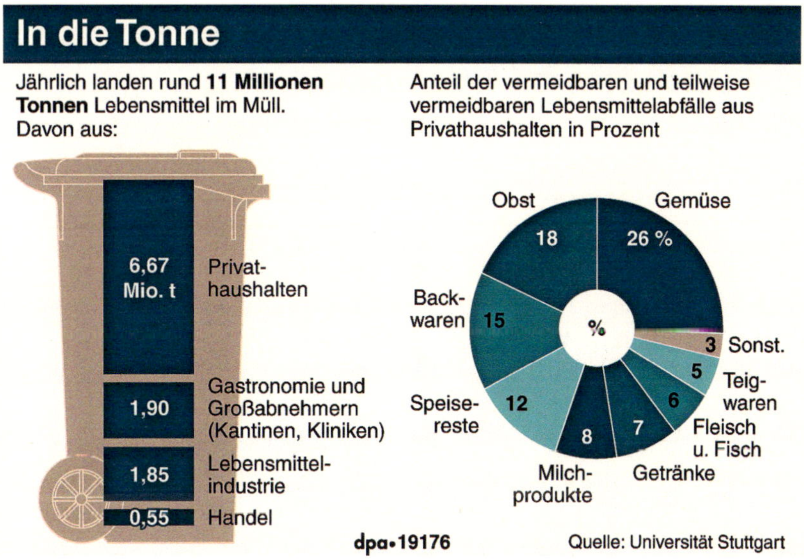

MATERIAL 3

The dominant paradigm of global food security is that humanity "needs" to increase food production by 50 to 100% by 2050. The consensus is that this is partly due to population growth, but mostly because this population is shifting towards more meat- and dairy-intensive diets. [...]
Food waste in the developed world suggests there's no guarantee that increasing global food production would eliminate world hunger. Food availability in rich countries in fact represents 150–200% of nutritional needs in calorific terms.

Source: Tristram Stuart, "Food: how much does the world need?", the website of World Economic Forum, 07.05.2015

Exploring the topic

SITUATION

You and your friends have just seen an action film in which drones play a big part. You write to an English friend of yours on your common messaging platform and tell him how much you enjoyed the film. Your friend, however, worries about a future in which drones play an even bigger part in life. He has just read a novel called *Sting of the Drone* by the American writer Richard A. Clarke. He recommends a passage from the novel to you about drone strikes that shows the complexity of the decision-making process and the various human factors at play. You read the passage and then, on your common messaging platform, send him a reply to his view that drone warfare is unethical.

1 **In small groups, exchange what you know about drones used in warfare. These questions may help: What do you know about the technical side of drone deployment? Where did you get your information? What do you think it must be like for the soldiers who operate drones?**

2 **Read the following text and make notes on the following.**

a the decision-making process in drone warfare
b the three main characters:
- Bruce Dougherty
- Erik Parsons
- Sandra Vittonelli

STING OF THE DRONE

FRIDAY, JUNE 26
GLOBAL COORDINATION CENTER
CREECH AIR FORCE BASE, NEVADA

The room five thousand miles to the east was also cool, dark, quiet. Lit by the glow of the screen in front of him, the red-haired Air Force pilot suddenly sat straight up in his specially designed ergonomic chair. He was one of thirty Air Force pilots in the room, each remotely flying a drone somewhere in the world. Each wore an olive-drab one-piece flight suit emblazoned with colorful unit patches and symbols.

In front of him were two large and six small screens, ten analog dials, and two sticks. The two large screens provided the live image feeds from two of the cameras onboard this drone, one a high-definition television-like video, the other an infrared or synthetic-aperture radar image for night operations. One stick directed the aircraft, up and down, right and left. Thumb dials on the side of the stick allowed the pilot to precisely control ailerons and wing flaps. The other stick armed weapons, launched them, and guided them to the target. For weapon release, a small red metal cover on the side of the stick had to be lifted and a button physically depressed before the selected missile launched or the chosen bomb dropped. Despite all of the on-screen controls, a hand had to touch metal before the death from above could be unleashed.

Next to the pilot a similar cockpit could be staffed by a non-commissioned officer to assist the pilot when needed on complicated missions, providing a second set of eyes to look at sensors, or perhaps to steer the aircraft while the pilot guided a missile to the target. Today, the second seat was empty. The pilot was on his own.

"Got somethin' here, boss," the pilot called out.

Colonel Erik Parsons spun around in his chair above and behind the pilots. Parsons was the squadron commander for the drone pilots at Creech Air Force Base, where there were more Unmanned Aerial Vehicle pilots than at any other of the twelve bases from which Americans directed their worldwide fleet of drones. If pilots were supposed to look like the cartoon hero Steve Canyon, tall and blond, Erik Parsons looked more like a wrestling coach, short, stocky, with closely cropped black hair.

Erik got out of his chair and walked purposefully, quickly down the row of pilot cubicles toward the pilot who had called out, Major Bruce Dougherty.

"Watchya got there, Carrot Top?"

"Goats, boss. I got goats. But I don't have goat herders. Water, but no people."

"Bruce, there is water all over the world without people nearby."

"Yes, sir, but not in these arid mountains in the summer. Besides, that was just the tell. I made a second pass with the synthetic-aperture radar imager turned on and ... presto ... two SUVs sitting under a camo tarp about a football field up the road from the water. Three more and a couple of pickups under netting farther up the canyon. Now, with the infrared on you can see a whole complex of shit nestled up against the canyon wall, hiding from view under the netting. Or so they thought."

Erik Parsons leaned over the pilot for a better look at the screen. "Throw it up on the Big Board, Bruce." As a series of green blobs flashed onto the main video screen, covering two hundred

6 ergonomic chair: work chair designed for efficiency and comfort
7 olive-drab: *in verblasstem Olivton*
7 emblazoned with sth: *mit etwas geschmückt*
11 synthetic-aperture radar: a form of radar that is used to create two- or three-dimensional images of objects, such as landscapes
13 aileron: *Querruder eines Flugzeugs*
13 wing flap: *Flügelklappe*
18 non-commissioned officer: *Unteroffizier/in*
24 squadron commander: leader of a unit of aircraft
25 Unmanned Aerial Vehicle: drone
31 Watchya: what have you

square feet on the front wall, Parsons picked up a red handset. "Sandy, we got any HVIs likely to be up in grid square A-08? I think I got a live one."

In the glass-walled room behind the pilots' cubicles, Sandra Vittonelli consulted her own small screen. "Maybe. We lost signals from a guy guarding a High Value Individual almost three hours ago in sector A-17. That's not too far away, he could be in A-08 by now. But that's hardly reason enough to get excited."

"Well, Sandy, even without a named target on screen, I am looking at enough suspicious activity here to designate this a signature-based strike. I think we got us a terrorist camp." As Erik Parsons spoke he patted Bruce Dougherty's shoulder.

Sandra Vittonelli stood and squinted through the glass at the Big Board in the next room. "I'll be right out to the floor."

Since she was far away from Washington, Sandra wore jeans, but in deference to standards she had learned at Headquarters over the years, she also wore a blue blazer. It helped to make clear the authority relationship. Sexism was officially taboo, but some of these jocks needed reminders sometimes. They were not all used to taking orders from a short, civilian woman in blue jeans. Although she was a CIA employee, as Director of the Joint Global Coordination Center for the program she owned the pilots. There had been a single integrated drone program for both the Pentagon and the Agency planes now for three months. When Erik had asked her about the blazer once, she had told him that she wore it because the air-conditioning was set too low in the Center and, moreover, the jacket also gave her lots of pockets for her "stuff". Then she had changed the subject to why the pilots felt the need to wear jumpsuits when the airplanes were thousands of miles away.

As she stood at Bruce's cubicle, she was aware that all the other pilots were watching her and not focusing on the video feeds from their aircraft. "I gotta admit, it does fit a signature," she told Erik and Bruce, "but how long you been looking at it?"

Bruce looked at the digital elapse clock running in his console. "I've been loitering for seventy-three minutes now. I've run electro-optical, infrared, and synthetic-aperture radar passes. This is one of the new birds with all three types of sensors. The analysis software has located thirty-two human life forms, identified all of them as adults. Except for seven guys on the hills, all of them are under the camouflage. No signatures of women or kids."

She looked at Erik, who shook his head in affirmation. "It's a good one, Sandy."

Vittonelli put on her poker face. "Let's loiter some more. And pull up any imagery of the place from past missions. Somebody must have passed over it before en route to somewhere else." Then she picked up the handset of a red phone. "This is the Director, GCC. Let's wake up the boys and girls in DC. I'm initiating a Kill Call."

(1081 words)

Source: Richard A Clarke, Sting of the Drone, *2014*

49 a signature-based strike: *ein allen Vorschriften genügender Angriff*
62 jumpsuit: *einteilige Uniform oder Einsatzbekleidung*
67 digital elapse clock: *Digitaluhr, die die verbleibende Zeit anzeigt*

3 Pay particular attention to lines 44–76 and discuss the following:

- the relationship between Parsons and Dougherty, and between Vittonelli and Dougherty.
- what kind of emotions may be at play in this scene.

4 Note down what this passage says about drone warfare. You will need the notes later for your response to your friend.

Testing your reading skills

1 Gapped summary

Copy the summary of the text and fill the gaps with appropriate words from the corresponding passages of the text (one word per gap). Do not make any changes. Please also provide the number of the line in which you found the word or expression.

The scene is set in a control room of an air force base, from which American pilots direct drones ___[1] (line ___) to a particular target. They watch the ___[2] ___[3] (line ___) supplied by the drones' cameras, and they control the aircrafts and the ___[4] (line ___) they carry. For missiles to actually strike, the pilots have to activate them ___[5] (line ___) by pushing a button. In situations where it is difficult for one pilot alone to make decisions, an officer is usually at hand to ___[6] (line ___) him or her. One of these pilots, Major Bruce Dougherty, calls his boss, Colonel Erik Parsons, because he thinks he may have discovered a ___[7] ___[8] (line ___) hidden in a mountain range ___[9] ___[10] (line ___) miles east of the base. Parsons believes Dougherty is correct in his assessment, and hopes the strike will hit one of the ___[11] (line ___) in the area. He consults CIA employee Sandra Vittonelli in the next room, as she is the person with the ___[12] (line ___) to order the strike. In order to convince Vittonelli that the strike will not cause collateral damage, Dougherty stresses the fact that his drone has located only ___[13] (line ___), and that ___[14] (line ___) and ___[15] (line ___) will not get caught up in an attack. Although Vittonelli wants assurance, she eventually tells everyone that she will be ___[16] (line ___) the process to launch an attack.

2 Short-answer questions

Answer the following questions. You may use words from the text.

1	What physical attribute does Parsons refer to with the expression "Carrot Top" (line 31)?
2	What does Sandra Vitonelli do to continually remind her colleagues of her position at the base?
3	What does "GCC" (line 75) stand for?

Developing Your Language Skills

Improving your listening skills

13

a Listen to the interview with Richard A. Clarke, the author of *Sting of the Drone*, and complete the sentences.

1. As former national coordinator for security and counterterrorism under three American presidents, Richard A Clarke could draw on his ___
2. With his fictional Air Force pilots, Clarke gives the drone programme of the US military ___
3. With this technology a pilot can kill people thousands of miles away and then ___
4. The good thing about drones is that the pilot ___
5. The bad thing is that sometimes there are innocent victims and then there is a ___
6. In the scene set in a hotel in Vienna, the pilots think they can strike without causing ___
7. Clarke warns that a drone strike in the USA might not be far away, as drones ___
8. Clarke wants to provide his readers with the unique opportunity to ___
9. At the end he wonders whether the drone programme has become ___

b Note down the arguments for and against drone warfare mentioned in this interview. You will need the notes later for your response to your friend.

Testing your writing skills

Material-based writing

Write a 300-word response to your friend's view that drone warfare is unethical. Make use of the materials below.

MATERIAL 1

Unsere Gesellschaft verdrängt gerne, wozu Militär eigentlich da ist und wozu es ausgebildet wird: schlichtweg zur Anwendung physischer Gewalt. Doch das ist der Kern des Militärischen. Und ob die Mittel der Gewaltanwendung nun Kampfdrohnen, Panzerhaubitzen oder Eurofighter heißen, ist letztlich ganz egal. [...] Letztendlich kann eine Drohne mit ihrer Bewaffnung nur das leisten, was ein bemanntes Flugsystem mindestens auch leisten kann: Sie kann aufklären und ein zuvor definiertes Ziel aus der Luft angreifen. Und dabei kann sie noch präziser feuern, als es bemannte Kampfflugzeuge mit ihrer Präzisionsbewaffnung heute können. Die wichtigsten Vorzüge von Drohnen sind die geringeren Kollateralschäden, ein geringeres Risiko für die eigenen Soldaten und geringere Kosten als für bemannte Flugzeuge.

Source: Detlef Buch, "Warum die Bundeswehr Drohnen braucht", the website of Deutschlandfunk Kultur, 12. 02. 2013

MATERIAL 2

Your notes on:
- the excerpt from the novel (page 100)
- the radio interview with the author (page 103)

Any other knowledge you have of the use of drones in warfare.

MATERIAL 3

GLOBALIZATION AND CONFLICT 4

FOCUS

1 Globalization encompasses many areas of life. Four of them are BUSINESS, MIGRATION, SEPARATISM and TERRORISM. Find the sets of four pictures which deal with one of the four aspects.

2 Decide which illustration best represents the most pressing issue facing society today. Then share your view in a group of four and decide on a ranking list of four which you all can agree upon. Be ready to present your ranking list to class and defend it.

3 Look at the following statement for a writing task. Decide which of the pictures above you would find most suitable as an illustration for the writing task. Present your ideas in class.

What unites humans is our aspiration for dignity, safety and a better future.

The effects of globalization

Globalization is the process of interaction and integration between different countries, cultures and economic systems around the world. Globalization has affected every aspect of life due to advances in transportation and communication technology. While primarily an economic process, globalization has also affected social and cultural norms throughout the world.

Deregulation has enabled financial and investment markets to operate internationally. The result has been the easy flow of capital, goods, services and human resources across national borders, thereby expanding global trade. By liberalizing markets, privatizing industries and reducing protectionist barriers, governments have created opportunities for business to flourish. International institutions such as the World Trade Organization (WTO) as well as the summits of the leading industrial states (the G7) and the emerging markets (Brazil, Russia, India and China) were established to promote globalization. Multinational corporations have used globalization to disperse their operations throughout the world and to outsource work to low-wage countries, thereby becoming more competitive.

Globalization has a technological and cultural side as well. The advent of the World Wide Web allows individuals everywhere to take advantage of computer-related services in order to connect to the rest of the world or to gain information instantaneously.

Opponents believe that globalization has benefitted large companies in developed countries rather than workers in the developing world. In the eyes of anti-globalists, trade agreements like TTIP and neo-liberal policies are the cause of the exploitation of developing countries, of sweatshops, child labour, cyclical financial crises, the reduction of social services and the declining influence of trade unions. The result is the erosion of social justice, as just a small minority benefit from globalization and the vast majority of workers live impoverished lives with little hope of betterment.

Critics also worry that cultural globalization will result in a standardization of cultural expression around the world. Propelled by the ease of shared experience in the form of popular culture or international travel, globalization has an impact on our taste in food, music and art and ultimately renders human experience everywhere more or less the same. A loss of uniqueness of less dominant cultures and the disappearance of cultural heritage may be the inevitable result of a world moving together. Supporters, however, argue that cultural globalization will give us a wider range of choices, as we pick and choose which elements of global culture we wish to enjoy.

The exploitation of natural resources on an unprecedented scale, leading to environmental degradation, animal extinction and climate change, has set off waves of migration from the poorer states to the rich, industrialized countries. Migrants often flee to escape from the bleak prospects and terrible living conditions in their home countries. Additionally, there are many war-ravaged countries, where political oppression, religious persecution and civil wars force people to leave. Many of those refugees become displaced people in their own countries or move across borders into neighbouring states, where they are often met with resistance.

The dissatisfaction with falling living standards and the loss of cultural identity has fuelled radical Islamic terror groups, which have devastated countries in the Middle East while bringing terror attacks in the form of suicide bombings, shootings and stabbings to the streets of European cities.

The international flow of migrant workers and refugees, the destruction of entire branches of industry due to outsourcing to low-wage countries and the fear of cultural homogeneity have encouraged both nationalist and separatist movements. The Brexit vote in the UK and separatist movements in various European countries show that globalization has left people with a feeling of fear, resentment and anger about their lost identity and about the influence of supranational institutions such as the European Union. Yet a move away from European unity could have detrimental effects for economic prosperity as well as for peace on the continent. (645 words)

Working with words

1 Which of the highlighted words in the text can be used correctly in all three sentences?

1 If we cannot stop the ___ of blood from the wound, the patient will die.
We must encourage the free ___ of information.
This word interrupts the smooth ___ of the text.

2 Many students are afraid of going abroad due to the language ___.
The crowd was kept behind a safety ___.
Not knowing English will be a ___ to professional success.

3 It's hoped that lowering tariffs will ___ economic growth.
The government wants to ___ the forest as a tourist destination.
They only ___ people after they have worked here for several years.

4 He is one of Germany's best ___ for the Olympic gold medal.
There are excellent career ___ in engineering.
As she has failed all her exams, her future ___ don't look very good.

2 Complete the second sentence so that it has a similar meaning to the first sentence. Use highlighted words and phrases from the text.

1	Globalization may make people and communities no longer be different but all be the same.	Globalization may lead to the ___ of local culture.
2	Civil wars often lead to the end of old and unique traditions and history as communities are destroyed and displaced.	Civil wars often lead to the ___ as communities are destroyed and displaced.
3	Europe faced a refugee crisis of a size that had never occurred before.	Europe faced a refugee crisis ___
4	Many refugees come from places in the world which have been destroyed by fighting.	Many refugees come from ___.

3 Your American friend Kyle is spending his vacation at your home. He meets your German friends Jonas and Lena, and together you discuss the state of the world. As you're the only one who masters both languages, it is up to you to interpret what each person says.

1 Jonas: Welche staatlich unterstützten Terrorgruppen gibt es?
2 Lena: Globalisierung fördert die kulturelle Gleichschaltung.
3 Jonas: Ist die Aushöhlung der sozialen Gerechtigkeit eine Folge der Globalisierung?
4 Kyle: Why are there so many separatist movements in Europe?
5 Lena: Ist Kyle der Begriff „Schwellenländer" bekannt?
6 Jonas: Meiner Meinung nach sind Bürgerkrieg, Unterdrückung und Verfolgung die Hauptursachen von Migration.

4 A THE GLOBAL WORLD

Exploring the topic

SITUATION

Globalization seems to have reached a tipping point. People throughout Europe and the world are speaking up against globalization, as can be seen in the examples of Brexit in the UK, the rise of populist parties in Europe and the emergence of protectionist policies in the USA. Your school's radio station wants you to broadcast a short report in its next programme on the challenges globalization faces nowadays.

1 **Look at the photos and try to give a short overview on what they represent.**

2 **Work in groups of three and write down your ideas on the positive and negative aspects of globalization. Come up with a pro-and-con list, which you can present to the class.**

3 **Read the text "Brexit is a rejection of globalization" and make notes on relevant information the text provides. Don't forget to write down vocabulary that might be helpful for your report.**

BREXIT IS A REJECTION OF GLOBALIZATION

A The age of globalization began on the day the Berlin Wall came down. From that moment, the trends evident in the late 1970s and throughout the 1980s accelerated: the free movement of capital, people and goods; trickle-down economics; a much diminished role for nation states; and a belief that market forces, now unleashed, were unstoppable.

B There has been push back against globalization over the years. The violent protests seen in Seattle during the World Trade Organization meeting in December 1999 were the first sign that not everyone saw the move towards untrammelled freedom in a positive light. One conclusion from the 9/11 attacks on New York and Washington in September 2001 was that it was not only trade and financial markets that had gone global. The collapse of the investment bank Lehman Brothers seven years later put paid to the idea that the best thing governments could do when confronted with the power of global capital was to get out of the way and let the banks supervise themselves.

C Now we have Britain's rejection of the EU. This was more than a protest against the career opportunities that never knock and the affordable homes that never get built. It was a protest against the economic model that has been in place for the past three decades. To be sure, not all Britain's problems are the result of its EU membership. It is not the European Commission's fault that productivity is so weak or that the trains don't run on time. The deep-seated failings that were there when Britain voted in the referendum were still there when the country woke up to the result. Evidence of just how unbalanced the economy is will be provided when the latest figures for Britain's

current account are released later this week. These show whether the country's trade and investment income is in the black or the red.

D In another sense, however, the EU is culpable. In the shiny new world created when former communist countries were integrated into the global model, Europe was supposed to be powerful enough to protect its citizens against the worst excesses of the market. Nation states had previously been the guarantor of full employment and welfare. The controls they imposed on the free movement of capital and people ensured that trade unions could bargain for higher pay without the threat of work being off-shored, or cheaper labour being brought into the country. In the age of globalization, the idea was that a more integrated Europe would collectively serve as the bulwark that nation states could no longer provide. Britain, France, Germany or Italy could not individually resist the power of trans-national capital, but the EU potentially could. The way forward was clear. Move on from a single market to a single currency, a single banking system, a single budget and eventually a single political entity.

E That dream is now over. As the director of a thinktank put it: "Brexit is a momentous event in the history of Europe and from now on the narrative will be one of disintegration not integration." The reason is obvious. Europe has failed to fulfil the historic role allocated to it. Jobs, living standards and welfare states were all better protected in the heyday of nation states in the 1950s and 1960s than they have been in the age of globalization. Unemployment across the eurozone is more than 10%. Greece's economy has shrunk by almost a third. Austerity has eroded welfare provision. Labour market protections have been stripped away.

F Inevitably, there has been a backlash, manifested in the rise of populist parties on the left and right. An increasing number of voters believe there is not much on offer from the current system and are at odds with it. They think globalization has benefited a small, privileged elite, but not them. They think it is unfair that they should pay the price for bankers' failings. They hanker after a return to the security that the nation state provided, even if that means curbs on the core freedoms

20 to put paid to sth.: *etwas zunichte machen*
88 to hanker after sth.: *sich nach etwas sehnen*

that underpin globalization, including the free movement of people.

G This has caused great difficulties for Europe's mainstream parties, but especially those of the centre left. They have been perfectly happy to countenance the idea of curbs on capital movements such as a financial transaction tax, and have no problems with imposing tariffs to prevent the dumping of Chinese steel. They feel uncomfortable, however, with the idea that there should be limits on the free movement of people. The risk is that if the mainstream parties don't respond to the demands of their traditional supporters, they will be replaced by populist parties who will. The French Socialist party has effectively lost most of its old blue-collar working class base to the hard left and the hard right.

H There are those who argue that globalization is now like the weather, something we can moan about but not alter. This is a false comparison. The global market economy was created by a set of political decisions in the past and it can be shaped by political decisions taken in the future. Torsten Bell, the director of the Resolution Foundation thinktank, analysed the voting patterns in the referendum and found that those parts of Britain with the strongest support for Brexit were those that had been poor for a long time. The result was affected by "deeply entrenched national geographical inequality", he said. There has been much lazy thinking in the past quarter of a century about globalization.

I Self-evidently, large numbers of people across Europe do not believe a flexible, globalized economy is working for them. One response to the Brexit vote from the rest of Europe has been that a tough line should be taken with Britain to show other countries that dissent has consequences. This would only make matters worse. Voters have legitimate grievances about an economic system that has failed them. Punishing Britain will not safeguard the EU. It will hasten its dissolution.

(996 words)
Source: Larry Elliott, The Guardian, *26. 06. 2016*

4 **Compare your information in a small group, and together prepare a list of ideas that should be included in your radio broadcast. If necessary, do some research on issues you are not sure about.**

Testing your reading skills

1 Short-answer questions (paragraphs A–C)

Answer the following questions. You may use words from the text.

1 What has globalization allowed both people and goods to do?

2 What lesson was learned from the collapse of Lehman Brothers?

3 What were the British who voted to leave the EU protesting about?

4 Which phrase is used for "profits or losses"?

2 Multiple-choice questions (paragraphs D–I)

Choose the most suitable option in each case.

1 According to the text, the EU has failed its citizens as it …

- a hasn't improved the living standards in Eastern European countries.
- b doesn't care about the needs of the nation states and their citizens.
- c never worked as a strong powerhouse to protect against the worst effects of globalization.
- d is more interested in pursuing political unity than economic success.

2 Which of the following was seen as a possible aim of the EU?

- a to match the military might of the USA
- b to become one state
- c to offer outsourcing possibilities for firms
- d to lower labour costs

3 The phrase "a momentous event" (paragraph E) in this context means …

- a immediate
- b historic
- c inconsequential
- d prominent

4 Which of the following areas is not mentioned as one in which the EU has failed its citizens?

- a job creation
- b improving the quality of life
- c support for those in need
- d the integration of foreigners

5 Which statement is true about many of today's voters?

a	They don't mind sacrificing individual liberties.
b	They value the present political system.
c	They feel they have caught up with the elite.
d	They feel more secure than in former times.

6 Which statement best represents the main idea of paragraph G?

a	The major parties find it difficult to support the demands of the working class.
b	Populist parties have better policies than most major parties.
c	Centre-left parties are at odds with some of the demands of their voters.
d	Socialist parties are willing to yield to the demands of their voters.

7 According to the author, the comparison of globalization and weather is …

a	fake.
b	uninformative.
c	unintentional.
d	misleading.

8 According to Torsten Bell, the Brexit vote showed a regional divide between …

a	wealthy and impoverished areas.
b	the various ethnic groups.
c	the city and the country.
d	the north and the south.

9 The concerns about the effects of globalization are …

a	greatly exaggerated.
b	specific to the UK.
c	felt throughout Europe.
d	rejected by other European countries.

10 The author predicts that a tough stance towards the British over Brexit by the EU …

a	will help unite the EU.
b	will bring back the UK into the EU.
c	is bound to be detrimental for the EU.
d	will fail to destroy the UK's global power.

11 All in all, the article provides a/an … analysis of the issue.

a	pedantic
b	momentous
c	in-depth
d	sensational

Developing your language skills

1 Improving your vocabulary

Another student has also written a short text on the topic of globalization for the radio station. His text – though grammatically faultless – could have used better vocabulary and expressions. The editor of your radio team has checked it and underlined parts which need some polishing. Use words and phrases from the text to improve the style. The letters in the margin refer to the paragraphs where you can find the words or expressions.

There is no doubt that globalization has led to countries selling and buying things from each other[1]. Most governments accept that the competitive pressures of a free system of trade in which prices rise and fall without being controlled by the government[2] benefit our economies. [1] A [2] A

However, critics claim that supporters of globalization close their eyes to the mistakes, which are not superficial[3], of the system that has led to lower levels of income and comfort[4]. [3] C [4] E

They take the view that the EU has failed, as it hasn't worked as a defence[5] against uncontrolled capitalism. And now the grave economic situation has led to the imposition of harsh financial steps to save money[6] in many countries. [5] D [6] E

As a result of this, the EU has eroded the trust of its citizens. Brexit is just one manifestation of the fact that European citizens don't agree with[7] the economic policy and system of the EU. [7] F

Many now wish to introduce limits on who can come and live in a country[8]. [8] F

2 Formulating questions

You've put together a whole list of questions in German, but you're not sure how to phrase them in English. Use vocabulary from the text for your questions. The letter of the paragraph in which you can find useful vocabulary is at the end of the line.

1 Ist Ungleichheit in unserer globalen Gesellschaft wirklich tief verwurzelt? **H**
2 Sollte die EU einen harten Kurs in den Verhandlungen mit Großbritannien fahren? **I**
3 Sind die Klagen der Bürger hinsichtlich der Globalisierung wirklich berechtigt? **I**
4 Werden Zolltarife in zehn Jahren noch bestehen? **C**
5 Müssen wir wirklich einen Abbau des Arbeitsschutzes durch die Globalisierung fürchten? **E**
6 Muss nicht letztlich die politische Einheit das Resultat eines einheitlichen Wirtschaftsraums sein? **D**
7 Können die Gewerkschaften das Abwandern von Arbeitsplätzen ins Ausland verhindern? **D**
8 Beschleunigt die Globalisierung die Auflösung der EU? **I**
9 Sind der Aufstieg populistischer Parteien und der Niedergang der Volksparteien wirklich Folgen der Ablehnung der Globalisierung? **F/G**

3 Improving your viewing skills

Watch a video about which countries benefit from globalization.

08

While watching, look out for the following aspects or statements mentioned or shown in the talk and recreate the order in which they occur. The starting point (1) is already marked. Copy the table and put numbers 2–14 into the correct boxes. There are two aspects that are not discussed in the video. Mark their boxes with an X.

	Findings: first, all 42 countries benefitted from globalization in the period under review.
	Supporters of globalization claim it is the key 21st-century growth motor.
	Study's approach: globalization index which measures the overall effect of economic, social and political interconnection.
	African countries have little hope of joining the party.
	Second, average net benefit: a 0.35 per cent increase in the growth rate of real per capita GDP.
	Emerging markets should be given every opportunity to join the party.
	Opponents of globalization argue it facilitates inequality and lowers standards.
	It is believed that losers of globalization come disproportionately from disadvantaged communities.
	An average per capita income rise of about EUR100 in countries like China, Brazil and Mexico.
	In the long run, this trend could exacerbate global inequalities, especially as emerging markets could lose out from regional trade pacts like TTIP.
	However, there is a difference in benefit: emerging markets benefitted significantly less than developed nations.
	Finland was the country that benefitted most from globalization.
	Gains to developed countries far outweigh those to emerging markets.
	Comparison of real growth to estimated growth if global interconnectedness had remained at 1990 levels.
1	Belief that globalized interconnectedness creates winners and losers.
	In the long run globalization is not sustainable.
	Although interconnectedness is generally beneficial, globalization opportunities are not evenly dispersed.
	Germany was ranked fourth in terms of benefitting from globalization.

4 Writing a report for a radio programme

Write the report for a 3–4-minute contribution to be be aired on the next school radio programme.

Testing your writing and speaking skills

1 Mediation Deutsch – English

Für einen Beitrag in der bilingualen Schülerzeitung zum Themenkomplex „Globalisierung" haben Sie den nachfolgenden Artikel entdeckt. Die Redaktion der Schülerzeitung will einen Artikel zum Thema in englischer Sprache veröffentlichen. Fassen Sie den Artikel in ca. 150 Wörtern nach folgenden Gesichtspunkten zusammen:

- **(historische) Ereignisse, die die Globalisierung beschleunigten**
- **Zusammenhang zwischen Globalisierung und dem Ende des Sozialismus**
- **Einfluss der Globalisierung auf die politische Ordnung auf europäischer und internationaler Ebene**

DIE MENSCHEN RÜCKEN ZUSAMMEN, ABER DIE INTERNATIONALE ZUSAMMENARBEIT KOLLABIERT

Die Globalisierung ist keine Erfindung finsterer City-Banker sondern ein Produkt – nun ja: der Umstände. Am Ende ist alles gar nicht so kompliziert, Geschichte ist eine Aneinanderreihung von Ereignissen, und es sind diese Ereignisse, die den Schub in der Globalisierung ermöglicht haben. Zwei Umstände waren es im Besonderen: der Epochenbruch von 1989 mit dem Kollaps der Sowjetunion; und das Internet, also die Digitalisierung der Welt unter dem Präfix www. Nie zuvor hat die Globalisierung so viel ökonomische Verflechtung und kulturelle Angleichung bewirkt, nie zuvor war dank weltumspannender Echtzeitkommunikation ein Gefühl entstanden, als wäre die Erde ein Dorf und jede Krise eine Provokation im eigenen Vorgarten.

Die Globalisierung hatte ihren Anteil am Zusammenbruch des Sozialismus. Noch denkt man bemerkenswert wenig über die Jahre nach dem Epochenbruch nach, vielleicht weil noch immer die irrige Vorstellung von den 1990er-Jahre als Wohlstands- und Konsolidierungsjahre vorherrscht, einer weitgehend guten, aber ereignisarmen Zeit also. Diese Vorstellung ist falsch. Bereits in den Achtzigerjahren des vorigen Jahrhunderts hat die Beschleunigung im Globalisierungskarussell Fliehkräfte entwickelt. Diesen Kräften ausgesetzt war das autoritär-sozialistische System der UdSSR samt seinen Satelliten. Sie hatten am Ende dem inneren Druck ihrer Gesellschaften, dem Freiheitswunsch und der Sehnsucht nach Wohlstand nichts entgegenzusetzen. Geschichte ist nie monokausal, aber man wird der Globalisierung ihren Anteil an dieser Zäsur nicht verweigern können. Nach dem Mauerfall triumphierten die USA und das westliche Modell; ihre politische, ökonomische und kulturelle Vormacht waren unangefochten. Aber füllten sie das ideologische Vakuum auch aus, das der Kollaps geschaffen hatte? Platz für Krisengewinnler und neue Probleme gab es jedenfalls ausreichend. Wer diese fast dreißig Jahre im Schnelldurchlauf abspult, der stellt vor allem fest: Eine stabile politische Ordnung hat es nie wirklich gegeben, vielmehr ein Wirrwarr konkurrierender Kräfte, die Geburt neuer Ordnungsvorstellungen und den Abschied von gescheiterten Modellen. Die Europäische Union etwa entwickelte sich von einer überschaubaren Handelsgemeinschaft hin zu einer Werte- und Rechtsallianz, die qua Statuten keine geografischen Grenzen kennen durfte. Manche fantasierten gar vom Superstaat, dann reduzierte man die Sache ein banales Bündnis von Nationalstaaten. Die Verschiebung der politischen Kräfte in dreißig Jahren lässt sich gut am Beispiel der Zahl der jeweiligen Kraftzentren der Welt. Da wandelte sich die internationale Ordnung von der Bipolarität (zwischen dem westlichen Bündnis und dem Ostblock), hin zur Unipolarität (mit dem Hegemon USA) bis hin zur Multipolarität (getragen von vielen Akteuren wie den USA, China, der EU, Russland). Ist das also das Ergebnis der Globalisierung, die Auflösung aller politischen Ordnung?

Source: Stefan Kornelius, Süddeutsche Zeitung, *13.04.2017*

2 Material-based writing

On an online platform you find the following comment by someone:

Globalization has not only benefited the majority of people throughout the world economically but it has also enriched the world culturally.

Write a 300-word response to the statement, using the materials below.

MATERIAL 1

Source: Cagle.com

MATERIAL 2

While open economies are always subject to new competition and structural changes that affect firms and jobs, [...] the same economic processes create a lot of new jobs and business opportunities, and – ultimately – improve living standards. Moreover, the new jobs that are created tend to be better rewarded and come with better working conditions.

Source: Fredrik Erixon, the website of the European Centre for International Political Economy, 01.2018

MATERIAL 3

Von jedem Standort in der Welt mit einem Internetanschluss ist jetzt der Zugriff auf ein riesiges und rasch wachsendes Volumen von Informationen möglich, die alle Bereiche abdecken. Ideen können über das Internet mühelos verbreitet und diskutiert werden. Die Auswirkungen der Technologien der Globalisierung machen den beispiellosen Charakter des gegenwärtigen Prozesses aus. Die natürlichen Grenzen von Zeit und Raum spielen in vielen Bereichen eine immer geringere Rolle.

Source: Sascha Meinert, Michael Stollt, "Vernetzte Welten – Die technische Infrastruktur der Globalisierung", the website of Bundeszentrale für politische Bildung, 18.04.2011

3 Group discussion

Situation: The threat of global dangers accompanies us on a daily basis. You and a group of like-minded students want to get involved in campaigns and decide to join one organization dedicated to improving the world. You each do some research on an organization dealing with a global danger. The organizations can be found on page 145.

Presentation phase: Present your organization, explaining why you think it is the best choice to fight pressing global issues.

Interaction phase: Exchange arguments and try to persuade your group members that your proposal is the most convincing one. Be willing to compromise. Decide in the end which organization you want to join.

Optional *(if you have time at the end of the discussion):* Discuss whether non-governmental organizations can really change things or whether this is actually the domain of governments.

B MIGRATION

Exploring the topic

SITUATION

The topic of migration has become increasingly divisive. Mass international migration is a response to extreme global inequality, war and oppression, and has a profound impact on societies throughout the world. Often, information on the topic is lacking or inaccurate. As part of a student visit to the European Parliament, you have been given the opportunity to interview a leading European politician on the topic of migration. In order to prepare yourself, you do some research so that you can formulate your questions.

1 Have a look at the following pictures and write down a statement which sums up the main idea of each picture. Which aspects of migration or the migration crisis do they convey?

2 Work in groups of four: think of background information you will need for the interview and the questions you would ask a European politician on the issue of migration.

The following terms may be of help:

- Dublin Regulation
- Schengen area
- FRONTEX
- EU-Turkey refugee agreement
- European Agenda on Migration
- people smuggling
- Visegrad group and EU migration policy
- right to asylum (Human Rights Declaration)

3 Read the following text about Europe and its attitude to refugees.

EUROPE'S FAILURE ON REFUGEES ECHOES THE MORAL COLLAPSE OF THE 1930S

A British MPs have voted down a plan to admit just 600 child refugees a year. With governments across the continent abdicating responsibility, this is an ethical catastrophe of historic proportions. In 1938, representatives from 32 western states gathered in the pretty resort town of Evian, southern France. They were there to discuss whether to admit a growing number of Jewish refugees fleeing persecution in Germany and Austria. After several days of negotiations, most countries, including Britain, decided to do nothing.

B I was reminded of the Evian conference when British MPs voted against welcoming just 600 child refugees a year over the next half-decade. The two moments are not exactly comparable. History doesn't necessarily repeat itself. But it does echo, and it does remind us of the consequences of ethical failure. Looking back at their inaction at Evian, delegates could claim they were unaware of what was to come. In 2016, we no longer have that excuse.

C Nevertheless, both in Britain and across Europe and America, we currently seem keen to forget the lessons of the past. In Britain, many of those MPs who voted against admitting a few thousand refugees are also campaigning to unravel a mechanism – the European Union – that was created, at least in part, to heal the divisions that tore apart the continent during the first and second world wars. Across Europe, leaders recently ripped up the 1951 refugee convention in order to justify deporting Syrians back to Turkey, a country where most can't work legally; where some have allegedly been deported back to Syria; and still more have been shot at the border.

D Emboldened by this, the Italian and German governments have since joined the British Prime Minister in calling for refugees to be sent back to Libya, a war zone where – in a startling display of cognitive dissonance – some of the same governments are also mulling a military intervention. Where many migrants work in conditions tantamount to slavery. Where three separate governments are vying for control. In Greece, Europe's leaders have forced the bankrupt government to lock up all arriving asylum seekers – and then reneged on a promise to help care for them, or move them to better-resourced countries elsewhere on the continent. The result is a dire situation on the Greek islands, where the world's richest continent has contrived to jail babies.

E In Denmark, asylum seekers are forced to hand over valuables to pay for their stay, and volunteers have been prosecuted as smugglers for giving them lifts. In America, where boatloads of refugees were turned away from US ports in the 30s, more than 30 governors have refused to accept Muslim refugees. **1** .

F On Saturday afternoon, I came face to face with a similar kind of wilful blindness, close to Turkey's border with Syria. European politicians were visiting a Syrian refugee camp. **2** . They were at the camp to highlight the first beneficiaries of this cash, and to show that life

in Turkey can be every bit as nice as life in Europe.

G The camp was pleasant enough – but it does not represent the lived reality of most Syrians in Turkey, 90% of whom live in urban poverty outside the camps. To really understand their limbo the politicians should have visited the sweatshops on the other side of town, where thousands of Syrian children work 12-hour days to support their families. **3** .

H Instead, they visited a sanitised refugee camp for 45 minutes. **4** . It was a PR stunt stage-managed for the benefit of a hundred waiting journalists – a visual metaphor for the see-no-evil excuses that Europe has used to justify deporting refugees back to Turkey.

I **5** . Invoking a religion named after a man who was at times both a refugee and a migrant, several European politicians have used Christianity to justify their rejection of refugees. "Is it not worrying in itself that European Christianity is now barely able to keep Europe Christian?" asks Hungary's prime minister. **6** . By turning a blind eye to reality, by forgetting the lessons of the past, Europe risks an ethical catastrophe that would return us to the moral collapse of the 1930s. With the far right on the rise across Europe, it has been argued that deporting refugees back to places such as Turkey and Libya will save the continent from relapsing into the extremism of the interwar years. But I wonder if the opposite is true.

J **7** . It reminds us that we, as humans, balance on the very lip of the unspeakable; always far closer to toppling than we might wish to admit. A few hours before the European politicians arrived at the refugee camp, I was at a sweatshop full of Syrians making shoes. The manager hadn't heard of anything like the Evian conference. But he knows about Europe, and its reputation for morality. **8** . "Cats and dogs in Germany can get pet passports – and they're closing the borders to humans?" he asked. "History will document this."

(985 words)

Source: Patrick Kingsley, The Guardian, *26.04.2016*

42 cognitive dissonance: *Widerspruch*
45 tantamount to: *gleichwertig mit*
74 limbo: *Schwebezustand*
80 PR stunt: *PR-Gag*
103 lip: *(hier) Rand*

Testing your reading skills

1 Gapped summary (paragraphs A–D)

Copy the summary and fill the gaps with appropriate words from the corresponding passages of the text (one word per gap). Do not make any changes. Please also provide the number of the line in which you found the word or expression.

Hearing about the refusal of the British MPs to admit 600 child refugees a year, the writer wonders if history is repeating itself, as it reminds him of a tragic decision in 1938 which was a mistake of ___[1] ___[2] (line ___). The recent ___[3] (line ___) concerned child refugees rather than Jewish refugees. While the two cases might not be directly ___[4] (line ___), nevertheless both groups were forced to flee their homelands in order to escape ___[5] (line ___) or war. The question remains whether we can learn from the ___[6] (line ___) of history. Unfortunately, European leaders have decided to ignore a ___[7] (line ___) that guarantees the safety of those fleeing war and oppression and now prefer ___[8] (line ___) refugees to third countries in which they have no future or which are a ___[9] ___[10] (line ___). However, even in Europe, refugees are living in ___[11] (line ___) conditions, as European politicians have ___[12] (line ___) on their commitments to the Greek government to provide support and assistance.

2 Multiple matching (paragraphs E–J)

Match the sentences (A–J) with the gaps (1–8) in the text. Two sentences do not fit.

A	The Evian conference may have happened long ago, but we can still learn its lessons
B	Or, even better, they might have peered over the border wall to the south, to watch Turkish soldiers shoot at Syrians as they try to escape the battlegrounds of northern Syria
C	And he thinks it's now undeserved
D	In exchange for Turkey readmitting asylum seekers deported back from Europe, Europe is giving Turkey several billion euros to help care for the Syrians now stranded on its soil
E	Some called for an outright ban on anyone fleeing a war that is ironically the partial result of catastrophic mistakes in American foreign policy over the past two decades.
F	Europe's abdication of responsibility is usually justified in the name of cultural superiority
G	Europe still deserves this image
H	But citing religion and morality shouldn't obscure the truth
I	Most camp residents were ordered out of sight for the duration of the visit
J	America has always been a beacon of freedom and never turned a cold shoulder on refugees whatever their religion or country of origin

3 Mediation Englisch – Deutsch

Beantworten Sie folgende Fragen auf Deutsch.

1 Welche Länder vergleicht der Autor, wenn er von „better-resourced countries“ (Zeile 51) spricht?

2 Wem kreidet der Autor Blindheit (Zeile 63) an und worin besteht diese? Erläutern Sie Ihre Antwort an einem Beispiel aus dem Text.

3 Wie wurde aus dem syrischen Flüchtlingslager in der Türkei das „sanitised refugee camp“ (Zeilen 79–80), das die Besucher zu Gesicht bekamen?

Developing your language skills

1 Improving your vocabulary

Writing any text requires appropriate and varied language. Repetitions and monotonous vocabulary should be avoided.

Look at the text below and decide which of the alternatives for the words (1–22) does *not* fit?

Migration is an important [1] thing [2] for Europe today. We very often [3] see scenes on TV which are not good [4]. They show [5] what a big [6] problem migration has become for the world. Migrants are often poor [7] and come mainly [8] from war-ravaged countries. Some people say [9] that migrants can easily be welcomed into our rich [10] Western societies. But others want [11] a different solution: that migrants should be housed separately and not in their area [12]. Many think [13] that solutions are needed in the countries they come from [14]. There are some interesting [15] ideas to deal with this problem [16]. It is clear [17] to many [18] politicians that financial aid could be helpful. Others say [19] that human rights and the rule of law must be secured in those countries, and that once these have been achieved, refugees can quickly [20] return home. But [21] many refugees prefer to stay in the new country where they are staying [22].

1	a major	a significant	an urgent
2	issue	theme	topic
3	constantly	frequently	usually
4	dreadful	horrible	remarkable
5	demonstrate	mention	prove
6	enormous	magnanimous	massive
7	destitute	discriminated	impoverished
8	altogether	predominantly	to a large extent
9	argue	deliver	insist
10	opulent	prosperous	wealthy
11	favour	improve	prefer
12	neighbourhood	outskirts	vicinity
13	are of the opinion	feel	mean
14	their destinations	their countries of origin	their home countries
15	fascinating	inquisitive	thought-provoking
16	affair	predicament	situation
17	apparent	bright	evident
18	manifold	numerous	plenty of
19	claim	maintain	intend
20	suddenly	rapidly	swiftly
21	Because of this,	Nevertheless,	Yet,
22	host country	receiving country	transit country

2 Improving your listening skills

15

The current US administration has proposed several plans to cut immigration to the USA. Besides building a border to Mexico, it has demanded an end to the system of "chain migration". Listen and make notes with the help of the prompts below. At the end you should be able to give an overview of the matter and the different views held. Listen to the recording twice.

1	Chain migration is …	a by-product of … part of the US …
2	Who can make a request for spouses and young children to be allowed into the USA?	… …
3	If you have US citizenship the circle of those you can invite is widened; who else is allowed in?	… … …
4	Critics of the current system of "chain migration" claim:	… … …
5	What immigration scheme do Trump and his supporters favour?	…
6	Under this scheme immigrants must:	… … …
7	Opponents of Trump accuse him of "fear-mongering" because:	…
8	Business community's view on the matter:	… … …
9	NumbersUSA, an anti-immigration group, claims "a single illegal immigrant means hundreds of family members coming". What is the current practice concerning limits or caps on immigration?	no caps on: … … caps on: … … …
10	What is the current trend concerning family-based visas?	…

3 Writing questions for an interview

a In your group, draft questions for an interview with a European politician. The questions should be inspired by the information given in the text. If you need further information, do some research on the internet.

b Perform the interviews with a partner in front of the class and ask the rest of the students to evaluate the performance.

Testing your writing skills

1 Mediation Deutsch – English

Im Fokus einer Sozialkundeeinheit steht das Thema „Migration". Balkanroute, Mittelmeerroute, Ceuta und Griechenlandroute sind Thema einer Unterrichtsstunde. In diesem Zusammenhang haben Sie einen Beitrag vorbereitet, der die europäische Migrationspolitik in Afrika zum Thema hat. Ein Artikel zum EU-Afrika-Gipfel in Abidjan, der Hauptstadt der Elfenbeinküste, den Sie recherchiert haben, bietet eine Fülle von interessanten Einblicken. Da die Sozialkundeklasse bilingual unterrichtet wird, ist der Beitrag in englischer Sprache zu verfassen. Sie fassen den Artikel in ca. 150 Wörtern im Hinblick auf nachfolgende Aspekte zusammen:

- **Forderung von Frau Muyumba und der Grund dafür**
- **konkret beschlossene humanitäre Maßnahme des EU-Afrika-Gipfels**
- **Problem der jungen Generation in Afrika und die Gründe dafür**
- **Lösungsansätze des EU-Gipfels**
- **Die Haltung der Bundesregierung zur Migrationsfrage**

Afrika bleibt der Bloß-weg-hier-Kontinent

Es kommt nicht oft vor, dass Dutzende Staatsoberhäupter und Regierungschefs von einer jungen Frau eine Standpauke bekommen. […] „Sie müssen die Jugend und das Unternehmertum fördern und Jobs schaffen", sagte Francine Muyumba, Präsidentin der Pan-Afrikanischen Jugendunion. „Junge Menschen würden sich nur in Richtung Europa aufmachen, „weil sie die Nase voll haben von dem Leben, das sie in Afrika führen müssen."

Unter Teilnehmern des EU-Afrika-Gipfels in Abidjan sorgte die Rede für hochgezogene Augenbrauen, doch viel mehr offenbar nicht: Der Gipfel ging mit einer wachsweichen Erklärung zu Ende, die viele wohlklingende Ankündigungen, aber wenig Konkretes enthält.

Die einzige belastbare Ankündigung war die der Afrikanischen Union (AU), schnellstmöglich 3800 Flüchtlinge aus Libyen zu evakuieren. Auslöser war ein Video des US-Senders CNN über Sklavenmärkte in Libyen, die auf dem Gipfel ein zentrales Gesprächsthema waren. […] Dass Migranten in Libyen misshandelt, missbraucht und mitunter ermordet werden, „ist lange bekannt". […] Ohnehin sei die Evakuierung „nur eine Notmaßnahme", meint Friederike Röder von der Hilfsorganisation One. An den eigentlichen Problemen ändert sie nichts.

Die bestehen vor allem darin, dass ein bedeutender Teil von Afrikas extrem junger Bevölkerung keine Perspektive auf dem Kontinent hat; […] in vielen afrikanischen Staaten politische Instabilität, Korruption und ein Mangel an Rechtsstaatlichkeit herrschen; und dringend notwendige Investitionen ausbleiben […].

Wie man diesen Teufelskreis theoretisch durchbrechen könnte, zählt das Abschlussdokument des Gipfels zwar durchaus auf: Investitionen in Ausbildung und Technologie, die Stärkung von politischer Stabilität und Sicherheit, ein nachhaltiger struktureller Wandel Afrikas. Allerdings: Wie das alles in der Praxis geschehen soll, verrät das Gipfel-Kommunique nicht.

EU-Ratspräsident Donald Tusk sprach von einem „erfolgreichen Gipfel", die Hilfsorganisation One dagegen von einer „bitteren Enttäuschung" für Afrikas Jugend. Alle Staats- und Regierungschefs seien sich darin einig gewesen, dass man in die Jugend investieren müsse und vor einer einmaligen demografischen Herausforderung stehe, die – richtig angefasst – eine Chance sei. […] „Dieser Gipfel hätte die Zukunft vorbereiten müssen, aber er hat die notwendige Grundlage nicht geschaffen", sagt Friederike Röder. […]

Auch zum Thema Migration findet sich im Abschlussdokument kaum Konkretes. Man strebe an, einen „positiven, konstruktiven und mehrdimensionalen Ansatz" zu fördern, der auf „sichere, geordnete und reguläre Art" durchgeführt wird. […] Die Bundesregierung hat dafür aber eine klare Bedingung. „Afrikanische Staaten müssen abgelehnte Asylbewerber zurücknehmen, das ist eine Voraussetzung für mehr legale Migration", sagt Günter Nooke, Afrika-Beauftragter von Kanzlerin Angela Merkel. […] „Bei Rückführungen dürfen wir bei den Mindeststandards von Rechtsstaatlichkeit und Menschenrechten keine Kompromisse machen." Im Abschlussdokument heißt es jedoch lediglich, dass die Rückführung abgelehnter Asylbewerber „in allen Aspekten untersucht" werden soll.

Source: Marcus Becker, Der Spiegel, *30. 11. 2017*

2 Material-based writing

When reading about a demonstration in favour of welcoming migrants, you come across the following line by the British-Somali poet Warsan Shire, which has become a rallying cry for refugees around the world:

"No one leaves home unless home is the mouth of a shark."

Comment on the slogan using the material given below. Write 300 words.

MATERIAL 1

Gesellschaftliche Wanderungsfaktoren sind eng mit politischen Faktoren verbunden. Druckfaktoren können beispielsweise vorliegen, wenn ein Gegensatz zwischen laizistischen und religiös-fundamentalistischen Gruppen besteht, bei dem es oft um die grundsätzliche Frage geht, wie Staat und Gesellschaft organisiert sein sollen.

Auf der anderen Seite sind moderne liberale Gesellschaften, in denen Staat und Kirche häufig getrennt sind oder in denen zumindest Religionsfreiheit herrscht und bürgerliche Freiheiten gewahrt sind, für viele Menschen attraktiv.

Source: Steffen Angenendt, "Gesellschaftliche Wanderungsfaktoren", the website of Bundeszentrale für politische Bildung, 01. 06. 2009

MATERIAL 2

Disaster-induced displacement

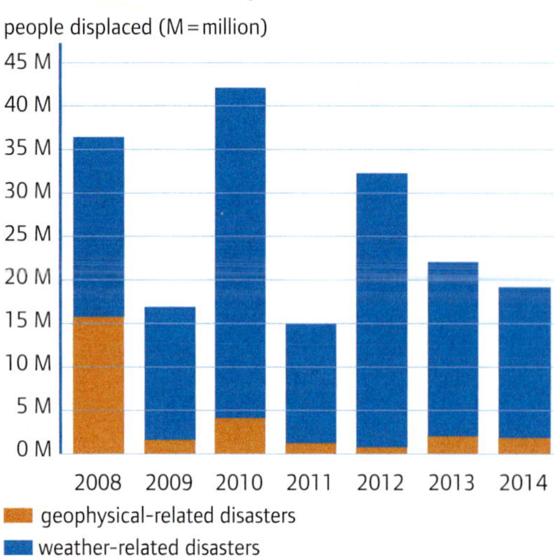

Source: IDMC, 2014

MATERIAL 3

SUNDAY EXPRESS

SHOCK FIGURES: Seven out of 10 migrants crossing to Europe are not refugees, UN reveals

The United Nations (UN) has made shocking claims that the majority of migrants are not refugees but are in fact economic migrants searching for a better life.

Source: Rebecca Flood, Sunday Express, *04. 07. 2017*

Exploring the topic

SITUATION

Europe is under pressure: the EU is losing Britain as a member and other nations may follow; separatist movements are pushing their agenda in many countries; and the EU seems to be losing the support of its allies. Your school is a member of the Erasmus+ programme, with exchange students from Belgium, the Czech Republic and Spain attending class with you. Together with these students you hold a discussion about proposals to make young Europeans more aware and prouder of their European identity.

1 **Do a brainstorming exercise in class to find out what you already know about separatism in Europe. Give your personal view on the matter.**

2 **Have a look at the map below and speculate on the reasons why the coloured regions might want more self-government or independence from their nation state.**

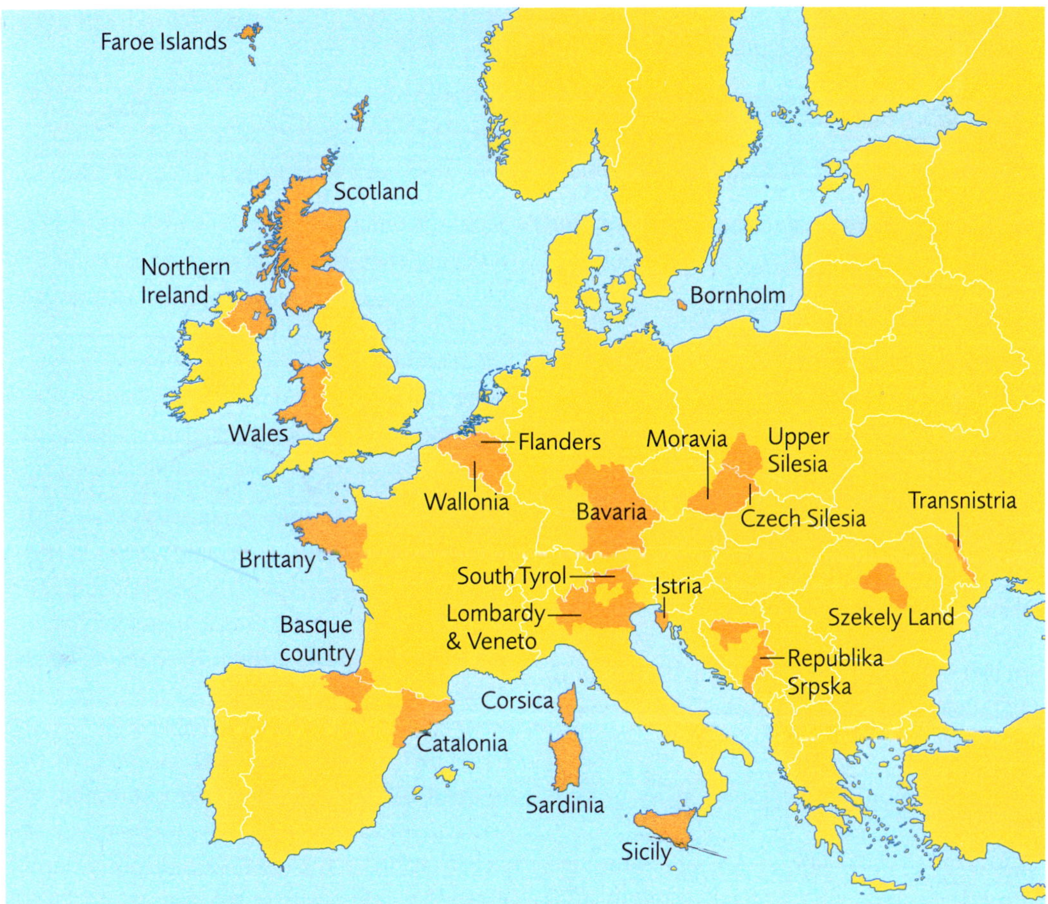

3 **Read the text on the next page about separatism in Europe.**

RIPPLES FROM CATALAN REFERENDUM COULD EXTEND BEYOND SPAIN

A The Spanish government's attempted suppression of Catalonia's independence referendum by brute force has raised urgent questions for fellow EU members about Spain's adherence to democratic norms, 42 years after the death of the fascist dictator, Francisco Franco. Belgium's prime minister spoke for many in Europe when he tweeted: "Violence can never be the answer!" Madrid's pugnacious stance, while widely condemned as a gross and shameful over-reaction, has nevertheless sent a problematic message to would-be secessionists everywhere. It is that peaceful campaigns in line with the UN charter's universal right to self-determination, campaigns that eschew violence and rely on conventional political means, are ultimately doomed to fail. In other words, violence is the only answer. [...]

B Spain's prime minister, Mariano Rajoy, did everything he could to derail a referendum that the courts had deemed illegal, but his pleas and threats were not persuasive. That is democracy. Rajoy's subsequent choice to employ physical force to impose his will on civilians exercising a basic democratic right carried a chill echo of Spain's past and a dire warning for the future. That is dictatorship. Surely no one believes the cause of Catalan independence will fade away after Sunday's bloody confrontations that left hundreds injured. Rajoy's actions may have ensured, on the contrary, that the campaign enters a new, more radical phase, potentially giving rise to ongoing clashes, reciprocal violence, and copycat protests elsewhere, for example in Galicia.

C In Spain's Basque country, where ETA separatists waged a decades-long terror campaign that killed more than 800 people and injured thousands, the dream of independence is on ice – but not forgotten. The danger is that a new generation of younger Basques who feel ignored by Madrid, and repelled by what happened in Barcelona, may be tempted to revisit ETA's unilateral 2010 ceasefire and its subsequent disarmament. The ripple effect of the Catalan crackdown could potentially extend beyond Spain. There were covert links at one time between ETA and the IRA during Northern Ireland's Troubles, with the two groups comparing notes and sharing expertise.

D Belfast, like Bilbao, is another place where a dissident minority remains unimpressed by placatory measures such as devolution, limited autonomy and power-sharing. Fringe outfits such as the New IRA, responsible for several attacks since 2012, find self-justification in the violence of the state.

E Similarities between Catalonia and other supposed secessionist hotspots in Europe can be exaggerated. The Lega Nord (Northern League) is influential in parts of northern Italy, but is not serious about independence. The same may be said of conservative Bavarian nationalists in southern Germany [...], whose frustrations have often found release through the CSU, sister party to Angela Merkel's ruling centre-right CDU. A closer comparison is with Scotland's SNP.

F What all these groups do have in common with the Catalan nationalists is their dislike, if not rejection, of the centralised authority of the state. Previous polls suggest most Catalans do not support independence from Madrid. But not unlike Scotland, a majority does appear to question the legitimacy of a distant central government that speaks a different language, hands down political diktats, levies unfair taxes and allegedly gives back less than it takes. The attempt by Rajoy and his ministers to depict the Catalan independence movement as belonging to the wider, recent phenomenon of right-wing European nationalism, xenophobia and populism was an obvious smear. Many Catalans distrust rule by Madrid. That does not mean they have renounced values of tolerance and inclusion. Quite the opposite, as any visitor to Barcelona knows.

G But the distinctions can get blurred. Politicians such as the new Lega Nord leader, Matteo Salvini, are only too happy to exploit voters' distrust and disillusion with central government to advance their particular anti-immigrant, Islamophobic and extreme nationalist-populist agendas. In France, the Front National's key presidential election message was that the state was broken. Upon that basic premise were heaped its objectionable policies. Nigel Farage's Ukip did something similar in Britain last year, playing on a basic distrust of "establishment elites" to whip up support for Brexit. In last month's German elections, the insurrectionary, hard-right Alternative für Deutschland ambushed the two main parties, which polled at record low levels. The AfD's success was not, for the most part, an endorsement of neo-Nazism. It was a rejection of the status quo.

H Looked at in this broader context, the upheavals in Catalonia are part of a chaotic, Europe-wide, multifaceted fracturing of the authority and legitimacy of the traditional, all-powerful, uniform nation state, and of the control exercised by mainstream centre-left and centre-right political parties. Catalonia's brave and battered voters are in the vanguard of a new movement towards a Europe where identity is being radically redefined. If leaders and governments such as Rajoy's remain stubbornly inflexible and refuse to bend, they risk being broken.

(805 words)

Source: Simon Tisdall, The Guardian, *02. 10. 2017*

26 chill echo: *frostiger Nachklang*
84 smear: *Verleumdung*
89 Matteo Salvini: since 2018, deputy prime minister and interior minister of Italy
100 whip up support: *Unterstützung auftreiben*
102 insurrectionary: *aufständisch*

4 **a** Work in groups of four. Create a poster that gives an overview of "Separatism in Europe", in which you outline the separatist movements in Europe, their aims and any aspect that is mentioned in the text.

b Walk around: Have a look at the posters, evaluate them and ask questions. Two members of the group should always be ready to answer questions.

Testing your reading skills

1 Short-answer questions (paragraphs A–B)

Answer the following questions. You may use words from the text.

1	What does the Spanish government's use of force in Catalonia call into question?
2	How did European leaders view Madrid's violent response to the referendum in Catalonia?
3	What might be the conclusion that potential secessionists draw from Madrid's action against Catalonia?
4	What consequences might Madrid's crackdown on Catalonia have in other parts of Spain?

2 Mediation Englisch – Deutsch (paragraphs C–D)

Beantworten Sie folgende Fragen auf Deutsch.

1	Das Baskenland war jahrzehntelang von Terroranschlägen der ETA heimgesucht. Was ist der gegenwärtige Stand des Unabhängigkeitsstrebens der Basken?
2	Erläutern Sie den Ausdruck „ripple effect" (Zeile 45) im Textzusammenhang.
3	Mit welchen konkreten Maßnahmen hat London versucht die Situation in Nordirland zu entschärfen?

3 Multiple-choice questions (paragraphs E–H)

Choose the most suitable option.

1 The phrase "secessionist hotspots" (line 59) means …

a	regions where significant numbers of people want autonomy or independence.
b	areas where separatists are conducting a campaign of violence.
c	places where people follow parties which are neo-Nazi.
d	regions without autonomous government.

2 What do all the secessionist movements share?

a	the understanding that violence can help them achieve their goals
b	the hope of preserving their language
c	an antipathy towards the central government
d	the desire to stop paying taxes

3 When Spain's Prime Minister claimed the Catalan independence movement was little different from the populist nationalist parties, it was …

- a a lie intending to destroy the reputation of the separatists.
- b an attempt to divert attention from his unpopular economic policies.
- c an example of intolerance towards political groups with different views.
- d a sign of a return to fascism.

4 The author believes that the political agenda of the French Front National is …

- a offensive and unpleasant.
- b intended to destroy the state.
- c unconstitutional and dangerous.
- d a recipe for disaster.

5 The common political strategy of Ukip, the AfD, the Front National and the Lega Nord is …

- a to put forward sound political and economic ideas.
- b to exploit the negative attitude of people towards their governments.
- c to attack the current political system and destroy democracy.
- d to give a voice to the poor and oppressed people of their countries.

6 When a party polls "at record low levels" (line 104), voters …

- a support it in the election.
- b are unsure of whether to vote for it or not.
- c give it the cold shoulder in the voting booth.
- d avoid going to the polls.

7 The Catalan crisis shows that European nation states …

- a are facing a major political crisis.
- b are divided between the centre-right and centre-left.
- c still rely on mainstream parties for good government.
- d are not going to break up into smaller entities.

8 The author believes that Catalans …

- a are feeling defensive about their policies.
- b are strong believers in a united Europe.
- c are unsure about who they are.
- d are pioneers of a new trend.

Developing your language skills

1 Using advanced structures

In the following excerpt from a student's text the sentences are all rather simple, with the result that the text does not read well. Rewrite the text using complex structures such as *if*-clauses, the gerund, infinitive or participle constructions. The information in the second column will help you.

Advanced writing uses complex structures and avoids monotonous and simple sentence constructions.

The European Union has been in existence since 1957.	
Robert Schuman had a vision. Because of this vision, a unified and peaceful Europe has become a reality.	*if*-clause
Following two terrible wars, everyone in Europe wanted a permanent peace but didn't know how they could achieve it.	*to*-infinitive
Adenauer and Schuman agreed that Europe needed to come together. They then went on to convince their countries that an economic and political union was the way forward.	*after* + gerund
West Germany and France were the first which joined the new union. Italy and the Benelux countries joined at the same time.	*to*-infinitive; *along with*
Other countries decided that they would join it too at a later date. Joining it meant that they had to give up some of their sovereign rights.	*to*-infinitive; *which;* *mean* + gerund
The European Union has brought benefits to its members and citizens. We should definitely support it.	*so; worth* + gerund
Some of the problems, which the EU is facing, are difficult to solve.	present participle
Here are a few ideas that we can use to improve the EU.	*for* + gerund
To start with, governments should give orders to the Commission, so that the Commission draws up a clear social and economic programme that its citizens can identify with.	*make* + object + verb
Politicians must put forward a positive image of Europe. They should offer EU citizens more participation in political decisions.	*by* + gerund
The European Parliament was founded in 1979. But the European Parliament still does not exercise much power 40 years later.	past participle
The European Parliament needs more power. Then it would be taken more seriously by the public.	*if*-clause
The MEPs are directly elected by EU citizens. This means that its citizens often identify more with the Parliament than with the Commission.	*as*

2 Using idiomatic language

Students try hard to come up with adequate idiomatic phrases in their writing, but sometimes they translate directly from German. With the help of a dictionary, correct the highlighted expressions using the words on the right.

1	The new regulations on how to apply for citizenship step into power next week.	EFFECT
2	Joining the party was just a means to the purpose – he really wanted power.	END
3	The situation in the Third World makes people flee from their countries. It is difficult to solve the problem, it is a devil's cycle.	VICIOUS
4	If populist parties believe that tough entrance requirements will solve the migration problem, they are on the wrong steamboat.	BARK
5	It's time their intentions were made public.	INTO THE OPEN
6	In the opinion polls the populists are winning on soil on the mainstream parties.	GROUND
7	You mustn't take all the information you find on the internet at bare coins.	FACE
8	Readers see it as obvious that journalists research their information before publishing it.	GRANT
9	The news of the government crackdown was spread by mouth propaganda.	WORD
10	The media concentration on separatist parties is making an elephant out of a mosquito.	MOUNTAIN
11	Sometimes politicians press an eye to the plight of the refugees.	BLIND
12	Immigration has been a strong element of America ever since the arrival of the first Europeans.	PARCEL
13	Refugees have to be in a serious emergency if they are willing to face death crossing the sea.	DIRE
14	If we don't choke it in the seed, the violence will get worse.	BUD

3 Expressing yourself in good English

A student has written a first draft of a text about secessionist movements in Europe. He was not sure how to phrase some parts adequately, so he wrote them down in German in his draft. Find English phrases which match the German ones in order to complete the sentences.

What can we learn from the crisis in Catalonia? First of all, a government should not *(den Willen nicht aufzwingen)* ▬ [1] with *(brutaler Gewalt)* ▬ [2]. The strategy should be to find an agreement *(in Übereinstimmung mit)* ▬ [3] international law. Even when the goals of secessionist movements might *(auf Eis liegen)* ▬ [4], they are rarely forgotten. Despite the setbacks they face, secessionist parties *(haben demokratische Werten nicht abgeschworen)* ▬ [5]. Their struggle is usually characterized by campaigns for referenda and attacks on *(die zentrale Staatsgewalt)* ▬ [6]. Through peaceful protests independence movements have created *(einen Welleneffekt)* ▬ [7]. Sometimes *(verschwimmen die Unterschiede)* ▬ [8] between those who are actually fighting for independence and those who are seeking to undermine national governments.

Testing your writing and speaking skills

1 Mediation Deutsch–Englisch

Zum Abschluss einer Unterrichtseinheit zum Thema „Rückfall in die Kleinstaaterei in Europa" lesen Sie einen Artikel „Europa im Sezessionsfieber". Sie fassen den Artikel in ca. 150 Wörtern zusammen, wobei Sie sich auf folgende Aspekte konzentrieren:

- **die Politik der EU hinsichtlich separatistischer Tendenzen in Europa**
- **die Ziele des bzw. Gründe für das Unabhängigkeitsstreben in Korsika und Norditalien**
- **Leitgedanke der EU-Kommission im Hinblick auf separatistische Tendenzen**

EUROPA
IM SEZESSIONSFIEBER

South Tyrol: a German-speaking region of Italy that has a strong secessionist movement

Ob Katalonien, Südtirol, Schottland oder auf Korsika: In der Europäischen Union gibt es viele Länder oder Regionen, die nach Unabhängigkeit streben. Dabei setzen die Separatisten höchst unterschiedliche Methoden ein.

Aber die EU will unbedingt verhindern, dass Europa in Kleinstaaten zerfällt. Die Krise zwischen Katalonien und Spanien – sie bringt auch die EU in eine vertrackte Lage. Bislang hat sich die Kommission nicht als Vermittlerin angeboten und ist dafür scharf kritisiert worden. Doch mischt sich die Brüsseler Behörde in den Konflikt ein, riskiert sie, den Separatisten Legitimität zu verleihen. Denn was jetzt für Katalonien gilt, müsste später wohl auch für andere Regionen in Europa gelten, die unabhängig werden wollen.

Und davon gibt es einige. Zum Beispiel für die französische Insel Korsika. Dort gibt es seit Jahrzehnten Unabhängigkeitsbestrebungen. 2014 legte die „Korsische Nationale Befreiungsfront" zwar ihre Waffen nieder. Zugleich gewannen separatistische Kräfte in der Politik aber an Macht. Der Präsident des korsischen Parlaments will Korsika zu einem unabhängigen Staat machen. Er fordert, politische Gefangene freizulassen und Korsisch neben Französisch als offizielle Inselsprache einzuführen.

Abspaltung aus historischen Gründen: Das kennt man auch in Großbritannien. 2014 hatten die Schotten mit knapper Mehrheit gegen die Unabhängigkeit entschieden. Doch die Pläne für ein neues Referendum liegen nur auf Eis.

the building of the European Commission

Auch Italien hat mit Abspaltungskräften zu kämpfen. In Südtirol wollen sich viele seit langem von Italien loszusagen. In der deutschsprachigen Region liegt das Bruttosozialprodukt deutlich über dem italienischen Durchschnitt. Neue Unabhängigkeitstendenzen kommen aus der Lombardei und Venetien. Die wohlhabenden Regionen in Norditalien wollen am 22. Oktober nichtbindende Referenden abhalten. „Es soll darum gehen, wie unsere Bürger zu mehr Autonomie von Rom stehen", sagt der lombardische Regionalpräsident Roberto Maroni von der rechtspopulistischen Partei „Lega Nord". Man wolle sich nicht von Italien abspalten. Es gehe vielmehr um finanzielle Unabhängigkeit. Die Lombardei und Venetien machen zusammen fast ein Drittel der Wirtschaftskraft Italiens aus und fordern mehr Zugriff auf ihr Steueraufkommen.

Die Regierungen in Rom, Paris und Madrid haben kein Interesse daran, dass ihre Länder zersplittern. Und die EU-Kommission will verhindern, dass Europa in Kleinstaaten zerfällt. „Wir haben viele unterschiedliche regionale Traditionen, das gehört zu den Besonderheiten Europas", meint Kommissionspräsident Jean-Claude Juncker. Diese regionalen Besonderheiten dürften aber nicht zu Separatismus in Europa führen, fügte Juncker hinzu. Heute Katalonien, morgen Korsika, übermorgen Südtirol? Damit die EU nicht zerbröckelt, versucht die Kommission sie zusammenzuhalten. Ohne laute Worte vor Kameras und Mikrofonen, eher still im Hintergrund. Nach dem Motto: Einigkeit statt Unabhängigkeit.

Source: Karin Bensch,
the website of Deutschlandfunk, 09. 10. 2017

2 Group discussion

Situation: The European ideal is under threat. National governments are questioning the future of Europe, separatists want to divide the continent into smaller entities, and citizens are questioning the Euro, the lack of border controls and the common refugee policy. As part of your Erasmus+ programme your class and the European exchange students decide to start a campaign to show what Europe stands for and why it is worth defending.
Each of you has found something which in your eyes makes the European Union a wonderful idea. You need to decide which of the suggestions (page 146) might be the most convincing and should therefore be used in your campaign.

Presentation phase: Each of you presents the suggestion you feel would be the most effective in the campaign.

Interaction phase: Exchange arguments and discuss the strengths as well as the weaknesses of the different suggestions and try to convince the other members of your proposal. In the end you should agree on the best option and a runner-up. Be willing to compromise.

Optional *(if you have time at the end of the discussion):* Discuss which other countries should join the EU.

4 D COPING WITH TERRORISM

Exploring the topic

SITUATION

Terrorism seems to have the world in a stranglehold. Suicide bombings, stabbings, shootings and truck attacks have become common news. Whereas previously it was separatist groups like the IRA and ETA that perpetrated terror attacks, now it is young radicalized jihadists. A European-wide programme has asked youngsters to send in videos they have made that show how they see the process of radicalization.

1 **You read an excerpt from John Updike's novel *Terrorist* and decide to turn this text into a screenplay before filming it. Your intention is to show the mindset of the protagonist. Make notes on Ahmad, his reflections and thoughts as they shed light on his personality. Write down what props might be necessary, which other characters should be portrayed and how, etc. You could use a table like the one below to collect information.**

CHARACTERS	QUOTES	TRAITS	PROPS	DRESS	GESTURES
Ahmad					
Shaikh					
teachers					
female students					
males students					

TERRORIST

John Updike's novel Terrorist *is the story of 18-year-old Ahmad, son of an Irish-American mother and an Egyptian father who left the family when Ahmad was very young. Ahmad's search for identity, acceptance and a set of values he can believe in has made the vulnerable teen the perfect target for radicalization.*

A *Devils,* Ahmad thinks. *These devils seek to take away my God.* All day long, at Central High School, girls sway and sneer and expose their soft bodies and alluring hair. Their bare bellies, adorned with shining navel studs and low-down purple tattoos, ask, *What else is there to see?* Boys strut and saunter along and look dead-eyed, indicating with their edgy killer gestures and careless scornful laughs that this world is all there is – a noisy varnished hall lined

with metal lockers and having at its end a blank wall desecrated by graffiti and roller-painted over so often it feels to be coming closer by millimeters.

The teachers, weak Christians and non-observant Jews, make a show of teaching virtue and righteous self-restraint, but their shifty eyes and hollow voices betray their lack of belief. They are paid to say these things, by the city of New Prospect and the state of New Jersey. They lack true faith; they are not on the Straight Path; they are unclean. Ahmad and the two thousand other students can see them scuttling after school into their cars on the crackling, trash-speckled parking lot like pale crabs or dark ones restored to their shells, and they are men and women like any others, full of lust and fear and infatuation with things that can be bought. Infidels, they think safety lies in accumulation of the things of this world, and in the corrupting diversions of the television set. They are slaves to images, false ones of happiness and affluence. But even true images are sinful imitations of God, who can alone create. Relief at escaping their students unscathed for another day makes the teachers' chatter of farewell in the halls and on the parking lot too loud, like the rising excitement of drunks.

The teachers revel when they are away from the school. Some have the pink lids and bad breaths and puffy bodies of those who habitually drink too much. Some get divorces; some live with others unmarried. Their lives away from the school are disorderly and wanton and self-indulgent. They are paid to instill virtue and democratic values by the state government down in Trenton, and that Satanic government farther down, in Washington, but the values they believe in are Godless: biology and chemistry and physics. On the facts and formulas of these their false voices firmly rest, ringing out into the classroom. They say that all comes out of merciless blind atoms, which cause the cold weight of iron, the transparency of glass, the stillness of clay, the agitation of flesh. Electrons pour through copper threads and computer gates and the air itself when stirred to lightning by the interaction of water droplets. Only what we can measure and deduce from measurement is true. The rest is the passing dream that we call ourselves.

B Ahmad is eighteen. **1** ; again green sneaks, seed by seed, into the drab city's earthy crevices. He looks down from his new height and thinks that to the insects unseen in the grass he would be, if they had a consciousness like his, God. In the year past he has grown three inches, to six feet – more unseen materialist forces, working their will upon him. **2** . If there is a next, an inner devil murmurs. What evidence beyond the Prophet's blazing and divinely inspired words proves that there is a next? Where would it be hidden? Who would forever stoke Hell's boilers? What infinite source of energy would maintain opulent Eden, feeding its dark-eyed houris, swelling its heavy-hanging fruits, renewing the streams and splashing fountains in which God, as described in the ninth sura of the Qur'an, takes eternal good pleasure? What of the second law of thermodynamics?

The deaths of insects and worms, their bodies so quickly absorbed by earth and weeds and road tar, devilishly strive to tell Ahmad that his own death will be just as small and final. Walking to school, he has noticed a sign, a spiral traced on the pavement in luminous ichor, angelic slime from the body of some low creature, a worm or snail of which only this trace remains. **3** ? If it was seeking to remove itself from the hot sidewalk that was roasting it to death as the burning sun beat down, it failed and moved in fatal circles. But no little worm-body was left at the spiral's center.

So where did that body fly to? **4** . Ahmad's teacher, Shaikh Rashid, the imam at the mosque upstairs at 2781½ West Main Street, tells him that according to the sacred tradition of the Hadith such things happen: the Messenger, riding the winged white horse Buraq, was guided through the seven heavens by the angel Gabriel to a certain place, where he prayed with Jesus, Moses, and Abraham before returning to Earth, to become the last of the prophets, the ultimate one. His adventures that day are proved by the hoof print, sharp and clear, that Buraq left on the Rock beneath the sacred Dome in the center of Al-Quds, called Jerusalem by the infidels and Zionists,

62 houri: virgin found in paradise
63 sura: chapter of the Quran
67 ichor: slimy bodily fluid
73 Hadith: collection of texts containing things said by Muhammad and descriptions of his daily life

whose torments in the furnaces of Jahannam are well described in the seventh and eleventh and fiftieth of the suras of the Book of Books.
Shaikh Rashid recites with great beauty of pronunciation the one hundred fourth sura, concerning Hutama, the Crushing Fire:

And who shall teach thee what the Crushing Fire is?
It is God's kindled fire,
Which shall mount above the hearts of the damned;
It shall verily rise over them like a vault,
On outstretched columns.

When Ahmad seeks to extract from the images in the Qur'an's Arabic – the outstretched columns, *fi 'amadin mumaddada,* and the vault high above the hearts of those huddled in terror and straining to see into the towering mist of white heat, *naru 'l-lahi 'l-muqada* – some hint of the Merciful's relenting at some point in time, and calling a halt to Hutama, the imam casts down his eyes, which are an unexpectedly pale gray, as milky and elusive as a kafir woman's, and says that these visionary descriptions by the Prophet are figurative. They are truly about the burning misery of separation from God and the scorching of our remorse for our sins against His commands. **5** . It reminds him of the unconvincing voices of his teachers at Central High. He hears Satan's undertone in it, a denying voice within an affirming voice. The Prophet meant physical fire when he preached unforgiving fire; Mohammed could not proclaim the fact of eternal fire too often.
Shaikh Rashid is not much older than Ahmad – perhaps ten years, perhaps twenty. He has few wrinkles in the white skin of his face. He is diffident though precise in his movements. **6** . When the murmuring of the devils gnawing within him tinges the imam's voice, Ahmad feels in his own self a desire to rise up and crush him, as God roasted that poor worm at the center of the spiral. The student's faith exceeds the master's; it frightens Shaikh Rashid to be riding the winged white steed of Islam, its irresistible onrushing. He seeks to soften the Prophet's words, to make them blend with human reason, but they were not meant to blend: they invade our human softness like a sword. **7** . There is no God but He, the Living, the Self-Subsistent; He is the light by which the sun looks black. He does not blend with our reason but makes our reason bow low, its forehead scraping the dust and bearing like Cain the mark of that dust. Mohammed was a mortal man but visited Paradise and consorted with the realities there. Our deeds and thoughts were written in the Prophet's consciousness in letters of gold, like the burning words of electrons that a computer creates of pixels as we tap the keyboard. (1368 words)

Source: John Updike, Terrorist, *2006*

79 Jahannam: *Hölle*
92 kafir: unbeliever

Test your reading skills

1 Gapped summary (section A)

Copy the summary and fill the gaps with appropriate words from the corresponding passages of the text (one word per gap). Do not make any changes. Please also provide the number of the line in which you have found the word.

Ahmad is repulsed by what he sees at his high school. The ___[1] (line ___) charms of the female students, be it their gait, bodies or hair, repel him, while the ___[2] (line ___) attitude of the male students reveals lives with no meaning. The school building, with its vain attempts to hide graffiti on its walls, seems ___[3] (line ___) to him. Even the teachers don't believe in the values of goodness and ___[4] (line ___) they are supposed to teach their students. They are all fake, as they don't have ___[5] (line ___). Their ___[6] (line ___) with materialism blinds them to the truth. As ___[7] (line ___), they don't understand that the ___[8] (line ___) of possessions and the ___[9] (line ___) of the media offer no solution. The teachers' ___[10] (line ___) at leaving school at the end of the day hides the fact that even at home their lives are ___[11] (line ___), immoral and chaotic: they consume too much alcohol and cohabit with their partners. As they are paid by the local authorities and, even worse, the ___[12] (line ___) US administration to teach so-called Western ___[13] (line ___), they teach ___[14] (line ___) science instead of truth. They believe only in ___[15] (line ___), which they ___[16] (line ___) from measuring and examining. In the process, they treat the soul like a ___[17] (line ___) that is here today and gone tomorrow.

2 Multiple matching (section B)

The sentences below were deleted from the text and replaced by a small grey gap with a number. Match them to the gaps in the text (1–7) where they belong. There are three sentences that do not belong in any of the gaps.

A	Why was the worm moving so swiftly
B	In the years by which he is older, the world has weakened him
C	Perhaps it was snatched up by God and taken straight to Heaven
D	This is early April
E	It probably was snatched up by a caring student
F	Where was the creature going, its path spiralling inward to no purpose
G	He will not grow any taller, he thinks, in this life or the next
H	Thinking of his body height is infatuation and makes him a slave of images
I	But Ahmad does not like Shaikh Rashid's voice when he says this
J	Allah is sublime beyond all particulars

3 Mediation Englisch–Deutsch (section B)

Beantworten Sie folgende Fragen auf Deutsch.

1	Warum ist Ahmad ein Produkt seiner säkularen schulischen Bildung?
2	Für Ahmad sind Scheich Rashids Ansichten nicht annehmbar. Wo sieht Ahmad Parallelen zwischen dem Scheich und seinen Lehrern an der Schule?
3	Wie zeigt sich Ahmads Arroganz, die Arroganz eines Radikalen?

Developing your language skills

1 Improving your listening skills

16

Listen to an interview between Renee Montagne and Jane Harman, a former Congresswoman who is an expert on terror prevention. Listen and make notes with the help of the prompts below.

Montagne	■ Harman played a key role in:	…
Harman	■ results of her effort/work: ■ how Bush and Obama helped ■ steps to need to be taken in the Middle East: ■ steps to be taken in the USA:	… … avoided … promote … debate about …
Montagne	■ polls show:	…
Harman	■ kinds of terror attacks she is afraid of: ■ most afraid of:	… … … like the one in Boston
Montagne	■ Europe faces:	… … by people quickly radicalized or who have emotional problems
Harman	■ who can help to fight against radicals: ■ example for positive effect of internet and social media:	… … and … …
Montagne	■ example of a new event feeding terrorism:	…
Harman	■ sees Syria as an example of: ■ destabilizing factor for Syria's neighbouring countries: ■ her personal conclusion is: ■ the new potential feeder system for terrorists:	… … … … in Syria, Iran, etc

2 Writing and filming a screenplay

a Work in small groups.
- Decide which characters you want to appear in the video, and how they should dress and move. List words from the scene that will help you decide.
- Decide what the plot, atmosphere and setting should be.
- Should there be a narrator? Should there be dialogue? Which sentences from the extract should be used?
- Discuss what is necessary for the screenplay and what can be skipped.
- What should be the focus of the scene – a confused youth, a radical demagogue, a desperate situation?

b Write the screenplay based on the extract.

c Shoot your film and show it to the class, which will evaluate it.

Testing your writing and speaking skills

1 Material-based writing

The programme that asked you to make a video about the process of radicalization has also asked for a short essay to be handed in that relates in some way to the video.

Using the materials below, write about 300 words on the following question:

Is religion the cause of terrorism?

MATERIAL 1

IDPS: internally displaced persons; **UNHCR:** the UN refugee agency *Source: Global Peace Index 2017*

MATERIAL 2

Religion is a secondary motivation for most terrorists. What inspires the most uncompromisingly lethal actors in the world today is not so much the Qur'an or religious teachings. It's a thrilling cause that promises glory and esteem.

Source: Scott Atran, "Mindless terrorists? The truth about Isis is much worse", The Guardian, *15.11.2015*

MATERIAL 3

Wer berichtet über die berechtigten Proteste im marokkanischen Rif-Gebirge, die vom Staat unterdrückt werden? Die Demonstrationen hatten begonnen, nachdem ein Fischverkäufer seine von der Polizei beschlagnahmte Ware aus einem Mülltransporter retten wollte und dabei zu Tode gequetscht worden war. Hier liegen die Ursachen von Flucht und Terror – nicht in einer falschen Islamauslegung, sondern in Raffgier, Reformunfähigkeit, krasser Verteilungsungerechtigkeit und Ausgrenzung auf allen Ebenen, sowohl in der islamischen Welt wie inzwischen auch in vielen westlichen Gesellschaften. Es sind vor allem muslimische Einwanderer, die in Europa an den Rand gedrängt werden.

Source: Stefan Weidner, "Was Terroristen antreibt", Die Zeit, *12.07.2017*

2 Group discussion

Situation: Terror attacks have become commonplace: there have been suicide bombings in the UK, France and Belgium, truck attacks in the UK, France, Spain and Germany, as well as knife and gun attacks. Many of the terrorists perpetrating these bloody acts claim to do so in the name of God. But what can be done by European countries to overcome the threat of terrorism? You discuss the proposals of various think tanks and decide on the one you find most suitable to tackle terrorism. Make a ranking list.

Presentation phase: Each of you presents one of the proposals. Explain why you think it is the most convincing strategy.

Interaction phase: Exchange arguments and try to convince the others that your strategy is the most promising one or why it should at least be second on the list. Be willing to compromise.

Optional *(if there is time left at the end of the discussion):* Is terrorism the number one issue facing Europe today?

Strategy 1: More government aid for areas which are terrorist hotbeds. The aim is to end social and economic hardship, poverty and injustice, which are often the causes of terrorism. Political pressure should be applied in those states to end oppression.

Strategy 2: The "an-eye-for-an-eye" solution. Military force should be used to attack terrorist hotbeds and destroy their infrastructure. Every effort should be made to eliminate radical forces that attempt to destroy Western societies. Once the military intervention has been completed, Western governments should ensure that states adopt democratic structures (nation building).

Strategy 3: Tighten security measures in Western countries. Introduce CCTV in most public spaces, more surveillance of suspected radicals, stricter punishment as a deterrent (including taking away citizenship).

Strategy 4: Show tolerance towards different cultures. Launch projects to foster mutual understanding of different cultures and religions. Even radical supporters of Islam should be invited to public discussions and schools. Launch exchange programmes between Islamic countries and Western countries.

Strategy 5: Stop the influx of refugees and asylum seekers from countries which nurture radical extremism. Make Europe a "fortress" and keep out all potential terrorists.

APPENDIX

Unit 1, Topic A page 18

1 MORE ENGLISH LESSONS

English for everyone in primary school plus a maximum of four lessons per week throughout secondary education. More remedial English classes for those who need it instead of a second foreign language. The more lessons young students have, the better their English will become.

2 MORE BILINGUAL EDUCATION

After five years of formal English classes, subjects like chemistry, biology, technology or economics should be taught partly in English instead. This does happen in some schools but not enough. The students' grades should also reflect the fact that the language of instruction is English, so that students will not fear losing marks by studying in a foreign language.

3 VOLUNTEERS

English native speakers should be brought into every school to support German teachers of English at least twice a week. This could also be extra-curricular and be conducted by volunteers. The native speakers could lead discussions about any subject the students are interested in. If there aren't enough English native speakers, the school could look for exchange meetings with newly arrived refugees who speak sufficient English so that the communication can take place in English.

4 SCHOOL PARTNERSHIPS

School partnerships with common web-based projects and visits should be a compulsory part of English lessons. Working together with schools from different countries underlines the importance of English as the international language. This is especially true if the partner schools are in non-English-speaking countries, as all the students will have the same level of English.

5 USING THE BIG AND THE SMALL SCREEN

In every country where the population speaks good English, there is no dubbing on television. Time should be set aside every week for watching TV series or movies in English. The films and series should be watched for entertainment purposes with a short discussion afterwards just to see how much the students understood.

1 INDEPENDENCE FOR YOU

People who cannot drive anymore can connect with drivers who offer rides in their free time. Volunteer drivers can store up transportation credits for the time when they can no longer drive, or they can collect transportation credits for their parents.

2 ONLINE? OF COURSE!

Volunteers teach seniors to use computers. Classes include anything from using internet services to installing apps on their digital devices. The programme enables older adults to use the computer to stay up to date with the requirements of online services of any kind. In exchange, "Grannies" and "Grandpas" can be booked for younger children in order to get them acquainted with the wisdom and life stories of elderly people who have experienced a less digital world.

3 BUCKET LIST TICKERS

This programme helps people living in long-term care communities, nursing homes or even hospice facilities to tick off their last wishes still left on their bucket lists. The seniors' dreams range from reuniting with a lost family member to attending a live concert by their favourite artist. Sponsors, donators and organizers of these wishes can store up credit points for their own dream journey.

4 HOLIDAYS – NO PROBLEM

A group of people visits lonely senior citizens during the various holidays (e.g. Christmas, New Year's Eve, Easter) to make their lives more joyful over the festive period. In exchange, volunteers learn about the background, the food and other customs now lost in a modern, hectic environment.

5 MULTI-GENERATION HOMES

Several generations sign up to live in one huge house together. This saves on natural resources and building space in crowded towns, since there is only one private room for each couple or single person, while the rest of the rooms (kitchen, living room, laundry room, garden, library, sports facilities, etc.) are for communal use. People help each other and therefore live for very little rent in these houses.

Unit 3, Topic A

page 85

PHOTO 1

PHOTO 2

PHOTO 3

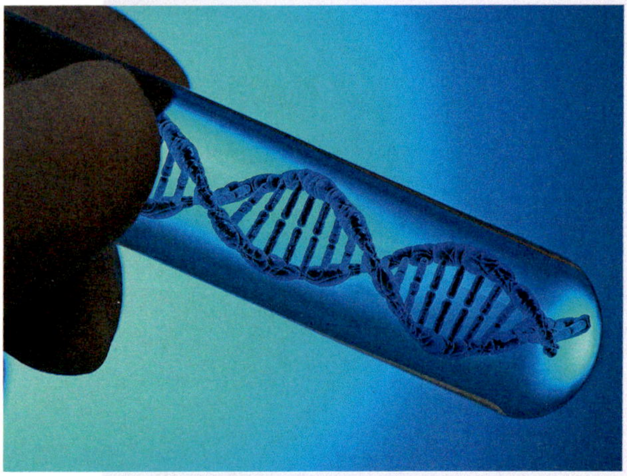

PHOTO 4

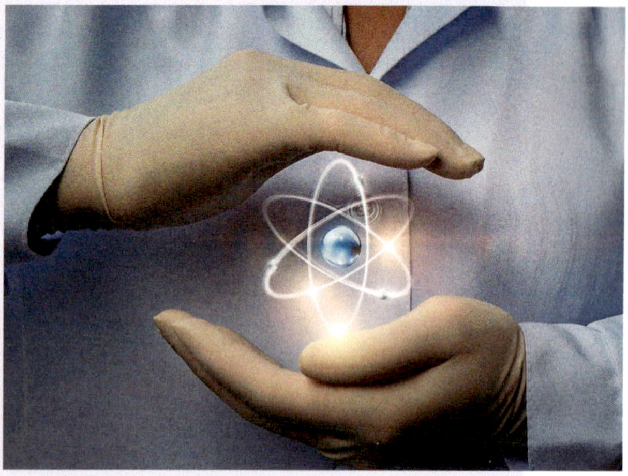

PHOTO 5

PROPOSAL 1

ATTAC is part of the alter-globalization movement, which opposes neo-liberal globalization. Active in 40 countries, it protests against global organizations and their actions. It believes that global economic competition and free markets enslave rather than liberate humanity. It also believes that the preservation of our planet cannot be attained through technological progress and the commercialization of natural resources. ATTAC promotes social, ecological and democratic alternatives which guarantee fundamental rights for all. It believes that the common goods of humanity such as health care, education, water, climate and biodiversity must be given a protected status so that everyone can use them.

PROPOSAL 2

350.org is an environmental organization which fights for a greener climate. It opposes new coal, oil and gas projects, urges divestment from fossil fuel companies and campaigns for 100% clean energy solutions that work for all. Its aim is to build a zero-carbon economy and promote investment in community-based sustainability solutions.

PROPOSAL 3

Human Rights Watch is a non-profit, non-governmental organization which defends the rights of people worldwide. It pressures democratic governments to denounce human rights abuses and urges oppressive governments to respect human rights and promote justice. It often works on behalf of refugees, children, migrants and political prisoners. In an era of disinformation, it is strictly non-partisan and maintains neutrality in areas of conflict. It insists on keeping high standards of accuracy and fairness.

PROPOSAL 4

Oxfam believes that poverty and powerlessness can be overcome by human action and political will. While its main focus was initially on the eradication of poverty worldwide by providing food in times of famine, it is now committed to development work to combat the causes of poverty. It explores strategies that enable people to become self-supporting, as only long-term, sustainable solutions will end poverty and give everyone a sustainable livelihood. It also lobbies to influence policy decisions on different levels to promote the right to life and security as well as to basic social services.

PROPOSAL 5

BICE is a network of organizations committed to the defence of the dignity and rights of children around the world. It fights the mistreatment, sexual abuse, exploitation and discrimination of children. It develops programmes and projects which benefit thousands of children worldwide, by providing access to formal or informal education and vocational training. It offers emergency hotlines for children in danger and shelters for sexually abused children, while raising public awareness of the issue.

Unit 4, Topic C page 133

1 THE SCHENGEN AREA

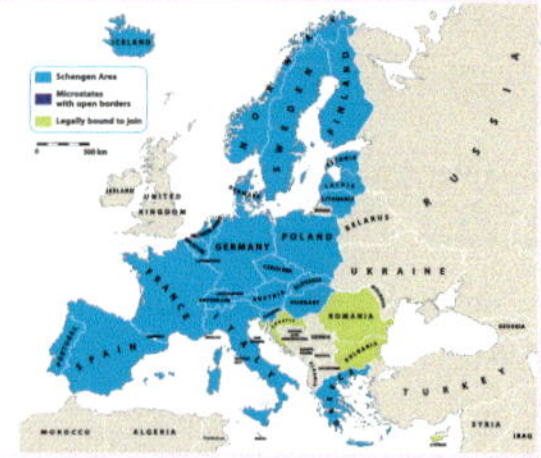

The Schengen Area encompasses most of Europe, ensuring that national borders exist only on maps. The free movement of people and also of goods and services are the positive outcome. As almost every European country has opened its doors to its European neighbours, a unified European continent without borders and visas has become reality.

2 INTERRAIL

Europe, with its abundance of historical sites and wonderful customs, is a wonderful continent to explore. Interrail provides the freedom and flexibility to choose from multiple itineraries throughout Europe. It is the ultimate backpacker experience. It is not just the treasures of Europe that youngsters can discover but also the incredible people they can meet along the way. Interrail stands for Europe and international understanding.

3 THE EURO

The Euro is without doubt the most tangible proof of European integration. European citizens don't have to worry any longer about exchange rates or which coin works in which country. Europeans can go abroad in Europe without paying extra exchange fees. The single European currency also has economic benefits for companies, as they are able to trade easily throughout Europe with a secure currency. The Euro is a symbol of a unified Europe.

4 EASTWARD ENLARGEMENT OF THE EU

When former Eastern bloc countries started to join the EU, this was a manifestation of the end of the Cold War. The reunification of the European continent had become a reality and former enemies had become friends. A pan-European community of democracies respecting freedom, human rights and the rule of law had become reality. Europe has finally become Europe again.

5 THE SCHUMAN DECLARATION

The main idea was, in the words of Schuman, to "make war not only unthinkable but materially impossible". Historic enemies – Germany and France – were willing to give some of their sovereignty to a supranational, European institution to overcome competition between European nation states over natural resources, thereby encouraging peace. When further European states joined the institution, it marked the birth of a united Europe. Just a decade after a devastating war Europe had changed to become a continent in pursuit of permanent peace.

GENERAL LANGUAGE SKILLS

DEALING WITH UNKNOWN WORDS

When you read a text, you usually won't understand every word. When you come across a word you don't know, ask yourself whether it is really necessary to understand that word in order to understand the overall message of the text. Looking up words takes time and often doesn't help you to understand the most important points. However, if the meaning of a word is essential to a sentence, there are some techniques that can help you work it out.

Working out the meaning from the context

Looking at the word in the context of the sentence can give you more information. First think about what part of speech you are dealing with. Are you looking for a noun? What does the noun you are looking for represent – a person or an abstract idea? If you're looking for an adjective, is it one which describes an exact situation or someone's character? Look at the following sentences and try to work out the meanings of the words in bold from the context:

The average amount of time spent in front of the computer playing games ***soared*** *from 8.5 minutes in 2004 to 17.8 minutes in 2014.*

Because the number of minutes has increased, you can deduct that the verb 'soar' means 'increase' in one form or another. The fact that the number of minutes has doubled can lead you to conclude that the increase was considerable. So the meaning is 'to rise very quickly'.

Working out the meaning from similar words

A word that you don't know could be related to another word that you already know. Always think of similar words that may belong to the same word family (e.g. *aggressor/aggressive*).

Some words are also similar to German words, especially those of foreign origin (compare *initial* and 'Initialen' or *potential* and 'potenziell').

However, watch out for 'false friends': actual does not mean 'aktuell' *(= current, present)* but 'tatsächlich' or 'eigentlich'.

Understanding the meaning from word formation

Words can be formed by adding a prefix or a suffix to a root word.

Prefixes: *un-*, *in-* (both indicate a negative), *mis-* (means 'wrongly'), *multi-* (means 'many'), *pre-* (means 'before', 'in front of').

Examples: *comfort → discomfort, comfortable; understand → misunderstand; coloured → multicoloured; school → preschool.*

Suffixes: Suffixes are often used to form adjectives and nouns: *-ful, -ible, -able, -hood, -ity, -ment.*

Examples: *wonderful, responsible, comfortable, childhood, stupdity, amazement.*

LEARNING NEW WORDS

Learning vocabulary is a lifelong activity. There are different methods for expanding your vocabulary in a foreign language. Try out a variety of methods until you find the one that works best for you.

Step 1

Identify words that could be useful to you. These might be:

- Thematic vocabulary that is related to the topic you are dealing with (e.g. the environment).
- Useful phrases that help you talk or write about texts or topics in class (see the flap on the back cover of this book).
- Collocations, i.e. words that go together with other words, e.g. *take a photo* (~~make a photo~~).
- Words that belong to a word family that you already know.

Step 2

Arrange your words in a suitable form. This could be a mind map or a list – or you might want to use index cards. Indicate the meaning of your words by:

- giving synonyms (e.g. *dogma = belief/principle*).
- giving antonyms (e.g. *upheaval ≠ stability*).
- making sketches/drawings.
- giving examples (e.g. *the arts = art, music, literature,* etc.).
- giving the German equivalent (e.g. achievement = *Errungenschaft*).

Step 3

Write down words in a context, in complete sentences or as part of a collocation; this will help you to use them in a sentence (e.g. *be torn between:* 'I was torn between going and remaining'; *be remembered for:* 'Shakespeare is remembered for his many plays').

Step 4

Use your new vocabulary as soon and as often as possible, e.g. include it in a short text.

Step 5

Study your index cards often so that you remember the new words.

VARYING YOUR VOCABULARY

With a large vocabulary you will be able to express yourself in a more interesting way. Here are some ideas on how to vary the vocabulary you use when you write. Remember to use your monolingual dictionary to see exactly how words are used – often the dictionaries offer sample sentences.

Use more interesting verbs

We often stick to simple verbs, but more interesting and specific verbs will improve your writing and speaking. Here is a list of simple words with some suggestions of what you could say instead:

be about	→	deal with, concern, have to do with, discuss, explore
do	→	carry out, perform
feel	→	realize, consider, experience
get	→	come into possession of, obtain, receive
have	→	possess, comprise, consist of, contain, include, be made up of
like	→	be fond of (+ gerund), be keen on (+ gerund), cherish, enjoy
make	→	build, assemble, put together, manufacture, produce
say	→	mention, remark, state, argue, express, claim
see	→	notice, observe, recognize, regard, understand, realize
show	→	demonstrate, indicate, reveal, prove
think	→	believe, be of the opinion, imagine, suppose
use	→	employ, make use of

Use a greater variety of adjectives

beautiful	→	*attractive, good-looking, gorgeous, lovely, stunning*
clear	→	*plain, explicit, evident*
important	→	*significant, major, essential, notable*
interesting	→	*absorbing, fascinating, gripping, engaging, thought-provoking*
main	→	*principal, major, foremost*
nice	→	*agreeable, charming, delightful, enjoyable, pleasant*
not good	→	*awful, disgusting, dreadful, horrible, terrible, unpleasant*
unclear	→	*ambiguous, uncertain, in doubt*
very good	→	*great, magnificent, outstanding, superb, wonderful*

Avoid repeating other words

about	→	*approximately, around, roughly*
mainly	→	*mostly, on the whole, to a large extent, predominantly*
part (of a text)	→	*passage, paragraph, section*
theme	→	*topic, subject*
very	→	*extremely, highly, remarkably, really*

AVOIDING INTERFERENCE FROM GERMAN

It's always tempting to translate directly from your mother tongue into English, but unfortunately this doesn't always work, as every language follows different unwritten laws of combining words.

Here is a list of typical mistakes speakers of German often make. You can avoid making these mistakes and others if you learn to work regularly with a monolingual dictionary whenever you have to write something in English or when you have to revise a piece of written work. Your monolingual dictionary won't help you find words that you don't know, but it does help you to use the words you know correctly. Also, you should treat word combinations like the ones below just like any other vocabulary: Note them down and learn them.

Note: Some of the expressions in English are correct but are not the equivalent of the German phrase given.

incorrect expression	German	correct expression
~~in the TV~~	*im Fernsehen*	on TV
~~look / see TV~~	*fernsehen*	watch TV
~~hear radio~~	*Radio hören*	listen to the radio
~~drive with the car~~	*mit dem Auto fahren*	go by car / take the car / drive
~~make a party~~	*Party machen*	have a party
~~bring (a bottle) with~~	*(eine Flasche) mitbringen*	bring (a bottle)
~~make sth together~~	*etwas zusammen machen*	do sth together
~~Let's meet us tomorrow.~~	*Lass uns morgen treffen.*	Let's meet tomorrow.
~~What do you take?~~	*Was nimmst du?*	What are you having?
~~it makes fun~~	*es macht Spaß*	it's fun
~~be lucky~~	*glücklich / froh sein*	be happy
~~I'm interested on / for sth~~	*ich bin an etwas interessiert / ich interessiere mich für etwas*	I'm interested in sth
~~spend money for sth~~	*Geld für etwas ausgeben*	spend money on sth
~~in the near~~	*in der Nähe*	near / close by
~~in few days/weeks~~	*in wenigen Tagen/Wochen*	in a few days/weeks
~~in the last time~~	*in letzter Zeit*	recently / in recent weeks/years
~~in the next time~~	*in nächster Zeit*	in the near future / soon
~~in the time of (the internet)~~	*in der Zeit (des Internet)*	in the days / age of (the internet)
~~in our (today's) time~~	*in unserer heutigen Zeit*	in our day and age / nowadays
~~over the whole year~~	*das ganze Jahr über*	all year long / throughout the whole year
~~in this time~~	*in dieser Zeit/Zeitraum*	in this period of time / during this time

incorrect expression	German	correct expression
~~for a long time~~	*vor langer Zeit*	a long time ago
~~since a long time~~	*seit langer Zeit*	for a long time
~~in former times~~	*früher / in früheren Zeiten*	in the past
~~at first~~	*als erstes*	first (of all)
~~The next is …~~	*Das Nächste ist …*	The next thing/point is …
~~It's the wrong/right way …~~	*Das ist das Falsche/Richtige …*	It's the wrong/right thing to do
~~Also a reason is …~~	*Auch/Noch ein Grund ist …*	Another reason is …
~~the most people~~	*die meisten Leute*	most of the people / most people
~~a small/big part of people~~	*einer kleiner/großer Teil der Leute*	a few / many people
~~Two persons were there.~~	*Zwei Personen waren da.*	There were two people there.
~~I mean~~	*ich meine*	I think/believe
~~in my meaning~~	*meiner Meinung nach*	in my opinion
~~I remember me~~	*Ich erinnere mich*	I remember
~~It's the best for you.~~	*Das ist das Beste für dich.*	It's the best thing for you.
~~visit the school~~	*die Schule besuchen*	attend school / go to school
~~study on the university~~	*an der Uni studieren*	study at university
~~I must learn for my exams~~	*Ich muss auf meine Prüfungen lernen*	I have to revise for my exams
~~I have informed me about sth~~	*Ich habe mich über etwas informiert*	I've found some information about/on sth
~~informations~~	*Informationen*	information
~~search for a workplace~~	*einen Arbeitsplatz suchen*	look for a job
~~find a work~~	*eine Arbeit finden*	find work / find a job
~~on the workplace~~	*am Arbeitsplatz*	in the workplace
~~I'm engineer/doctor~~	*Ich bin Ingenieur/Arzt*	I'm an engineer / a doctor
~~on the table stands …~~	*auf dem Tisch steht …*	There is a … on the table
~~In the room is/are …~~	*Im Zimmer ist/sind …*	In the room there is/are …
~~in how far~~	*inwiefern*	to what extent/degree
~~how he/she/it looks like~~	*wie er/sie/es aussieht*	what he/she/it looks like
~~Hello/Goodbye together~~	*Hallo/Auf Wiedersehen zusammen*	Hello/Goodbye everybody
~~How do you call …~~	*Wie heißt …?*	What do you call …?
~~be good/bad in sth~~	*gut/schlecht in etwas sein*	be good/bad at sth

incorrect expression	German	correct expression
~~spend money for sth~~	*Geld für etwas ausgeben*	spend money on sth
~~the opposite from~~	*das Gegenteil von*	the opposite of
~~by my own~~	*ganz alleine*	by myself / on my own
~~it gave a lot of food~~	*Es gab viel zu essen*	There was a lot of food
~~so to say~~	*sozusagen*	so to speak
~~stand up late/early~~	*spät/früh aufstehen*	get up late/early
~~make an exam~~	*ein Examen machen*	take/sit/do an exam
~~You will come, or?~~	*Du kommst doch, oder?*	You will come, won't you.
~~hold a talk / presentation~~	*einen Vortrag halten*	give a talk/presentation
~~discuss about an issue~~	*über ein Problem diskutieren*	discuss an issue
~~make a good experience~~	*eine gute Erfahrung machen*	have a good experience
~~it is self-evident that~~	*es ist selbstverständlich, dass*	it stands to reason / it goes without saying that
~~easy to oversee~~	*leicht zu übersehen*	easily overlooked
~~the pause between …~~	*die Pause zwischen …*	the break between …
~~private TV programmes~~	*private Fernsehsender*	private TV channels
~~get a baby~~	*ein Kind bekommen*	have a baby
~~She's my chef / chief~~	*Sie ist meine Chefin*	She's my boss
~~my free day~~	*mein freier Tag*	my day off
~~What's about …?~~	*Was ist mit …?*	What about
~~I have my birthday on …~~	*Ich habe am … Geburtstag*	My birthday is on …
~~I am born in …~~	*Ich bin in … geboren*	I was born in …
~~I'm 19 years~~	*Ich bin 19 Jahre*	I'm 19 years old / of age
~~She is a single~~	*Sie ist ein Single*	She is single
~~a recipe from the doctor~~	*ein Rezept vom Arzt*	a prescription from the doctor
~~get a credit from the bank~~	*einen Bankkredit bekommen*	get a loan from the bank
~~a free parking place~~	*ein freier Parkplatz*	a free parking space
~~discriminate women~~	*Frauen diskriminieren*	discriminate against women
~~offer and demand~~	*Angebot und Nachfrage*	supply and demand
~~the tourist branch~~	*die Reisebranche*	the tourist industry
~~in the (free) ecomony~~	*in der (freien) Wirtschaft*	in business/industry

READING SKILLS

READING DIFFICULT TEXTS

Texts are read for different reasons. Apart from reading just for fun and entertainment, we read in order to acquire new knowledge, to form an opinion on an issue or to have our opinion confirmed. Sometimes you just want a rough idea of what the text is about, so it is usually enough just to **skim** the text carefully. Look at the title and sub-headings, words in bold, pictures and their captions. Read the first and last sentences of each paragraph. The former often states the main idea of that paragraph and the latter often contains a summary.

When specific information has to be found, the important thing is to **scan** the text for keywords.

As language learners, you are often asked to skim or scan a text in order to be able to discuss the whole text or parts of it in class.

At other times you are asked to read a text and **answer comprehension questions** on it to prove that you've understood some or most of it. This is usually done for test purposes. The reading comprehension tasks which you are given test your understanding of a text by requiring you to find specific pieces of information quickly. These can take the following forms:
- Multiple-choice questions
- Gapped summary
- Mediation
- Multiple matching
- Short-answer questions

You should always make it a habit to tackle the comprehension questions strategically, which means:

Step 1 Read the whole text from beginning to end before you start answering the comprehension questions. Don't spend a lot of time looking up words or worrying about difficult passages.

Step 2 After you've gained an overview of the whole text, look for keywords in the text that are similar to the keywords in the questions in order to relate the questions to the relevant text passages. (But watch out for multiple-choice and multiple matching tasks, as the options will probably contain words from the text or similar to ones in the text.)

Step 3 Highlight the main ideas or take some very brief notes in the margin while reading. When working with photocopied texts or printouts, mark the place in the text where the keywords occur. If you are dealing with several tasks, use different colours for each task. However, one text passage will never be used for two different tasks.

If you have an overview of the whole text, it will be much easier and less time-consuming for you to find the text passages that the questions refer to. If you don't have this overview, you will have to look through the whole text anew to answer every new question. Since the texts you read are rather long, comprehension questions need to be tackled strategically in the way suggested above. You also need to have a strategy to deal with unknown words (cf. 147).

LISTENING / VIEWING SKILLS

Listening tasks at school usually require you to listen to a recording or watch a video and then do tasks related to what you heard or saw. After reading the tasks, you are usually allowed to listen or watch the recording twice.

Before you listen/watch

- Read the tasks carefully to find out exactly what you are expected to listen for. These tasks come in lots of different forms, e.g. multiple-choice tasks, short-answer questions, matching tasks and note-taking. There are more possible listening/viewing tasks than reading tasks.
- If possible, write down keywords connected to the tasks, so you can listen out for them.

First listening/viewing

- Try to get as many answers as possible. Don't look up words while listening/viewing. If need be, you can look up words before the second listening/viewing.

Second listening/viewing

- During the second listening/viewing, you need to listen out for the answers you missed in the first hearing. Concentrate only on those areas you did not get the first time.

After listening/viewing

- If there are some details you haven't understood when writing your answers, then make a guess based on what you have understood.

There are plenty of useful websites where you can listen to radio broadcasts to practise your listening skills. The best place to find British English is www.bbc.co.uk where you can choose programmes from a huge radio archive. The British Council offers transcripts to their listening material: www.britishcouncil.org. If you prefer to listen to American programmes, go to www.npr.org, the National Public Radio website. And, of course, there are plenty of websites where you can watch videos in English.

SPEAKING SKILLS

TAKING PART IN A GROUP DISCUSSION

One of the basic skills of life is knowing how to take part in a meeting or discussion. It is important to know how to put forward your ideas, how to argue, how to listen to and appreciate the arguments of other people and how to reach compromises.

The aim of a group discussion is to find a solution to an issue during a discussion. You are given various pieces of information, different options or visuals and have to decide which one(s) you wish to use for a certain purpose or to make a ranking of the material, depending on the situation you have been put in.

Preparation phase

Step 1 Familiarize yourself with useful phrases for discussion. These will help you structure your thoughts and take turns in presenting your views.

Step 2 Look at the task you are given. Make sure you know what the situation is and what you are expected to do during the discussion and what the result of the discussion should be.

Step 3 Examine the material you have been given. Decide how best to present it according to the task you have been given.

Presentation phase

In about one minute present your material, explaining what it is about and why it is the best option for the task in question.

Interaction phase

- Every member joins in the discussion about the pros and cons of each option.
- Try to connect your arguments to what has been said beforehand. Make sure that you do not just list arguments – you need to conduct a real discussion and conversation.
- Keep the discussion friendly, as it is easier to convince someone to compromise if they feel you are not hostile.
- Reach a conclusion by finding a solution or reaching a compromise or making a ranking. Remember that it is not important if your idea or suggestion is not chosen – you will be examined according to your language competence, to your contribution to the group discussion and its outcome and to your strategic competence (i.e. your ability to engage in a meaningful exchange with others).

PRESENTING INFORMATION

Presenting information is an essential part of life. In preparation you have to research individual aspects and find specific information. Here are some ways to make your presentation more effective.

The preparation stage

- Think carefully about what your topic is, then brainstorm it. Decide what information you need so that you can structure your research accordingly.
- If you work in a group, discuss how everybody can contribute best to the project and assign the tasks accordingly. Use digital online appointment-making tools so that everyone is up to date with the work.
- Agree on a schedule, including regular group meetings at which all group members give status reports, present their results as they stand at the moment and discuss problems.
- Agree on a cloud service to work on your project without having to send thousands of mails to each other.
- Decide which sources are helpful for your research: the internet, textbooks, encyclopaedias, newspapers or magazines.

The research stage

- Concentrate on English language sources. Using German information and translating it into English will take a long time and often leads to unidiomatic English.
- Check your sources: Older publications may contain outdated information; information published by individuals, interest groups or companies may be biased. Talk to your teacher if you are unsure about the reliability of your sources. Do not just rely on one source.
- Make notes on the information you find. Using index cards might make it easier to organize the information later.
- When quoting, copy the exact wording from your source. Note down the source, as this normally needs to be provided in a bibliography (an alphabetical list of sources used).
- Write a report that shows how you worked, e.g. how you divided the work up, how you kept to a schedule, etc.

Organizing the presentation

- Organize your findings and start preparing your final result and/or any kind of written material (e.g. a wall display, a written text to be handed in, your web page, etc. Bear in mind any specific instructions you were given by your teacher (e.g. length of presentation or text, etc.).
- Visual aids help you:
  - to structure information before writing a text.
  - to present information to accompany a presentation.

  Some typical examples of visual aids are
  - timelines: order of events, dates.
  - flow charts: cause and effect.
  - pie charts: percentages, amounts.
  - clusters/mind maps: structured ideas.
- Ask yourself what kind of presentation software (if required) you want to use, but remember: your audience is more interested in you and not in an endless slideshow of facts and figures.
- Check your written and visual material. Is it well organized and clear? Is the English correct? Give your product to someone else in your group to check it again.

WRITING SKILLS

MATERIAL-BASED WRITING

One form of writing you will be required to do at school is to write a text based upon a situation and three different pieces of material, in which you are asked to address an issue. The material on offer may be illustrations, cartoons, statistics, quotes, headlines or short texts. At least one piece of material will be in German. One of the three pieces of material may come from a biased, unreliable or problematic source – you need to take this into consideration when examining the sources.

Rules

- You have to use the messages or information contained in all three pieces of material to examine the issue and/or support your line of argumentation in your text, but you need not describe or explain the pieces of material themselves or explain them in depth.
- You must write a coherent and cohesive text.
- Make sure your writing looks professional and tidy, as the appearance of your text will have an influence on your final mark.

Procedure

Step 1 Organize your thoughts.

- Make sure that you fully understand what you have to write about.
- Think about what you want to say and how you want to structure your arguments.
- Look at the material and turn the information or message contained in the material into ideas for your text.
- Decide where best to include the material in your text, e.g. in the introduction, as an argument or an example. As you cannot quote directly from the material (unless it is a short quote or slogan), make sure you know how to use indirect speech.

Step 2 Write your text.

- Write an **introduction** in which you name and explain the topic. You may link your introduction to the main part by hinting at your own opinion already. If you cannot think of a sophisticated way to link your introduction to the main part, you can use fixed phrases like:

  In the following, I shall deal with / discuss the problem/subject/issue of… …

- Write the **main part** of the text, in which you present each of your arguments in a well-structured paragraph with evidence to support your arguments (e.g. information from a graph or a text that is in the material you were given).
- Write a **conclusion** in which you offer a solution, a personal opinion or a possible outcome.

  Concluding a comment
  - *All in all, I think it can be said that …*
  - *In conclusion, I would like to say that …*
  - *I would like to conclude by saying that …*

- Make sure your writing looks professional and tidy and that your paragraphs are signalled clearly by an indentation.

Step 3 Proofread your text to make sure that there are no mistakes and that you have used all three pieces of material in your text.

MEDIATION (DEUTSCH–ENGLISH)

Another form of writing is to render certain information from a German text into English. You are given a situation and a text and are asked to present certain contents of the text.

Step 1 Study the task to find out which aspects need to be in your English text. Then mark the keywords relating to the aspects in the German text. Use different colours for different aspects.

Step 2 Translate the keywords from the text into English. If you can't remember the exact English word or expression, think of a way of paraphrasing it.

Step 3 Write the text ensuring that you cover all aspects asked for in the task. Make sure that your text is coherent and cohesive.

WRITING A GOOD TEXT

Whatever form of text you are writing, you will need to make sure that your argumentation flows well and your sentences read well.

Using complex structures

It is easy to write a simple English sentence and you are less likely to make mistakes, but simple English won't impress your examiner.

- To improve your style, it is necessary to combine simple sentences to make more complex sentences. This can be done by using subordinate sentences.
  Example:
  In the foreground we see a man. He is spraying a cornfield with chemical fertilizer.
  In the foreground we see a man spraying a cornfield with chemical fertilizer.
- Use the gerund to make your sentences sound more English. Some verbs and prepositions can be followed by the gerund.
  Examples:
  I prefer ***watching*** *love stories.*
  He improved his English by ***learning*** *ten new words every day.*
  He passed his exam without ***working*** *very hard.*
  Travelling *around the world is the best way to learn about different cultures.*
  After ***seeing*** *the ad on TV, people often want to buy the product.*
  Before ***discussing*** *this aspect, I want to point out one important fact.*
- Use participle constructions. English, especially written English, is full of sentences shortened by a participle. This automatically sounds more elegant.
  Examples:
  The food ***advertized*** *on TV promotes an unhealthy diet.*
  One ad ***promoting*** *toys was criticized because it used racial stereotypes.*
- Inversion is particularly effective in argumentative texts. Note that it is usually with negative adverbs *(never, rarely, seldom).*
  Examples:
  Under no circumstances should we accept the claims of those who deny that climate change is happening.
  Never has this issue been as controversial as it is today.

Connecting arguments and making transitions

When you outline a new argument, start a new paragraph or conclude your composition, it is good style to use connectors.

Listing	besides, equally important, first (second, etc.), further, furthermore, in addition, in the first place, moreover
Giving examples	for example, for instance, in fact, to illustrate
Comparing	likewise, similarly
Contrasting	although, and yet, despite, even though, however, on the other hand
Summarizing or concluding	all in all, in conclusion, in other words, in short, in summary, on the whole, therefore, to sum up
Showing your argument is logical	accordingly, as a result, because, consequently, for this reason

PROOFREADING

Whenever you write a text, it is important to check the correctness and the style of the English you have used. Ideally ask someone else to read it through. Others will often see more because they are not as involved with the text as you are. If possible, read your text out loud. This will help you spot if you have accidently left out any words.

Step 1 Checking structure

- Check that you have included an introduction and a conclusion.
- Check that you have followed all the rules for a sensible text structure, e.g. topic sentences, paragraphs, etc.
- Make sure that your paragraphs include more than one sentence but still focus on one basic thought, argument or idea.

Step 2 Checking style

- Look at your sentences. If your text consists of lots of unconnected main clauses, then add linking words to express logical connections between your ideas and thus make your text more readable.
- Make sure you used the right collocations. If in doubt, look them up in a dictionary.
- Check for repetitions. Substitute words you have used repeatedly with synonyms.

Step 3 Checking correctness

- Keep a checklist of mistakes you have regularly made in the past, e.g. correct tenses in the if-clause, the use of adverbs, etc. Look specifically for these mistakes when reading your text.
- Check spelling and punctuation. If possible take advantage of your computer's spell-checker, but always double-check its suggestions rather than accepting them blindly.

REFERENCING A TEXT

Citing a text

It is important to know how to reference a work in your text and in your bibliography.

1. MONOGRAPHS AND BOOKS IN GENERAL

type	in running text	in reference section
monograph, one author	(Culler 1997: 56–59)	Culler, Jonathan. 1997. *Literary Theory: A Very Short Introduction.* Oxford: Oxford University Press.
monograph, more than one author	(Baugh and Cable 2002: 103)	Baugh, Albert C. and Thomas Cable. 2002. *A History of the English Language.* 5th ed. London: Routledge.
edited volume	(Schabert 2000)	Schabert, Ina, ed. 2000. *Shakespeare-Handbuch: Die Zeit – Der Mensch – Das Werk – Die Nachwelt.* 4th ed. Stuttgart: Kröner.
more than three authors or editors	(Crenshaw et al. 1995)	Crenshaw, Kimberlé, Neil Gotanda, Gary Peller, and Kendall Thomas, eds. 1995. *Critical Race Theory: The Key Writings that Formed the Movement.* New York: New Press.

2. ARTICLES IN BOOKS AND JOURNALS, WEB SOURCES AND OTHER SOURCES

type	in running text	in reference section
article in a book/ journal	(Kastovsky 1992: 290–297)	Kastovsky, Dieter. 1992. 'Semantics and Vocabulary'. *The Cambridge History of the English Language. Volume I: The Beginnings to 1066.* Ed. Richard M. Hogg. Cambridge: Cambridge University Press. 290–407.
article in a magazine	(Jones 1989: 5)	Jones, Mick. 1989. "My Life with the Stones". *Time* Nov. 14: 1–20.
web source	(Willey 2003)	Willey, David. 2003. 'Italy Gets Globe Theatre Replica'. BBC News Oct. 14 < http://news.bbc.co.uk/2/hi/europe/3190268.stm> (accessed 18.01.2016).
dictionary entry	(OED s.v. speed, n.)	OED = The Oxford English Dictionary. 2000 –. Ed. John A. Simpson. 3rd ed. Oxford: Oxford University Press. <http://www.oed.com> (accessed 18.01.2018)

3. LITERARY TEXTS, TEXT EDITIONS, PLAYS, MOVIES AND TELEVISION SERIES

type	in running text	in reference section
novel/play	(The Sea 35) or (Banville 2005: 35)	Banville, John. 2005. *The Sea.* London: Picador.
text edition	(Pride and Prejudice 56) or (Austen [1813] 1999: 56)	Austen, Jane. [1813] 1999. *Pride and Prejudice.* Ed. William Trevor. Oxford: Oxford University Press.
short story	('Conversation' 100) or (McEwan [1975] 2003: 100)	McEwan, Ian. [1975] 2003. 'Conversation with a Cupboard Man'. First Love, Last Rites. New York: Anchor. 97–114.
poem	('Journey' ll. 11–16) or (Eliot [1927] 2000: l. 11–16)	Eliot, T. S. [1927] 2000. 'Journey of the Magi'. *The Norton Anthology of English Literature.* Ed. M. H. Abrams et al. Vol. 2. New York: Norton. 2386–2387.
film and television series	(Dracula 1:14:12)	*Bram Stoker's Dracula.* 1992. Dir. Francis Ford Coppola.

Quoting a text in your writing

Quoting is used when you want to support your own statements by giving evidence from other texts or the text you are working on. You can either paraphrase (i.e. use your own words to express ideas from a text) or you can use a direct quote (i.e. use the exact words of the text).

Here are some rules for quoting properly:

- With a direct quote, repeat exactly what the author wrote – this also refers to spelling, punctuation, etc.
- Use quotation marks to show where the direct quote begins and ends: A direct quote must be clearly indicated as someone else's thoughts to avoid giving the impression of plagiarism. Remember that in English, quotation marks start and end above the line ("…").

STRATEGY	EXAMPLE
Indirect quotes If you use an indirect quote (i.e. you paraphrase or summarize ideas from a text in your own words) you do not use quotation marks, but you must indicate that you are referring to somebody else's ideas.	President Obama claimed that ignorance was not a virtue and that one should know what one was talking about (Obama, 2016).
Direct quotes: complete sentences When quoting complete sentences make sure to use quotation marks at the beginning and the end of the quote. Use a colon (:) to separate the quotation from your introductory phrase or sentence.	Iceland is the first country to introduce a law that requires firms to prove that they pay men and women equally: "The new law requires employers to show, through certification by an accredited auditor, that their pay management system complies with a national equal pay standard." (Henley 2017)
Direct quotes: words or phrases If you want to refer to individual words from the text, you can incorporate words/phrases into your own sentence. Work the quotations into your sentences as smoothly as possible so that they fit syntactically.	According to Graddol, the widespread use of English throughout the world "is largely a product of economic globalisation" but he concedes that it "may not prove to be a permanent phenomenon" (Graddol 2005).
Deleting from or adding to a direct quote If you want to leave out part of a quote indicate this by using square brackets […]. If you need to add to a quote, for example to make it fit into your sentence syntactically or logically, indicate this by adding words in square brackets, too. Make sure that you don't change the meaning of the quote and that it is still syntactically correct.	"Keep in mind that cultural traits should never be taken as absolutes. […] While particular communication style may be fairly common in a certain culture, individual people, businesses and industries also have their own styles." (Martinez-Carter 2014)
Direct quotes: texts containing quotation mark When quoting a passage that includes quotation marks (e.g. in direct speech), use two different kinds of quotation marks, i.e. "…" for the main quote and '…' for the secondary quote.	"In recent years 'trigger warnings' have been adopted by many universities in America to alert students to syllabus material that might be distressing." (Anthony 2016)

IRREGULAR VERBS

arise	arose	arisen	*entstehen*
be	was/were	been	*sein*
beat	beat	beaten	*schlagen*
become	became	become	*werden*
begin	began	begun	*starten, anfangen*
bind	bound	bound	*fesseln, binden*
break	broke	broken	*brechen, kaputtmachen*
bring	brought	brought	*bringen*
broadcast	broadcast	broadcast	*senden, ausstrahlen*
build	built	built	*bauen*
burn	burnt/burned	burnt/burned	*brennen*
buy	bought	bought	*kaufen*
catch	caught	caught	*fangen*
choose	chose	chosen	*wählen*
come	came	come	*kommen*
cost	cost	cost	*kosten*
cut	cut	cut	*schneiden*
deal	dealt	dealt	*handeln, sich beschäftigen mit*
dig	dug	dug	*graben, bohren*
do	did	done	*tun, machen*
draw	drew	drawn	*zeichnen*
dream	dreamt/dreamed	dreamt/dreamed	*träumen*
drink	drank	drunk	*trinken*
drive	drove	driven	*fahren*
eat	ate	eaten	*essen*
fall	fell	fallen	*fallen*
feel	felt	felt	*fühlen*
fight	fought	fought	*(be)kämpfen*
find	found	found	*finden*
fly	flew	flown	*fliegen*
forget	forgot	forgotten	*vergessen*
freeze	froze	frozen	*frieren*
get	got	got	*bekommen*
give	gave	given	*geben*
go	went	gone	*gehen*
grow	grew	grown	*wachsen*
have	had	had	*haben*
hear	heard	heard	*hören*
hide	hid	hidden	*(sich) verstecken*
hit	hit	hit	*schlagen*
hold	held	held	*halten*
hurt	hurt	hurt	*weh tun*
input	input	input	*eingeben*
keep	kept	kept	*behalten*
know	knew	known	*wissen, kennen*
lay	laid	laid	*legen*
lead	led	led	*führen*

learn	learnt/learned	learnt/learned	*lernen*
leave	left	left	*(weg)gehen, (ver)lassen*
let	let	let	*lassen, erlauben*
light	lit	lit	*erleuchten, entzünden*
lose	lost	lost	*verlieren*
make	made	made	*machen, tun*
mean	meant	meant	*bedeuten*
meet	met	met	*treffen*
pay	paid	paid	*bezahlen*
put	put	put	*legen, stellen*
read	read	read	*lesen*
ride	rode	ridden	*fahren, reiten*
rise	rose	risen	*steigen, sich erheben*
ring	rang	rung	*klingeln, anrufen*
run	ran	run	*laufen, verwalten*
say	said	said	*sagen*
see	saw	seen	*sehen*
seek	sought	sought	*suchen*
sell	sold	sold	*verkaufen*
send	sent	sent	*senden*
set	set	set	*setzen, stellen, legen*
shake	shook	shaken	*schütteln*
show	showed	shown	*zeigen*
shut	shut	shut	*schließen*
sing	sang	sung	*singen*
sink	sank	sunk	*(ver)senken*
sit	sat	sat	*sitzen*
sleep	slept	slept	*schlafen*
smell	smelt/smelled	smelt/smelled	*riechen*
speak	spoke	spoken	*sprechen*
speed	sped	sped	*rasen*
spell	spelt/spelled	spelt/spelled	*buchstabieren*
spend	spent	spent	*ausgeben, verbringen*
stand	stood	stood	*stehen*
steal	stole	stolen	*stehlen*
swim	swam	swum	*schwimmen*
take	took	taken	*nehmen*
teach	taught	taught	*unterrichten*
tear	tore	torn	*zerreißen*
tell	told	told	*erzählen*
think	thought	thought	*denken, meinen*
throw	threw	thrown	*werfen*
understand	understood	understood	*verstehen*
wake	woke	woken	*wecken*
wear	wore	worn	*tragen*
win	won	won	*gewinnen*
write	wrote	written	*schreiben*

UNIT WORD LIST

Der im Vokabelverzeichnis angegebene Wortschatz dient der Festigung des ggf. bereits vorhandenen Aufbauwortschatzes der Schüler und Schülerinnen und erweitert diesen auf die dem Fachabitur in Englisch entsprechende Niveaustufe. Die Wörter erscheinen in der Reihenfolge ihres Auftretens in **Focus on Success Plus 13.**

Wörter, die in den Audio- und Videotexten vorkommen, sind mit einem blauen Balken gekennzeichnet.

pl = Plural *AE* = amerikanisches Englisch *BE* = britisches Englisch *fml* = formell *infml* = informell, umgangssprachlich

UNIT 1

page 7

effort ['efət]	Bemühen, Unternehmung
to **appease sb** [ə'pi:z]	jdn beschwichtigen
mute [mju:t]	Stumme/r
to **allot sb sth** [ə'lɒt]	jdm etw zuteilen
to **point at sb/sth** ['pɔɪnt ət]	auf jdn/etw zeigen
to **adjust to sth** [ə'dʒʌst]	sich an etw gewöhnen, sich auf etw einstellen
long distance [ˌlɒŋ 'dɪstəns]	Fern-
lover ['lʌvə]	Geliebte/r, Liebhaber/in
to **respond** [rɪ'spɒnd]	antworten, reagieren
to **use up** [ˌju:z 'ʌp]	aufgebrauchen, verbrauchen
to **whisper** ['wɪspə]	flüstern
to **breathe** [bri:ð]	atmen
to **cope** [kəʊp]	zurechtkommen
entitled [ɪn'taɪtld]	betitelt, benannt
to **reflect sth** [rɪ'flekt]	etw reflektieren, etw widerspiegeln

page 8

psychologist [saɪ'kɒlədʒɪst]	Psychologe/-in
to **decipher sth** [dɪ'saɪfə]	etw entziffern, etw entschlüsseln
means, *pl* **means** [mi:nz]	Möglichkeit, Mittel
in the face of [feɪs]	trotz, angesichts
to **take notice of** [ˌteɪk 'nəʊtɪs]	beachten, aufmerksam werden auf
to **address sth** [ə'dres]	etw angehen, sich mit etw befassen
view [vju:]	Ansicht, Auffassung
indifference (to) [ɪn'dɪfrəns]	Gleichgültigkeit (gegenüber)
hostility [hɒ'stɪləti]	Feindseligkeit
to **come across as ...** [ˌkʌm 'əkrɒs əz]	... wirken, einen ... Eindruck machen
consideration [kənˌsɪdə'reɪʃn]	Rücksicht, Erwägung, Überlegung
empathy ['empəθi]	Einfühlungsvermögen
in addition to sth [ɪn ə'dɪʃn tə]	zusätzlich zu etw
posture ['pɒstʃə]	(Körper-)Haltung
gesture ['dʒestʃə]	Geste
facial ['feɪʃl]	Gesichts-
handwriting ['hændraɪtɪŋ]	Handschrift
typeface ['taɪpfeɪs]	Schrift(art)
decorative ['dekərətɪv]	dekorativ
to **add to sth** [æd]	beitragen zu etw, etw vergrößern
to **convey** [kən'veɪ]	übermitteln, vermitteln
to **intend** [ɪn'tend]	beabsichtigen, vorhaben
mother tongue ['mʌðə tʌŋ]	Muttersprache
foreign language [ˌfɒrən 'læŋgwɪdʒ]	Fremdsprache
to **acquire sth** [ə'kwaɪə]	etw erwerben
to **be likely to do sth** [bi 'laɪkli tə]	etw wahrscheinlich tun (werden)
guarantee [ˌgærən'ti:]	Garantie
fuzzy ['fʌzi]	verschwommen, unscharf
vague [veɪg]	vage, unbestimmt, ungenau
ambiguous [æm'bɪgjuəs]	mehrdeutig
thus [ðʌs]	daher, deshalb, somit
misunderstanding [ˌmɪsʌndə'stændɪŋ]	Missverständnis
essential (to) [ɪ'senʃl]	wesentlich, unerlässlich (für)
to **have (a) good command of English** [kəˌmɑ:nd əv 'ɪŋglɪʃ]	Englisch gut beherrschen
first language [ˌfɜ:st 'læŋgwɪdʒ]	Muttersprache
as well as [əz 'wel əz]	sowohl ... als auch ..., ebenso wie, sowie
first and foremost [ˌfɜ:st ən 'fɔ:məʊst]	vor allem, in erster Linie
rightly ['raɪtli]	mit/zu Recht
due to sth [dju:]	wegen etw
apart from [ə'pɑ:t frəm]	abgesehen von, außer
awareness [ə'weənəs]	Bewusstsein
i.e. (= that is) [ˌaɪ 'i:]	d.h. (= das heißt)
behaviour [bɪ'heɪvjə]	Benehmen, Verhalten
to **be used to sth** [bi 'ju:st tə]	gewöhnt sein an etw
elsewhere [ˌels'weə]	woanders, anderswo
for this reason [fə ðɪs 'ri:zn]	aus diesem Grund
to **provide sth** [prə'vaɪd]	etw (an)bieten, etw zur Verfügung stellen
intercultural [ˌɪntə'kʌltʃərəl]	interkulturell
senior ['si:niə]	leitend, älter, ranghöher
to **be aware of sth** [bi ə'weər əv]	etw wissen, sich einer Sache bewusst sein
communicator [kə'mju:nɪkeɪtə]	Kommunikator/in
purpose ['pɜ:pəs]	Absicht, Zweck
to **serve a purpose** [ˌsɜ:v ə 'pɜ:pəs]	einem Zweck dienen
deliberate [dɪ'lɪbərət]	absichtlich, (ganz) bewusst, vorsätzlich
to **manipulate** [mə'nɪpjuleɪt]	manipulieren
to **brainwash sb** ['breɪnwɒʃ]	jdn einer Gehirnwäsche unterziehen
since time immemorial [ˌɪmə'mɔ:riəl]	seit Menschengedenken, seit jeher
orator ['ɒrətə]	Redner/in, Rhetoriker/in
rhetorical device [rɪˌtɒrɪkl dɪ'vaɪs]	Stilmittel
for good or bad [fə ˌgʊd ɔ: 'bæd]	zum Guten oder zum Schlechten
to **strengthen** ['streŋθn]	kräftigen, stärken
cohesion [kəʊ'hi:ʒn]	Zusammenhalt
to **foster sth** ['fɒstə]	etw fördern
solidarity [ˌsɒlɪ'dærəti]	Solidarität
to **marginalize** ['mɑ:dʒɪnəlaɪz]	ins Abseits drängen, an den Rand drängen
to **ostracize** ['ɒstrəsaɪz]	ächten, ausschließen
marketer ['mɑ:kɪtə]	Vermarkter

persuasion [pə'sweɪʒn]	Überzeugung, Überzeugungskunst
era ['ɪərə]	Ära, Epoche
influencer ['ɪnfluənsə]	Einflussnehmer/in
hate [heɪt]	Hass
economy [ɪ'kɒnəmi]	Wirtschaft
for instance [fər 'ɪnstəns]	zum Beispiel
avoidance [ə'vɔɪdəns]	Vermeidung
sexist ['seksɪst]	sexistisch
manipulation [məˌnɪpju'leɪʃn]	Manipulation
basis, *pl* **bases** ['beɪsɪs, 'beɪsiːz]	Basis, Grundlage
poetry ['pəʊətri]	Dichtung, Lyrik
work of art [ˌwɜːk əv 'ɑːt]	Kunstwerk
vagueness ['veɪgnəs]	Unbestimmtheit, Unschärfe
ambiguity [ˌæmbɪ'gjuːəti]	Mehrdeutigkeit
enjoyable [ɪn'dʒɔɪəbl]	angenehm, schön

page 9

bracket ['brækɪt]	Klammer
to **gain** [geɪn]	erwerben, gewinnen, sammeln, erlangen
influential [ˌɪnflu'enʃl]	einflussreich
recipient [rɪ'sɪpiənt]	Empfänger/in
youngster ['jʌŋstə]	Jugendliche/r
opportunity [ˌɒpə'tjuːnəti]	Gelegenheit, Möglichkeit, Chance
persuasive [pə'sweɪsɪv]	überzeugend
to **translate** [træns'leɪt]	übersetzen, (sich) übertragen (lassen)
to **fit** [fɪt]	passen
to **number** ['nʌmbə]	nummerieren
former ['fɔːmə]	ehemalige/r/s
yet [jet]	(und) doch, dennoch
executive [ɪg'zekjətɪv]	leitende/r Angestellte/r
to **occur** [ə'kɜː]	passieren, geschehen, stattfinden
employer [ɪm'plɔɪə]	Arbeitgeber/in
keyword ['kiːwɜːd]	Schlagwort, Schlüsselwort
to **collocate** ['kɒləkeɪt]	kollokieren (eine gebräuchliche lexikalische Einheit bilden)
to **arouse sth** [ə'raʊz]	etw wecken, etw erregen
outright ['aʊtraɪt]	total, völlig, offen, direkt
mutual ['mjuːtʃuəl]	gegenseitige/r/s
lack (of) [læk]	Mangel (an)
collocation [ˌkɒlə'keɪʃn]	Kollokation (inhaltlich kombinierbare sprachliche Einheiten)

page 10

particular [pə'tɪkjələ]	bestimmt, speziell
adviser, advisor [əd'vaɪzə]	Berater/in
need [niːd]	Bedarf, Bedürfnis, Notwendigkeit
to **draw a conclusion** [ˌdrɔː ə kən'kluːʒn]	eine Schlussfolgerung ziehen
to **remain** [rɪ'meɪn]	bleiben

page 11

to **contradict** [ˌkɒntrə'dɪkt]	widersprechen
phenomenon, *pl* **phenomena** [fə'nɒmɪnən, fə'nɒmɪnə]	Phänomen, Erscheinung
sufficient [sə'fɪʃnt]	ausreichend, hinreichend
universal [juːnɪ'vɜːsl]	universell, allgemein, weltweit
largely ['lɑːdʒli]	größtenteils, überwiegend, weitgehend
communications *(pl)* [kəˌmjuːnɪ'keɪʃnz]	Nachrichten
indeed [ɪn'diːd]	tatsächlich, in der Tat
to **accelerate** [ək'seləreɪt]	beschleunigen
root [ruːt]	Wurzel
to **point to sth** ['pɔɪnt tə]	auf etw hindeuten
settlement ['setlmənt]	Siedlung, Kolonie
to **establish** [ɪ'stæblɪʃ]	etablieren, aufbauen, einrichten
labour ['leɪbə]	Arbeit, Arbeitskräfte
expansion [ɪk'spænʃn]	Ausdehnung, Expansion
variety [və'raɪəti]	Sorte, Art, Variante
to **refer to sb/sth as** [rɪ'fɜː]	jdn/etw bezeichnen als
to **emerge (from)** [ɪ'mɜːdʒ]	entstehen, hervorgehen (aus)
concern [kən'sɜːn]	Sorge, Befürchtung
to **diverge from** [daɪ'vɜːdʒ]	abweichen von
unintelligible [ˌʌnɪn'telɪdʒəbl]	unverständlich
to **evolve (from)** [ɪ'vɒlv]	sich (weiter) entwickeln, entstehen (aus)
linguistic [lɪŋ'gwɪstɪk]	sprachlich, Sprach-, sprachwissenschaftlich
major ['meɪdʒə]	Haupt-, wesentlich, größer

page 12

to **disperse** [dɪ'spɜːs]	(sich) verteilen, (sich) verbreiten, (sich) zerstreuen
air traffic control [ˌeə træfɪk kən'trəʊl]	Flugsicherung
microbiology [ˌmaɪkrəʊbaɪ'ɒlədʒi]	Mikrobiologie
to **stay in touch** [ˌsteɪ ɪn 'tʌtʃ]	in Verbindung/Kontakt bleiben
simultaneous [ˌsɪml'teɪniəs]	gleichzeitig
colleague ['kɒliːg]	Kollege/-in
evidence ['evɪdəns]	Anzeichen, Hinweis, Beweis
tolerance ['tɒlərəns]	Toleranz, Verständnis
fluidity [flu'ɪdəti]	Fluidität, Flüssigkeit, Geschmeidigkeit
mechanism ['mekənɪzəm]	Mechanismus, Mechanik
to **maintain** [meɪn'teɪn]	aufrecht erhalten, beibehalten
effectiveness [ɪ'fektɪvnəs]	Wirksamkeit, Effektivität
principle ['prɪnsəpl]	Grundsatz, Prinzip
intelligibility [ɪnˌtelɪdʒə'bɪləti]	Verständlichkeit
to **carry over** ['kæri əʊvə]	übernehmen, übertragen
provided (that) [prə'vaɪdɪd]	vorausgesetzt, (dass)
to **endanger** [ɪn'deɪndʒə]	bedrohen, gefährden
to **disregard** [ˌdɪsrɪ'gɑːd]	ignorieren, nicht beachten, unbeachtet lassen
native speaker [ˌneɪtɪv 'spiːkə]	Muttersprachler/in
articulation [ɑːˌtɪkju'leɪʃn]	Artikulation, Aussprache
mark [mɑːk]	(Kenn-)Zeichen, Markierung
distinction [dɪ'stɪŋkʃn]	Unterscheidung
vowel ['vaʊəl]	Vokal
crucial (to/for) ['kruːʃl]	äußerst wichtig, entscheidend (für)
skilled [skɪld]	erfahren, geübt
appeal [ə'piːl]	Appell, Ansprache
specific [spə'sɪfɪk]	bestimmt, speziell, spezifisch
to **tend to do sth** ['tend tə]	dazu neigen, etw zu tun
colloquial [kə'ləʊkwiəl]	umgangssprachlich

UNIT WORD LIST

comprehensible [ˌkɒmprɪˈhensəbl]	verständlich
to **cease** [siːs]	aufhören, eingestellt werden
primary school [ˈpraɪməri skuːl]	Grundschule
alongside [əˌlɒŋˈsaɪd]	neben

page 13

unprecedented [ʌnˈpresɪdentɪd]	beispiellos, einmalig, noch nie da gewesen
unrepeatable [ˌʌnrɪˈpiːtəbl]	nicht wiederholbar, einmalig
throughout ... [θruːˈaʊt]	der/die/das ganze ... (hindurch), überall in ...
intermediate [ˌɪntəˈmiːdiət]	mittlere/r/s (Niveau), für fortgeschrittene Anfänger/innen
to **subside** [səbˈsaɪd]	zurückgehen, verebben, zurückgehen
secondary school [ˈsekəndri skuːl]	weiterführende Schule
to **be expected to do sth** [ɪkˈspektɪd]	etw tun sollen/müssen, es wird erwartet, dass man etw tut
curriculum, *pl* **curriculums** *or* **curricula** [kəˈrɪkjələm, kəˈrɪkjələ]	Lehrplan
such as [ˈsʌtʃ əz]	wie (zum Beispiel)
undoubtedly [ʌnˈdaʊtɪdli]	zweifellos
decade [ˈdekeɪd]	Jahrzehnt
in demand [ɪn dɪˈmɑːnd]	(nach)gefragt, gesucht
overseas [ˌəʊvəˈsiːz]	nach/in Übersee
multinational [ˌmʌltiˈnæʃnəl]	multinational, multinationaler Konzern
to **be based in** [ˈbeɪst ɪn]	seinen (Firmen-)Sitz haben in
manufacturing [ˌmænjuˈfæktʃərɪŋ]	Fertigung, Herstellung
service [ˈsɜːvɪs]	Dienst, Dienstleistung
to **arise (arose, arisen)** [əˈraɪz]	entstehen, auftreten, sich ergeben
conspiracy [kənˈspɪrəsi]	Verschwörung, Komplott
otherwise [ˈʌðəwaɪz]	ansonsten, andernfalls
monolingual [ˌmɒnəˈlɪŋgwəl]	einsprachig
applicant [ˈæplɪkənt]	Bewerber/in
fluent [ˈfluːənt]	(Sprache:) fließend
gradually [ˈgrædʒuəli]	allmählich, langsam, nach und nach
to **fade away** [ˌfeɪd əˈweɪ]	schwächer werden, (nach und nach) verschwinden
to **prove** [pruːv]	sich erweisen (als)
to **decline** [dɪˈklaɪn]	zurückgehen, fallen, sinken
to **queue** [kjuː]	sich (in einer Warteschlage) anstellen, Schlange stehen
source [sɔːs]	Quelle, Herkunft

page 14

to **indicate sth** [ˈɪndɪkeɪt]	etw (an)zeigen, auf etw deuten, auf etw hinweisen
momentum [məˈmentəm]	Schwung, Fahrt
to **preserve sth** [prɪˈzɜːv]	etw bewahren, etw erhalten
foreigner [ˈfɒrənə]	Ausländer/in
aspect [ˈæspekt]	Gesichtspunkt, Aspekt
to **judge** [dʒʌdʒ]	(be)urteilen, ermessen
to **turn out to be ...** [ˌtɜːn ˈaʊt tə bi]	sich erweisen/herausstellen als ...
to **promote sth** [prəˈməʊt]	etw fördern, etw unterstützen
in the long run [ɪn ðə ˈlɒŋ rʌn]	auf lange Sicht, langfristig
to **master sth** [ˈmɑːstə]	etw meistern, etw bewältigen

page 15

to **stage sth** [steɪdʒ]	etw inszenieren, etw veranstalten, etw aufführen
introductory [ˌɪntrəˈdʌktəri]	einführend, einleitend
excerpt [ˈeksɜːpt]	Auszug, Ausschnitt
lecture [ˈlektʃə]	Vortrag, Vorlesung
rather than [ˈrɑːðə ðən]	anstatt
increasingly [ɪnˈkriːsɪŋli]	zunehmend, in zunehmendem Maße
to **adapt** [əˈdæpt]	sich anpassen
to **suit sb/sth** [suːt]	zu jdm/etw passen
slight [slaɪt]	gering
dozen [ˈdʌzn]	Dutzend
construction [kənˈstrʌkʃn]	Konstruktion
to **suppose** [səˈpəʊz]	annehmen
usage [ˈjuːsɪdʒ]	Nutzung
to **shape sth** [ʃeɪp]	etw formen
and so forth [ənd səʊ ˈfɔːθ]	und so weiter
to **diversify** [daɪˈvɜːsɪfaɪ]	(sich) differenzieren
to **fragment** [frægˈment]	zerfallen
vulgar Latin [ˌvʌlgə ˈlætɪn]	Vulgärlatein
pidgin [ˈpɪdʒɪn]	Pidgin, Mischsprache
to **derive** [dɪˈraɪv]	ableiten
mixture [ˈmɪkstʃə]	Mischung
thrown in for good measure [θrəʊn ˌɪn fə gʊd ˈmeʒə]	obendrein
amalgam [əˈmælgəm]	Amalgam, Verschmelzung
to **unify** [ˈjuːnɪfaɪ]	vereinigen, vereinheitlichen
homogeneity [ˌhɒmədʒəˈniːəti]	Homogenität, Gleichartigkeit
at grass-roots level [ˌgrɑːs ruːts ˈlevl]	an der Basis
dialect [ˈdaɪəlekt]	Dialekt
to **operate** [ˈɒpəreɪt]	arbeiten, wirken, funktionieren
to **represent sth** [ˌreprɪˈzent]	etw ausmachen, etw repräsentieren
to **strike sb** [straɪk]	jdn treffen, jdm auffallen
similarity [ˌsɪməˈlærəti]	Ähnlichkeit
hardly [ˈhɑːdli]	kaum
to **lock sb up** [ˌlɒk ˈʌp]	jdn wegsperren
to **achieve sth** [əˈtʃiːv]	etw erreichen, etw leisten
empire [ˈempaɪə]	(Welt-)Reich, Imperium
scientific [ˌsaɪənˈtɪfɪk]	wissenschaftlich
virtually [ˈvɜːtʃuəli]	praktisch, nahezu
to **facilitate sth** [fəˈsɪlɪteɪt]	etw ermöglichen, etw vermitteln, etw vereinfachen
to **diminish** [dɪˈmɪnɪʃ]	(sich) verringern, abnehmen
to **depend on/upon sb/sth** [dɪˈpend]	von jdm/etw abhängen
foreseeable [fɔːˈsiːəbl]	vorhersehbar
fortunes *pl* [ˈfɔːtʃuːnz]	Schicksal
concerned about [kənˈsɜːnd]	bedacht auf
evolution [ˌiːvəˈluːʃn]	Entwicklung
indication [ˌɪndɪˈkeɪʃn]	Hinweis, Anzeichen
to **split (up)** [splɪt]	sich trennen, sich aufteilen
to **consist of sth** [kənˈsɪst əv]	aus etw bestehen
distant [ˈdɪstənt]	entfernt
to **dominate** [ˈdɒmɪneɪt]	herrschen, dominieren
not least [nɒt ˈliːst]	nicht zuletzt

page 16

repetitive [rɪ'petətɪv]	sich ständig wiederholend, (z. B. Arbeit) monoton
varied ['veərid]	vielfältig, abwechslungsreich
advanced [əd'vɑːnst]	fortgeschritten, hochentwickelt
understandable [ˌʌndə'stændəbl]	verständlich
therefore ['ðeəfɔː]	daher, deshalb, demzufolge
Franconian [fræŋ'kəʊniən]	Fränkisch
titled ['taɪtld]	betitelt

page 18

federal ['fedərəl]	Bundes-
selection [sɪ'lekʃn]	Auswahl
to **conduct sth** [kən'dʌkt]	etw (durch)führen, etw leiten
Bavarian [bə'veəriən]	bayerisch
in favour of [ɪn 'feɪvər əv]	zugunsten von, für
measure ['meʒə]	Maßnahme
feasible ['fiːzəbl]	machbar, möglich
optional ['ɒpʃənl]	optional, freiwillig, freigestellt
to **aim at/for sth** ['eɪm]	etw anstreben

page 19

to **submit** [səb'mɪt]	einreichen, vorlegen, zusenden
to **admit sb** [əd'mɪt]	jdn aufnehmen, jdn zulassen
arrogant ['ærəgənt]	arrogant
patriotic [ˌpætri'ɒtɪk]	patriotisch
tactile ['tæktaɪl]	taktil (berührt gerne Menschen)
individualistic [ˌɪndɪˌvɪdʒuə'lɪstɪk]	individualistisch
humorous ['hjuːmərəs]	humorvoll
xenophobic [ˌzenə'fəʊbɪk]	fremdenfeindlich
self-confident [ˌself 'kɒnfɪdənt]	selbstsicher
disciplined ['dɪsəplɪnd]	diszipliniert
nationalistic [ˌnæʃnə'lɪstɪk]	nationalistisch
nostalgic [nɒ'stældʒɪk]	nostalgisch, wehmütig
industrious [ɪn'dʌstriəs]	fleißig, tüchtig
boisterous ['bɔɪstərəs]	ausgelassen, übermütig
characteristic [ˌkærəktə'rɪstɪk]	Merkmal, charakteristische Eigenschaft
client ['klaɪənt]	Kunde/Kundin
pitfall ['pɪtfɔːl]	(Stolper-)Falle, Schwierigkeit
costly ['kɒstli]	teuer, verlustreich
critical incident [ˌkrɪtɪkl 'ɪnsɪdənt]	kritisches Ereignis, kritischer Zwischenfall
cultural clash [ˌkʌltʃərəl 'klæʃ]	Kulturkonflikt
actual ['æktʃuəl]	tatsächlich, konkret

page 20

sales representative [ˌseɪlz reprɪ'zentətɪv]	Handelsvertreter/in
negotiation [nɪˌgəʊʃi'eɪʃn]	Verhandlung
tense [tens]	angespannt, verkrampft
upright ['ʌpraɪt]	aufrecht
subsidiary [səb'sɪdiəri]	Tochterunternehmen, Filiale
deadline ['dedlaɪn]	Frist, Termin
to **be keen to do sth** [bɪ 'kiːn tə]	etw unbedingt tun wollen
to **attend sth** [ə'tend]	an etw teilnehmen
lecturer ['lektʃərə]	Dozent/in, Hochschullehrer/in
uneasy [ʌn'iːzi]	besorgt, unbehaglich, mulmig
unpopular [ʌn'pɒpjələ]	unbeliebt, unpopulär
researcher [rɪ'sɜːtʃə]	Forscher/in, Wissenschaftler/in
businessman, *pl* **businessmen**, **businesspeople** ['bɪznəsmən]	Geschäftsmann
separately ['seprətli]	einzeln
ridiculous [rɪ'dɪkjələs]	lächerlich, unglaublich
to **explode** [ɪk'spləʊd]	explodieren
to **take sb aside** [ə'saɪd]	jdn beiseite nehmen
resignation [ˌrezɪg'neɪʃn]	Kündigung
academic [ˌækə'demɪk]	Akademiker/in
disturbed [dɪ'stɜːbd]	beunruhigt
tight schedule [ˌtaɪt 'ʃedjuːl]	enger Zeitplan
to **be able to afford sth** [ə'fɔːd]	sich etw leisten können
interruption [ˌɪntə'rʌpʃn]	Unterbrechung

page 21

explanation [ˌeksplə'neɪʃn]	Erläuterung, Erklärung
to **value sth** ['væljuː]	etw (wert)schätzen
hemisphere ['hemɪsfɪə]	Hemisphäre, Halbkugel
to **lose face** [ˌluːz 'feɪs]	an Prestige verlieren
openness ['əʊpənnəs]	Offenheit
honesty ['ɒnəstɪ]	Ehrlichkeit
disrespect [ˌdɪsrɪ'spekt]	Respektlosigkeit, Missachtung
to **associate sth with sth** [ə'səʊʃiət]	etw mit etw verbinden, etw mit etw assoziieren
seriousness ['sɪəriəsnəs]	Seriosität, Ernsthaftigkeit
to **signal** ['sɪgnəl]	signalisieren
attempt [ə'tempt]	Versuch
to **deflate** [dɪ'fleɪt]	Luft ablassen, dämpfen
to **gesture** ['dʒestʃə]	gestikulieren, eine Handbewegung machen
Slavic ['slɑːvɪk]	slawisch
to **misinterpret** [ˌmɪsɪn'tɜːprɪt]	fehlinterpretieren
to **treat** [triːt]	behandeln
sensitive ['sensətɪv]	empfindlich, sensibel
sexual harassment [ˌsekʃuəl 'hærəsmənt]	sexuelle Belästigung
predominantly [prɪ'dɒmɪnəntli]	überwiegend

page 22

abrupt [ə'brʌpt]	abrupt, plötzlich
annoyed [ə'nɔɪd]	verärgert
to **recall sth** [rɪ'kɔːl]	sich an etw erinnern
to **coach** [kəʊtʃ]	schulen, trainieren, unterrichten
caller ['kɔːlə]	Anrufer/in
down to business [ˌdaʊn tə 'bɪznəs]	zum Wesentlichen, Spaß beiseite
proper ['prɒpə]	ordentlich, angemessen
to **secure sth** [sɪ'kjuə]	(sich) etw sichern, etw sicherstellen
to **crumble** ['krʌmbl]	zerbröseln
crossed wires [ˌkrɒst 'waɪəz]	vertauschte Leitungen, Missverständnisse
burned ground [ˌbɜːnd 'graʊnd]	verbrannte Erde
to **err** [ɜː]	sich irren

to **assume sth** [ə'sju:m]	etw annehmen, von etw ausgehen
to **perceive sth** [pə'si:v]	etw wahrnehmen, etw erkennen
authority [ɔ:'θɒrəti]	Autorität, Kompetenz
vital ['vaɪtl]	wichtig, wesentlich
to **result in sth** [rɪ'zʌlt ɪn]	zu etw führen
miscommunication [ˌmɪskəˌmju:nɪ'keɪʃn]	Fehlkommunikation
to **focus on sth** ['fəʊkəs ɒn]	sich auf etw konzentrieren
sole (of your shoes) [səʊl]	(Schuh-)Sohle
seamless ['si:mləs]	nahtlos
standpoint ['stændpɔɪnt]	Standpunkt
to **keep in mind** [ˌki:p ɪn 'maɪnd]	daran denken, nicht vergessen
trait [treɪt]	Wesenszug, Eigenschaft
fairly ['feəli]	ziemlich, recht
hierarchical [ˌhaɪə'rɑ:kɪkl]	hierarchisch
honour ['ɒnə]	Ehre
prevailing [prɪ'veɪlɪŋ]	herrschend, allgemein geltend
apparent [ə'pærənt]	augenscheinlich
emphasis, *pl* **emphases** ['emfəsɪs]	Betonung, Schwerpunkt, Akzent
negotiator [nɪ'gəʊʃieɪtə]	Unterhändler/in, Verhandlungsführer/in
to **be considered sth** [kən'sɪdəd]	für etw gehalten werden, als etw angesehen werden
disrespectful [ˌdɪsrɪ'spektfl]	respektlos
equivalent [ɪ'kwɪvələnt]	Äquivalent, Entsprechung

page 23

priority [praɪ'ɒrəti]	Priorität, Vorrang
meaningful ['mi:nɪŋfl]	wichtig, bedeutend, sinnstiftend
necessity [nə'sesəti]	Notwendigkeit
to **engage in sth** [ɪn'geɪdʒ wɪð]	sich an etw beteiligen
in earnest [ɪn 'ɜ:nɪst]	ernsthaft, im Ernst
to **defer to sb** [dɪ'fɜ:]	sich jdm unterordnen, jdm nachgeben
to **voice** [vɔɪs]	äußern, ausdrücken
disagreement [ˌdɪsə'gri:mənt]	Ablehnung, Meinungsverschiedenheit
to **contribute (to)** [kən'trɪbju:t]	beitragen (zu)
outcome ['aʊtkʌm]	Ergebnis, Resultat
varying ['veəriɪŋ]	unterschiedlich
to **prioritise sth** [praɪ'ɒrətaɪz]	etw priorisieren
clarity ['klærəti]	Klarheit
negative ['negətɪv]	Verneinung, Kritik
distinct [dɪ'stɪŋkt]	deutlich, unterschiedlich
sandwiched between sth ['sænwɪtʃt]	zwischen etw gelegt, eingeklemmt von etw
positive ['pɒzətɪv]	Bejahung, Zustimmung
to **deliver sth** [dɪ'lɪvə]	etw liefern
to **appreciate sth** [ə'pri:ʃieɪt]	etw schätzen, etw zu schätzen wissen
unaccustomed [ˌʌnə'kʌstəmd]	ungewohnt, nicht gewöhnt
to **float** [fləʊt]	schweben, treiben
criticism (of sb/sth) ['krɪtɪsɪzəm]	Kritik (an jdm/etw)
conservative [kən'sɜ:vətɪv]	konservativ
to **involve** [ɪn'vɒlv]	einbeziehen, beteiligen
downgrader [ˌdaʊn'greɪdə]	Abschwächer
to **soften** ['sɒfn]	mildern, abmildern
insubordination [ˌɪnsəˌbɔ:dɪ'neɪʃn]	Gehorsamsverweigerung
oblique [ə'bli:k]	indirekt, versteckt
to **consider sth** [kən'sɪdə]	über etw nachdenken, etw in Erwägung ziehen
to **trace sth** [treɪs]	etw (zurück)verfolgen
objective [əb'dʒektɪv]	objektiv, zielorientiert
to **emphasise sth** ['emfəsaɪz]	etw betonen, etw hervorheben
pervasive [pə'veɪsɪv]	um sich greifend, durchdringend
egalitarian [igælɪ'teəriən]	egalitär, auf Gleichheit beruhend
outsider [ˌaʊt'saɪdə]	Außenstehende/r
thought [θɔ:t]	Gedanke

page 24

to **pursue sth** [pə'sju:]	einer Sache nachgehen, etw verfolgen
regardless of sth [rɪ'gɑ:dləs əv]	ungeachtet einer Sache
to **affect sth** [ə'fekt]	etw beeinflussen, sich auswirken auf etw
elementary school [ˌelɪ'mentri sku:l]	Grundschule
limited ['lɪmɪtɪd]	begrenzt
developing country [dɪˌveləpɪŋ 'kʌntri]	Entwicklungsland
corresponding [ˌkɒrɪ'spɒndɪŋ]	entsprechend, passend
reproach [rɪ'prəʊtʃ]	Vorwurf, Anschuldigung
instrumental [ˌɪnstrə'mentl]	behilflich, dienlich
to **negotiate** [nɪ'gəʊʃieɪt]	verhandeln, aushandeln
to **conclude** [tə kən'klu:d]	abschließen
everyday ['evrideɪ]	alltäglich, Alltags-
to **be to do sth** ['bi tə]	etw tun sollen
to **interact** [ˌɪntər'ækt]	interagieren, aufeinander eingehen
to **encounter sth** [ɪn'kaʊntə]	auf etw stoßen, etw begegnen
to **be bound to sth** ['baʊnd tə]	etwas erwarten können

page 25

to **offend sb** [ə'fend]	jdn beleidigen, verletzen; jdm zu nahe treten
to **classify** ['klæsɪfaɪ]	klassifizieren, einteilen
clothing ['kləʊðɪŋ]	Bekleidung, Kleidung
to **curtsy** ['kɜ:tsi]	knicksen
to **clap** [klæp]	(Beifall) klatschen
passionate ['pæʃənət]	leidenschaftlich
hospitable [hɒ'spɪtəbl]	gastfreundlich
to **regard** [rɪ'gɑ:d]	schätzen, würdigen
to **bargain** ['bɑ:gɪn]	(ver)handeln
auspicious [ɔ:'spɪʃəs]	vielversprechend, glückverheißend
gift [gɪft]	Geschenk
headshake ['hedʃəɪk]	Kopfschütteln
to **acknowledge sth** [ək'nɒlɪdʒ]	etw anerkennen
punctuality [ˌpʌŋktʃu'æləti]	Pünktlichkeit
pleasure ['pleʒə]	Vergnügen, Freude
surrounding [sə'raʊndɪŋ]	Umgebung
elder ['eldə]	älter
counterpart ['kaʊntəpɑ:t]	Gegenstück, Gegenüber, Pendant
elderly ['eldəli]	älter; Senioren

postgraduate diploma [ˌpəʊstˌɡrædʒuət dɪ'pləʊmə]	Aufbaustudium
representative [ˌreprɪ'zentətɪv]	Vertreter/in, Beauftragte/r
orientation [ˌɔːriən'teɪʃn]	Orientierung, Einführung
proverb ['prɒvɜːb]	Sprichwort
casual ['kæʒuəl]	leger, zwanglos
nude [nuːd]	nackt
pastel ['pæstl]	Pastell
jewellery ['dʒuːəlri]	Schmuck
flashy ['flæʃi]	auffällig, protzig
to **refuse sth** [rɪ'fjuːz]	etw verweigern, etw ablehnen
ignorance ['ɪɡnərəns]	Unwissenheit, Unkenntnis
traditionalist [trə'dɪʃənlɪst]	traditionell, traditionalistisch
to **waste sth** [weɪst]	etw verschwenden, etw vergeuden
bright [braɪt]	hell, strahlend, freundlich
to **dine** [daɪn]	speisen, Essen gehen
to **underestimate sb/sth** [ˌʌndər'estɪmeɪt]	jdn/etw unterschätzen
decent ['diːsnt]	anständig, ordentlich, annehmbar
hospitality [ˌhɒspɪ'tæləti]	Gastfreundschaft
sense (of) [sens]	Sinn (für)
page 26	
various ['veəriəs]	verschieden, mehrere, allerlei
session ['seʃn]	Sitzung, Termin, Treffen
content(s) ['kɒntent]	Inhalt
monotonous [mə'nɒtənəs]	eintönig, monoton
instructions *pl* [ɪn'strʌkʃnz]	Anleitung, Anweisung(en)
to **highlight sth** ['haɪlaɪt]	etw hervorheben
prospect ['prɒspekt]	Aussicht, Perspektive
apprenticeship [ə'prentɪʃɪp]	Ausbildung, Lehre
working life [ˌwɜːkɪŋ 'laɪf]	Arbeitsleben
to **get down to business** [get ˌdaʊn tə 'bɪznəs]	zur Sache kommen
placement ['pleɪsmənt]	Praktikum
repetition [ˌrepə'tɪʃn]	Wiederholung
composition [ˌkɒmpə'zɪʃn]	Aufsatz
page 27	
to **participate (in sth)** [pɑː'tɪsɪpeɪt]	(an etw) teilnehmen, sich (an etw) beteiligen
competence ['kɒmpɪtəns]	Kompetenz
pen pal ['pen pæl]	Brieffreund/in
scheme [skiːm]	Programm, Projekt
range [reɪndʒ]	Bereich, Bandbreite, Palette
awkward ['ɔːkwəd]	unangenehm, peinlich
realisation [ˌriːəlaɪ'zeɪʃn]	Erkenntnis
page 29	
relation [rɪ'leɪʃn]	Beziehung, Verhältnis
findings *(pl)* ['faɪndɪŋz]	Ergebnisse
fellow student [ˌfeləʊ 'stjuːdnt]	Kommilitone/in
award [ə'wɔːd]	Auszeichnung, Preis
to **insult sb** [ɪn'sʌlt]	jdn beleidigen
threat [θret]	Bedrohung
pigeon ['pɪdʒɪn]	Taube
facade [fə'sɑːd]	Fassade
to **erect** [ɪ'rekt]	errichten
to **depict** [dɪ'pɪkt]	darstellen, aufzeigen
arch [ɑːtʃ]	Erz-
imperialist [ɪm'pɪəriəlɪst]	Imperialist/in
one-time ['wʌn taɪm]	ehemalig
to **be aimed at sth** [bi 'eɪmd ət]	auf etw zielen, auf etw gerichtet sein
to **remove sth** [rɪ'muːv]	etw entfernen, etw beseitigen
offensive [ə'fensɪv]	beleidigend, anstößig
colonialism [kə'ləʊniəlɪzəm]	Kolonialismus
after all [ˌɑːftər 'ɔːl]	schließlich (doch), immerhin
supremacist [suː'preməsɪst]	Rassist/in, Verfechter/in der Rassentrennung
exploitation [ˌeksplɔɪ'teɪʃn]	Ausbeutung, Abbau (von Rohstoffen)
flashpoint ['flæʃpɔɪnt]	Krisenherd
to **be centred on sth** ['sentəd ɒn]	sich um etw drehen, sich auf etw konzentrieren
protection [prə'tekʃn]	Schutz, Schutzvorkehrung
offence [ə'fens]	Straftat, Vergehen
union ['juːniən]	Gewerkschaft
to **be committed to sth** [kə'mɪtɪd]	sich für etw engagieren, für etw engagiert sein
creation [kri'eɪʃn]	Schaffung
association [əˌsəʊʃi'eɪʃn]	Verband, Vereinigung
to **be concerned (with sth)** [kən'sɜːnd]	sich (mit etw) befassen
page 30	
to **challenge sth** ['tʃælɪndʒ]	etw infrage stellen, etw anzweifeln
campus ['kæmpəs]	Gelände (z. B. Universität)
to **trigger sth** ['trɪɡə]	etw auslösen
to **alert sb** [ə'lɜːt]	jdn alarmieren
syllabus ['sɪləbəs]	Lehrplan
distressing [dɪ'stresɪŋ]	beunruhigend, beängstigend
advised [əd'vaɪzd]	angehalten
goal [ɡəʊl]	Ziel, Absicht
agenda [ə'dʒendə]	Agenda, Tagesprogramm
curb [kɜːb]	Einschränkung
previous ['priːviəs]	vorherig, früher
to **reserve** [rɪ'zɜːv]	reservieren, sich vorbehalten
to **deem** [diːm]	erachten, halten
ranking (list) ['ræŋkɪŋ]	Rangfolge, Rangliste
explicit [ɪk'splɪsɪt]	klar, deutlich, ausdrücklich
restriction [rɪ'strɪkʃn]	Beschränkung, Einschränkung
to **cater to sb/sth** ['keɪtə tə]	auf jdn/etw ausgerichtet sein, jdm/etw gerecht werden
resourced [rɪ'sɔːst]	ausgestattet
to **bustle** ['bʌsl]	wimmeln, wuseln
amiable ['eɪmiəbl]	liebenswürdig
to **be happy to do sth** ['hæpi tə]	etw gern tun
to **speak on the record** [ˌspiːk ɒn ðə 'rekəd]	sich offiziell äußern
external [ɪk'stɜːnl]	extern, auswärtig
fascist ['fæʃɪst]	faschistisch, Faschist
to **capture** ['kæptʃə]	einfangen, erfassen
contradiction [ˌkɒntrə'dɪkʃn]	Widerspruch
to **surround sth** [sə'raʊnd]	etw umgeben
spokesperson ['spəʊkspɜːsn]	Sprecher/in
to **heckle** ['hekl]	(durch Zwischenrufe) stören
prolonged [prə'lɒŋd]	anhaltend, andauernd
disruption [dɪs'rʌpʃn]	Störung, Behinderung, Unterbrechung
to **refer to sb/sth** [rɪ'fɜː tə]	jdn/etw erwähnen, sich auf jdn/etw beziehen
to **hack** [hæk]	hacken

agitation [ˌædʒɪ'teɪʃn]	Aufregung
tension ['tenʃn]	Spannung
to **pervade** [pə'veɪd]	durchdringen
to **silence sb** ['saɪləns]	jdn zum Schweigen bringen
lone [ləʊn]	einzeln, einsam
close [kləʊs]	nah, dicht, eng
physical ['fɪzɪkl]	körperlich, physisch
intimidation [ɪnˌtɪmɪ'deɪʃn]	Einschüchterung

page 31

storm in a teapot [ˌstɔːm ɪn ə 'tiːpɒt]	Sturm im Wasserglas
to **demand** [dɪ'mɑːnd]	fordern, verlangen, nachfragen
justice ['dʒʌstɪs]	Gerechtigkeit
at the expense of [ɪk'spens]	auf Kosten
veteran ['vetərən]	Veteran/in
to **resist sth** [rɪ'zɪst]	einer Sache widerstehen
notion ['nəʊʃn]	Vorstellung, Auffassung
cross (with) [krɒs]	sauer (auf)
outraged ['aʊtreɪdʒ]	entrüstet, empört
to **provoke** [prə'vəʊk]	provozieren
to **inspire** [ɪn'spaɪə]	inspirieren, anregen
appalling [ə'pɔːlɪŋ]	entsetzlich, schrecklich
censorship ['sensəʃɪp]	Zensur
to **confront sb with sb/sth** [kən'frʌnt]	jdn mit jdm/etw konfrontieren
exaggeration [ɪgˌzædʒə'reɪʃn]	Übertreibung
crisis, *pl* **crises** ['kraɪsɪs, 'kraɪsiːz]	Krise
legitimate [lɪ'dʒɪtɪmət]	legitim, berechtigt
underway [ˌʌndə'weɪ]	im Gange, angelaufen
removal [rɪ'muːvl]	Entfernung
defeat [dɪ'fiːt]	Niederlage
bland [blænd]	fade, fadenscheinig
consensus [kən'sensəs]	Konsens
communal [kə'mjuːnl]	Gemeinschafts-, gemeinschaftlich, gemeinsam
incarnation [ˌɪnkɑː'neɪʃn]	Inkarnation, Verkörperung
closed mind [ˌkləʊzd 'maɪnd]	Engstirnigkeit
tabloid (newspaper) ['tæblɔɪd]	Boulevardzeitung
topless ['tɒpləs]	oben ohne
lyrics *(pl)* ['lɪrɪks]	Liedtext
demand [dɪ'mɑːnd]	Forderung

page 32

to **reject** [rɪ'dʒekt]	ablehnen, zurückweisen
nostalgia [nɒ'stældʒə]	Nostalgie
racial ['reɪʃl]	rassisch, Rassen-
to **overwhelm sb** [ˌəʊvə'welm]	jdn überwältigen, jdn überschütten
to **honour** ['ɒnə]	ehren
outstanding [aʊt'stændɪŋ]	hervorragend, überragend, außergewöhnlich
to **defend sb/sth** [dɪ'fend]	jdn/etw verteidigen
to **criticize sb/sth** ['krɪtɪsaɪz]	jdn/etw kritisieren
statistical [stə'tɪstɪkl]	statistisch
reflective [rɪ'flektɪv]	nachdenklich, reflektierend
unreasonable [ʌn'riːznəbl]	unvernünftig, unangemessen
festive ['festɪv]	festlich
laid-back [ˌleɪd 'bæk]	lässig, entspannt
to **insist** [ɪn'sɪst]	darauf bestehen

page 33

advocacy (of) ['ædvəkəsi]	Eintreten (für), Befürwortung (einer Sache)
amendment [ə'mendmənt]	Ergänzung, Zusatz
constitution [ˌkɒnstɪ'tjuːʃn]	Verfassung
to **recreate** [ˌriːkri'eɪt]	wiederherstellen, nachbauen
to **constitute sth** ['kɒnstɪtjuːt]	etw darstellen, etw ausmachen, etw bilden
to **veer** [vɪə]	umschlagen, umspringen
standard-bearer ['stændəd beərə]	Bannerträger/in, Vorkämpfer/in
problematic [ˌprɒblə'mætɪk]	problematisch
provocateur [prəˌvɒkə'tɜː]	Provokateur/in
to **instigate** ['ɪnstɪgeɪt]	aufhetzen, anstacheln
to **anger sb** ['æŋgə]	jdn ärgern, jdn beleidigen
to **sue** [suː]	verklagen
on … grounds [graʊndz]	aufgrund von …
to **grandstand** ['grænstænd]	Effekthascherei betreiben
to **fundraise** ['fʌndreɪz]	eine Spendenaktion betreiben
to **gallivant** ['gælɪvænt]	herumziehen
reprise [rɪ'priːz]	Reprise, Wiederholung
to **fizzle out** [ˌfɪzl 'aʊt]	im Sande verlaufen, verpuffen
essentially [ɪ'senʃəli]	im Wesentlichen
to **advocate sth** ['ædvəkeɪt]	etw befürworten, etw verfechten
capitalist ['kæpɪtəlɪst]	kapitalistisch
marketplace ['mɑːkɪtpleɪs]	Markt
verdict ['vɜːdɪkt]	Urteil
administration [ədˌmɪnɪ'streɪʃn]	Verwaltung
out of bounds [ˌaʊt əv 'baʊndz]	verboten
pure [pjʊə]	rein, schier
to **resolve sth** [rɪ'zɒlv]	etw (auf)lösen
on behalf of [ɒn bɪ'hɑːf]	im Namen von, im Interesse von, für
outer ['aʊtə]	äußere/r/s
limit ['lɪmɪt]	Grenze, Begrenzung
to **mount sth** [maʊnt]	etw auf die Beine stellen
eventually [ɪ'ventʃuəli]	letztendlich, schließlich
to **handle sth** ['hændl]	mit etw umgehen, etw handhaben
reverence ['revərəns]	Verehrung
exclusively [ɪk'skluːsɪvli]	ausschließlich
to **take stock** [ˌteɪk 'stɒk]	Bestand aufnehmen, Bilanz ziehen
scholar ['skɒlə]	Gelehrte/r
forebear ['fɔːbeə]	Vorfahr/in
to **invoke** [ɪn'vəʊk]	zitieren, anführen
slur [slɜː]	Verleumdung
to **be bent on doing sth** [bent]	unbedingt etw tun wollen
to **undercut** [ˌʌndə'kʌt]	untergraben
to **wage** [weɪdʒ]	führen
controversy ['kɒntrəvɜːsi]	Kontroverse, Auseinandersetzung
case [keɪs]	Fall
versus ['vɜːsəs]	gegen
generational [ˌdʒenə'reɪʃənl]	Generations-
expectation [ˌekspek'teɪʃn]	Erwartung
conscientiousness [ˌkɒnʃi'enʃəsnəs]	Gewissenhaftigkeit
to **scoff at sb/sth** [skɒf]	über jdn/etw spotten
accustomed [ə'kʌstəmd]	gewöhnt, gewohnt
jarring ['dʒɑːrɪŋ]	misstönend
to **rankle sb** ['ræŋkl]	jdm zu schaffen machen
boundary ['baʊndri]	Grenze, Trennlinie

right-wing [ˌraɪt ˈwɪŋ] (politisch) rechts
to **violate sth** [ˈvaɪəleɪt] gegen etw verstoßen, etw verletzen

wise [waɪz] klug, weise
concerning [kənˈsɜːnɪŋ] betreffend, hinsichtlich
to **exclude sb/sth** [ɪkˈskluːd] jdn/etw ausschließen
footnote [ˈfʊtnəʊt] Fußnote
to **approve of sth** [əˈpruːv əv] etw gut finden
personnel manager [ˌpɜːsəˈnel mænɪdʒə] Personalchef/in
administrator [ədˈmɪnɪstreɪtə] Verwalter/in, Verwaltungsangestellte/r
ruling [ˈruːlɪŋ] Entscheidung
to **take into account** [ˌteɪk ɪntu əˈkaʊnt] berücksichtigen

page 35

motivational [məʊtɪˈveɪʃənl] motivierend, Motivations-
inspirational [ˌɪnspɪˈreɪʃnəl] anregend, inspirierend
expertise [ˌekspɜːˈtiːz] Fachkenntnisse, Sachverstand

spectacular [spekˈtækjələ] sensationell, spektakulär
marketing [ˈmɑːkɪtɪŋ] Marketing, Vermarktung
e-commerce [ˈiː kɒmɜːs] Onlinehandel
agency [ˈeɪdʒənsi] Agentur
to **found sth** [faʊnd] etw gründen
to **pioneer sth** [ˌpaɪəˈnɪə] etw zum ersten Mal anwenden, etw entwickeln

missionary [ˈmɪʃənri] Missionar/in
disruptive [dɪsˈrʌptɪv] (zer)störend, zerreißend
to **initiate sth** [ɪˈnɪʃieɪt] etw einleiten, etw initiieren
to **meet a demand** [ˌmiːt ə dɪˈmɑːnd] eine Nachfrage befriedigen
to **optimize** [ˈɒptɪmaɪz] optimieren

page 36

dystopian [dɪsˈtəʊpiən] dystopisch
utopian [juːˈtəʊpiən] utopisch
parallel [ˈpærəlel] Parallele
low-ranking [ˈləʊ ræŋkɪŋ] niederrangig
seemingly [ˈsiːmɪŋli] scheinbar, anscheinend
back number [ˈbæk nʌmbə] frühere Ausgabe
omniscient [ɒmˈnɪsiənt] allwissend
currently [ˈkʌrəntli] zurzeit
implementation [ˌɪmplɪmenˈteɪʃn] Umsetzung, Durchführung
to **invent sth** [ɪnˈvent] etw erfinden, sich etw ausdenken

to **prevent sb from doing sth** [prɪˈvent] jdn davon abhalten, etw zu tun
rebellion [rɪˈbeljən] Rebellion, Aufstand
rebellious [rɪˈbeljəs] aufsässig, rebellisch
chapter [ˈtʃæptə] Kapitel
nearness [ˈnɪənəs] Nähe
telescreen [ˈtelɪskriːn] Televisor
to **utter** [ˈʌtə] von sich geben, ausstoßen
dust [dʌst] Staub
mouthpiece [ˈmaʊθpiːs] Mundstück
spectacles *(pl)* [ˈspektəkəlz] Brille
to **unroll** [ʌnˈrəʊl] ausrollen
to **clip sth together** [klɪp] etw zusammenheften
cylinder [ˈsɪlɪndə] Zylinder
to **flop out of sth** [ˌflɒp ˈaʊt] aus etw herausplumpsen
pneumatic tube [njuːˌmætɪk ˈtjuːb] Rohrpost
right-hand [ˈraɪt hænd] rechte/r/s, auf der rechten Seite

cubicle [ˈkjuːbɪkl] Kabine
orifice [ˈɒrɪfɪs] Öffnung, Loch
oblong [ˈɒblɒŋ] länglich, rechteckig
slit [slɪt] Schlitz
disposal [dɪˈspəʊzl] Entsorgung
interval [ˈɪntəvl] Abstand
corridor [ˈkɒrɪdɔː] Flur, Gang
to **nickname** [ˈnɪkneɪm] (mit Spitznamen) nennen
memory [ˈmeməri] Gedächtnis, Erinnerung
destruction [dɪˈstrʌkʃn] Zerstörung, Vernichtung
scrap [skræp] Stück, Fragment
automatic [ˌɔːtəˈmætɪk] automatisch
flap [flæp] Klappe
whereupon [ˌweərəˈpɒn] woraufhin
to **whirl** [wɜːl] wirbeln
current [ˈkʌrənt] Strom
enormous [ɪˈnɔːməs] enorm, gewaltig
furnace [ˈfɜːnɪs] (Industrie-)Ofen, Hochofen
recess [ˈriːses] Nische, Winkel

page 37

to **execute sb** [ˈeksɪkjuːt] jdn hinrichten
to **erase** [ɪˈreɪz] (aus)löschen, ausradieren
abbreviated [əˈbriːvieɪtɪd] abgekürzt
jargon [ˈdʒɑːgən] Fachsprache, Jargon
internal [ɪnˈtɜːnl] intern
to **dial** [ˈdaɪəl] wählen (Telefon)
to **alter sth** [ˈɔːltə] etw (ab)ändern
to **rectify** [ˈrektɪfaɪ] berichtigen, richtigstellen
shortly [ˈʃɔːtli] bald, in Kürze
to **launch sth** [lɔːntʃ] etw starten
output [ˈaʊtpʊt] Leistung, Produktion
consumption [kənˈsʌmpʃn] Verbrauch, Konsum
goods *(pl)* [gʊdz] Waren, Güter
instance [ˈɪnstəns] Beispiel, Fall
gross [ˈgrɒs] grob
error [ˈerə] Fehler, Irrtum
plenty [ˈplenti] Überfluss
to **issue** [ˈɪʃuː] herausgeben
categorical pledge [kætəˌgɒrɪkl ˈpledʒ] kategorische Garantie
reduction [rɪˈdʌkʃn] Verringerung, Senkung
ration [ˈræʃn] Ration, Zuteilung
to **substitute for sb/sth** [ˈsʌbstɪtjuːt fə] jdn/etw ersetzen
correction [kəˈrekʃn] Korrektur
to **crumple sth up** [ˌkrʌmpl ˈʌp] etw zerknüllen
to **devour sth** [dɪˈvaʊə] etw verschlingen
flame [fleɪm] Flamme
to **assemble sth** [əˈsembl] etw wzusammenbauen, etw montieren
to **collate** [kəˈleɪt] zusammentragen, zusammenstellen
to **reprint** [ˌriːˈprɪnt] nachdrucken, neu auflegen
in its stead [ɪn ɪts ˈsted] an seiner/ihrer Stelle
continuous [kənˈtɪnjuəs] kontinuierlich, anhaltend
alteration [ˌɔːltəˈreɪʃn] Änderung
periodical [ˌpɪəriˈɒdɪkl] Zeitschrift
pamphlet [ˈpæmflət] Broschüre
documentation [ˌdɒkjumenˈteɪʃn] Dokumentation, Unterlagen
conceivably [kənˈsiːvəbli] möglicherweise
ideological [ˌaɪdiəˈlɒdʒɪkl] ideologisch
significance [sɪgˈnɪfɪkəns] Bedeutung, Stellenwert
day by day [ˌdeɪ baɪ ˈdeɪ] tagtäglich

page 38

up to **date** [ˌʌp tə ˈdeɪt]	aktuell, auf dem/den neuesten Stand
nor [nɔː]	auch nicht, ebenso wenig, noch
item [ˈaɪtəm]	Artikel, Gegenstand, Punkt (auf einer Liste)
on record [ɒn ˈrekɔːd]	aktenkundig, dokumentiert
alignment [əˈlaɪnmənt]	Ausrichtung
mistaken [mɪˈsteɪkən]	falsch, irrig
prophecy [ˈprɒfəsi]	Prophezeiung
to **bear (bore, borne)** [beə]	tragen, ertragen
to **recall sth** [rɪˈkɔːl]	etw zurückrufen
invariably [ɪnˈveəriəbli]	ausnahmslos
to **reissue** [ˌriːˈɪʃuː]	neu auflegen
to **deal with sth** [ˈdiːl wɪð]	mit etw umgehen
to **state** [steɪt]	erklären, feststellen
to **imply sth** [ɪmˈplaɪ]	etw andeuten, etw nahelegen
forgery [ˈfɔːdʒəri]	Fälschung
slip [slɪp]	Versehen, Irrtum
misprint [ˈmɪsprɪnt]	Druckfehler, Fehldruck
misquotation [ˌmɪskwəʊˈteɪʃn]	falsches Zitat
accuracy [ˈækjərəsi]	Genauigkeit
merely [ˈmɪəli]	bloß, nur
substitution [ˌsʌbstɪˈtjuːʃn]	Austausch, Auswechslung
to **make sth up** [ˌmeɪk ˈʌp]	etw erfinden, sich etw ausdenken
forecast [ˈfɔːkɑːst]	Vorhersage
claim [kleɪm]	Behauptung
quota [ˈkwəʊtə]	Kontingent, Quote
overfulfilled [ˌəʊvəfʊlˈfɪld]	übererfüllt
quarter [ˈkwɔːtə]	Quartal
astronomical [ˌæstrəˈnɒmɪkl]	astronomisch
barefoot [ˈbeəfʊt]	barfuß
recorded [rɪˈkɔːdɪd]	dokumentiert, erfasst
to **fade away** [ˌfeɪd əˈweɪ]	verblassen, verhallen
uncertain [ʌnˈsɜːtn]	unsicher

page 39

address [əˈdres]	Ansprache
to **dispose of sth** [dɪˈspəʊz əv]	etw beseitigen, etw entsorgen
to **slide (slid, slid)** [slaɪd]	rutschen, gleiten
delay [dɪˈleɪ]	Verzögerung
to **retain sb/sth** [rɪˈteɪn]	jdn/etw behalten, etw beibehalten, etw bewahren
anthology [ænˈθɒlədʒi]	Sammelband, Zusammenstellung, Anthologie
deed [diːd]	Tat
to **conflict with** [kənˈflɪkt]	in Widerspruch stehen mit

page 40

fellow [ˈfeləʊ]	Fellow (Mitglied eines akademischen Instituts)
to **nominate** [ˈnɒmɪneɪt]	nominieren
official [əˈfɪʃl]	Beamte/r, Funktionär/in
interference [ˌɪntəˈfɪərəns]	Einmischung, Beeinflussung
presidential election [prezɪˌdenʃl ɪˈlekʃn]	Präsidentschaftswahl
division [dɪˈvɪʒn]	Spaltung
supporter [səˈpɔːtə]	Anhänger/in
affiliated [əˈfɪlieɪtɪd]	verbunden mit, nahestehend
brutality [bruːˈtæləti]	Brutalität
to **craft** [krɑːft]	herstellen
to **mistrust** [ˌmɪsˈtrʌst]	misstrauen
to **heighten** [ˈhaɪtn]	erhöhen, steigern
arousal [əˈraʊzl]	Erregung
belief [bɪˈliːf]	Glaube, Überzeugung
to **brutalize sb** [ˈbruːtəlaɪz]	jdm brutal behandeln
civilian [səˈvɪliən]	Zivilist/in
to **be/get exposed to sth** [ɪkˈspəʊzd tə]	einer Sache ausgesetzt sein, mit etw in Berührung kommen
to **enhance sth** [ɪnˈhɑːns]	etw steigern, etw erhöhen
anger [ˈæŋgə]	Zorn, Wut
divide-and-conquer approach [dɪˌvaɪd ən ˈkɒŋkə əprəʊtʃ]	Teile-und-Herrsche-Herangehensweise
ambassador [æmˈbæsədə]	Botschafter/in
polarization [ˌpəʊləraɪˈzeɪʃn]	Polarisierung
unofficial [ˌʌnəˈfɪʃl]	inoffiziell
reportedly [rɪˈpɔːtɪdli]	Berichten zufolge
to **set up (set, set)** [ˌset ˈʌp]	planen, arrangieren
falsely [ˈfɔːlsli]	fälschlicherweise
voter fraud [ˈvəʊtə frɔːd]	Wahlbetrug
plenty of [ˈplenti əv]	eine Menge, viel
amplification [ˌæmplɪfɪˈkeɪʃn]	Verstärkung
to **investigate sth** [ɪnˈvestɪgeɪt]	etw ermitteln, etw untersuchen
to **cite sth** [saɪt]	etw zitieren, etw angeben
operative [ˈɒpərətɪv]	Funktionär/in
exclusive [ɪkˈskluːsɪv]	exklusiv, alleinig
to **hand over** [ˌhænd ˈəʊvə]	übergeben
transparency [trænsˈpærənsi]	Transparenz
media outlet [ˈmiːdiə aʊtlet]	Pressekanal
to **disguise** [dɪsˈgaɪz]	verschleiern, tarnen
authoritarian [ɔːˌθɒrɪˈteəriən]	autoritär
to **claim** [kleɪm]	behaupten
self-defence [ˌself dɪˈfens]	Selbstverteidigung

page 42

respondent [rɪˈspɒndənt]	Befragte/r

UNIT 2

page 43

to **empower sb** [ɪmˈpaʊə]	jdn stärken, jdn befähigen, jdn ermächtigen
empowerment [ɪmˈpaʊəmənt]	Befähigung, Ermächtigung

page 44

transition [trænˈzɪʃn]	Übergang, Umstellung
to **undergo sth** [ˌʌndəˈgəʊ]	sich einer Sache unterziehen
demographic [ˌdeməˈgræfɪk]	demographisch
to **widen** [ˈwaɪdn]	(sich) erweitern, verbreitern
thereby [ˌðeəˈbaɪ]	dabei, dadurch
to **drift apart** [ˌdrɪft əˈpɑːt]	auseinandertreiben
homogenous [ˌhɒməˈdʒiːniəs]	homogen
acceptance [əkˈseptəns]	Akzeptanz, Annahme
nevertheless [ˌnevəðəˈles]	trotzdem, dennoch
opposition [ˌɒpəˈzɪʃn]	Widerstand
economical [ˌiːkəˈnɒmɪkl]	wirtschaftlich, sparsam
displacement [dɪsˈpleɪsmənt]	Verdrängung
liberalization [ˌlɪbrəlaɪˈzeɪʃn]	Liberalisierung
to **cling to sth (clung, clung)** [klɪŋ]	sich an etw klammern, an etw festhalten
ethnic [ˈeθnɪk]	ethnisch, Volks-

metropolitan [ˌmetrə'pɒlɪtən]	großstädtisch, Ballungs-
poverty ['pɒvəti]	Armut
destabilization [ˌdiːˌsteɪbəlaɪ'zeɪʃn]	Destabilisierung
populist ['pɒpjəlɪst]	populistisch
to **be at stake** [ət 'steɪk]	auf dem Spiel stehen
to **embed sth** [ɪm'bed]	etw integrieren, etw einbetten, etw einbauen
retreat [rɪ'triːt]	Rückzug, Rückgang
regime [reɪ'ʒiːm]	Regime
ardent ['ɑːdnt]	glühend, begeistert
extremist [ɪk'striːmɪst]	Extremist/in
non-governmental organization (NGO) [ˌnɒn gʌvənˌmentl ˌɔːgənaɪ'zeɪʃn]	Nichtregierungsorganisation
to **be under assault** [ə'sɔːlt]	angegriffen werden
climate change ['klaɪmət tʃeɪndʒ]	Klimawandel
to **shift** [ʃɪft]	(sich) verlagern, (sich) verändern
distribution [ˌdɪstrɪ'bjuːʃn]	Verteilung, Versorgung
wealth [welθ]	Wohlstand, Reichtum
in the wake of sth [weɪk]	infolge von etw
populism ['pɒpjəlɪzəm]	Populismus
misogynist [mɪ'sɒdʒɪnɪst]	frauenfeindlich
supposedly [sə'pəʊzɪdli]	vermeintlich, angeblich
ceiling ['siːlɪŋ]	(Zimmer-)Decke
gender bias ['dʒendə baɪəs]	geschlechtsspezifische Diskriminierung
to **be on the wane** [weɪn]	schwinden
limelight ['laɪmlaɪt]	Rampenlicht (Mittelpunkt des Interesses)
cause [kɔːz]	Ursache, Grund, Anliegen
hardship ['hɑːdʃɪp]	Not, Elend, Entbehrung(en)
acute [ə'kjuːt]	akut
degradation [ˌdegrə'deɪʃn]	Abbau, Schädigung
entrepreneurial [ˌɒntrəprə'nɜːriəl]	unternehmerisch
consumerist society [kənˌsjuːmərɪst sə'saɪəti]	Konsumgesellschaft
to **rethink (rethought, rethought)** ['riːθɪŋk]	überdenken
as opposed to [əz ə'pəʊzd tə]	im Gegensatz zu, gegenüber
compassionate [kəm'pæʃənət]	mitfühlend, mitleidig
predecessor ['priːdɪsesə]	Vorgänger/in, Vorläufer/in
at your fingertips ['fɪŋgətɪps]	zur Hand

page 45

to **freelance** ['friːlɑːns]	freiberuflich arbeiten
restructuring [ˌriː'strʌktʃərɪŋ]	Umstrukturierung
tax [tæks]	Steuer
surgery ['sɜːdʒəri]	Operation
intense [ɪn'tens]	intensiv
devoted [dɪ'vəʊtɪd]	zugetan, ergeben
to **be willing to do sth** [bi 'wɪlɪŋ tə]	bereit sein, etw zu tun
sensible ['sensəbl]	vernünftig, sinnvoll
judgement ['dʒʌdʒmənt]	Urteilsvermögen, Urteil, Einschätzung
sympathy ['sɪmpəθi]	Sympathie, Mitgefühl

page 46

to **come up with sth** [ˌkʌm 'ʌp wɪð]	auf etw kommen, etw erbringen
to **bridge sth** [brɪdʒ]	etw überbrücken
time frame ['taɪm freɪm]	Zeitrahmen
roughly ['rʌfli]	ungefähr, etwa
birth [bɜːθ]	Geburt
epidemic [ˌepɪ'demɪk]	Epidemie, Seuche
cautious ['kɔːʃəs]	vorsichtig, zurückhaltend
unimpressed [ˌʌnɪm'prest]	unbeeindruckt
to **stick to sth (stuck, stuck)** ['stɪk tə]	bei etw bleiben, sich an etw halten
to **conform** [kən'fɔːm]	sich anpassen
loyal ['lɔɪəl]	treu, loyal
housewife ['haʊswaɪf]	Hausfrau
assertive [ə'sɜːtɪv]	durchsetzungsfähig
to **envision** [ɪn'vɪʒn]	sich vorstellen, vorhaben
affinity [ə'fɪnəti]	Affinität
prone to [prəʊn]	anfällig für
civic duty [ˌsɪvɪk 'djuːti]	bürgerliche Pflicht
loyalty ['lɔɪəlti]	Treue, Loyalität
self-oriented ['self ɔːriəntɪd]	selbstbezogen

page 47

to **desire sth** [dɪ'zaɪə]	(sich) etw wünschen, nach etw verlangen
individualized [ˌɪndɪ'vɪdʒuəlaɪzd]	individualisiert
exception [ɪk'sepʃn]	Ausnahme
span [spæn]	Spanne
footprint ['fʊtprɪnt]	Fußabdruck
desperate ['despərət]	verzweifelt
to **hang on to sth** [ˌhæŋ 'ɒn tə]	sich an etw festhalten, sich an etw festklammern
walkout ['wɔːkaʊt]	Streik, Arbeitsniederlegung
to **blast sth** [blɑːst]	etw vernichten, etw scharf kritisieren
to **declare sth** [dɪ'kleə]	etw verkünden, etw erklären
hilarious [hɪ'leəriəs]	ausgelassen, vergnügt
to **go viral** [ˌgəʊ 'vaɪrəl]	sich (im Internet) rasend schnell verbreiten
to **stand out** [ˌstænd 'aʊt]	auffallen, herausstechen
abstract ['æbstrækt]	abstrakt
constitutional [ˌkɒnstɪ'tjuːʃənl]	verfassungsrechtlich
security blanket [sɪ'kjʊərəti blæŋkɪt]	Rettungsdecke
of choice [əv 'tʃɔɪs]	seiner/ihrer/... Wahl
to **flag sth** [flæg]	auf etw aufmerksam machen
to **stockpile** ['stɒkpaɪl]	horten
anxiety (about/over) [æŋ'zaɪəti]	Angst, Sorge (wegen), Ängstlichkeit
emasculation [iˌmæskju'leɪʃn]	Entmannung
attachment [ə'tætʃmənt]	Bindung, Verbundenheit
to **stem from sth** [stem]	sich ableiten von etw
woe [wəʊ]	Kummer, Weh, Sorge
breadwinner ['bredwɪnə]	Brotverdiener/in
to **reclaim** [rɪ'kleɪm]	zurückfordern, zurückerobern
to **oppose sth** [ə'pəʊz]	gegen etw opponieren, sich gegen etw widersetzen
shooting ['ʃuːtɪŋ]	Schießerei

page 48

masculinity [ˌmæskju'lɪnəti]	Männlichkeit
resentment [rɪ'zentmənt]	Unmut, Groll, Ressentiment
predictor [prɪ'dɪktə]	Prädiktor, Anzeichen (für)

steadfast ['stedfɑːst]	standhaft
irate [aɪ'reɪt]	zornig, wütend
lesbian ['lezbiən]	Lesbe, lesbisch
to **mock sb** [mɒk]	sich über jdn lustig machen
mass shooter ['mɑːs ʃuːtə]	Amokschütze /-schützin
domestic violence [dəˌmestɪk 'vaɪələns]	häusliche Gewalt
to **confound** [kən'faʊnd]	verwirren
nuanced ['njuːɑːnst]	differenziert, nuanciert
to **bolster** ['bɒlstə]	unterstützen
to **abhor sth** [əb'hɔː]	verabscheuen, hassen
to **arm sb** [ɑːm]	jdn bewaffnen
to **dedicate sth to sb** ['dedɪkeɪt]	jdm etw widmen
savvy ['sævi]	versiert, gewieft, erfahren
to **cow sb** [kaʊ]	jdn einschüchtern
to **stump sb** [stʌmp]	jdn verwirren, jdn aus der Fassung bringen
to **hesitate** ['hezɪteɪt]	zögern
to **boo** [buː]	buhen
to **appeal to sb/sth** [ə'piːl tə]	an jdn/etw appellieren
rape [reɪp]	Vergewaltigung
rhetorical [rɪ'tɒrɪkl]	rhetorisch
posturing ['pɒstʃərɪŋ]	Getue
accordingly [ək'ɔːdɪŋli]	(dem)entsprechend
to **fail** [feɪl]	versagen, scheitern
abusive [ə'bjuːsɪv]	gewalttätig, missbrauchend
failure ['feɪljə]	Versagen, Ausfall, Zusammenbruch
well-funded ['wel fʌndɪd]	kapitalkräftig
to **call bullshit** [ˌkɔːl 'bʊlʃɪt]	Blödsinn reden
to **succeed** [sək'siːd]	erfolgreich sein, Erfolg haben
to **deserve sth** [dɪ'zɜːv]	etw verdienen
cue [kjuː]	Zeichen, Hinweis
insane [ɪn'seɪn]	irrsinnig, verrückt
babe [beɪb]	junges Mädchen
participation (in) [pɑːˌtɪsɪ'peɪʃn]	Teilnahme, Beteiligung (an)

page 49

protester [prə'testə]	Demonstrant/in
to **excel in/at sth** [ɪk'sel]	sich auszeichnen in etw, ausgezeichnet sein in etw
creativity [ˌkriːeɪ'tɪvəti]	schöpferische Begabung, Kreativität
to **ridicule sb** ['rɪdɪkjuːl]	jdn lächerlich machen
hatred ['heɪtrɪd]	Hass, Abscheu
to **fuel sth** ['fjuːəl]	etw anheizen, etw anfachen
irrational [ɪ'ræʃənl]	irrational

page 50

stubborn ['stʌbən]	störrisch
to **observe sth** [əb'zɜːv]	etw beobachten
ownership ['əʊnəʃɪp]	Besitz
tons of ['tʌnz əv]	jede Menge
corporation [ˌkɔːpə'reɪʃn]	Konzern
in charge of sth [ɪn 'tʃɑːdʒ]	verantwortlich für etw, (feder)führend bei etw
thrilled ['θrɪld]	begeistert
actually ['æktʃuəli]	eigentlich, wirklich, in der Tat
bay [beɪ]	Bucht
game changer ['geɪm tʃeɪndʒə]	Wendpunkt
not necessarily [nɒt ˌnesə'serəli]	nicht unbedingt
frugal ['fruːgl]	genügsam, bescheiden
to **scare sb** [skeə]	jdn erschrecken, jdm Angst machen
ride-hailing ['raɪd heɪlɪŋ]	einen Fahrdienst in Anspruch nehmen
brand [brænd]	Marke
to **redefine sth** [ˌriːdɪ'faɪn]	etwas neu umbenennen, etw neu definieren
preference ['prefrəns]	Präferenz, Vorliebe
to **purchase sth** ['pɜːtʃəs]	etw kaufen
manufacturer [ˌmænju'fæktʃərə]	Hersteller, Produzent

page 52

to **age** [eɪdʒ]	altern
to **tackle a problem** [ˌtækl ə 'prɒbləm]	ein Problem angehen
to **implement sth** ['ɪmplɪmənt]	etw einführen, etw umsetzen, etw einsetzen
feasibility [ˌfiːzə'bɪləti]	Machbarkeit, Umsetzbarkeit
impact ['ɪmpækt]	Einfluss, Auswirkung
to **come into account** [ˌkʌm ɪntə ə'kaʊnt]	in Betracht kommen
additional [ə'dɪʃənl]	zusätzlich

page 53

symposium [sɪm'pəʊziəm]	Fachkonferenz
participant [pɑː'tɪsɪpənt]	Teilnehmer/in
unjust [ˌʌn'dʒʌst]	ungerecht
to **enforce sth** [ɪn'fɔːs]	etw durchsetzen, etw vollstrecken
case study ['keɪs stʌdi]	Fallstudie
to **overcome sth (overcame, overcome)** [ˌəʊvə'kʌm]	etw bewältigen, über etw hinwegkommen
legislative ['ledʒɪslətɪv]	gesetzgebend, legislativ
failure to comply (with sth) [ˌfeɪljə tə kəm'plaɪ]	Nichteinhaltung (von etw)

page 54

despite [dɪ'spaɪt]	trotz
to **rate** [reɪt]	bewerten, beurteilen
MP (Member of Parliament) [ˌem 'piː, ˌmembər əv 'pɑːləmənt]	Parlamentsabgeordnete/r
day care ['deɪ keə]	Kinderbetreuung
parental leave [pəˌrentl 'liːv]	Elternzeit, Erziehungsurlaub
to **ensure sth/that** [ɪn'ʃʊə]	etw sicherstellen, dafür sorgen, dass
key team ['kiː tiːm]	Kernmannschaft
home carer ['həʊm keərə]	Hauspfleger/in
chair [tʃeə]	Vorsitzende/r
to **date back ...** [ˌdeɪt 'bæk]	... alt sein, stammen aus ...
on average [ɒn 'ævərɪdʒ]	im Durchschnitt
to **employ sb** [ɪm'plɔɪ]	jdn beschäftigen, jdn einstellen (Personal)
to **certify** ['sɜːtɪfaɪ]	zertifizieren
legislation [ˌledʒɪs'leɪʃn]	Gesetzgebung
head [hed]	Leiter/in, Chef/in
welfare ['welfeə]	Wohl, Wohlergehen
welfare ministry ['welfeə mɪnɪstri]	Sozialministerium
mandatory ['mændətəri]	verpflichtend, vorgeschrieben, obligatorisch
albeit [ˌɔːl'biːɪt]	wenngleich
certification [ˌsɜːtɪfɪ'keɪʃn]	Bescheinigung
to **comply with sth** [kəm'plaɪ wɪð]	etw erfüllen, etw befolgen, sich an etw halten

to **model sth on sth** ['mɒdl] etw einer Sache zum Vorbild nehmen, etw einer Sache nachbilden
to **assess sth** [ə'ses] etw beurteilen
occupation [ˌɒkju'peɪʃn] Beruf, Tätigkeit, Beschäftigung
agreement [ə'gri:mənt] Vereinbarung, Absprache
confederation [kənˌfedə'reɪʃn] Bund, Konföderation
to **stagger** ['stægə] staffeln
workforce ['wɜ:kfɔ:s] Erwerbstätige, Belegschaft
bottom-up [bɒtəm 'ʌp] von unten nach oben

page 55

delighted [dɪ'laɪtɪd] (sehr) erfreut, entzückt
to **eliminate sth** [ɪ'lɪmɪneɪt] etw eliminieren, etw unterbinden
trade union [ˌtreɪd 'ju:niən] Gewerkschaft
toolbox ['tu:lbɒks] Werkzeugkasten
in the aftermath of ['ɑ:ftəmæθ] in der Folge von
to **seize on sth** ['si:z ɒn] etw aufgreifen, etw ergreifen
subsequent ['sʌbsɪkwənt] nachfolgend, anschließend
to **boost sth** [bu:st] etw stärken, etw ankurbeln, einer Sache Auftrieb geben
proportion [prə'pɔ:ʃn] Anteil
to **shrink** [ʃrɪŋk] schrumpfen
chief executive [ˌtʃi:f ɪg'zekjətɪv] Hauptgeschäftsführer/in
satisfaction [ˌsætɪs'fækʃn] Zufriedenheit
morale ['mɒrəl] Moral, geistig-seelische Verfassung
crude [kru:d] roh, grob
toxic ['tɒksɪk] toxisch, giftig, Gift-
broad [brɔ:d] breit, weit
nursing ['nɜ:sɪŋ] Pflege, Krankenpflege
confidence ['kɒnfɪdəns] (Selbst-)Vertrauen, Zuversicht
to **justify sth** ['dʒʌstɪfaɪ] etw begründen, etw rechtfertigen
irrelevant [ɪ'reləvənt] irrelevant
entitlement (to) [ɪn'taɪtlmənt] Anspruch (auf)
impetus ['ɪmpɪtəs] Impuls, Anstoß

page 56

voluntary ['vɒləntri] freiwillig, ehrenamtlich
payment ['peɪmənt] (Be-)Zahlung
particularly [pə'tɪkjələli] besonders, insbesondere
to **compel** [kəm'pel] zwingen
managerial [ˌmænə'dʒɪəriəl] Management-, Führungs-

page 57

to **grade sb** [greɪd] jdn benoten
wordy ['wɜ:di] wortreich, langatmig
stylistic [staɪ'lɪstɪk] stilistisch
to **take care of sb** [teɪk 'keə əv] sich um jdn kümmern
to **enable sb to do sth** [ɪ'neɪbl] es jdm ermöglichen / jdn befähigen, etw zu tun
income ['ɪnkʌm] Einkommen
amount [ə'maʊnt] Menge, Ausmaß, Umfang
hesitant ['hesitənt] zögernd, zögerlich
employment [ɪm'plɔɪmənt] Anstellung, Beschäftigung, Arbeit
cohabitation [ˌkəʊˌhæbɪ'teɪʃn] Zusammenleben, (eheähnliche) Gemeinschaft
camaraderie [ˌkæmə'rɑ:dəri] Kameradschaft
conscription [kən'skrɪpʃn] Wehrpflicht, Wehrdienst, Einberufung
compulsory [kəm'pʌlsəri] Pflicht-, obligatorisch
recruit [rɪ'kru:t] Rekrut/in
to **be eligible (for sth / to do sth)** ['elɪdʒəbl] berechtigt sein (zu etw / etw zu tun)
rank [ræŋk] Dienstgrad
conscript ['kɒnskrɪpt] Wehrpflichtige/r
to **whittle sth down** ['wɪtl] reduzieren
to **come into force** [ˌkʌm ɪntə 'fɔ:s] in Kraft treten
dormitory ['dɔ:mətri] Wohnheim
to **combat sth** ['kɒmbæt] etw bekämpfen
commander [kə'mɑ:ndə] Kommandant/in, Anführer/in
operation [ˌɒpə'reɪʃn] Operation, Einsatz
intelligence gathering [ɪn'telɪdʒəns gæðərɪŋ] Informationsgewinnung
dependent on sth [dɪ'pendənt ɒn] von etw abhängig
defence minister [dɪ'fens mɪnɪstə] Verteidigungsminister/in
to **oust sth** [aʊst] etw verdrängen
once and for all [ˌwʌns ən fər 'ɔ:l] ein für allemal, endgültig
to **accompany sb/sth** [ə'kʌmpəni] jdn/etw begleiten, mit etw einhergehen

page 58

Lieutenant Colonel [lefˌtenənt 'kɜ:nl] Oberstleutnant
to **have sth in common** [ɪn 'kɒmən] etw (miteinander) gemeinsam haben
umbilical cord [ʌm'bɪlɪkl kɔ:d] Nabelschnur
urbanization [ˌɜ:bənaɪ'zeɪʃn] Verstädterung, Urbanisierung
respective [rɪ'spektɪv] jeweilig
to **position sb/sth** [pə'zɪʃn] jdn/etw platzieren, jdn/etw positionieren
corporate board [ˌkɔ:pərət 'bɔ:d] Unternehmensleitung
co-founder [ˌkəʊ'faʊndəl] Mitbegründer/in
donation [dəʊ'neɪʃn] Spende
downside ['daʊnsaɪd] Nachteil
to **align with sb** [ə'laɪn] sich mit jdm verbünden, sich auf jds Seite stellen
to **demonstrate sth** ['demənstreɪt] etw zeigen, etw demonstrieren
frankly ['fræŋkli] ehrlich (gesagt)
outgrowth ['aʊtgrəʊθ] Folge, Konsequenz
to **chair sth** [tʃeə] etw leiten (als Vorsitzende/r)
senior position ['si:niə pəzɪʃn] leitende Position
overall [ˌəʊvər'ɔ:l] allgemein, insgesamt, im Großen und Ganzen
to **comprise sth** [kəm'praɪz] etw umfassen, aus etw bestehen
inconsistent [ˌɪnkən'sɪstənt] inkonsequent
leadership ['li:dəʃɪp] Führung
admirable ['ædmərəbl] bewundernswert
to **extend** [ɪk'stend] sich erstrecken, sich ausweiten

to **settle a lawsuit** [ˌsetl ə ˈlɔːsuːt]	einen Rechtsstreit beilegen
contractor [kənˈtræktə]	Auftragnehmer/in
unemployment [ˌʌnɪmˈplɔɪmənt]	Arbeitslosigkeit
benefits *pl* [ˈbenɪfɪts]	Sozialleistungen
conscience [ˈkɒnʃəns]	Gewissen
care [keə]	Versorgung, Fürsorge
ordinary [ˈɔːdnri]	normal, gewöhnlich
ultimate [ˈʌltɪmət]	ultimativ, letzte/r/s
entire [ɪnˈtaɪə]	ganz, vollständig
portable [ˈpɔːtəbl]	tragbar, übertragbar
partnership [ˈpɑːtnəʃɪp]	Partnerschaft
affordable [əˈfɔːdəbl]	erschwinglich
health care [ˈhelθ keə]	Gesundheitswesen, medizinische Versorgung
to **figure sth out** [ˌfɪgər ˈaʊt]	etw (heraus)finden
gig economy [ˈgɪg ɪkɒnəmi]	Gig Economy (auf Freiberuflern basierendes Wirtschaftsmodell)
privacy [ˈprɪvəsi]	Privatsphäre
leak [liːk]	Leck, undichte Stelle
breach [briːtʃ]	Verletzung, Bruch
revelation [ˌrevəˈleɪʃn]	Enthüllung
to **invest in sth** [ɪnˈvest]	in etw investieren
to **restrict** [rɪˈstrɪkt]	einschränken, beschränken
CEO (Chief Executive Officer) [ˌsiː iː ˈəʊ]	Vorstandsvorsitzende/r
red envelope [ˈenvələʊp]	roter Umschlag (in dem Netflix Videos an US-Abonnenten zuschickte)
iteration [ˌɪtəˈreɪʃn]	Iteration, Wiederholung
to **subscribe to sth** [səbˈskraɪb tə]	etw abonnieren
convenience [kənˈviːniəns]	Bequemlichkeit, Annehmlichkeit, Komfort
in terms of … [ɪn ˈtɜːmz əv]	was … betrifft/angeht
affordability [əˌfɔːdəˈbɪləti]	Erschwinglichkeit, Bezahlbarkeit
to **clarify sth** [ˈklærəfaɪ]	etw klären, etw verdeutlichen
zip code *(AE)* [ˈzɪp kəʊd]	Postleitzahl
host [həʊst]	Gastgeber/in
to **distinguish** [dɪˈstɪŋgwɪʃ]	unterscheiden
inference [ˈɪnfərəns]	Schlussfolgerung

page 59

affirmative action *(AE)* [əˌfɜːmətɪv ˈækʃn]	Fördermaßnahmen (zugunsten benachteiligter Gruppen)
educational [ˌedʒuˈkeɪʃənl]	Erziehungs-, Bildungs-
lifetime [ˈlaɪftaɪm]	Lebenszeit
economics [ˌiːkəˈnɒmɪks]	Ökonomie, Wirtschaft(swissenschaft)

page 61

preselection [ˈpriːsɪlekʃn]	Vorauswahl
slim [slɪm]	schlank

page 62

to **have yet to do sth** [jet]	etw erst noch tun müssen
to **crest** [krest]	den Gipfel erreichen
sobering [ˈsəʊbərɪŋ]	ernüchternd
to **resonate** [ˈrezəneɪt]	widerhallen, mitschwingen
to **double down on sth** [ˌdʌbl ˈdaʊn]	etw signifikant erhöhen
base [beɪs]	Basis
to **wreck sth** [rek]	etw demolieren
to **remake (remade, remade)** [ˈriːmeɪk]	erneuern
remedy [ˈremədi]	Heilmittel
demise [dɪˈmaɪz]	Ende, Untergang
disproportionate [ˌdɪsprəˈpɔːʃənət]	unverhältnismäßig
blue-collar worker [ˈbluː kɒlə wɜːkə]	Arbeiter/in
to **back sb/sth** [bæk]	jdn/etw unterstützen
to **defeat sb** [dɪˈfiːt]	jdn besiegen, jdn schlagen
to **blunt** [blʌnt]	dämpfen, abschwächen
appeal [əˈpiːl]	Anziehungskraft, Reiz
vocation [vəˈkeɪʃn]	Berufung, Beruf
inequality [ˌɪnɪˈkwɒləti]	Ungleichheit
investment [ɪnˈvestmənt]	Anlage, Investition
to **bear sth out** [ˌbeər ˈaʊt]	etw bestätigen
to **narrow** [ˈnærəʊ]	sich verengen
affluent [ˈæfluənt]	wohlhabend
divergence [daɪˈvɜːdʒəns]	Divergenz, Auseinanderklaffen
wealthy [ˈwelθi]	wohlhabend, reich
scale [skeɪl]	Ausmaß, Umfang
hoard [hɔːd]	Vorrat, Schatz

page 63

stock exchange [ˈstɒk ɪkstʃeɪndʒ]	(Wertpapier-)Börse
return [rɪˈtɜːn]	Ertrag, Rendite
clustered [ˈklʌstəd]	geballt, angehäuft
disparity [dɪsˈpærəti]	Ungleichheit, Unterschied
percentage [pəˈsentɪdʒ]	Prozentsatz, Anteil
footloose [ˈfʊtluːs]	frei, ungebunden
shift [ʃɪft]	Verschiebung, Verlagerung, Wandel
earner [ˈɜːnə]	Verdiener/in
household [ˈhaʊshəʊld]	Haushalt
culprit [ˈkʌlprɪt]	Schuldige/r, Übeltäter/in
to **soar** [sɔː]	steigen
housing [ˈhaʊzɪŋ]	Wohnungsbau, Wohnungen
prosperous [ˈprɒspərəs]	florierend, wohlhabend
scarcity [ˈskeəsəti]	Mangel, Knappheit
occupational licensing [ˌɒkjuˌpeɪʃənl ˈlaɪsnsɪŋ]	Berufszulassung
to **punish sb** [ˈpʌnɪʃ]	jdn bestrafen
pension [ˈpenʃn]	Rente, Pension
perverse [pəˈvɜːs]	pervers, widersinnig
unintentional [ˌʌnɪnˈtenʃənəl]	unbeabsichtigt
to **exacerbate sth** [ɪgˈzæsəbeɪt]	etw verschärfen, etw verschlimmern
plight [plaɪt]	Notlage
employable [ɪmˈplɔɪəbl]	arbeitsfähig
capitalism [ˈkæpɪtəlɪzəm]	Kapitalismus
to **perpetuate sth** [pəˈpetʃueɪt]	etw aufrechterhalten
thriving [ˈθraɪvɪŋ]	florierend, blühend, gedeihend
to **accommodate sb** [əˈkɒmədeɪt]	jdn unterbringen
reciprocal [rɪˈsɪprəkl]	reziprok, gegenseitig
recognition [ˌrekəgˈnɪʃn]	(An-)Erkennung, (Wieder-)Erkennen
border [ˈbɔːdə]	Grenze
to **drain** [dreɪn]	entleeren, austrocknen
moribund [ˈmɒrɪbʌnd]	sterbend, todgeweiht
talented [ˈtæləntɪd]	begabt, talentiert
trouble [ˈtrʌbl]	Ärger, Problem(e)
to **erode** [ɪˈrəʊd]	erodieren, aushöhlen

obligation [ˌɒblɪˈgeɪʃn]	Pflicht, Verpflichtung
to **mount** [maʊnt]	(allmählich) wachsen
trade [treɪd]	Handel

page 64

subsidy [ˈsʌbsədi]	Subvention
patchy [ˈpætʃi]	fleckig, durchwachsen
to **lure sb/sth** [lʊə]	jdn/etw locken, ködern
automotive [ˌɔːtəˈməʊtɪv]	Automobil-
cluster [ˈklʌstə]	Cluster, Anhäufung
structural [ˈstrʌktʃərəl]	Struktur-, strukturell
funds *(pl)* [fʌndz]	Gelder, Fördermittel
funding [ˈfʌndɪŋ]	Finanzierung, Geldmittel
enterprise [ˈentəpraɪz]	Unternehmen
diffusion [dɪˈfjuːʒn]	Verbreitung, Streuung
to **sap** [sæp]	schwächen, untergraben
dynamism [ˈdaɪnəmɪzəm]	Tatendrang
bold [bəʊld]	kühn, mutig
to **set off sth** [ˌset ˈɒf]	etw in Gang setzen
scramble (for sth) [ˈskræmbl]	Gerangel (um etw)
mould [məʊld]	Form, Gussform
retailer [ˈriːteɪlə]	Einzelhändler/in
reform [rɪˈfɔːm]	Reform
aid [eɪd]	Hilfe
incentive [ɪnˈsentɪv]	Anreiz
mindset [ˈmaɪndset]	Mentalität, Denkweise
to **alleviate sth** [əˈliːvieɪt]	etw mildern, etw lindern
insufficient [ˌɪnsəˈfɪʃnt]	ungenügend, nicht ausreichend, unzureichend
to **assuage sb** [əˈsweɪdʒ]	jdn beschwichtigen
to **limit sth** [ˈlɪmɪt]	etw begrenzen, etw einschränken
to **concentrate on sth** [ˈkɒnsntreɪt ɒn]	sich auf etw konzentrieren
to **visualize sth** [ˈvɪʒuəlaɪz]	etw bildlich darstellen, etw visualisieren
outline [ˈaʊtlaɪn]	Umriss, Entwurf

page 65

sedentary [ˈsedntri]	sitzend
counterproductive [ˌkaʊntəprəˈdʌktɪv]	kontraproduktiv
to **hinder** [ˈhɪndə]	(be-, ver-)hindern, hemmen

page 66

life expectancy [ˈlaɪf ɪkspektənsi]	Lebenserwartung
divergent [divergent]	abweichend, auseinandergehend
competitive [kəmˈpetətɪv]	umkämpft, wettbewerbsintensiv
to **programme sth** [ˈprəʊgræm]	etw programmieren
implicit [ɪmˈplɪsɪt]	implizit, stillschweigend
bias [ˈbaɪəs]	Voreingenommenheit
perception [pəˈsepʃn]	Wahrnehmung
to **process sth** [ˈprəʊses]	etw (weiter)verarbeiten
oftentimes *(AE)* [ˈɒfntaɪmz]	oftmals
conscious [ˈkɒnʃəs]	bewusst
to **recircuit sth** [ˌriːˈsɜːkɪt]	etw neu verdrahten, etw neu verschalten
to **retrain** [ˌriːˈtreɪn]	umlernen, umschulen
schema [ˈskiːmə]	Schema
concerted [kənˈsɜːtɪd]	abgestimmt, konzertiert
intentional [ɪnˈtenʃənl]	absichtlich, beabsichtigt
to **cultivate sth** [ˈkʌltɪveɪt]	etw kultivieren
disarming [dɪsˈɑːmɪŋ]	entwaffnend
to **account for sth** [əˈkaʊnt fə]	etw ausmachen
flawed [flɔːd]	fehlerhaft, mangelhaft
colour-blind [ˈkʌlə blaɪnd]	farbenblind
to **evaluate sb/sth** [ɪˈvæljueɪt]	jdn/etw bewerten, jdn/etw beurteilen
to **override sth** [ˌəʊvəˈraɪd]	sich über etw hinwegsetzen, etw außer Kraft setzen
spoke [spəʊk]	Speiche
yolk [jəʊk]	Eigelb
to **anticipate sth** [ænˈtɪsɪpeɪt]	mit etw rechnen, etw erwarten
pairing [ˈpeərɪŋ]	Paarung
to **navigate** [ˈnævɪgeɪt]	navigieren, den Weg finden
unconscious [ʌnˈkɒnʃəs]	unbewusst, unterbewusst
to **rejig** *(BE)* **/ rejigger** *(AE)* **sth** [ˌriːˈdʒɪg]	etw ändern
to **accomplish sth** [əˈkʌmplɪʃ]	etw erreichen, etw leisten
to **spark** [spɑːk]	zünden, Feuer fangen
curiosity [ˌkjʊəriˈɒsəti]	Neugier
capacity [kəˈpæsəti]	Kapazität, Leistung
mental [ˈmentl]	geistig, psychisch, seelisch

page 67

for the sake of sth [seɪk]	einer Sache zuliebe, einer Sache wegen
parity [ˈpærəti]	Gleichheit, Parität

page 69

fiction [ˈfɪkʃn]	Belletristik, Prosa(literatur)
prompt [prɒmpt]	Stichwort, Vorgabe
for heaven's sake [fə ˌhevnz ˈseɪk]	um Himmels willen
be afflicted with sth [əˈflɪktɪd]	an etw leiden
to **break the news to sb** [ˌbreɪk ðə ˈnjuːz]	jdm eine Nachricht überbringen
veiled [veɪld]	verschleiert, versteckt
hint [hɪnt]	Hinweis
to **conceal** [kənˈsiːl]	verbergen
railroad *(AE)* [ˈreɪlrəʊd]	Eisenbahn
to **assure sb of sth** [əˈʃʊə]	jdm etw versichern
to **hasten** [ˈheɪsn]	eilen
to **forestall sb/sth** [fɔːˈstɔːl]	jdm/etw zuvorkommen
tender [ˈtendə]	zart
to **paralyze** [ˈpærəlaɪz]	lähmen
inability [ˌɪnəˈbɪləti]	Unfähigkeit
to **weep (wept, wept)** [wiːp]	weinen
abandonment [əˈbændənmənt]	Aufgabe, Verlassenheit
grief [griːf]	Kummer, Leid, Trauer
roomy [ˈruːmi]	geräumig
armchair [ˈɑːmtʃeə]	Sessel
exhaustion [ɪgˈzɔːstʃən]	Erschöpfung
to **haunt sb** [hɔːnt]	jdn heimsuchen
soul [səʊl]	Seele
aquiver [əˈkwɪvə]	erwartungsvoll, erregt
peddler [ˈpedlə]	Bettler/in
ware [weə]	Ware
faint [feɪnt]	schwach, matt
countless [ˈkaʊntləs]	zahllose, unzählige
sparrow [ˈspærəʊ]	Spatz, Sperling
to **twitter** [ˈtwɪtə]	zwitschern
eave [iːv]	Dachvorsprung, Dachrinne

page 70

patch [pætʃ]	Fleck, Bereich
to **pile** [paɪl]	sich häufen, sich auftürmen
upon [ə'pɒn]	auf
motionless ['məʊʃnləs]	regungslos
sob [sɒb]	Schluchzer
to **sob** [sɒb]	schluchzen
to **bespeak sth (bespoke, bespoken)** [bɪ'spiːk]	etw erkennen lassen, etw verraten
repression [rɪ'preʃn]	Verdrängung, Zurückdrängung
dull [dʌl]	dumpf, trüb
stare [steə]	starrer Blick
gaze [geɪz]	Blick
yonder ['jɒndə]	(dort) drüben
reflection [rɪ'flekʃn]	Reflexion, Nachdenken
suspension [sə'spenʃn]	Aussetzung
fearful ['fɪəfl]	ängstlich
subtle ['sʌtl]	subtil, fein
elusive [i'luːsɪv]	trügerisch, schwer definierbar
scent [sent]	Duft
bosom ['bʊzəm]	Busen
tumultuous [tjuː'mʌltʃuəs]	tumultartig, ungestüm
to **possess sth** [pə'zes]	etw besitzen
to **strive** [straɪv]	streben, bemüht sein
powerless ['paʊələs]	machtlos, unfähig
slender ['slendə]	schmal, feingliedrig
to **abandon oneself** [ə'bændən]	sich hingeben
parted lips [ˌpɑːtɪd 'lɪps]	geöffnete Lippen
under her breath [ʌndə hɜː 'breθ]	flüsternd
vacant ['veɪkənt]	leer, ausdruckslos
pulse [pʌls]	Puls
to **course** [kɔːs]	strömen
to **warm sth** [wɔːm]	etw erwärmen
monstrous ['mɒnstrəs]	monströs
joy [dʒɔɪ]	Freude
exalted [ɪg'zɔːltɪd]	überschwänglich
to **dismiss sth as sth** [dɪs'mɪs]	etw als etw abtun
trivial ['trɪviəl]	belanglos
to **fold sth** [fəʊld]	etw falten
save [seɪv]	außer
beyond [bɪ'jɒnd]	jenseits, außerhalb
procession [prə'seʃn]	Prozession
to **bend sth (bent, bent)** [bend]	etw beugen
persistence [pə'sɪstəns]	Beharrlichkeit, Ausdauer
to **impose sth on/upon sb** [ɪm'pəʊz]	jdm etw aufdrängen
fellow ['feləʊ]	Mit-, andere
creature ['kriːtʃə]	Geschöpf, (Lebe-)Wesen
intention [ɪn'tenʃn]	Absicht
cruel [kruːəl]	grausam, gemein
illumination [ɪˌluːmɪ'neɪʃn]	Erleuchtung

page 71

unsolved [ˌʌn'sɔːlvd]	ungelost
mystery ['mɪstri]	Rätsel, Rätselhaftigkeit
possession [pə'zeʃn]	Besitz, Besitztum
self-assertion [ˌself ə'sɜːʃn]	Selbstbehauptung
to **kneel** [niːl]	knien
keyhole ['kiːhəʊl]	Schlüsselloch
to **implore sb** [ɪm'plɔː]	jdn anflehen, jdn inständig bitten
to **beg** [beg]	flehen, eindringlich bitten
elixir of life [ɪˌlɪksə əv 'laɪf]	Lebenselixier
to **run riot** [ˌrʌn 'raɪət]	randalieren, toben
prayer [preə]	Gebet
shudder ['ʃʌdə]	Schauder, Zittern
at length [ət 'leŋθ]	schließlich
importunity [ˌɪmpə'tjuːnəti]	Aufdringlichkeit, beharrliches Drängen
feverish ['fiːvərɪʃ]	fiebrig, fieberhaft
triumph ['traɪʌmf]	Triumph
unwitting [ʌn'wɪtɪŋ]	ahnungslos, unwissentlich
goddess of victory [ˌgɒdes əv 'vɪktəri]	Siegesgöttin
to **clasp sth** [klɑːsp]	sich in etw einhaken, etw umklammern
waist [weɪst]	Taille
to **descend** [dɪ'send]	hinabsteigen
latchkey ['lætʃkiː]	Haustürschlüssel
travel-stained ['trævl steɪnd]	schmutzig von der Reise
composed [kəm'pəʊzd]	gelassen, beherrscht
grip-sack *(AE)* ['grɪp sæk]	Reisetasche
amazed [ə'meɪzd]	erstaunt
motion ['məʊʃn]	Bewegung
to **screen sb from sth** [skriːn]	jdn von etw abschirmen
piercing ['pɪəsɪŋ]	durchdringend

page 72

adjustment [ə'dʒʌstmənt]	Anpassung, Veränderung
casualty ['kæʒuəlti]	Verlust, Opfer
harsh [hɑːʃ]	brutal, harsch
to **retire** [rɪ'taɪə]	sich zurückziehen
exhausted [ɪg'zɔːstɪd]	erschöpft
stillness ['stɪlnəs]	Stille
occasional [ə'keɪʒənl]	gelegentlich
odd [ɒd]	gelegentlich
countenance ['kaʊntənəns]	Gesichtsausdruck, Fassung
suicide ['suːɪsaɪd]	Selbstmord
ill health [ˌɪl 'helθ]	schlechter Gesundheitszustand
luggage ['lʌgɪdʒ]	Gepäck

page 73

attitudinal [ˌætɪ'tjuːdɪnl]	einstellungsbezogen

page 74

cf. [ˌsiː 'ef]	vgl.
gallery walk ['gæləri wɔːk]	Galerierundgang
to **have relevance** ['reləvəns]	von Bedeutung sein
initially [ɪ'nɪʃəli]	anfangs, anfänglich

UNIT 3

page 75

ethics *(pl)* ['eθɪks]	Ethik
organic [ɔː'gænɪk]	biologisch, Bio-
battery-cage hen [ˌbætəri keɪdʒ 'hen]	Legebatteriehuhn
to **testify** ['testɪfaɪ]	aussagen
globe [gləʊb]	Globus
nuclear fission ['njuːkliə]	Kernspaltung

page 76

improvement in/to sth [ɪm'pruːvmənt]	Verbesserung bei etw
prevalent ['prevələnt]	(weit) verbreitet, vorherrschend
to **revolve** [rɪ'vɒlv]	rotieren, sich drehen
to **belittle sth** [bɪ'lɪtl]	etw herabsetzen, etw schmälern

humanity [hjuːˈmænəti]	Menschheit, Menschlichkeit
creation [kriˈeɪʃn]	Geschöpf
to **renounce sth** [riːˈnaʊns]	etw widerrufen
to **comprehend sth** [ˌkɒmprɪˈhend]	etw verstehen
rational [ˈræʃnəl]	vernünftig, vernunftbegabt
agent [ˈeɪdʒənt]	Akteur, Handelnde/r
end [end]	Zweck, Ziel
foundation [faʊnˈdeɪʃn]	Grundlage, Fundament
to **further sth** [ˈfɜːðə]	etw voranbringen
oppressive [əˈpresɪv]	unterdrückend, repressiv
discovery [dɪˈskʌvəri]	Entdeckung
to **exercise sth** [ˈeksəsaɪz]	etw ausüben
warfare [ˈwɔːfeə]	Krieg(führung)
unimaginable [ˌʌnɪˈmædʒɪnəbl]	unvorstellbar
in our day and age [ɪn ɑː ˌdeɪ ən ˈeɪdʒ]	in unserer Zeit, heutzutage
deployment [dɪˈplɔɪmənt]	Stationierung, Einsatz
technical [ˈteknɪkl]	technisch
collateral damage [kəˌlætərəl ˈdæmɪdʒ]	Kollateralschaden
to **rule out sth** [ˌruːl ˈaʊt]	etw ausschließen
grave [ɡreɪv]	erst, schwerwiegend
misconduct [ˌmɪsˈkɒndʌkt]	Fehlverhalten
lapse [læps]	Fehler, Aussetzer, Lapsus
harm [hɑːm]	Schaden
fabricated [ˈfæbrɪkeɪtɪd]	fingiert
clinical trial [ˌklɪnɪkl ˈtraɪəl]	klinische Prüfung, klinische Studie
to **harm sb** [hɑːm]	jdm schaden, jdn schädigen
patient [ˈpeɪʃnt]	Patient/in
to **neglect sb/sth** [nɪˈɡlekt]	jdn/etw vernachlässigen
safety regulations *(pl)* [ˌseɪfti reɡjuˈleɪʃnz]	Sicherheitsvorschriften, Arbeitsschutzvorschriften
radiation [ˌreɪdiˈeɪʃn]	Strahlung
to **jeopardize sb/sth** [ˈdʒepədaɪz]	jdn/etw gefährden
artificial intelligence [ɑːtɪˌfɪʃl ɪnˈtelɪdʒəns]	künstliche Intelligenz
involvement [ɪnˈvɒlvmənt]	Beteiligung
moreover [mɔːrˈəʊvə]	überdies, zudem
humankind [ˌhjuːmənˈkaɪnd]	(die) Menschheit
pest [pest]	Schädling
careless [ˈkeələs]	nachlässig
extensive [ɪkˈstensɪv]	ausgedehnt, erheblich
to **pose sth** [pəʊz]	etw darstellen
realm [relm]	Bereich
reproductive medicine [ˌriːprəˈdʌktɪv medsn]	Reproduktionsmedizin
blessing [ˈblesɪŋ]	Segen
to **conceive** [kənˈsiːv]	empfangen
questionable [ˈkwestʃənəbl]	fragwürdig, bedenklich
to **liberate sb** [ˈlɪbəreɪt]	jdn befreien
to **enslave sb** [ɪnˈsleɪv]	jdn versklaven
to **foresee sth** [fɔːˈsiː]	etw voraussehen, etw vorhersehen
ramification [ˌræmɪfɪˈkeɪʃn]	Auswirkung, Effekt

page 77

row [rəʊ]	Reihe, Zeile
sophisticated [səˈfɪstɪkeɪtɪd]	raffiniert, anspruchsvoll
greatly [ˈɡreɪtli]	erheblich
obsessed (with/by) [əbˈsest]	besessen (von)
to **dispute sth** [dɪˈspjuːt]	etw abstreiten, etw bestreiten
medical [ˈmedɪkl]	medizinisch
to **postulate sth** [ˈpɒstjuleɪt]	etw annehmen (These), etw postulieren
practitioner [prækˈtɪʃənə]	Fachmann/frau, Praktizierende/r
physicist [ˈfɪzɪsɪst]	Physiker/in
anatomist [əˈnætəmɪst]	Anatom/in
mathematician [ˌmæθəməˈtɪʃn]	Mathematiker/in
chemist [ˈkemɪst]	Chemiker/in, Drogist/in, Apotheker/in
naturalist [ˈnætʃrəlɪst]	Naturforscher/in

page 78

to **jumble sth up** [ˌdʒʌmbl ˈʌp]	etw (kunterbunt) durcheinanderwerfen
grid [ɡrɪd]	Schema, Tabelle
to **activate sth** [ˈæktɪveɪt]	etw aktivieren
cyanide [ˈsaɪənaɪd]	Zyanid
extermination camp [ɪkˌstɜːmɪˈneɪʃn kæmp]	Vernichtungslager
knowingly [ˈnəʊɪŋli]	wissentlich
apology [əˈpɒlədʒi]	Entschuldigung
to **shut down (shut, shut)** [ˌʃʌt ˈdaʊn]	schließen
surveillance [sɜːˈveɪləns]	Überwachung
to **prosecute sb** [ˈprɒsɪkjuːt]	jdn strafrechtlich verfolgen
theft [θeft]	Diebstahl
covert [ˈkʌvətli]	verdeckt
to **surveil sb/sth** [səˈveɪl]	jdn/etw überwachen
image loss [ˈɪmɪdʒ lɒs]	Imageverlust, Imageschaden
to **package sth** [ˈpækɪdʒ]	etw (ver)packen
canister [ˈkænɪstə]	Dose, Büchse
to **infiltrate sth** [ˈɪnfɪltreɪt]	etw infiltrieren
to **select sb/sth** [sɪˈlekt]	jdn/etw (aus)wählen
contribution [ˌkɒntrɪˈbjuːʃn]	Beitrag
to **be related to sth** [bi rɪˈleɪtɪd tə]	mit etw in Zusammenhang setzen
obvious [ˈɒbviəs]	offensichtlich, klar

page 79

impenetrable [ɪmˈpenɪtrəbl]	undurchdringlich
flesh [fleʃ]	Fleisch
to **be mindful of sth** [ˈmaɪndfl]	etw berücksichtigen, an etw denken
misuse [ˌmɪsˈjuːs]	Missbrauch
to **hold sb responsible** [həʊld rɪˈspɒnsəbl]	jdn zur Verantwortung ziehen
defence [dɪˈfens]	Verteidigung
honourable [ˈɒnərəbl]	achtbar, ehrenwert
coup [kuː]	Putsch
anatomy [əˈnætəmi]	Anatomie
unambiguously [ˌʌnæmˈbɪɡjuəsli]	eindeutig
profession [prəˈfeʃn]	Beruf
lawyer [ˈlɔːjə]	(Rechts-)Anwalt/Anwältin
custodian [kʌˈstəʊdiən]	Bewahrer/in
to **embody sth** [ɪmˈbɒdi]	etw verkörpern
arguably [ˈɑːɡjuəbli]	wohl
exultant [ɪɡˈzʌltənt]	frohlockend
gas chamber [ˈɡæs tʃeɪmbə]	Gaskammer
awful [ˈɔːfl]	furchtbar, schrecklich
scope [skəʊp]	Rahmen, Umfang

page 80

force [fɔːs]	Kraft, Macht
unintended [ˌʌnɪnˈtendɪd]	unbeabsichtigt
to **hire sb** [ˈhaɪə]	jdn engagieren, jdn anstellen
wholesale [ˈhəʊlseɪl]	pauschal, summarisch
at a remove [rɪˈmuːv]	mit Abstand
at sb's disposal [dɪˈspəʊzl]	zu jds Verfügung

UNIT WORD LIST

drawback ['drɔːbæk]	Nachteil
autonomy [ɔː'tɒnəmi]	Autonomie, Unabhängigkeit
to **cut corners** [kʌt 'kɔːnəz]	Abkürzungen nehmen, pfuschen
to **utilize sth** ['juːtəlaɪz]	etw einsetzen, etw (be) nutzen
amoral [ˌeɪ'mɒrəl]	amoralisch (sich über die Moral hinwegsetzend)
to **steer sth** [stɪə]	etw steuern, etw lenken
morality [mə'ræləti]	Moral (Wertesystem)
reductionist [rɪ'dʌkʃənɪst]	reduktionistisch
code [kəʊd]	Code, Kodex, Regeln
to **redraft sth** [ˌriː'drɑːft]	etw neu entwerfen
to **redesign sth** [ˌriːdɪ'zaɪn]	etw überarbeiten, etw umgestalten
in-depth [ˌɪn 'depθ]	ausführlich
valuable ['væljuəbl]	wertvoll
unpleasant [ʌn'pleznt]	unangenehm, unschön
vested interest [ˌvestɪd 'ɪntrəst]	Eigennutz, persönliches Interesse
rightfully ['raɪtfəli]	rechtmäßig, zu Recht
to **invade sth** [ɪn'veɪd]	in etw eindringen
part and parcel [ˌpɑːt ən 'pɑːsl]	fester Bestandteil
modernity [mə'dɜːnəti]	Moderne
flaw [flɔː]	Schwachstelle, Fehler, Mangel
to **flourish** ['flʌrɪʃ]	florieren, blühen, gedeihen
capable of sth ['keɪpəbl əv]	zu etw fähig, zu etw imstande
alike [ə'laɪk]	gleichermaßen, in gleicher Weise
will [wɪl]	Wille
page 81	
to **adhere to sth** [əd'hɪə]	etw einhalten
producer [prə'djuːsə]	Produzent/in
coverage ['kʌvərɪdʒ]	Berichterstattung, Behandlung (eines Themas)
abhorrent [əb'hɒrənt]	abscheulich
to **advance sth** [əd'vɑːns]	etw verbessern, etw voranbringen
integral part [ˌɪntɪgrəl 'pɑːt]	fester Bestandteil
page 82	
permissible [pə'mɪsəbl]	zulässig
laureate ['lɒriət]	Preisträger/in
apace [ə'peɪs]	rasch
backdrop ['bækdrɒp]	Hintergrund
to **deliberate** [dɪ'lɪbəreɪt]	sich beraten, reiflich durchdenken
intergenerational [ˌɪntəˌdʒenə'reɪʃənl]	zwischen den Generationen
philosophical [ˌfɪlə'sɒfɪkl]	philosophisch
to **back sth up** [ˌbæk 'ʌp]	etw untermauern, etw bekräftigen, etw belegen
molecule ['mɒlɪkjuːl]	Molekül
to **synthesize sth** ['sɪnθəsaɪz]	etw synthetisieren, etw künstlich herstellen
equation [ɪ'kweɪʒn]	Gleichung
inventor [ɪn'ventə]	Erfinder/in
core [kɔː]	Kern-, Haupt-
declaration [ˌdeklə'reɪʃn]	Erklärung
human rights *(pl)* [ˌhjuːmən 'raɪts]	Menschenrechte
to **progress** [prə'gres]	vorankommen, weiterkommen
prosperity [prɒ'sperəti]	Wohlstand
faith [feɪθ]	Glaube, Vertrauen
limitless ['lɪmɪtləs]	unbegrenzt
capability [ˌkeɪpə'bɪləti]	Fähigkeit, Potenzial
miscalculation [ˌmɪskælkju'leɪʃn]	Fehleinschätzung
vigorous ['vɪgərəs]	kräftig, energisch
reasonable ['riːznəbl]	vernünftig
to **conquer sth** ['kɒŋkə]	etw bezwingen, sich etw unterwerfen
sentiment ['sentɪmənt]	Geisteshaltung
physician [fɪ'zɪʃn]	Arzt/Ärztin
routed ['ruːtɪd]	verwurzelt
objectivity [ˌɒbdʒek'tɪvəti]	Objektivität
reliability [rɪˌlaɪə'bɪləti]	Zuverlässigkeit, Verlässlichkeit
sociologist [ˌsəʊsi'ɒlədʒɪst]	Soziologe/-in
economist [ɪ'kɒnəmɪst]	Volkswirt/in, Wirtschaftswissenschaftler/in
stance [stæns]	Haltung, Einstellung
epistemic [ˌepɪ'stiːmɪk]	epistemisch, erkenntnistheoretisch
verifiable ['verɪfaɪəbl]	verifizierbar, beweisbar
to **question sth** ['kwestʃən]	etw infrage stellen
along with [ə'lɒŋ wɪð]	(zusammen) mit, neben
pollution [pə'luːʃn]	(Umwelt-)Verschmutzung
to **dwindle** ['dwɪndl]	schwinden, nachlassen
overpopulation [ˌəʊvəˌpɒpju'leɪʃn]	Überbevölkerung
domain [də'meɪn]	Domäne, Bereich, Gebiet
humanities *(pl)* [hjuː'mænətiz]	Geisteswissenschaften
to **persist** [pə'sɪst]	fortbestehen
worlds apart [ˌwɜːldz ə'pɑːt]	getrennte Welten
to **seek out sth (sought, sought)** [siːk]	etw ausfindig machen
reunification [ˌriːˌjuːnɪfɪ'keɪʃn]	Wiedervereinigung
assistance [ə'sɪstəns]	Hilfe, Unterstützung
prerequisite [ˌpriː'rekwəzɪt]	erforderlich, notwendig
sibling ['sɪblɪŋ]	Geschwister
to **disrupt sth** [dɪs'rʌpt]	etw trennen
inquiry [ɪn'kwaɪəri]	Untersuchung, Recherche
to **wither (away)** ['wɪðə]	verkümmern
to **put sth forward** [ˌpʊt 'fɔːwəd]	(Argument/Vorschlag) vorbringen, etw zur Diskussion stellen
well-being ['wel biːɪŋ]	Wohl(befinden)
nomination [ˌnɒmɪ'neɪʃn]	Nominierung
genetically modified [dʒəˌnetɪkli 'mɒdɪfaɪd]	genetisch verändert
crop [krɒp]	Nutzpflanze, Feldfrucht
laboratory [lə'bɒrətri]	Labor
premised ['premɪst]	vorausgesetzt
code of conduct [ˌkəʊd əv 'kɒndʌkt]	Verhaltenskodex
oath [əʊθ]	Eid
guiding ethical principle [ˌgaɪdɪŋ ˌeθɪkl 'prɪnsəpl]	ethische Leitlinie
ethics commission ['eθɪks kəmɪʃn]	Ethikkommission
trial ['traɪəl]	Untersuchung, Studie
to **lack sth** [læk]	etw nicht haben
safeguard ['seɪfgɑːd]	Schutzmaßnahme
to **remedy sth** ['remədi]	etw abhelfen
to **conceive sth** [kən'siːv]	etw konzipieren
addendum [ə'dendəm]	Zusatz, Ergänzung
compulsion [kəm'pʌlʃn]	Zwang, Druck
tendency ['tendənsi]	Neigung, Tendenz
intra- ['ɪntrə]	-intern
selfishness ['selfɪʃnəs]	Egoismus, Selbstsucht

inter- ['ɪntə]	zwischen-
savannah [sə'vænə]	Savanne
genetic [dʒə'netɪk]	genetisch
extinction [ɪk'stɪŋkʃn]	Vernichtung, Ausrottung, Aussterben
apocalyptic [əˌpɒkə'lɪptɪk]	apokalyptisch
to **make a mess of things** [mes]	es vermasseln, es verpfuschen
evolutionary [ˌiːvə'luːʃənri]	evolutionär, entwicklungsgeschichtlich

page 83

column ['kɒləm]	Spalte
to **emit sth** [ɪ'mɪt]	etw emittieren, etw ausstoßen, etw abstrahlen
particulates *(pl)* [pɑː'tɪkjələts]	Feinstaub
senior ['siːniə]	Vorgesetzte/r
to **let sb off (let, let)** [ˌlet 'ɒf]	jdm (ein Strafe) erlassen

page 85

verbal ['vɜːbl]	verbal, sprachlich

page 86

venture capitalist ['ventʃə kæpɪtlɪst]	Risikokapitalgeber/in
to **sustain sth** [sə'steɪn]	etw (aufrecht)erhalten, etw (unter)stützen
to **uphold sth (upheld, upheld)** [ʌp'həʊld]	etw aufrechterhalten, etw hochhalten
data collection ['deɪtə kəlekʃn]	Datensammlung
entrepreneur [ˌɒntrəprə'nɜː]	Unternehmer/in
addiction (to) [ə'dɪkʃn]	Sucht (nach), Abhängigkeit (von)
to **monitor sth** ['mɒnɪtə]	etw überwachen
third-party [ˌθɜːd 'pɑːti]	von dritter Seite
regulatory agency [ˌregjələtəri 'eɪdʒənsi]	Aufsichtsbehörde, Regulierungsagentur
to **coin sth** [kɔɪn]	etw prägen
to **advise against sth** [ədˌvaɪz ə'genst]	von etw abraten

page 87

to **hijack sth** ['haɪdʒæk]	etw kapern
dystopia [dɪs'təʊpiə]	Dystopie, Schreckensvision
to **brand sb (as) sth** [brænd]	jdn als etw abstempeln
ubiquitous [juː'bɪkwɪtəs]	allgegenwärtig
to **be unaware of sth** [ˌʌnə'weə]	sich einer Sache nicht bewusst sein
to **revere sb** [rɪ'vɪə]	jdn verehren
to **go rogue** [rəʊg]	abtrünnig werden
of sorts [əv ' sɔːts]	so etwas wie
vast [vɑːst]	riesig, sehr groß
to **accumulate sth** [ə'kjuːmjəleɪt]	etw ansammeln, etw anhäufen
urgent ['ɜːdʒənt]	dringend
lawmaker ['lɔːmeɪkə]	Abgeordnete/r
to **campaign for/against sth** [kæm'peɪn]	sich für/gegen etw einsetzen
to **circulate sth** ['sɜːkjəleɪt]	etw verschicken
memo ['meməʊ]	Memo, Notiz
distraction [dɪ'strækʃn]	Ablenkung
to **strike a chord with sb (struck, struck)** [ˌstraɪk ə 'kɔːd]	bei jdm auf Anklang stoßen
to **reward sb** [rɪ'wɔːd]	jdn belohnen
impressive [ɪm'presɪv]	beeindruckend, eindrucksvoll
ethicist [ˌeθɪ'sɪst]	Ethiker/in
marginal ['mɑːdʒɪnl]	marginal, geringfügig
to **exploit sth** [ɪk'splɔɪt]	etw ausnutzen
to **deprive sb of sth** [dɪ'praɪv]	jdn etw berauben, jdm etw vorenthalten
addictive [ə'dɪktɪv]	süchtig machend

page 88

snap streak ['snæp striːk]	Schnappschuss-Serie, „Flamme“ (Snapchat)
tailored ['teɪləd]	maßgeschneidert
to **leak sth** [liːk]	etw durchsickern lassen, etw durchstechen
insecure [ˌɪnsɪ'kjʊə]	unsicher
worthless ['wɜːθləs]	wertlos
boost [buːst]	(schnelle) Steigerung, Auftrieb
vulnerability [ˌvʌlnərə'bɪləti]	Empfindlichkeit, Schwachstelle
to **keep sb hooked** [ˌkiːp 'hʊkt]	jdn süchtig halten, jdn bei der Stange halten
vulnerable ['vʌlnərəbl]	verletzlich, verwundbar
to **be in need of sth** [ɪn 'niːd]	etw brauchen, etw benötigen
approval [ə'pruːvl]	Bestätigung, Anerkennung
to **stumble across sth** [ˌstʌmbl ə'krɒs]	zufällig über etw stolpern
notification [ˌnəʊtɪfɪ'keɪʃn]	Benachrichtigung, Mitteilung, Bescheid
seductive [sɪ'dʌktɪv]	verführerisch
psychological [ˌsaɪkə'lɒdʒɪkl]	psychologisch
susceptibility [səˌseptə'bɪləti]	Empfänglichkeit, Anfälligkeit
gambling ['gæmbliŋ]	Glücksspiel
compulsive [kəm'pʌlsɪv]	zwanghaft
variable ['veəriəbl]	variabel, wechselnd
reward [rɪ'wɔːd]	Belohnung
avalanche ['ævəlɑːnʃ]	Lawine
pull-to-refresh [ˌpʊl tə rɪ'freʃ]	Pull to Refresh (Ziehen zum Aktualisieren)
whereby [weə'baɪ]	wobei
to **swipe** [swaɪp]	wischen (auf dem Touchscreen)
disenchanted [ˌdɪsɪn'tʃɑːntɪd]	desillusioniert
mission ['mɪʃn]	Auftrag, Mission
distorted [dɪ'stɔːtɪd]	entstellt
advent (of sth) ['ædvent]	Ankunft, Beginn (einer Sache)
to **raise the stakes** [ˌreɪz ðə 'steɪks]	den Einsatz erhöhen
arms race ['ɑːmz reɪs]	Wettrüsten
to **assert sth** [ə'sɜːt]	etw behaupten
merit ['merɪt]	Verdienst, Wert, Leistung
tobacco [tə'bækəʊ]	Tabak
drug dealer ['drʌg diːlə]	Drogenhändler/in
to **oversee sth (oversaw, overseen)** [ˌəʊvə'siː]	etw leiten
chief operating officer [ˌtʃiːf ˌɒpəreɪtɪŋ 'ɒfɪsə]	leitende/r Geschäftsführer/in
to **come in handy** [ˌkʌm ɪn 'hændi]	sich als nützlich erweisen, gelegen kommen

page 89

bidder ['bɪdə]	Bieter/in

UNIT WORD LIST

handful ['hændfʊl]	Handvoll
to **emulate sth** ['emjuleɪt]	etw nachbilden
harmful ['hɑːmfl]	schädlich
immoral [ɪ'mɒrəl]	unmoralisch
granular information [ˌɡrænjələ ɪnfə'meɪʃn]	detaillierte Informationen
disappointment [ˌdɪsə'pɔɪntmənt]	Enttäuschung

page 90

epic ['epɪk]	episch, unglaublich
net neutrality [ˌnet njuː'træləti]	Netzneutralität
merchant ['mɜːtʃənt]	Händler/in
abyss [ə'bɪs]	Abgrund
clickbait ['klɪkbeɪt]	Klickfang, Klickköder
subscription [səb'skrɪpʃn]	Abonnement
walled [wɔːld]	ummauert, eingefriedet
socialization [ˌsəʊʃəlaɪ'zeɪʃn]	Sozialisierung
delivery [dɪ'lɪvəri]	Lieferung
revenue ['revənjuː]	Einkünfte, Einnahmen
one way or another [ˌwʌn weɪ ɔːr ən'ʌðə]	so oder so, auf die eine oder andere Art
Securities and Exchange Commission [sɪˌkjʊərətiz ən ɪks'tʃeɪndʒ kəˌmɪʃn]	Börsenaufsichtsbehörde (USA)
founder ['faʊndə]	Gründer/in
idealistic [ˌaɪdiə'lɪstɪk]	idealistisch
appendix [ə'pendɪks]	Anhang (am Ende eines Buches)
to **corrupt sth** [kə'rʌpt]	etw verderben, etw korrumpieren
to **keep sb/sth at bay** [ət 'beɪ]	jdn/etw fernhalten, sich jdn/etw vom Leib halten
payload ['peɪləʊd]	Nutzdaten
to **degrade sth** [dɪ'ɡreɪd]	etw abbauen
cautionary tale ['kɔːʃənəri teɪl]	abschreckendes Beispiel
primarily [praɪ'merəli]	vorrangig, hauptsächlich
mental state [ˌmentl 'steɪt]	psychische Verfassung
fishing hook ['fɪʃɪŋ hʊk]	Angelhaken
marriage counselling ['mærɪdʒ kaʊnsəlɪŋ]	Eheberatung
micromental ['maɪkrəmentl]	mikromental
primacy of sth ['praɪməsi]	Primat von etw
to **cheat on sb** [tʃiːt]	jdn betrügen
to **shorten sth** ['ʃɔːtn]	etw (ver)kürzen

page 91

humane [hjuː'meɪn]	human, menschenwürdig
common sense [ˌkɒmən 'sens]	gesunder Menschenverstand
to **beware of sth** [bɪ'weər əv]	sich vor etw hüten, etw vermeiden
marriage proposal ['mærɪdʒ prəpəʊzl]	Heiratsantrag

page 92

arable farming [ˌærəbl 'fɑːmɪŋ]	Ackerbau
powerhouse ['paʊəhaʊs]	treibende Kraft
poultry ['pəʊltri]	Geflügel
fishery ['fɪʃəri]	Fischerei
forestry ['fɒrɪstri]	Forstwirtschaft
biofuel [ˌbaɪəʊ'fjuːəl]	Biokraftstoff
to **decrease** [dɪ'kriːs]	abnehmen, zurückgehen
livestock ['laɪvstɒk]	Vieh
to **domesticate sth** [də'mestɪkeɪt]	etw zähmen, etw domestizieren
respectively [rɪ'spektɪvli]	beziehungsweise
yield [jiːld]	Ertrag
cultivation [ˌkʌltɪ'veɪʃn]	Kultivierung, Anbau
fertilizer ['fɜːtəlaɪzə]	Dünger, Düngemittel
to **rear sb/sth** [rɪə]	jdn/etw aufziehen
commodity [kə'mɒdəti]	Erzeugnis, Ware
to **forbid sth (forbade, forbidden)** [fə'bɪd]	etw verbieten, etw untersagen

page 93

to **propose sth** [prə'pəʊz]	etw vorschlagen, etw unterbreiten, etw darlegen
cruelty ['kruːəlti]	Grausamkeit
beyond [bɪ'jɒnd]	darüber hinaus
niche [niːʃ, nɪtʃ]	Nische
to **contend** [kən'tend]	behaupten
shrouded [ʃraʊdɪd]	verschleiert, eingehüllt
mythology [mɪ'θɒlədʒi]	Mythologie, Sagenwelt
myth [mɪθ]	Mythos, Märchen
inefficient [ˌɪnɪ'fɪʃnt]	ineffizient, unwirtschaftlich
wasteful ['weɪstfl]	verschwenderisch
surface ['sɜːfɪs]	Oberfläche
plausible ['plɔːzəbl]	plausibel, glaubwürdig
to **cram sth into sth** [kræm]	etw in etw einpferchen
confinement [kən'faɪnmənt]	Gefangenschaft
to **overlook sth** [ˌəʊvə'lʊk]	etw übersehen
acreage ['eɪkərɪdʒ]	Anbaufläche
scarce [skeəs]	knapp, rar
arable ['ærəbl]	urbar, kultivierbar
deforestation [diːˌfɒrɪ'steɪʃn]	Waldzerstörung
soil erosion ['sɔɪl ɪrəʊʒn]	Bodenerosion
marine [mə'riːn]	Meeres-
soybean *(AE)* ['sɔɪbiːn]	Sojabohne
trawling net ['trɔːlɪŋ net]	Schleppnetz

page 94

soil [sɔɪl]	Erde, Boden
to **bail sb out** [ˌbeɪl 'aʊt]	jdm aus der Patsche helfen
the likes of sth [laɪks]	solche wie etw
to **raze sth** [reɪz]	etw zerstören
plantation [plæn'teɪʃn]	Anpflanzung, Plantage
habitat ['hæbɪtæt]	natürlicher Lebensraum
to **strip sth away** [ˌstrɪp ə'weɪ]	etw wegräumen
quantity ['kwɒntəti]	Menge, Quantität
to **scoop up sth** [ˌskuːp 'ʌp]	etw an Bord holen
species, *pl* **species** ['spiːʃiːz]	Art (Biologie)
to **starve** [stɑːv]	verhungern
resistant (to sth) [rɪ'zɪstənt]	resistent (gegen etw)
superbugs ['suːpəbʌɡz]	Superkeime
treatable ['triːtəbl]	behandelbar
unregulated [ʌn'reɡjuleɪtɪd]	ungeregelt
to **prescribe sth** [prɪ'skraɪb]	etw verschreiben
to **administer sth** [əd'mɪnɪstə]	etw anwenden
compassion [kəm'pæʃən]	Mitgefühl
regenerative [rɪ'dʒenərətɪv]	regenerativ, erneuerbar
rotational grazing [rəʊˌteɪʃənl 'ɡreɪzɪŋ]	Rotationsweiden
groundswell ['ɡraʊndswel]	starke öffentliche Bewegung
civil society [ˌsɪvl sə'saɪəti]	Zivilgesellschaft
sustainability [səˌsteɪnə'bɪləti]	Nachhaltigkeit

regeneration [rɪˌdʒenə'reɪʃn]	Wiederherstellung, Erneuerung
notable ['nəʊtəbl]	bedeutend, bemerkenswert
to **finance sth** ['faɪnæns]	etw finanzieren
appointee [əˌpɔɪn'tiː]	Benannte/r
appointment [ə'pɔɪntmənt]	Ernennung, Berufung
campaigner [kæm'peɪnə]	Aktivist/in
editorial [ˌedɪ'tɔːriəl]	Leitartikel

page 95

to **be opposed to sth** [bi ə'pəʊzd tə]	gegen etw sein
to **breed sth (bred, bred)** [briːd]	etw züchten
opponent [ə'pəʊnənt]	Gegner/in
caged [keɪdʒd]	eingesperrt (in Käfighaltung)
acidity [ə'sɪdəti]	Säure, Säuregehalt
barren ['bærən]	ausgedörrt, unfruchtbar
considerable [kən'sɪdərəbl]	erheblich, beträchtlich
to **rely on sb/sth** [rɪ'laɪ ɒn]	sich auf jdn/etw verlassen

page 96

to **cure sb/sth** [kjʊə]	jdn/etw heilen
to **contract sth** [kən'trækt]	sich mit etw infizieren
malnutrition [ˌmælnjuː'trɪʃn]	Unterernährung, falsche Ernährung
curable ['kjʊərəbl]	heilbar
at present [ət 'preznt]	momentan, derzeit, zurzeit
deregulation [ˌdiːˌregju'leɪʃn]	Liberalisierung, Freigabe
to **graze** [greɪz]	grasen
to **enrich sth** [ɪn'rɪtʃ]	etw bereichern
to **reverse sth** [rɪ'vɜːs]	etw rückgängig machen

page 97

impactful [ɪm'pæktfl]	wirkungsvoll
staggering ['stægərɪŋ]	niederschmetternd
soya [sɔɪ]	Soja
palm [pɑːm]	Palme
to **haul sth out** [ˌhɔːl 'aʊt]	etw herausziehen
to **stagger sb** ['stægə]	jdn überwältigen
grain [greɪn]	Getreide
madness ['mædnəs]	Wahnsinn
presumably [prɪ'zjuːməbli]	vermutlich
affluence ['æfluəns]	Wohlstand
commerce ['kɒmɜːs]	Handel
vicious circle [ˌvɪʃəs 'sɜːkl]	Teufelskreis
inhumane [ˌɪnhjuː'meɪn]	unmenschlich, menschenunwürdig
pasture ['pɑːstʃə]	Weide
free range [friː 'reɪndʒ]	Freiland(haltung)
to **overload sth** [ˌəʊvə'ləʊd]	etw überladen, etw überbeanspruchen
checkout ['tʃekaʊt]	Kasse
clean-up cost ['kliːn ʌp kɒst]	Sanierungskosten
public health [ˌpʌblɪk 'helθ]	öffentliches Gesundheitswesen
to **be geared to/towards sth** [gɪəd]	auf etw ausgerichtet sein
environmentally friendly [ɪnˌvaɪrənˌmentəli 'frendli]	umweltfreundlich
nutritious [nju'trɪʃəs]	nahrhaft, nährstoffreich
to **be predicated on sth** ['predɪkeɪtɪd]	auf etw basieren
infinite ['ɪnfɪnət]	unendlich, unerschöpflich
finite ['faɪnaɪt]	begrenzt, endlich
pollinator ['pɒləneɪtə]	Bestäuber
to **pollinate sth** ['pɒləneɪt]	etw bestäuben
depletion [dɪ'pliːʃn]	Verringerung, Abbau
to **unscramble sth** [ˌʌn'skræmbl]	etw entflechten
efficiency [ɪ'fɪʃnsi]	Leistungsfähigkeit, Wirksamkeit, Wirkungsgrad
unique [ju'niːk]	einzigartig
to **restore sth** [rɪ'stɔː]	etw restaurieren, etw wieder aufbauen
forage ['fɒrɪdʒ]	Viehfutter
intensification [ɪnˌtensɪfɪ'keɪʃn]	Intensivierung
to **drive sth** [draɪv]	etw vorantreiben, etw stärken
environmental credentials *(pl)* [ɪnˌvaɪrənˌmentl krə'denʃlz]	Umweltverträglichkeit
to **trash sth** [træʃ]	etw demolieren

page 99

inevitable [ɪn'evɪtəbl]	unausweichlich, unvermeidbar
paradigm ['pærədaɪm]	Paradigma, Modell
dairy ['deəri]	Molkerei, Milch-, Molkerei-
availability [əˌveɪlə'bɪləti]	Verfügbarkeit
nutritional [nju'trɪʃənl]	Nahrungs-, Ernährungs-, Nähr-
in calorific terms [ɪn ˌkælə'rɪfɪk tɜːzm]	in kalorischer Hinsicht

page 100

unethical [ʌn'eθɪkl]	unethisch
glow [gləʊ]	Schein, Schimmer
remotely [rɪ'məʊtli]	aus der Ferne
onboard sth [ˌɒn'bɔːd]	an Bord von etw, auf etw
infrared [ˌinfrə'red]	infrarot
to **direct sb/sth** [də'rekt]	etw leiten, jdm den Weg sagen/zeigen
aircraft, *pl* **aircraft** ['eəkrɑːft]	Flugzeug
to **guide sb/sth** [gaɪd]	jdn/etw führen
weapon release [ˌwepən rɪ'liːs]	Waffenfreigabe, -abwurf
to **depress sth** [dɪ'pres]	etw drücken
missile ['mɪsaɪl]	Rakete, Flugkörper
to **unleash sth** [ʌn'liːʃ]	etw auslösen, etw entfesseln
staffed [stɑːft]	(mit Personal) besetzt

page 101

to **spin around (spun, spun)** [ˌspɪn ə'raʊnd]	sich drehen, herumwirbeln
fleet [fliːt]	Flotte
stocky ['stɒki]	untersetzt
closely cropped [ˌkləʊsli 'krɒpt]	kurzgeschoren
purposeful ['pɜːpəsfl]	zielgerichtet, zielstrebig
herder ['hɜːdə]	Hirt/in
arid ['ærɪd]	trocken, ausgedörrt
tell [tel]	verräterisches Zeichen, Hinweis
camo tarp ['kæmə tɑːp]	Tarnplane
netting ['netɪŋ]	Netz, Geflecht
nestled up [ˌnesld 'ʌp]	angeschmiegt
blob [blɒb]	Klecks

page 102

handset ['hændset]	Handapparat, Telefonhörer
High Value Individual (HVI) [haɪ ˌvæljuː ˌɪndɪ'vɪdʒuəl]	wichtige (feindliche) Person

grid [grɪd]	Gitter(netz)
square [skweə]	Planquadrat
to **consult sth** [kən'sʌlt]	in etw nachsehen, in etw nachlesen
to **guard sb** [gɑːd]	jdn überwachen
named target [ˌneɪmd 'tɑːgɪt]	benanntes Ziel, namentlich bekannte Zielperson
to **designate sth sth** ['dezɪgneɪt]	etw als etw benennen, etw als etw ausweisen
to **pat sb/sth** [pæt]	jdn/etw tätscheln
to **squint** [skwɪnt]	schielen, spähen
in deference to ['defərəns]	mit Rücksicht auf
jock [dʒɒk]	Sportler/in, Sportskanone
reminder [rɪ'maɪndə]	Erinnerung, Mahnung
joint [dʒɔɪnt]	gemeinsam, gemeinschaftlich
air conditioning ['eə kəndɪʃnɪŋ]	Klimaanlage
airplane *(AE)* ['eəpleɪn]	Flugzeug
to **loiter** ['lɔɪtə]	herumhängen, warten
to **locate sth** [ləʊ'keɪt]	etw ausfindig machen
camouflage ['kæməflɑːʒ]	Tarnung
affirmation [ˌæfə'meɪʃn]	Bestätigung
imagery ['ɪmɪdʒəri]	Bildaufnahmen
en route [ˌɒn 'ruːt]	auf dem Weg

page 103

to **supply sth** [sə'plaɪ]	etw liefern, etw bieten, etw bereitstellen
mountain range ['maʊntən reɪndʒ]	Gebirge, Gebirgszug
assessment [ə'sesmənt]	Beurteilung, Einstufung
to **consult sb** [kən'sʌlt]	jdn um Rat fragen, jdn hinzuziehen
to **stress sth** [stres]	etw betonen, etw hervorheben
assurance [ə'ʃʊərəns]	Zusage, Vergewisserung
continual [kən'tɪnjuəl]	ständig, ununterbrochen, kontinuierlich
counterterrorism [ˌkaʊntə'terərɪzəm]	Terrorismusabwehr, Terrorismusbekämpfung
boardroom ['bɔːdruːm]	Sitzungssaal
sensation [sen'seɪʃn]	Gefühl, Empfinden
prior ['praɪə]	vorrangig
lethal ['liːθl]	tödlich
to **blow up sth (blew, blown)** [ˌbləʊ 'ʌp]	etw in die Luft jagen
innocent ['ɪnəsnt]	unschuldig
revenge killing [rɪ'vendʒ kɪlɪŋ]	Rachemord
luxury hotel ['lʌkʃəri həʊtel]	Luxushotel
authorities *(pl)* [ɔː'θɒrətiz]	Behörden
to **wink** [wɪŋk]	zwinkern
to **fight back (fought, fought)** [ˌfaɪt 'bæk]	sich wehren
to **allege sb sth** [ə'ledʒ]	jdm etw vorwerfen, jdm etw unterstellen
to **plot to do sth** [plɒt]	(heimlich) planen, etw zu tun
explosive [ɪk'spləʊsɪv]	Sprengstoff

page 104

control-alt-delete [kənˌtrəʊl ˌɔːlt dɪ'liːt]	Strg-Alt-Entf (Windows-Computertastatur-Kürzel für das „Abschießen" eines Programms)

UNIT 4

page 105

to **encompass sth** [ɪn'kʌmpəs]	etw umfassen
separatism ['seprətɪzəm]	Separatismus, Loslösungsbestreben
to **unite** [ju'naɪt]	etw vereinen, etw vereinigen
aspiration [ˌæspə'reɪʃn]	Ambition, Bestreben
dignity ['dɪgnət]	Würde

page 106

to **liberalize sth** ['lɪbrəlaɪz]	etw liberalisieren
to **privatize sth** ['praɪvətaɪz]	etw privatisieren
protectionist [prə'tekʃənɪst]	protektionistisch
barrier ['bæriə]	Barriere, Schranke, Grenze
summit ['sʌmɪt]	Gipfel(treffen)
to **take advantage of sth** [ˌteɪk əd'vɑːntɪdʒ əv]	sich etw zunutze machen, etw ausnutzen
instantaneous [ˌɪnstən'teɪniəs]	sofort, unmittelbar
cyclical ['saɪklɪkl, 'sɪklɪkl]	zyklisch
impoverished [ɪm'pɒvərɪʃt]	verarmt
betterment ['betəmənt]	Besserung
to **propel sth** [prə'pel]	etw (an)treiben
ultimately ['ʌltɪmətli]	letztlich, letztendlich
to **render** ['rendə]	machen
uniqueness [ju'niːknəs]	Einzigartigkeit
disappearance [ˌdɪsə'pɪərəns]	Verschwinden
to **flee** [fliː]	flüchten, fliehen
to **escape from sth** [ɪ'skeɪp frəm]	einer Sache entkommen
bleak [bliːk]	trostlos, freudlos
ravaged ['rævɪdʒd]	verwüstet
oppression [ə'preʃn]	Unterdrückung
persecution [ˌpɜːsɪ'kjuːʃn]	Verfolgung
civil war [ˌsɪvɪl 'wɔː]	Bürgerkrieg
to **displace sb** [dɪs'pleɪs]	jdn vertreiben
resistance [rɪ'zɪstəns]	Widerstand
dissatisfaction [ˌdɪsˌsætɪs'fækʃn]	Unzufriedenheit
to **devastate sth** ['devəsteɪt]	zerstören, verwüsten
stabbing ['stæbɪŋ]	Messerstecherei
branch [brɑːntʃ]	Zweig
supranational [ˌsuːprə'næʃnəl]	länderübergreifend
unity ['juːnəti]	Einheit
detrimental (to/for) [ˌdetrɪ'mentl]	schädlich (für)
peace [piːs]	Frieden

page 107

wound [wuːnd]	Wunde
to **lower sth** ['ləʊə]	etw senken, etw herabsetzen
tariff ['tærɪf]	Tarif

page 108

tipping point ['tɪpɪŋ pɔɪnt]	Kipppunkt, kritischer Punkt, Wendepunkt
emergence [i'mɜːdʒəns]	Entstehen, Aufkommen
to **broadcast (broadcast, broadcast)** ['brɔːdkɑːst]	senden
rejection [rɪ'dʒekʃn]	Ablehnung
evident ['evɪdənt]	offensichtlich

trickle-down economics ['trɪkl daʊn]	Trickle-Down-Wirtschaft (Theorie, dass Wirtschaftswachstum allen zugute kommt)
unstoppable [,ʌn'stɒpəbl]	unaufhaltsam
untrammelled [ʌn'træmld]	uneingeschränkt, ungehindert
collapse [kə'læps]	Einsturz, Kollaps
to **supervise sb** ['su:pəvaɪz]	jdn beaufsichtigen
membership ['membəʃɪp]	Mitgliedschaft
failing ['feɪlɪŋ]	Mangel, Missstand

page 109

culpable [kʌlpəbl]	schuldig
shiny ['ʃaɪni]	glänzend
communist ['kɒmjənɪst]	kommunistisch, Kommunist/in
excess [ɪk'ses]	Exzess, Überschuss
guarantor [,gærən'tɔ:]	Garant/in
to **offshore sth** [,ɒf'ʃɔ:]	etw ins Ausland verlagern
bulwark ['bʊlwək]	Bollwerk
individual [,ɪndɪ'vɪdʒʊəl]	einzeln, individuell
transnational [,trænz'næʃnəl]	transnational, grenzübergreifend
currency ['kʌrənsi]	Währung
entity ['entəti]	Einheit
think tank ['θɪŋk tæŋk]	Expertenkommission, Denkfabrik
momentous [mə'mentəs]	bedeutsam, folgenreich
narrative ['nærətɪv]	Erzählung, Geschichte
disintegration [dɪs,ɪntɪ'greɪʃn]	Zerfall
to **fulfil sth** [fʊl'fɪl]	etw erfüllen, etw ausführen
to **allocate sth to sb** ['æləkeɪt]	jdm etw zuweisen, jdm etw zuteilen
heyday ['heɪdeɪ]	Blütezeit
austerity [ɒ'sterəti]	wirtschaftliche Einschränkung, Entbehrung
provision [rə'vɪʒn]	Bereitstellung, Versorgung
inevitably [ɪn'evɪtəbli]	zwangsläufig
backlash ['bæklæʃ]	Gegenreaktion, Gegenbewegung
to **manifest in sth** ['mænɪfest]	sich in etw zeigen
to **be at odds with sth** [ət 'ɒdz]	mit etw hadern

page 110

to **underpin sth** [,ʌndə'pɪn]	etw (ab)stützen, etw untermauern
to **impose sth on/upon sb** [ɪm'pəʊz]	jdm etw auferlegen
tariff ['tærɪf]	Handelszoll
dumping ['dʌmpɪŋ]	Preisunterbietung, Dumping
steel [sti:l]	Stahl
to **moan** [məʊn]	stöhnen, jammern, klagen
resolution [,rezə'lu:ʃn]	Vorsatz, Entschluss
to **entrench sth** [ɪn'trenʃ]	etw etablieren
self-evidently [,self 'evɪdəntli]	selbstverständlich
dissent [dɪ'sent]	Widerspruch, Einwand
grievance ['gri:vəns]	Beschwerde
to **hasten sth** ['heɪsn]	etw beschleunigen
dissolution [,dɪsə'lu:ʃn]	Auflösung, Verfall

page 111

loss [lɒs]	Verlust
inconsequential [ɪn,kɒnsɪ'kwenʃl]	unbedeutend, belanglos
prominent ['prɒmɪnənt]	bekannt, bedeutend

page 112

to **sacrifice sth** ['sækrɪfaɪs]	etw opfern
liberty ['lɪbəti]	Freiheit
to **catch up with sb (caught, caught)** [,kætʃ 'ʌp]	zu jdm aufschließen
misleading [,mɪs'li:dɪŋ]	irreführend
the haves and the have-nots [hævs, ,hæv 'nɒts]	die Besitzenden und die Habenichtse
to **exaggerate sth** [ɪg'zædʒəreɪt]	etw übertreiben
pedantic [pɪ'dæntɪk]	kleinlich, spitzfindig
sensational [sen'seɪʃənl]	reißerisch, effekthascherisch

page 113

faultless ['fɔ:ltləs]	einwandfrei, makellos
to **polish sth** ['pɒlɪʃ]	etw (auf)polieren
margin ['mɑ:dʒɪn]	Rand, Randspalte
superficial [,su:pə'fɪʃl]	oberflächlich, vordergründig
imposition [,ɪmpə'zɪʃn]	Auferlegung, Verhängung
manifestation [,mænɪfe'steɪʃn]	Manifestation, Erscheinungsform

page 114

edition [ɪ'dɪʃn]	Ausgabe (z. B. einer Sendung/Zeitschrift)
cutting-edge [,kʌtɪŋ 'edʒ]	Spitzen-, auf dem neusten Stand
insight (into) ['ɪnsaɪt]	Einblick (in), Verständnis (von)
to **simmer** ['sɪmə]	köcheln
interconnectedness [,ɪntəkə'nektɪdnəs]	Vernetzung
rhetoric ['retərɪk]	Redekunst, Phrasendrescherei
to **devise sth** [dɪ'vaɪz]	etw entwickeln
index ['ɪndeks]	Index, Verzeichnis, Register
to **measure sth** ['meʒə]	etw messen
per capita [pə 'kæpɪtə]	pro Kopf
gross domestic product (GDP) [,grəʊs də,mestɪk 'prɒdʌkt]	Bruttosozialprodukt
across the board [ə,krɒs ðə 'bɔ:d]	durch die Bank
net [net]	netto, Netto-
to **review sth** [rɪ'vju:]	etw bewerten, etw prüfen
annual ['ænjuəl]	jährlich
gain [geɪn]	Gewinn, Vorteil
evenly ['i:vnli]	ausgeglichen, gleichmäßig
to **lose out on sth** [,lu:z 'aʊt]	bei etw schlecht wegkommen
trade pact ['treɪd pækt]	Handelsabkommen
beneficial [,benɪ'fɪʃl]	nützlich, vorteilhaft
to **rank sb/sth** [ræŋk]	jdn/etw einstufen, jdn/etw (ein-)ordnen
to **air sth** [eə]	etw senden

page 116

working conditions *(pl)* [,wɜ:kɪŋ kən'dɪʃnz]	Arbeitsbedingungen
like-minded [,laɪk 'maɪndɪd]	gleichgesinnt
to **compromise** ['kɒmprəmaɪz]	Kompromisse eingehen

page 117

divisive [dɪ'vaɪsɪv]	polarisierend, umstritten
profound [prə'faʊnd]	tief greifend, tief gehend, fundiert
inaccurate [ɪn'ækjərət]	ungenau, unrichtig
people smuggling ['pi:pl smʌglɪŋ]	Menschenschmuggel

page 118

to **abdicate responsibility** [ˌæbdɪkeɪt rɪˌspɒnsə'bɪləti]	sich aus der Verantwortung ziehen
comparable ['kɒmpərəbl]	vergleichbar
inaction [ɪn'ækʃn]	Tatenlosigkeit
delegate ['delɪgət]	Delegierte/r
to **unravel sth** [ʌn'rævl]	etw entwirren, etw enträtseln
to **heal sth** [hi:l]	etw heilen
to **tear apart (tore, torn)** [ˌteə ə'pɑ:t]	auseinanderreißen
to **rip sth up** [ˌrɪp 'ʌp]	etw zerreißen
to **deport sb** [dɪ'pɔ:t]	jdn abschieben
allegedly [ə'ledʒɪdli]	angeblich
to **embolden sb to do sth** [ɪm'bəʊldən]	jdm Mut machen, etw zu tun
startling ['stɑ:tlɪŋ]	alarmierend, erschreckend, erstaunlich
to **mull sth** [mʌl]	etw überdenken
to **vie for sth** [vaɪ]	um etw konkurrieren
to **renege on sth** [rɪ'ni:g]	etw nicht einhalten
to **care for sb** ['keə fə]	für jdn sorgen, sich um jdn kümmern, auf jdn aufpassen
dire situation [ˌdaɪə sɪtʃu'eɪʃn]	bedrohliche Lage
to **contrive sth** [kən'traɪv]	etw bewerkstelligen
to **jail sb** [dʒeɪl]	jdn einsperren, jdn ins Gefängnis werfen
valuable ['væljuəbl]	Wertsache
boatload ['bəʊtləʊd]	Bootladung
wilful blindness [ˌwɪlfl 'blaɪndnəs]	vorsätzliche Blindheit
beneficiary [ˌbenɪ'fɪʃəri]	Nutznießer/in

page 119

pleasant ['pleznt]	angenehm
sweatshop ['swetʃɒp]	Ausbeutungsbetrieb
to **sanitize sth** ['sænɪtaɪz]	etw säubern, etw zensieren
metaphor ['metəfə]	Metapher
barely ['beəli]	kaum
to **relapse into sth** ['ri:læps]	wieder in etw zurückfallen
interwar [ˌɪntə'wɔ:]	zwischen den Weltkriegen
unspeakable [ʌn'spi:kəbl]	unsäglich, unaussprechlich
to **topple** ['tɒpl]	stürzen
reputation [ˌrepju'teɪʃn]	Ansehen, Ruf

page 120

refusal [rɪ'fju:zl]	Ablehnung, Verweigerung
tragic ['trædʒɪk]	tragisch
homeland ['həʊmlənd]	Heimat(land)
commitment (to) [kə'mɪtmənt]	Engagement (für), Bekenntnis (zu)
to **peer** [pɪə]	prüfend blicken
battleground ['bætlgraʊnd]	Schlachtfeld
undeserved [ˌʌndɪ'zɜ:vd]	unverdient
to **readmit sb** [ˌri:əd'mɪt]	jdn wieder aufnehmen
to **be stranded** ['strændɪd]	festsitzen, gestrandet sein
ironic [aɪ'rɒnɪk]	ironisch
partial ['pɑ:ʃəl]	teilweise, Teil-
catastrophic [ˌkætə'strɒfɪk]	katastrophal, verhängnisvoll
abdication [ˌæbdɪ'keɪʃn]	Verzicht
superiority [su:ˌpɪəri'ɒrəti]	Überlegenheit
to **obscure sth** [əb'skjʊə]	verbergen, verdunkeln
duration [dju'reɪʃn]	Dauer
beacon ['bi:kən]	Leuchtfeuer

page 121

to **house sb** [haʊz]	jdn unterbringen
dreadful ['dredfl]	schrecklich, furchtbar
magnanimous [mæg'nænɪməs]	großherzig; großmütig
destitute ['destɪtju:t]	mittellos
discriminated [dɪ'skrɪmɪneɪtɪd]	diskriminiert
extent [ɪk'stent]	Umfang, Ausmaß
opulent ['ɒpjələnt]	superreich
outskirts *(pl)* ['aʊtskɜ:ts]	Stadtrand, Randbezirk(e)
vicinity [və'sɪnəti]	Nähe, nähere Umgebung
inquisitive [ɪn'kwɪzətɪv]	neugierig, wissbegierig
predicament [prɪ'dɪkəmənt]	Notlage
manifold ['mænɪfəʊld]	vielfältig, mannigfaltig
numerous ['nju:mərəs]	zahlreich
swiftly ['swɪftli]	rasch, flugs

page 122

recording [rɪ'kɔ:dɪŋ]	Aufnahme, Aufzeichnung
congressional [kən'greʃənl]	Kongress-
to **reside** [rɪ'zaɪd]	residieren, ansässig sein
to **grant sb sth** [grɑ:nt]	jdm etw gewähren
holder ['həʊldə]	Inhaber/in
spouse [spaʊz]	Ehepartner/in
minor ['maɪnə]	minderjährig
petitioner [pə'tɪʃənə]	Antragsteller/in
citizenship ['sɪtɪzənʃɪp]	Staatsbürgerschaft, Staatsbürgerkunde
restrictionist [rɪ'strɪkʃnɪst]	Restriktionist (Befürworter der Beschränkung)
to **slash sth** [slæʃ]	etw (drastisch) reduzieren, etw senken
proponent [prə'pəʊnənt]	Befürworter/in
pipe bomb ['paɪp bɒm]	Rohrbombe
proficiency [prə'fɪʃnsi]	Können, Kenntnisse, Fähigkeiten
defender [dɪ'fendə]	Verteidiger/in
fearmongering ['fɪəmɒŋgerɪŋ]	Panikmache
rigorous ['rɪgərəs]	streng, drastisch, rigoros
to **radicalize** ['rædɪkəlaɪz]	sich radikalisieren
genius ['dʒi:niəs]	Genie, Geistesgröße
cap [kæp]	Deckel, Obergrenze
to **accuse sb of sth** [ə'kju:z]	jdn einer Sache beschuldigen, jdm etw vorwerfen
to **draft sth** [drɑ:ft]	etw entwerfen

page 124

to **induce sth** [ɪn'dju:s]	etw verursachen
rallying cry ['rælɪŋ kraɪ]	Parole, Schlachtruf
displacement [dɪs'pleɪsmənt]	Vertreibung

page 125

ally ['ælaɪ]	Alliierte/r, Verbündete/r
proposal [prə'pəʊzl]	Vorschlag
to **brainstorm** ['breɪnstɔ:m]	Ideen (ungeordnet) sammeln
to **speculate on/about sth** ['spekjuleɪt]	sich über etw Gedanken machen

page 126

ripple ['rɪpl] Welle
suppression [sə'preʃn] Unterdrückung
brute force [ˌbruːt 'fɔːs] brutale Gewalt
adherence [əd'hɪərəns] Einhaltung
pugnacious [pʌg'neɪʃəs] kampflustig, streitsüchtig
to **condemn sth** [kən'dem] etw verdammen, etw verurteilen
shameful ['ʃeɪmfl] schändlich
secessionist [sɪ'seʃənɪst] Abtrünnige/r
charter ['tʃɑːtə] Charta, Satzung
self-determination [ˌself dɪˌtɜːmɪ'neɪʃn] Selbstbestimmung
to **eschew sth** [ɪs'tʃuː] etw (ver)meiden
conventional [kən'venʃənl] konventionell, herkömmlich
doomed to fail [ˌduːmd tə 'feɪl] zum Scheitern verurteilt
to **derail** [dɪ'reɪl] entgleisen
plea [pliː] Bitte
dictatorship [ˌdɪk'teɪtəʃɪp] Diktatur
confrontation [ˌkɒnfrʌn'teɪʃn] Auseinandersetzung
to **injure sb** ['ɪndʒə] jdn verletzen
on the contrary [ɒn ðə 'kɒntrəri] im Gegenteil
ongoing ['ɒngəʊɪŋ] laufend
clash [klæʃ] Konflikt
copycat ['kɒpikæt] Nachahmungs-
to **repel sb** [rɪ'pel] jdn abstoßen
tempted ['temptɪd] versucht
to **revisit sth** [ˌriː'vɪzɪt] nochmals zurückkommen auf etw
unilateral [ˌjuːnɪ'lætrəl] einseitig
ceasefire ['siːsfaɪə] Waffenstillstand
disarmament [dɪs'ɑːməmənt] Entwaffnung
crackdown ['krækdaʊn] Durchgreifen, Bekämpfung
dissident ['dɪsɪdənt] abtrünnig, regimekritisch
placatory [plə'keɪtəri] beschwichtigend
devolution [ˌdiːvə'luːʃn] Dezentralisierung

page 127

fringe outfit [ˌfrɪndʒ 'aʊtfɪt] Randorganisation
justification [ˌdʒʌstəfə'keɪʃn] Rechtfertigung
hot spot ['hɒt spɒt] Krisenherd
centralised ['sentrəlaɪzd] zentralisiert
poll [pəʊl] Umfrage, Wahl
legitimacy [lɪ'dʒɪtɪməsi] Legitimität, Rechtmäßigkeit
to **levy sth** ['levi] etw erheben
xenophobia [ˌzenə'fəʊbiə] Fremdenfeindlichkeit, Ausländerhass
to **distrust sb/sth** [dɪs'trʌst] jdm/etw misstrauen
inclusion [ɪn'kluːʒn] Einbeziehung, Einbindung, Inklusion
to **get blurred** [blɜːd] verschwimmen
distrust [dɪs'trʌst] Misstrauen
disillusion [ˌdɪsɪ'luːʒn] Ernüchterung
premise ['premɪs] Prämisse, Voraussetzung
to **heap sth** [hiːp] etw anhäufen
objectionable [əb'dʒekʃənəbl] unangenehm, bedenklich
to **ambush sb** ['æmbʊʃ] jdn überfallen, jdn in einen Hinterhalt locken
to **poll** [pəʊl] abschneiden (in einer Umfrage/Wahl)
endorsement [ɪn'dɔːsmənt] Werbung, Unterstützung
upheaval [ʌp'hiːvl] Aufruhr
chaotic [keɪ'ɒtɪk] chaotisch

multifaceted [ˌmʌlti'fæsɪtɪd] facettenreich
to **fracture sth** ['fræktʃə] etw brechen, etw aufbrechen
all-powerful [ˌɔːl 'paʊəfl] allmächtig
battered ['bætəd] (an)geschlagen
in the vanguard of sth ['vængɑːd] an der Spitze etw (einer Bewegung) sein
inflexible [ɪn'fleksəbl] unflexibel, unbeweglich

page 128

antipathy [æn'tɪpəθi] Antipathie, Abneigung
desire [dɪ'zaɪə] Verlangen

page 129

to **divert sth from sth** [daɪ'vɜːt] etw ablenken von etw
fascism ['fæʃɪzəm] Faschismus
unconstitutional [ˌʌnˌkɒnstɪ'tjuːʃənl] verfassungswidrig
sound [saʊnd] solide, vernünftig
oppressed [ə'prest] unterdrückt
voting booth *(AE)* ['vəʊtɪŋ buːð] Wahlkabine
to **be a believer in sth** [bɪ'liːvə] von etw überzeugt sein

page 130

sovereign right [ˌsɒvrɪn 'raɪt] Hoheitsrecht
to **draw sth up** [ˌdrɔː 'ʌp] etw erstellen

page 131

adequate ['ædɪkwət] angemessen, geeignet
regulation [ˌregju'leɪʃn] Vorschrift
devil ['devl] Teufel
steamboat ['stiːmbəʊt] Dampfer
to **bark** [bɑːk] bellen
bare [beə] kahl, nackt, bar
coin [kɔɪn] Münze
mosquito [məs'kiːtəʊ] Mücke
to **choke sb/sth** [tʃəʊk] jdn/etw ersticken
seed [siːd] Samen, Saat(gut), Keim
bud [bʌd] Knospe
setback ['setbæk] Rückschlag

page 134

stranglehold ['stræŋglhəʊld] Würgegriff
whereas [ˌweər'æz] während, wohingegen
to **perpetrate sth** ['pɜːpətreɪt] etw begehen, etw verüben (Verbrechen)
radicalization [ˌrædɪklaɪ'zeɪʃn] Radikalisierung
screenplay ['skriːnpleɪ] Drehbuch
prop [prɒp] Requisite
to **portray sb** [pɔː'treɪ] jdn porträtieren, jdn darstellen
to **sway** [sweɪ] sich wiegen
to **sneer** [snɪə] grinsen
alluring [ə'lʊərɪŋ] verlockend, verführerisch
belly ['beli] Bauch
to **adorn sth** [ə'dɔːn] etw zieren, etw schmücken
navel stud ['neɪvl stʌd] Nabelstecker
to **strut** [strʌt] stolzieren
to **saunter** ['sɔːntə] schlendern
edgy ['edʒi] nervös, unruhig
scornful ['skɔːnfl] spöttisch, verächtlich
varnished ['vɑːnɪʃt] lackiert
lined [laɪnd] gesäumt, ausgekleidet

blank [blæŋk]	leer, frei
desecrated ['desɪkreɪtɪd]	entweiht
non-observant [ˌnɒn əb'zɜːvənt]	nicht praktizierend
Jew [dʒuː]	Jude/Jüdin
virtue ['vɜːtʃuː]	Tugend
righteous ['raɪtʃəs]	rechtschaffen, gerecht
self-restraint [ˌself rɪ'streɪnt]	Selbstbeherrschung
shifty eyes [ˌʃɪfti 'aɪz]	unsteter Blick
hollow ['hɒləʊ]	hohl, leer
to **betray sb/sth (to sb)** [bɪ'treɪ]	jdn/etw (an jdn) verraten, preisgeben

page 135

unclean [ˌʌn'kliːn]	unrein
to **scuttle** ['skʌtl]	trippeln
crackling ['kræklɪŋ]	knisternd
trash-speckled ['træʃ spekld]	mit Müll gesprenkelt
shell [ʃel]	Muschel, Gehäuse
lust [lʌst]	Wollust, Gier
infatuation [ɪnˌfætʃu'eɪʃn]	Verliebtheit, Vernarrtheit
infidel ['ɪnfɪdəl]	Ungläubige/r
accumulation [əˌkjuːmjə'leɪʃn]	Anhäufung
diversion [daɪ'vɜːʃn]	Ablenkung, Umleitung
sinful ['sɪnfl]	sündig
imitation [ˌɪmɪ'teɪʃn]	Imitation, Nachahmung
relief [rɪ'liːf]	Erleichterung, Entlastung, Linderung
unscathed [ʌn'skeɪðd]	unversehrt
chatter ['tʃætər]	Geschwätz, Geplapper
farewell [ˌfeə'wel]	Abschied, Verabschiedung
drunk [drʌŋk]	Betrunkene/r
to **revel** ['revl]	feiern, schwelgen, ausgelassen sein
lid [lɪd]	Augenlid
puffy ['pʌfi]	geschwollen, aufgedunsen
habitual [hə'bɪtʃuəl]	gewohnheitsmäßig, Gewohnheits-
disorderly [dɪs'ɔːdəli]	undiszipliniert, zügellos
wanton [wɒntən]	liederlich, schamlos
self-indulgent [ˌself ɪn'dʌldʒənt]	ausschweifend, maßlos
to **instill** *(BE)* / **instil** *(AE)* **sth** [ɪn'stɪl]	etw vermitteln
satanic [sə'tænɪk]	satanisch, unmoralisch
godless ['gɒdləs]	gottlos
firm [fɜːm]	fest, sicher
to **ring out (rang, rung)** [ˌrɪŋ 'aʊt]	erschallen
merciless ['mɜːsɪləs]	gnadenlos
clay [kleɪ]	Ton, Lehm
to **pour** [pɔː]	strömen
copper ['kɒpə]	Kupfer
thread [θred]	Faden, Strang
to **stir sth** [stɜː]	etw rühren, etw mischen
lightning ['laɪtnɪŋ]	Blitz(e) (bei Gewitter)
droplet ['drɒplət]	Tröpfchen
to **deduce sth from sth** [dɪ'djuːs]	etw von etw ableiten, etw von etw herleiten
to **sneak** [sniːk]	schleichen
measurement ['meʃəmənt]	Abmessung, Maß
drab [dræb]	grau, trostlos
earthy ['ɜːθi]	erdig
crevice ['krevɪs]	Spalte
consciousness ['kɒnʃəsnəs]	Bewusstsein
materialist [mə'tɪəriəlɪst]	materialistisch
to **murmur** ['mɜːmə]	murmeln
to **blaze** [bleɪz]	leuchten, funkeln
divine [dɪ'vaɪn]	göttlich
to **stoke sth** [stəʊk]	etw schüren, etw anfachen
boiler ['bɔɪlə]	Kessel, Heizkessel
to **swell sth** [swel]	etw anschwellen lassen
fountain ['faʊntən]	(Spring-)Brunnen
eternal [ɪ'tɜːnl]	ewig
absorbed [əb'sɔːbd]	aufgenommen, absorbiert
tar [tɑː]	Teer
devilish ['devəlɪʃ]	teuflisch
spiral ['spaɪrəl]	Spirale
luminous ['luːmɪnəs]	leuchtend
angelic [æn'dʒelɪk]	Engels-, englisch
slime [slaɪm]	Schleim
worm [wɜːm]	Wurm
snail [sneɪl]	Schnecke (mit Schneckenhaus)
fatal ['feɪtl]	tödlich, verhängnisvoll
mosque [mɒsk]	Moschee
sacred ['seɪkrɪd]	heilig
messenger ['mesɪndʒə]	Bote, Kurier
winged [wɪŋd]	geflügelt
heaven [hevn]	Himmel
angel ['eɪndʒl]	Engel
to **pray** [preɪ]	beten
prophet ['prɒfɪt]	Prophet/in
hoof print ['huːf prɪnt]	Hufabdruck
sharp [ʃɑːp]	scharf
beneath [bɪ'niːθ]	unterhalb, unter
dome [dəʊm]	Kuppel

page 136

torment ['tɔːmənt]	Folter, Qual
to **recite** [rɪ'saɪt]	etw vortragen
beauty ['bjuːti]	Schönheit
crushing ['krʌʃɪŋ]	vernichtend
thee [ðiː]	dich, dir (veraltet oder auf Gott bezogen)
to **kindle sth** ['kɪndl]	etw entzünden
the damned *(pl)* [dæmd]	die Verdammten
verily ['verɪli]	wahrhaftig, wahrlich
vault [vɔːlt]	Gewölbe
outstretched [ˌaʊt'stretʃt]	ausgestreckt, ausgebreitet
column ['kɒləm]	Säule
to **huddle** ['hʌdl]	sich zusammendrängen
to **strain to do sth** [streɪn]	sich anstrengen etw zu tun
towering ['taʊərɪŋ]	emporragend, gewaltig
mist [mɪst]	Nebel, Dunst
merciful ['mɜːsɪfl]	barmherzig
to **relent** [rɪ'lent]	einlenken, nachgeben
halt [hɔːlt]	Halt
unexpected [ˌʌnɪk'spektɪd]	unerwartet
milky ['mɪlki]	milchig
visionary ['vɪʒənri]	visionär, seherisch
figurative ['fɪgərətɪv]	symbolisch, metaphorisch
truly ['truːli]	in Wahrheit
misery ['mɪzəri]	Elend
separation [sepə'reɪʃn]	Trennung
scorching ['skɔːtʃɪŋ]	Brennen
remorse [rɪ'mɔːs]	Reue
sin [sɪn]	Sünde
unconvincing [ˌʌnkən'vɪnsɪŋ]	nicht überzeugend
undertone ['ʌndətəʊn]	Unterton, Grundstimmung
to **deny sth** [dɪ'naɪ]	etw leugnen, etw bestreiten
to **affirm sth** [ə'fɜːm]	etw bestätigen

to **preach sth** [priːtʃ]	etw predigen
unforgiving [ˌʌnfə'gɪvɪŋ]	gnadenlos, unerbittlich
to **proclaim sth** [prə'kleɪm]	etw verkündigen
wrinkle ['rɪŋkl]	Falte
diffident ['dɪfɪdənt]	zurückhaltend, bescheiden
to **gnaw** [nɔː]	nagen
to **tinge sth** [tɪndʒ]	etw färben
to **crush sb/sth** [krʌʃ]	jdn/etw zerdrücken, jdn/etw vernichten
to **exceed sth** [ɪk'siːd]	etw übertreffen
steed [stiːd]	Ross
irresistible [ˌɪrɪ'zɪstəbl]	unwiderstehlich
onrushing ['ɒnrʌʃɪŋ]	Heranpreschen
to **blend sth** [blend]	etw (ver)mischen
softness ['sɒftnəs]	Sanftheit, Schwäche
self-subsistent [ˌself səb'sɪstənt]	selbsterhaltend
to **bow** [baʊ]	sich (ver)beugen
forehead ['fɔːhed]	Stirn
to **scrape sth** [skreɪp]	sich an etw kratzen, schrammen
mortal ['mɔːtl]	sterblich
to **consort with sb** [kən'sɔːt]	mit jdm verkehren
reality [ri'æləti]	Gegebenheit

page 137

repulsed [rɪ'pʌlst]	angewidert
charm [tʃɑːm]	Charme, Zauber
gait [geɪt]	Gang
goodness ['gʊdnəs]	Güte, Tugend
to **blind sb** [blaɪnd]	jdn blenden
to **consume sth** [kən'sjuːm]	etw verbrauchen, etw konsumieren, (Kalorien) aufnehmen
to **cohabit with sb** [kəʊ'hæbɪt]	mit jdm zusammenleben (in eheähnlicher Gemeinschaft)
to **weaken sb** ['wiːkən]	jdn schwächen, jdn schwach machen
to **snatch sth up** [ˌsnætʃ 'ʌp]	etw ergreifen
to **spiral** ['spaɪrəl]	sich schrauben, sich winden
inward ['ɪnwəd]	nach innen
sublime [sə'blaɪm]	unvergleichlich, erhaben
particular [pə'tɪkjələ]	Einzelheit

page 138

prevention [prɪ'venʃn]	Prävention, Vorbeugung
lawn [lɔːn]	Rasen(fläche)
to **unfold** [ʌn'fəʊld]	sich entwickeln, sich abspielen
intelligence subcommittee [ɪnˌtelɪdʒəns 'sʌbkəmɪti]	Geheimdienstunterausschuss
courageous [kə'reɪdʒəs]	mutig, couragiert
security [sɪ'kjʊərəti]	Sicherheit
to **decapitate sb** [dɪ'kæpɪteɪt]	jdn enthaupten
tenet ['tenɪt]	Grundsatz, Lehre
to **bury** ['beri]	begraben, beerdigen
to **demonize** ['diːmənaɪz]	dämonisieren, verteufeln
crucial ['kruːʃl]	entscheidend
to **figure out** [ˌfɪgər 'aʊt]	herausfinden, ausrechnen
to **thwart sth** [θwɔːt]	etw verhindern, etw vereiteln
kinetic power [kɪˌnetɪk 'paʊə]	Bewegungsenergie
to **strap on sth** [ˌstræp 'ɒn]	sich etw umschnallen
vest [vest]	Weste
trade-off ['treɪd ɒf]	Ausgleich, Abwägung, Kompromiss
to **elevate sth** ['elɪveɪt]	etw anheben
to **level with sb** ['levl]	mit jdm offen reden
home-grown [ˌhəʊm 'grəʊn]	einheimisch
lone wolf [ˌləʊn 'wʊlf]	Einzelkämpfer (einsamer Wolf)
to **exhibit sth** [ɪg'zɪbɪt]	etw zeigen, etw ausstellen
aircraft carrier ['eəkrɑːft kæriə]	Flugzeugträger
imperative [ɪm'perətɪv]	zwingend, unerlässlich
to **surface sth** ['sɜːfɪs]	etw aufgreifen
fruit vendor ['fruːt vendə]	Obstverkäufer/in
to **immolate oneself** ['ɪməleɪt]	sich selbst verbrennen
to **dislocate sth** ['dɪsləkeɪt]	etw ausrenken, etw zum Erliegen bringen
outflow ['aʊtfləʊ]	Abfluss, Abwanderung
to **destabilize sth** [ˌdiː'steɪbəlaɪz]	etw destabilisieren
to **confine sth to sth** [kən'faɪn]	etw auf etw beschränken
feeder system ['fiːdə sɪstəm]	Zuführungssystem
to **skip sth** [skɪp]	etw überspringen, etw auslassen
demagogue ['deməgɒg]	Volksverhetzer/in, Demagoge/-in

page 139

to **hand sth in** [ˌhænd 'ɪn]	etw abgeben
to **relate to sb/sth** [rɪ'leɪt tə]	einen Bezug zu jdm/etw haben, mit jdm/etw in Zusammenhang stehen
to **deteriorate** [dɪ'tɪəriəreɪt]	(sich) verschlechtern
to **double** ['dʌbl]	(sich) verdoppeln
internal [ɪn'tɜːnl]	inländisch, Inlands-
secondary ['sekəndri]	sekundär, zweitrangig
thrilling ['θrɪlɪŋ]	aufregend, erregend
glory ['glɔːri]	Ruhm
esteem [ɪ'stiːm]	Achtung, Ansehen
mindless ['maɪndləs]	hirnlos, blindwütig

page 140

commonplace ['kɒmənpleɪs]	alltäglich, gewöhnlich
hotbed ['hɒtbed]	Brutstätte
injustice [ɪn'dʒʌstɪs]	Unrecht, Ungerechtigkeit
to **tighten sth** ['taɪtn]	etw anziehen, etw verschärfen
CCTV (closed-circuit television) [ˌsiː siː tiː 'viː]	Videoüberwachung
suspected [sə'spektɪd]	mutmaßlich
punishment ['pʌnɪʃmənt]	Strafe, Bestrafung
deterrent [dɪ'terənt]	Abschreckung(smittel)
influx ['ɪnflʌks]	Zustrom
to **nurture sth** ['nɜːtʃə]	etw entwickeln, etw pflegen, etw fördern
fortress ['fɔːtrəs]	Festung

A–Z WORD LIST

Dieses Wörterverzeichnis enthält alle Wörter aus **Focus on Success Plus 13** in alphabetischer Reihenfolge. Wörter, die in den Hörverständnisübungen vorkommen, sind mit einem *T* gekennzeichnet.

A

to **abandon oneself** *70* sich hingeben
abandonment *69* Aufgabe, Verlassenheit
abbreviated *37* abgekürzt
to **abdicate responsibility** *118* sich aus der Verantwortung ziehen
abdication *120* Verzicht
to **abhor sth** *48* verabscheuen, hassen
abhorrent *81* abscheulich
abrupt *22* abrupt, plötzlich
absorbed *135* aufgenommen, absorbiert
abstract *47* abstrakt
abusive *48* gewalttätig, missbrauchend
abyss *90T* Abgrund
academic *20* Akademiker/in
to **accelerate** *11* beschleunigen
acceptance *44* Akzeptanz, Annahme
to **accommodate sb** *63* jdn unterbringen
to **accompany sb/sth** *57* jdn/etw begleiten, mit etw einhergehen
to **accomplish sth** *66T* etw erreichen, etw leisten
accordingly *48* (dem)entsprechend
account: to ~ **for sth** *66T* etw ausmachen; to **come into** ~ *52* in Betracht kommen; to **take into** ~ *33* berücksichtigen
to **accumulate sth** *87* etw ansammeln, etw anhäufen
accumulation *135* Anhäufung
accuracy *38* Genauigkeit
to **accuse sb of sth** *122* jdn einer Sache beschuldigen, jdm etw vorwerfen
accustomed *33T* gewöhnt, gewohnt
to **achieve sth** *15T* etw erreichen, etw leisten
acidity *95* Säure, Säuregehalt
to **acknowledge sth** *25V* etw anerkennen
to **acquire sth** *8* etw erwerben
acreage *93* Anbaufläche
across: ~ **the board** *114V* durch die Bank; to **come** ~ **as …** *8* … wirken, einen … Eindruck machen
to **activate sth** *78* etw aktivieren
actual *19* tatsächlich, konkret
actually *50T* eigentlich, wirklich, in der Tat
acute *44* akut
to **adapt** *15T* sich anpassen
to **add to sth** *8* beitragen zu etw, etw vergrößern
addendum *82V* Zusatz, Ergänzung
addiction (to) *86* Sucht (nach), Abhängigkeit (von)
addictive *87* süchtig machend
addition: in ~ **to sth** *8* zusätzlich zu etw
additional *52* zusätzlich
address *39* Ansprache; to ~ **sth** *8* etw angehen, sich mit etw befassen
adequate *131* angemessen, geeignet
to **adhere to sth** *81* etw einhalten
adherence *126* Einhaltung
to **adjust to sth** *7* sich an etw gewöhnen, sich auf etw einstellen
adjustment *72* Anpassung, Veränderung
to **administer sth** *94* etw anwenden
administration *33T* Verwaltung
administrator *33* Verwalter/in, Verwaltungsangestellte/r
admirable *58T* bewundernswert
to **admit sb** *19* jdn aufnehmen, jdn zulassen
to **adorn sth** *134* etw zieren, etw schmücken
to **advance sth** *81* etw verbessern, etw voranbringen
advanced *16* fortgeschritten, hochentwickelt
advantage: to **take** ~ **of sth** *106* sich etw zunutze machen, etw ausnutzen
advent (of sth) *88* Ankunft, Beginn (einer Sache)
to **advise against sth** *86* von etw abraten
advised *30* angehalten
adviser, advisor *10* Berater/in
advocacy (of) *33* Eintreten (für), Befürwortung *(einer Sache)*
to **advocate sth** *33T* etw befürworten, etw verfechten
to **affect sth** *24* etw beeinflussen, sich auswirken auf etw
affiliated *40T* verbunden mit, nahestehend
affinity *46* Affinität
to **affirm sth** *136* etw bestätigen
affirmation *102* Bestätigung
affirmative action *(AE)* *59* Fördermaßnahmen *(zugunsten benachteiligter Gruppen)*
afflicted: be ~ **with sth** *69* an etw leiden
affluence *97T* Wohlstand
affluent *62* wohlhabend
afford: to **be able to** ~ **sth** *20* sich etw leisten können
affordability *58T* Erschwinglichkeit, Bezahlbarkeit
affordable *58T* erschwinglich
after all *29* schließlich (doch), immerhin
aftermath: in the ~ **of** *55* in der Folge von
to **age** *52* altern; **in our day and** ~ *76* in unserer Zeit, heutzutage
agency *35* Agentur; **regulatory** ~ *86* Aufsichtsbehörde, Regulierungsagentur
agenda *30* Agenda, Tagesprogramm
agent *76* Akteur, Handelnde/r
agitation *30* Aufregung
agreement *54* Vereinbarung, Absprache
aid *64* Hilfe
to **aim at/for sth** *18* etw anstreben
aimed: to **be** ~ **at sth** *29* auf etw zielen, auf etw gerichtet sein
air: to ~ **sth** *114* etw senden; ~ **conditioning** *102* Klimaanlage
air traffic control *12* Flugsicherung
aircraft, *pl* **aircraft** *100* Flugzeug; ~ **carrier** *138T* Flugzeugträger
airplane *(AE)* *102* Flugzeug
albeit *54* wenngleich
to **alert sb** *30* jdn alarmieren
to **align with sb** *58T* sich mit jdm verbünden, sich auf jds Seite stellen
alignment *38* Ausrichtung
alike *80* gleichermaßen, in gleicher Weise
all: once (and) for ~ *57V* ein für allemal, endgültig
to **allege sb sth** *103T* jdm etw vorwerfen, jdm etw unterstellen
allegedly *118* angeblich
to **alleviate sth** *64* etw mildern, etw lindern
to **allocate sth to sb** *109* jdm etw zuweisen, jdm etw zuteilen
to **allot sb sth** *7* jdm etw zuteilen
all-powerful *127* allmächtig
alluring *134* verlockend, verführerisch
ally *125* Alliierte/r, Verbündete/r
along with *82V* (zusammen) mit, neben
alongside *12* neben
to **alter sth** *37* etw (ab)ändern
alteration *37* Änderung
amalgam *15T* Amalgam, Verschmelzung
amazed *71* erstaunt
ambassador *40T* Botschafter/in
ambiguity *8* Mehrdeutigkeit
ambiguous *8* mehrdeutig
to **ambush sb** *127* jdn überfallen, jdn in einen Hinterhalt locken
amendment *33* Ergänzung, Zusatz
amiable *30* liebenswürdig
amoral *80* amoralisch *(sich über die Moral hinwegsetzend)*
amount *57* Menge, Ausmaß, Umfang
amplification *40T* Verstärkung
anatomist *77* Anatom/in
anatomy *79* Anatomie
angel *135* Engel
angelic *135* Engels-, englisch
anger *40T* Zorn, Wut; to ~ **sb** *33T* jdn ärgern, jdn beleidigen
annoyed *22* verärgert
annual *114V* jährlich
another: one way or ~ *90T* so oder so, auf die eine oder andere Art
anthology *39* Sammelband, Zusammenstellung, Anthologie
to **anticipate sth** *66T* mit etw rechnen, etw erwarten
antipathy *128* Antipathie, Abneigung
anxiety (about/over) *47* Angst, Sorge (wegen), Ängstlichkeit
apace *82V* rasch
apart: worlds ~ *82V* getrennte Welten

apart from *8* abgesehen von, außer
apocalyptic *82V* apokalyptisch
apology *78* Entschuldigung
appalling *31* entsetzlich, schrecklich
apparent *22* augenscheinlich
appeal *12* Appell, Ansprache; *62* Anziehungskraft, Reiz; to ~ **to sb/sth** *48* an jdn/etw appellieren
to **appease sb** *7* jdn beschwichtigen
appendix *90T* Anhang *(am Ende eines Buches)*
applicant *13* Bewerber/in
appointee *94* Benannte/r
appointment *94* Ernennung, Berufung
to **appreciate sth** *23* etw schätzen, etw zu schätzen wissen
apprenticeship *26* Ausbildung, Lehre
approach: divide-and-conquer ~ *40T* Teile-und-Herrsche-Herangehensweise
approval *88* Bestätigung, Anerkennung
to **approve of sth** *33* etw gut finden
aquiver *69* erwartungsvoll, erregt
arable *93* urbar, kultivierbar; **~ farming** *92* Ackerbau
arch *29* Erz-
ardent *44* glühend, begeistert
arguably *79* wohl
arid *101* trocken, ausgedörrt
to **arise (arose, arisen)** *13* entstehen, auftreten, sich ergeben
to **arm sb** *48* jdn bewaffnen
armchair *69* Sessel
arms race *88* Wettrüsten
arousal *40T* Erregung
to **arouse sth** *9* etw wecken, etw erregen
arrogant *19* arrogant
art: work of ~ *8* Kunstwerk
articulation *12* Artikulation, Aussprache
artificial intelligence *76* künstliche Intelligenz
as: ~ well ~ *8* sowohl … als auch …, ebenso wie, sowie; **such ~** *13* wie (zum Beispiel)
aside: to **take sb ~** *20* jdn beiseite nehmen
aspect *14* Gesichtspunkt, Aspekt
aspiration *105* Ambition, Bestreben
assault: to **be under ~** *44* angegriffen werden
to **assemble sth** *37* etw wzusammenbauen, etw montieren
to **assert sth** *88* etw behaupten
assertion: self-~ *71* Selbstbehauptung
assertive *46* durchsetzungsfähig
to **assess sth** *54* etw beurteilen
assessment *103* Beurteilung, Einstufung
assistance *82V* Hilfe, Unterstützung
to **associate sth with sth** *21* etw mit etw verbinden, etw mit etw assoziieren
association *29* Verband, Vereinigung
to **assuage sb** *64* jdn beschwichtigen
to **assume sth** *22* etw annehmen, von etw ausgehen
assurance *103* Zusage, Vergewisserung
to **assure sb of sth** *69* jdm etw versichern
astronomical *38* astronomisch
at present *96* momentan, derzeit, zurzeit
attachment *47* Bindung, Verbundenheit
attempt *21* Versuch
to **attend sth** *20* an etw teilnehmen
attitudinal *73* einstellungsbezogen
auspicious *25V* vielversprechend, glückverheißend
austerity *109* wirtschaftliche Einschränkung, Entbehrung
authoritarian *40* autoritär
authorities *(pl)* *103T* Behörden
authority *22* Autorität, Kompetenz
automatic *36* automatisch
automotive *64* Automobil-
autonomy *80* Autonomie, Unabhängigkeit
availability *99* Verfügbarkeit
avalanche *88* Lawine
average: on ~ *54* im Durchschnitt
avoidance *8* Vermeidung
award *29* Auszeichnung, Preis
aware: to **be ~ of sth** *8* etw wissen, sich einer Sache bewusst sein
awareness *8* Bewusstsein
awful *79* furchtbar, schrecklich
awkward *27* unangenehm, peinlich

B

babe *48* junges Mädchen
back: to **~ sb/sth** *62* jdn/etw unterstützen; to **~ sth up** *82V* etw untermauern, etw bekräftigen, etw belegen
back number *36* frühere Ausgabe
backdrop *82V* Hintergrund
backlash *109* Gegenreaktion, Gegenbewegung
to **bail sb out** *94* jdm aus der Patsche helfen
bare *131* kahl, nackt, bar
barefoot *38* barfuß
barely *119* kaum
to **bargain** *25V* (ver)handeln
to **bark** *131*
barren *95* ausgedörrt, unfruchtbar
barrier *106* Barriere, Schranke, Grenze
base *62* Basis
based: to **be ~ in** *13* seinen (Firmen-)Sitz haben in
basis, *pl* **bases** *8* Basis, Grundlage
battered *127* (an)geschlagen
battery-cage hen *75* Legebatteriehuhn
battleground *120* Schlachtfeld
Bavarian *18* bayerisch
bay *50T* Bucht; to **keep sb/sth at ~** *90T* jdn/etw fernhalten, sich jdn/etw vom Leib halten
to **be to do sth** *24* etw tun sollen
beacon *120* Leuchtfeuer
bear: to **~ (bore, borne)** *38* tragen, ertragen; to **~ sth out** *62* etw bestätigen
beauty *136* Schönheit
to **beg** *71* flehen, eindringlich bitten
behalf: on ~ of *33T* im Namen von, im Interesse von, für
behaviour *8* Benehmen, Verhalten
belief *40T* Glaube, Überzeugung
believer: to **be a ~ in sth** *129* von etw überzeugt sein
to **belittle sth** *76* etw herabsetzen, etw schmälern
belly *134* Bauch
to **bend sth (bent, bent)** *70* etw beugen
beneath *135* unterhalb, unter
beneficial *114* nützlich, vorteilhaft
beneficiary *118* Nutznießer/in
benefits *pl* *58T* Sozialleistungen
bent: to **be ~ on doing sth** *33T* unbedingt etw tun wollen
to **bespeak sth (bespoke, bespoken)** *70* etw erkennen lassen, etw verraten
to **betray sb/sth (to sb)** *134* jdn/etw (an jdn) verraten, preisgeben
betterment *106* Besserung
to **beware of sth** *91* sich vor etw hüten, etw vermeiden
beyond *70* jenseits, außerhalb; *93* darüber hinaus
bias *66T* Voreingenommenheit; **gender ~** *44* geschlechtsspezifische Diskriminierung
bidder *89* Bieter/in
biofuel *92* Biokraftstoff
birth *46* Geburt
bland *31* fade, fadenscheinig
blank *134* leer, frei
to **blast sth** *47* etw vernichten, etw scharf kritisieren
to **blaze** *135* leuchten, funkeln
bleak *106* trostlos, freudlos
to **blend sth** *136* etw (ver)mischen
blessing *76* Segen
to **blind sb** *137* jdn blenden
blindness: wilful ~ *118* vorsätzliche Blindheit
blob *101* Klecks
to **blow up sth (blew, blown)** *103T* etw in die Luft jagen
blue-collar worker *62* Arbeiter/in
to **blunt** *62* dämpfen, abschwächen
blurred: to **get ~** *127* verschwimmen
board: across the ~ *114V* durch die Bank; **corporate ~** *58T* Unternehmensleitung
boardroom *103T* Sitzungssaal
boatload *118* Bootladung
boiler *135* Kessel, Heizkessel
boisterous *19* ausgelassen, übermütig
bold *64* kühn, mutig
to **bolster** *48* unterstützen
bomb: pipe ~ *122T* Rohrbombe
to **boo** *48* buhen
boost *88* (schnelle) Steigerung, Auftrieb; to **~ sth** *55* etw stärken, etw ankurbeln, einer Sache Auftrieb geben
booth: voting ~ *(AE)* *129* Wahlkabine
border *63* Grenze
bosom *70* Busen
bottom-up *54* von unten nach oben
bound: to **be ~ to sth** *24* etwas erwarten können
boundary *33T* Grenze, Trennlinie
bounds: out of ~ *33T* verboten
to **bow** *136* sich (ver)beugen
bracket *9* Klammer
to **brainstorm** *125* Ideen (ungeordnet) sammeln
to **brainwash sb** *8* jdn einer Gehirnwäsche unterziehen

branch *106* Zweig
brand *50T* Marke; to ~ **sb (as) sth** *87* jdn als etw abstempeln
breach *58T* Verletzung, Bruch
breadwinner *47* Brotverdiener/in
to **break the news to sb** *69* jdm eine Nachricht überbringen
breath: under her ~ *70* flüsternd
to **breathe** *7* atmen
to **breed sth (bred, bred)** *95* etw züchten
to **bridge sth** *46* etw überbrücken
bright *25* hell, strahlend, freundlich
broad *55* breit, weit
to **broadcast (broadcast, broadcast)** *108* senden
brutality *40T* Brutalität
to **brutalize sb** *40T* jdm brutal behandeln
brute force *126* brutale Gewalt
bud *131* Knospe
bullshit: to **call ~** *48* Blödsinn reden
bulwark *109* Bollwerk
burned ground *22* verbrannte Erde
to **bury** *138T* begraben, beerdigen
business: to **get down to ~** *26* zur Sache kommen
businessman, *pl* **businessmen, businesspeople** *20* Geschäftsmann
to **bustle** *30* wimmeln, wuseln

C

cage: battery-~ hen *75* Legebatteriehuhn
caged *95* eingesperrt *(in Käfighaltung)*
to **call bullshit** *48* Blödsinn reden
caller *22* Anrufer/in
calorific: in ~ terms *99* in kalorischer Hinsicht
camaraderie *57* Kameradschaft
camo tarp *101* Tarnplane
camouflage *102* Tarnung
camp: extermination ~ *78* Vernichtungslager
to **campaign for/against sth** *87* sich für/gegen etw einsetzen
campaigner *94* Aktivist/in
campus *30* Gelände *(z.B. Schule, Unternehmen)*
canister *78* Dose, Büchse
cap *122T* Deckel, Obergrenze
capability *82V* Fähigkeit, Potenzial
capable of sth *80* zu etw fähig, zu etw imstande
capacity *66T* Kapazität, Leistung
capita: per ~ *114V* pro Kopf
capitalism *63* Kapitalismus
capitalist *33T* kapitalistisch; **venture ~** *86* Risikokapitalgeber/in
to **capture** *30* einfangen, erfassen
care *58T* Versorgung, Fürsorge; to ~ **for sb** *118* für jdn sorgen, sich um jdn kümmern, auf jdn aufpassen; **health ~** *58T* Gesundheitswesen, medizinische Versorgung; to **take ~ of sb** *57* sich um jdn kümmern
careless *76* nachlässig
carer: home ~ *54* Hauspfleger/in
carrier: aircraft ~ *138T* Flugzeugträger
to **carry over** *12* übernehmen, übertragen

case *33T* Fall; ~ **study** *53* Fallstudie
casual *25V* leger, zwanglos
casualty *72* Verlust, Opfer
catastrophic *120* katastrophal, verhängnisvoll
to **catch up with sb (caught, caught)** *112* zu jdm aufschließen
categorical pledge *37* kategorische Garantie
to **cater to sb/sth** *30* auf jdn/etw ausgerichtet sein, jdm/etw gerecht werden
cause *44* Ursache, Grund, Anliegen
cautionary tale *90T* abschreckendes Beispiel
cautious *46* vorsichtig, zurückhaltend
CCTV (closed-circuit television) *140* Videoüberwachung
to **cease** *12* aufhören, eingestellt werden
ceasefire *126* Waffenstillstand
ceiling *44* (Zimmer-)Decke
censorship *31* Zensur
centralised *127* zentralisiert
centred on: to **be ~ sth** *29* sich um etw drehen, sich auf etw konzentrieren
CEO (Chief Executive Officer) *58T* Vorstandsvorsitzende/r
certification *54* Bescheinigung
to **certify** *54* zertifizieren
cf. *74* vgl.
chair *54* Vorsitzende/r; to ~ **sth** *58T* etw leiten *(als Vorsitzende/r)*
to **challenge sth** *30* etw infrage stellen, etw anzweifeln
chamber: gas ~ *79* Gaskammer
changer: game ~ *50T* Wendpunkt
chaotic *127* chaotisch
chapter *36* Kapitel
characteristic *19* Merkmal, charakteristische Eigenschaft
charge: in ~ of sth *50T* verantwortlich für etw, (feder)führend bei etw
charm *137* Charme, Zauber
charter *126* Charta, Satzung
chatter *135* Geschwätz, Geplapper
to **cheat on sb** *90* jdn betrügen
checkout *97T* Kasse
chemist *77* Chemiker/in, Drogist/in, Apotheker/in
chief: ~ executive *55* Hauptgeschäftsführer/in; ~ **operating officer** *88* leitende/r Geschäftsführer/in
choice: of ~ *47* seiner/ihrer/... Wahl
to **choke sb/sth** *131* jdn/etw ersticken
chord: to **strike a ~ with sb (struck, struck)** *87* auf Anklang stoßen
to **circulate sth** *87* etw verschicken
to **cite sth** *40T* etw zitieren, etw angeben
citizenship *122T* Staatsbürgerschaft, Staatsbürgerkunde
civic duty *46* bürgerliche Pflicht
civil: ~ society *94* Zivilgesellschaft; ~ **war** *106* Bürgerkrieg
civilian *40T* Zivilist/in
claim *38* Behauptung; to ~ *40* behaupten
to **clap** *25V* (Beifall) klatschen
to **clarify sth** *58T* etw klären, etw verdeutlichen

clarity *23* Klarheit
clash *126* Konflikt; **cultural ~** *19* Kulturkonflikt
to **clasp sth** *71* sich in etw einhaken, etw umklammern
to **classify** *25V* klassifizieren, einteilen
clay *135* Ton, Lehm
clean-up cost *97T* Sanierungskosten
clickbait *90T* Klickfang, Klickköder
client *19* Kunde/Kundin
climate change *44* Klimawandel
to **cling to sth (clung, clung)** *44* sich an etw klammern, an etw festhalten
clinical trial *76* klinische Prüfung, klinische Studie
to **clip sth together** *36* etw zusammenheften
close *30* nah, dicht, eng
closed mind *31* Engstirnigkeit
closely cropped *101* kurzgeschoren
clothing *25V* Bekleidung, Kleidung
cluster *64* Cluster, Anhäufung
clustered *63* geballt, angehäuft
to **coach** *22* schulen, trainieren, unterrichten
code *80* Code, Kodex, Regeln; ~ **of conduct** *82V* Verhaltenskodex
co-founder *58T* Mitbegründer/in
to **cohabit with sb** *137* mit jdm zusammenleben *(in eheähnlicher Gemeinschaft)*
cohabitation *57* Zusammenleben, (eheähnliche) Gemeinschaft
cohesion *8* Zusammenhalt
coin *131* Münze; to ~ **sth** *86* etw prägen
collapse *108* Einsturz, Kollaps
collar: blue-~ worker *62* Arbeiter/in
to **collate** *37T* zusammentragen, zusammenstellen
collateral damage *76* Kollateralschaden
colleague *12* Kollege/-in
collection: data ~ *86* Datensammlung
to **collocate** *9* kollokieren *(eine gebräuchliche lexikalische Einheit bilden)*
collocation *9* Kollokation *(inhaltlich kombinierbare sprachliche Einheiten)*
colloquial *12* umgangssprachlich
colonialism *29* Kolonialismus
colour-blind *66T* farbenblind
column *83* Spalte; *136* Säule
to **combat sth** *57V* etw bekämpfen
come: to ~ **across as ...** *8* ... wirken, einen ... Eindruck machen; to ~ **into force** *57V* in Kraft treten; to ~ **up with sth** *46* etw erbringen
comission: ethics commission *82V* Ethikkommission
command: to **have (a) good ~ of English** *8* Englisch gut beherrschen
commander *57V* Kommandant/in, Anführer/in
commerce *97T* Handel
commission: Securities and Exchange Commission *90T* Börsenaufsichtsbehörde *(USA)*
commitment (to) *120* Engagement (für), Bekenntnis (zu)
committed: to **be ~ to sth** *29* sich für etw engagieren, für etw engagiert sein

commodity *92* Erzeugnis, Ware
common: ~ sense *91* gesunder Menschenverstand; to **have sth in ~** *58* etw (miteinander) gemeinsam haben
commonplace *140* alltäglich, gewöhnlich
communal *31* Gemeinschafts-, gemeinschaftlich, gemeinsam
communications *(pl)*: **communications** *(pl)* *11* Nachrichten
communicator *8* Kommunikator/in
communist *109* kommunistisch, Kommunist/in
comparable *118* vergleichbar
compassion *94* Mitgefühl
compassionate *44* mitfühlend, mitleidig
to **compel** *56* zwingen
competence *27* Kompetenz
competitive *66* umkämpft, wettbewerbsintensiv
comply: failure to ~ (with sth) *53* Nichteinhaltung (von etw)
to **comply with sth** *54* etw erfüllen, etw befolgen, sich an etw halten
composed *71* gelassen, beherrscht
composition *26* Aufsatz
to **comprehend sth** *76* etw verstehen
comprehensible *12* verständlich
to **comprise sth** *58T* etw umfassen, aus etw bestehen
to **compromise** *116* Kompromisse eingehen
compulsion *82V* Zwang, Druck
compulsive *88* zwanghaft
compulsory *57V* Pflicht-, obligatorisch
to **conceal** *69* verbergen
conceivably *37* möglicherweise
to **conceive** *76* empfangen; to **~ sth** *82V* etw konzipieren
to **concentrate on sth** *64* sich auf etw konzentrieren
concern *11* Sorge, Befürchtung
concerned: to **be ~ (with sth)** *29* sich (mit etw) befassen
concerned about *15T* bedacht auf
concerning *33* betreffend, hinsichtlich
concerted *66T* abgestimmt, konzertiert
to **conclude** *24* abschließen
conclusion: to **draw a ~** *10* eine Schlussfolgerung ziehen
to **condemn sth** *126* etw verdammen, etw verurteilen
conditioning: air ~ *102* Klimaanlage
conditions: working ~ *(pl)* *116* Arbeitsbedingungen
conduct: to **~ sth** *18* etw (durch) führen, etw leiten; **code of ~** *82V* Verhaltenskodex
confederation *54* Bund, Konföderation
confidence *55* (Selbst-)Vertrauen, Zuversicht
to **confine sth to sth** *138T* etw auf etw beschränken
confinement *93* Gefangenschaft
to **conflict with** *39* in Widerspruch stehen mit
to **conform** *46* sich anpassen
to **confound** *48* verwirren
to **confront sb with sb/sth** *31* jdn mit jdm/etw konfrontieren
confrontation *126* Auseinandersetzung
congressional *122T* Kongress-
conquer: to **~ sth** *82V* etw bezwingen, sich etw unterwerfen; **divide-and-~ approach** *40T* Teile-und-Herrsche-Herangehensweise
conscience *58T* Gewissen
conscientiousness *33T* Gewissenhaftigkeit
conscious *66T* bewusst
consciousness *135* Bewusstsein
conscript *57* Wehrpflichtige/r
conscription *57V* Wehrpflicht, Wehrdienst, Einberufung
consensus *31* Konsens
conservative *23* konservativ
to **consider sth** *23* über etw nachdenken, etw in Erwägung ziehen
considerable *95* erheblich, beträchtlich
consideration *8* Rücksicht, Erwägung, Überlegung
considered: to **be ~ sth** *22* für etw gehalten werden, als etw angesehen werden
to **consist of sth** *15* aus etw bestehen
to **consort with sb** *136* mit jdm verkehren
conspiracy *13* Verschwörung, Komplott
to **constitute sth** *33T* etw darstellen, etw ausmachen, etw bilden
constitution *33* Verfassung
constitutional *47* verfassungsrechtlich
construction *15T* Konstruktion
consult: to **~ sb** *103* jdn um Rat fragen, jdn hinzuziehen; to **~ sth** *102* in etw nachsehen, in etw nachlesen
to **consume sth** *137* etw verbrauchen, etw konsumieren, *(Kalorien)* aufnehmen
consumerist society *44* Konsumgesellschaft
consumption *37* Verbrauch, Konsum
to **contend** *93* behaupten
content(s) *26* Inhalt
continual *103* ständig, ununterbrochen, kontinuierlich
continuous *37* kontinuierlich, anhaltend
to **contract sth** *96* sich mit etw infizieren
contractor *58T* Auftragnehmer/in
to **contradict** *11* widersprechen
contradiction *30* Widerspruch
contrary: on the ~ *126* im Gegenteil
to **contribute (to)** *23* beitragen (zu)
contribution *78* Beitrag
to **contrive sth** *118* etw bewerkstelligen
control-alt-delete *104* Strg-Alt-Entf *(Windows-Computertastatur-Kürzel für das „Abschießen" eines Programms)*
controversy *33T* Kontroverse, Auseinandersetzung
convenience *58T* Bequemlichkeit, Annehmlichkeit, Komfort
conventional *126* konventionell, herkömmlich
to **convey** *8* übermitteln, vermitteln
to **cope** *7* zurechtkommen
copper *135* Kupfer
copycat *126* Nachahmungs-
cord: umbilical ~ *58* Nabelschnur
core *82V* Kern-, Haupt-
corners: to **cut ~** *80* Abkürzungen nehmen, pfuschen
corporate board *58T* Unternehmensleitung
corporation *50T* Konzern
correction *37* Korrektur
corresponding *24* entsprechend, passend
corridor *36* Flur, Gang
to **corrupt sth** *90T* etw verderben, etw korrumpieren
cost: clean-up ~ *97T* Sanierungskosten
costly *19* teuer, verlustreich
counselling: marriage ~ *90T* Eheberatung
countenance *72* Gesichtsausdruck, Fassung
counterpart *25V* Gegenstück, Gegenüber, Pendant
counterproductive *65* kontraproduktiv
counterterrorism *103T* Terrorismusabwehr, Terrorismusbekämpfung
countless *69* zahllose, unzählige
coup *79* Putsch
courageous *138T* mutig, couragiert
to **course** *70* strömen
coverage *81* Berichterstattung, Behandlung *(eines Themas)*
covert *78* verdeckt
to **cow sb** *48* jdn einschüchtern
crackdown *126* Durchgreifen, Bekämpfung
crackling *135* knisternd
to **craft** *40T* herstellen
to **cram sth into sth** *93* etw in etw einpferchen
creation *29* Schaffung; *76* Geschöpf
creativity *49* schöpferische Begabung, Kreativität
creature *70* Geschöpf, (Lebe-)Wesen
credentials: environmental ~ *(pl)* *97T* Umweltverträglichkeit
to **crest** *62* den Gipfel erreichen
crevice *135* Spalte
crisis, *pl* **crises** *31* Krise
critical incident *19* kritisches Ereignis, kritischer Zwischenfall
criticism (of sb/sth) *23* Kritik (an jdm/etw)
to **criticize sb/sth** *32* jdn/etw kritisieren
crop *82V* Nutzpflanze, Feldfrucht
cropped: closely ~ *101* kurzgeschoren
cross (with) *31* sauer (auf)
crossed wires *22* vertauschte Leitungen, Missverständnisse
crucial *138T* entscheidend
crucial (to/for) *12* äußerst wichtig, entscheidend (für)
crude *55* roh, grob
cruel *70* grausam, gemein
cruelty *93* Grausamkeit
to **crumble** *22* zerbröseln
to **crumple sth up** *37* etw zerknüllen
to **crush sb/sth** *136* jdn/etw zerdrücken, jdn/etw vernichten
crushing *136* vernichtend

cry: rallying ~ *124* Parole, Schlachtruf
cubicle *36* Kabine
cue *48* Zeichen, Hinweis
culpable *109* schuldig
culprit *63* Schuldige/r, Übeltäter/in
to **cultivate sth** *66T* etw kultivieren
cultivation *92* Kultivierung, Anbau
cultural clash *19* Kulturkonflikt
curable *96* heilbar
curb *30* Einschränkung
to **cure sb/sth** *96* jdn/etw heilen
curiosity *66T* Neugier
currency *109* Währung
current *36* Strom
currently *36* zurzeit
curriculum, *pl* **curriculums** *or* **curricula: curriculum,** *pl* **curriculums** *or* **curricula** *13* Lehrplan
to **curtsy** *25V* knicksen
custodian *79* Bewahrer/in
to **cut corners** *80* Abkürzungen nehmen, pfuschen
cutting-edge *114V* Spitzen-, auf dem neusten Stand
cyanide *78* Zyanid
cyclical *106* zyklisch
cylinder *36* Zylinder

D

dairy *99* Molkerei, Milch-, Molkerei-
damage: collateral ~ *76* Kollateralschaden
damned: the ~ *(pl)* *136* die Verdammten
data collection *86* Datensammlung
date: to **~ back …** *54* … alt sein, stammen aus …; **up to ~** *38* aktuell, auf dem/den neuesten Stand
day: in our ~ and age *76* in unserer Zeit, heutzutage
day by day *37* tagtäglich
day care *54* Kinderbetreuung
deadline *20* Frist, Termin
to **deal with sth** *38* mit etw umgehen
dealer: drug ~ *88* Drogenhändler/in
decade *13* Jahrzehnt
to **decapitate sb** *138T* jdn enthaupten
decent *25* anständig, ordentlich, annehmbar
to **decipher sth** *8* etw entziffern, etw entschlüsseln
declaration *82V* Erklärung
to **declare sth** *47* etw verkünden, etw erklären
to **decline** *13* zurückgehen, fallen, sinken
decorative *8* dekorativ
to **decrease** *92* abnehmen, zurückgehen
to **dedicate sth to sb** *48* jdm etw widmen
to **deduce sth from sth** *135* etw von etw ableiten, etw von etw herleiten
deed *39* Tat
to **deem** *30* erachten, halten
defeat *31* Niederlage
to **defeat sb** *62* jdn besiegen, jdn schlagen
defence *79* Verteidigung
defence minister *57V* Verteidigungsminister/in
to **defend sb/sth** *32* jdn/etw verteidigen
defender *122T* Verteidiger/in
to **defer to sb** *23* sich jdm unterordnen, jdm nachgeben
deference: in ~ to *102* mit Rücksicht auf
to **deflate** *21* Luft ablassen, dämpfen
deforestation *93* Waldzerstörung
degradation *44* Abbau, Schädigung
to **degrade sth** *90T* etw abbauen
delay *39* Verzögerung
delegate *118* Delegierte/r
deliberate *8* absichtlich, (ganz) bewusst, vorsätzlich; to **~** *82V* sich beraten, reiflich durchdenken
delighted *55* (sehr) erfreut, entzückt
to **deliver sth** *23* etw liefern
delivery *90T* Lieferung
demagogue *138* Volksverhetzer/in, Demagoge/-in
demand *31* Forderung; to **~** *31* fordern, verlangen, nachfragen; **in ~** *13* (nach)gefragt, gesucht; to **meet a ~** *35* eine Nachfrage befriedigen
demise *62* Ende, Untergang
demographic *44* demographisch
to **demonize** *138T* dämonisieren, verteufeln
to **demonstrate sth** *58T* etw zeigen, etw demonstrieren
to **deny sth** *136* etw leugnen, etw bestreiten
to **depend on/upon sb/sth** *15T* von jdm/etw abhängen
dependent on sth *57V* von etw abhängig
to **depict** *29* darstellen, aufzeigen
depletion *97T* Verringerung, Abbau
deployment *76* Stationierung, Einsatz
to **deport sb** *118* jdn abschieben
to **depress sth** *100* etw drücken
to **deprive sb of sth** *87* jdn etw berauben, jdm etw vorenthalten
to **derail** *126* entgleisen
deregulation *96* Liberalisierung, Freigabe
to **derive** *15T* ableiten
to **descend** *71* hinabsteigen
desecrated *134* entweiht
to **deserve sth** *48* etw verdienen
to **designate sth sth** *102* etw als etw benennen, etw als etw ausweisen
desire *128* Verlangen; to **~ sth** *47* (sich) etw wünschen, nach etw verlangen
desperate *47* verzweifelt
despite *54* trotz
destabilization *44* Destabilisierung
to **destabilize sth** *138T* etw destabilisieren
destitute *121* mittellos
destruction *36* Zerstörung, Vernichtung
to **deteriorate** *139* (sich) verschlechtern
deterrent *140* Abschreckung(smittel)
detrimental (to/for) *106* schädlich (für)
to **devastate sth** *106* zerstören, verwüsten
developing country *24* Entwicklungsland
devil *131* Teufel
devilish *135* teuflisch
to **devise sth** *114V* etw entwickeln
devolution *126* Dezentralisierung
devoted *45* zugetan, ergeben
to **devour sth** *37* etw verschlingen
to **dial** *37* wählen *(Telefon)*
dialect *15T* Dialekt
dictatorship *126* Diktatur
diffident *136* zurückhaltend, bescheiden
diffusion *64* Verbreitung, Streuung
dignity *105* Würde
to **diminish** *15T* (sich) verringern, abnehmen
to **dine** *25* speisen, Essen gehen
dire situation *118* bedrohliche Lage
to **direct sb/sth** *100* etw leiten, jdm den Weg sagen/zeigen
disagreement *23* Ablehnung, Meinungsverschiedenheit
disappearance *106* Verschwinden
disappointment *89* Enttäuschung
disarmament *126* Entwaffnung
disarming *66T* entwaffnend
disciplined *19* diszipliniert
discovery *76* Entdeckung
discriminated *121* diskriminiert
disenchanted *88* desillusioniert
to **disguise** *40* verschleiern, tarnen
disillusion *127* Ernüchterung
disintegration *109* Zerfall
to **dislocate sth** *138T* etw ausrenken, etw zum Erliegen bringen
to **dismiss sth as sth** *70* etw als etw abtun
disorderly *135* undiszipliniert, zügellos
disparity *63* Ungleichheit, Unterschied
to **disperse** *12* (sich) verteilen, (sich) verbreiten, (sich) zerstreuen
to **displace sb** *106* jdn vertreiben
displacement *44* Verdrängung; *124* Vertreibung
disposal *36* Entsorgung; **at sb's ~** *80* zu jds Verfügung
to **dispose of sth** *39* etw beseitigen, etw entsorgen
disproportionate *62* unverhältnismäßig
to **dispute sth** *77* etw abstreiten, etw bestreiten
to **disregard** *12* ignorieren, nicht beachten, unbeachtet lassen
disrespect *21* Respektlosigkeit, Missachtung
disrespectful *22* respektlos
to **disrupt sth** *82V* etw trennen
disruption *30* Störung, Behinderung, Unterbrechung
disruptive *35* (zer)störend, zerreißend
dissatisfaction *106* Unzufriedenheit
dissent *110* Widerspruch, Einwand
dissident *126* abtrünnig, regimekritisch
dissolution *110* Auflösung, Verfall
distance: long ~ *7* Fern-
distant *15* entfernt
distinct *23* deutlich, unterschiedlich
distinction *12* Unterscheidung

to **distinguish** *58* unterscheiden
distorted *88* entstellt
distraction *87* Ablenkung
distressing *30* beunruhigend, beängstigend
distribution *44* Verteilung, Versorgung
distrust *127* Misstrauen; to ~ **sb/sth** *127* jdm/etw misstrauen
disturbed *20* beunruhigt
to **diverge from** *11* abweichen von
divergence *62* Divergenz, Auseinanderklaffen
divergent *66* abweichend, auseinandergehend
to **diversify** *15T* (sich) differenzieren
diversion *135* Ablenkung, Umleitung
to **divert sth from sth** *129* etw ablenken von etw
divide-and-conquer approach *40T* Teile-und-Herrsche-Herangehensweise
divine *135* göttlich
division *40T* Spaltung
divisive *117* polarisierend, umstritten
documentation *37* Dokumentation, Unterlagen
domain *82V* Domäne, Bereich, Gebiet
dome *135* Kuppel
domestic: ~ **violence** *48* häusliche Gewalt; **gross ~ product (GDP)** *114V* Bruttosozialprodukt
to **domesticate sth** *92* etw zähmen, etw domestizieren
to **dominate** *15* herrschen, dominieren
donation *58T* Spende
doomed to fail *126* zum Scheitern verurteilt
dormitory *57V* Wohnheim
to **double** *139* (sich) verdoppeln; to ~ **down on sth** *62* etw signifikant erhöhen
down: ~ **to business** *22* zum Wesentlichen, Spaß beiseite; to **get ~ to business** *26* zur Sache kommen
downgrader *23* Abschwächer
downside *58T* Nachteil
dozen *15T* Dutzend
drab *135* grau, trostlos
to **draft sth** *122* etw entwerfen
to **drain** *63* entleeren, austrocknen
draw: to ~ **a conclusion** *10* eine Schlussfolgerung ziehen; to ~ **sth up** *130* etw erstellen
drawback *80* Nachteil
dreadful *121* schrecklich, furchtbar
to **drift apart** *44* auseinandertreiben
to **drive sth** *97T* etw vorantreiben, etw stärken
droplet *135* Tröpfchen
drug dealer *88* Drogenhändler/in
drunk *135* Betrunkene/r
due to sth *8* wegen etw
dull *70* dumpf, trüb
dumping *110* Preisunterbietung, Dumping
duration *120* Dauer
dust *36* Staub
duty: civic ~ *46* bürgerliche Pflicht
to **dwindle** *82V* schwinden, nachlassen
dynamism *64* Tatendrang
dystopia *87* Dystopie, Schreckensvision
dystopian *36* dystopisch

E

earner *63* Verdiener/in
earnest: in ~ *23* ernsthaft, im Ernst
earthy *135* erdig
eave *69* Dachvorsprung, Dachrinne
e-commerce *35* Onlinehandel
economical *44* wirtschaftlich, sparsam
economics *59* Ökonomie, Wirtschaft(swissenschaft); **trickle-down ~** *108* Trickle-Down-Wirtschaft *(Theorie, dass Wirtschaftswachstum allen zugute kommt)*
economist *82V* Volkswirt/in, Wirtschaftswissenschaftler/in
economy *8* Wirtschaft; **gig ~** *58T* Gig Economy *(auf Freiberuflern basierendes Wirtschaftsmodell)*
edgy *134* nervös, unruhig
edition *114V* Ausgabe *(z.B. einer Sendung/Zeitschrift)*
editorial *94* Leitartikel
educational *59* Erziehungs-, Bildungs-
effectiveness *12* Wirksamkeit, Effektivität
efficiency *97T* Leistungsfähigkeit, Wirksamkeit, Wirkungsgrad
effort *7* Bemühen, Unternehmung
egalitarian *23* egalitär, auf Gleichheit beruhend
elder *25V* älter
elderly *25V* älter; Senioren
election: presidential ~ *40T* Präsidentschaftswahl
elementary school *24* Grundschule
to **elevate sth** *138T* etw anheben
eligible: to **be ~ (for sth / to do sth)** *57V* berechtigt sein (zu etw / etw zu tun)
to **eliminate sth** *55* etw eliminieren, etw unterbinden
elixir of life *71* Lebenselixier
elsewhere *8* woanders, anderswo
elusive *70* trügerisch, schwer definierbar
emasculation *47* Entmannung
to **embed sth** *44* etw integrieren, etw einbetten, etw einbauen
to **embody sth** *79* etw verkörpern
to **embolden sb to do sth** *118* jdm Mut machen, etw zu tun
to **emerge (from)** *11* entstehen, hervorgehen (aus)
emergence *108* Entstehen, Aufkommen
to **emit sth** *83* etw emittieren, etw ausstoßen, etw abstrahlen
empathy *8* Einfühlungsvermögen
emphasis, *pl* **emphases** *22* Betonung, Schwerpunkt, Akzent
to **emphasise sth** *23* etw betonen, etw hervorheben
empire *15T* (Welt-)Reich, Imperium
to **employ sb** *54* jdn beschäftigen, jdn einstellen *(Personal)*
employable *63* arbeitsfähig
employer *9* Arbeitgeber/in
employment *57* Anstellung, Beschäftigung, Arbeit
to **empower sb** *43* jdn stärken, jdn befähigen, jdn ermächtigen
empowerment *43* Befähigung, Ermächtigung
to **emulate sth** *89* etw nachbilden
en route *102* auf dem Weg
to **enable sb to do sth** *57* es jdm ermöglichen / jdn befähigen, etw zu tun
to **encompass sth** *105* etw umfassen
to **encounter sth** *24* auf etw stoßen, etw begegnen
end *76* Zweck, Ziel
to **endanger** *12* bedrohen, gefährden
endorsement *127* Werbung, Unterstützung
to **enforce sth** *53* etw durchsetzen, etw vollstrecken
to **engage in sth** *23* sich an etw beteiligen
to **enhance sth** *40T* etw steigern, etw erhöhen
enjoyable *8* angenehm, schön
enormous *36* enorm, gewaltig
to **enrich sth** *96* etw bereichern
to **enslave sb** *76* jdn versklaven
to **ensure sth/that** *54* etw sicherstellen, dafür sorgen, dass
enterprise *64* Unternehmen
entire *58T* ganz, vollständig
entitled *7* betitelt, benannt
entitlement (to) *55* Anspruch (auf)
entity *109* Einheit
to **entrench sth** *110* etw etablieren
entrepreneur *86* Unternehmer/in
entrepreneurial *44* unternehmerisch
red envelope *58T* roter Umschlag *(in dem Netflix Videos an US-Abonnenten zuschickte)*
environmental credentials *(pl)* *97T* Umweltverträglichkeit
environmentally friendly *97T* umweltfreundlich
to **envision** *46* sich vorstellen, vorhaben
epic *90* episch, unglaublich
epidemic *46* Epidemie, Seuche
epistemic *82V* epistemisch, erkenntnistheoretisch
equation *82V* Gleichung
equivalent *22* Äquivalent, Entsprechung
era *8* Ära, Epoche
to **erase** *37* (aus)löschen, ausradieren
to **erect** *29* errichten
to **erode** *63* erodieren, aushöhlen
erosion: soil ~ *93* Bodenerosion
to **err** *22* sich irren
error *37* Fehler, Irrtum
to **escape from sth** *106* einer Sache entkommen
to **eschew sth** *126* etw (ver)meiden
essential (to) *8* wesentlich, unerlässlich (für)
essentially *33T* im Wesentlichen
to **establish** *11* etablieren, aufbauen, einrichten
esteem *139* Achtung, Ansehen
eternal *135* ewig
ethical: guiding ~ principle *82V* ethische Leitlinie
ethicist *87* Ethiker/in

ethics *(pl) 75* Ethik; **~ commission** *82V* Ethikkommission
ethnic *44* ethnisch, Volks-
to **evaluate sb/sth** *66T* jdn/etw bewerten, jdn/etw beurteilen
evenly *114V* ausgeglichen, gleichmäßig
eventually *33T* letztendlich, schließlich
everyday *24* alltäglich, Alltags-
evidence *12* Anzeichen, Hinweis, Beweis
evident *108* offensichtlich
evolution *15T* Entwicklung
evolutionary *82* evolutionär, entwicklungsgeschichtlich
to **evolve (from)** *11* sich (weiter) entwickeln, entstehen (aus)
to **exacerbate sth** *63* etw verschärfen, etw verschlimmern
to **exaggerate sth** *112* etw übertreiben
exaggeration *31* Übertreibung
exalted *70* überschwänglich
to **exceed sth** *136* etw übertreffen
to **excel in/at sth** *49* sich auszeichnen in etw, ausgezeichnet sein in etw
exception *47* Ausnahme
excerpt *15* Auszug, Ausschnitt
excess *109* Exzess, Überschuss
exchange: Securities and Exchange Commission *90T* Börsenaufsichtsbehörde *(USA)*; **stock ~** *63* (Wertpapier-)Börse
to **exclude sb/sth** *33* jdn/etw ausschließen
exclusive *40T* exklusiv, alleinig
exclusively *33T* ausschließlich
to **execute sb** *37* jdn hinrichten
executive *9* leitende/r Angestellte/r; **chief ~** *55* Hauptgeschäftsführer/in
to **exercise sth** *76* etw ausüben
exhausted *72* erschöpft
exhaustion *69* Erschöpfung
to **exhibit sth** *138T* etw zeigen, etw ausstellen
expansion *11* Ausdehnung, Expansion
expectancy: life ~ *66* Lebenserwartung
expectation *33T* Erwartung
expected: to **be ~ to do sth** *13* etw tun sollen/müssen, es wird erwartet, dass man etw tut
expense: at the ~ of *31* auf Kosten
expertise *35* Fachkenntnisse, Sachverstand
explanation *21* Erläuterung, Erklärung
explicit *30* klar, deutlich, ausdrücklich
to **explode** *20* explodieren
to **exploit sth** *87* etw ausnutzen
exploitation *29* Ausbeutung, Abbau *(von Rohstoffen)*
explosive *103T* Sprengstoff
exposed: to **be/get ~ to sth** *40T* einer Sache ausgesetzt sein, mit etw in Berührung kommen
to **extend** *58T* sich erstrecken, sich ausweiten
extensive *76* ausgedehnt, erheblich
extent *121* Umfang, Ausmaß
extermination camp *78* Vernichtungslager
external *30* extern, auswärtig
extinction *82V* Vernichtung, Ausrottung, Aussterben
extremist *44* Extremist/in
exultant *79* frohlockend

F

fabricated *76* fingiert
facade *29* Fassade
face: in the ~ of *8* trotz, angesichts; to **lose ~** *21* an Prestige verlieren
facial *8* Gesichts-
to **facilitate sth** *15T* etw ermöglichen, etw vermitteln, etw vereinfachen
to **fade away** *38* verblassen, verhallen; *13* schwächer werden, (nach und nach) verschwinden
to **fail** *48* versagen, scheitern
failing *108* Mangel, Missstand
failure *48* Versagen, Ausfall, Zusammenbruch; **~ to comply (with sth)** *53* Nichteinhaltung (von etw)
faint *69* schwach, matt
fairly *22* ziemlich, recht
faith *82V* Glaube, Vertrauen
falsely *40T* fälschlicherweise
farewell *135* Abschied, Verabschiedung
farming: arable ~ *92* Ackerbau
fascism *129* Faschismus
fascist *30* faschistisch, Faschist
fatal *135* tödlich, verhängnisvoll
faultless *113* einwandfrei, makellos
favour: in ~ of *18* zugunsten von, für
fearful *70* ängstlich
fearmongering *122T* Panikmache
feasibility *52* Machbarkeit, Umsetzbarkeit
feasible *18* machbar, möglich
federal *18* Bundes-
feeder system *138T* Zuführungssystem
fellow *40* Fellow *(Mitglied eines akademischen Instituts)*; *70* Mit-, andere
fellow student *29* Kommilitone/in
fertilizer *92* Dünger, Düngemittel
festive *32* festlich
feverish *71* fiebrig, fieberhaft
fiction *69* Belletristik, Prosa(literatur)
to **fight back (fought, fought)** *103T* sich wehren
figurative *136* symbolisch, metaphorisch
figure: to **~ out** *138T* herausfinden, ausrechnen; to **~ sth out** *58T* etw (heraus)finden
to **finance sth** *94* etw finanzieren
findings *(pl) 29* Ergebnisse
fingertips: at your ~ *44* zur Hand
finite *97T* begrenzt, endlich
firm *135* fest, sicher
first and foremost *8* vor allem, in erster Linie
first language *8* Muttersprache
fishery *92* Fischerei
fishing hook *90T* Angelhaken
fission: nuclear ~ *75* Kernspaltung
to **fit** *9* passen
to **fizzle out** *33T* im Sande verlaufen, verpuffen
to **flag sth** *47* auf etw aufmerksam machen
flame *37* Flamme
flap *36* Klappe
flashpoint *29* Krisenherd
flashy *25V* auffällig, protzig
flaw *80* Schwachstelle, Fehler, Mangel
flawed *66T* fehlerhaft, mangelhaft
to **flee** *106* flüchten, fliehen
fleet *101* Flotte
flesh *79* Fleisch
to **float** *23* schweben, treiben
to **flop out of sth** *36* aus etw herausplumpsen
to **flourish** *80* florieren, blühen, gedeihen
fluent *13* *(Sprache:)* fließend
fluidity *12* Fluidität, Flüssigkeit, Geschmeidigkeit
to **focus on sth** *22* sich auf etw konzentrieren
to **fold sth** *70* etw falten
footloose *63* frei, ungebunden
footnote *33* Fußnote
footprint *47* Fußabdruck
for good or bad *8* zum Guten oder zum Schlechten
forage *97T* Viehfutter
to **forbid sth (forbade, forbidden)** *92* etw verbieten, etw untersagen
force *80* Kraft, Macht; **brute ~** *126* brutale Gewalt; to **come into ~** *57V* in Kraft treten
forebear *33T* Vorfahr/in
forecast *38* Vorhersage
forehead *136* Stirn
foreign language *8* Fremdsprache
foreigner *14* Ausländer/in
foremost: first and ~ *8* vor allem, in erster Linie
to **foresee sth** *76* etw voraussehen, etw vorhersehen
foreseeable *15T* vorhersehbar
to **forestall sb/sth** *69* jdm/etw zuvorkommen
forestry *92* Forstwirtschaft
forgery *38* Fälschung
former *9* ehemalige/r/s
forth: and so ~ *15T* und so weiter
fortress *140* Festung
fortunes *pl 15T* Schicksal
forward: to **put sth ~** *82V* (Argument/Vorschlag) vorbringen, etw zur Diskussion stellen
to **foster sth** *8* etw fördern
to **found sth** *35* etw gründen
foundation *76* Grundlage, Fundament
founder *90T* Gründer/in; **co-~** *58T* Mitbegründer/in
fountain *135* (Spring-)Brunnen
to **fracture sth** *127* etw brechen, etw aufbrechen
to **fragment** *15T* zerfallen
frame: time ~ *46* Zeitrahmen
Franconian *16* Fränkisch
frankly *58T* ehrlich (gesagt)
fraud: voter ~ *40T* Wahlbetrug
to **freelance** *45* freiberuflich arbeiten
fringe outfit *127* Randorganisation
frugal *50T* genügsam, bescheiden
fruit vendor *138T* Obstverkäufer/in
to **fuel sth** *49* etw anheizen, etw anfachen
to **fulfil sth** *109* etw erfüllen, etw ausführen
funded: well-~ *48* kapitalkräftig
funding *64* Finanzierung, Geldmittel

to **fundraise** 33T eine Spendenaktion betreiben
funds *(pl)* 64 Gelder, Fördermittel
furnace 36 (Industrie-)Ofen, Hochofen
to **further sth** 76 etw voranbringen
fuzzy 8 verschwommen, unscharf

G

gain 114V Gewinn, Vorteil; to ~ 9 erwerben, gewinnen, sammeln, erlangen
gait 137 Gang
gallery walk 74 Galerierundgang
to **gallivant** 33T herumziehen
gambling 88 Glücksspiel
game changer 50T Wendpunkt
gas chamber 79 Gaskammer
gathering: intelligence ~ 57V Informationsgewinnung
gaze 70 Blick
geard: to **be geared to/towards sth** 97T auf etw ausgerichtet sein
gender bias 44 geschlechtsspezifische Diskriminierung
generational 33T Generations-
genetic 82V genetisch
genetically modified 82V genetisch verändert
genius 122T Genie, Geistesgröße
gesture 8 Geste; to ~ 21 gestikulieren, eine Handbewegung machen
gift 25V Geschenk
gig economy 58T Gig Economy *(auf Freiberuflern basierendes Wirtschaftsmodell)*
globe 75 Globus
glory 139 Ruhm
glow 100 Schein, Schimmer
to **gnaw** 136 nagen
goal 30 Ziel, Absicht
goddess of victory 71 Siegesgöttin
godless 135 gottlos
goodness 137 Güte, Tugend
goods *(pl)* 37 Waren, Güter
governmental: non-~ organization (NGO) 44 Nichtregierungsorganisation
to **grade sb** 57 jdn benoten
gradually 13 allmählich, langsam, nach und nach
grain 97T Getreide
to **grandstand** 33T Effekthascherei betreiben
to **grant sb sth** 122T jdm etw gewähren
granular information 89 detaillierte Informationen
grass-roots: at ~ level 15T an der Basis
grave 76 erst, schwerwiegend
to **graze** 96 grasen
greatly 77 erheblich
grid 78 Schema, Tabelle; 102 Gitter(netz)
grief 69 Kummer, Leid, Trauer
grievance 110 Beschwerde
grip-sack *(AE)* 71 Reisetasche
gross 37 grob; **~ domestic product (GDP)** 114V Bruttosozialprodukt
ground: burned ~ 22 verbrannte Erde
grounds: on … ~ 33T aufgrund von …
groundswell 94 starke öffentliche Bewegung
guarantee 8 Garantie
guarantor 109 Garant/in
guards: to **guard sb** 102 jdn überwachen
to **guide sb/sth** 100 jdn/etw führen
guiding ethical principle 82V ethische Leitlinie

H

habitat 94 natürlicher Lebensraum
habitual 135 gewohnheitsmäßig, Gewohnheits-
to **hack** 30 hacken
halt 136 Halt
hand: to **~ over** 40T übergeben; to **~ sth in** 139 etw abgeben
handful 89 Handvoll
to **handle sth** 33T mit etw umgehen, etw handhaben
handset 102 Handapparat, Telefonhörer
handwriting 8 Handschrift
handy: to **come in ~** 88 sich als nützlich erweisen, gelegen kommen
to **hang on to sth** 47 sich an etw festhalten, sich an etw festklammern
happy: to **be ~ to do sth** 30 etw gern tun
hardly 15T kaum
hardship 44 Not, Elend, Entbehrung(en)
harm 76 Schaden; to **~ sb** 76 jdm schaden, jdn schädigen
harmful 89 schädlich
harsh 72 brutal, harsch
to **hasten** 69 eilen; to **~ sth** 110 etw beschleunigen
hate 8 Hass
hatred 49 Hass, Abscheu
to **haul sth out** 97T etw herausziehen
to **haunt sb** 69 jdn heimsuchen
the haves and the have-nots 112 die Besitzenden und die Habenichtse
head 54 Leiter/in, Chef/in
headshake 25V Kopfschütteln
to **heal sth** 118 etw heilen
health: ~ care 58T Gesundheitswesen, medizinische Versorgung; **ill ~** 72 schlechter Gesundheitszustand
to **heap sth** 127 etw anhäufen
heaven 135 Himmel; **for ~'s sake** 69 um Himmels willen
to **heckle** 30 (durch Zwischenrufe) stören
to **heighten** 40T erhöhen, steigern
hemisphere 21 Hemisphäre, Halbkugel
hen: battery-cage ~ 75 Legebatteriehuhn
herder 101 Hirt/in
hesitant 57V zögernd, zögerlich
to **hesitate** 48 zögern
heyday 109 Blutezeit
hierarchical 22 hierarchisch
to **highlight sth** 26 etw hervorheben
to **hijack sth** 87 etw kapern
hilarious 47 ausgelassen, vergnügt
to **hinder** 65 (be-, ver-)hindern, hemmen
hint 69 Hinweis
to **hire sb** 80 jdn engagieren, jdn anstellen
hoard 62 Vorrat, Schatz
to **hold sb responsible** 79 jdn zur Verantwortung ziehen
holder 122T Inhaber/in
hollow 134 hohl, leer
home carer 54 Hauspfleger/in
home-grown 138T einheimisch
homeland 120 Heimat(land)
homogeneity 15T Homogenität, Gleichartigkeit
homogenous 44 homogen
honesty 21 Ehrlichkeit
honour 22 Ehre; to ~ 32 ehren
honourable 79 achtbar, ehrenwert
hoof print 135 Hufabdruck
hook: fishing ~ 90T Angelhaken
hooked: to **keep sb ~** 88 jdn süchtig halten, jdn bei der Stange halten
hospitable 25V gastfreundlich
hospitality 25 Gastfreundschaft
host 58 Gastgeber/in
hostility 8 Feindseligkeit
hot spot 127 Krisenherd
hotbed 140 Brutstätte
to **house sb** 121 jdn unterbringen
household 63 Haushalt
housewife 46 Hausfrau
housing 63 Wohnungsbau, Wohnungen
to **huddle** 136 sich zusammendrängen
human rights *(pl)* 82V Menschenrechte
humane 91 human, menschenwürdig
humanities *(pl)* 82V Geisteswissenschaften
humanity 76 Menschheit, Menschlichkeit
humankind 76 (die) Menschheit
humorous 19 humorvoll

I

i.e. (= that is) 8 d.h. (= das heißt)
idealistic 90T idealistisch
ideological 37 ideologisch
ignorance 25 Unwissenheit, Unkenntnis
ill health 72 schlechter Gesundheitszustand
illumination 70 Erleuchtung
image loss 78 Imageverlust, Imageschaden
imagery 102 Bildaufnahmen
imitation 135 Imitation, Nachahmung
immemorial: since time ~ 8 seit Menschengedenken, seit jeher
to **immolate oneself** 138T sich selbst verbrennen
immoral 89 unmoralisch
impact 52 Einfluss, Auswirkung
impactful 97T wirkungsvoll
impenetrable 79 undurchdringlich
imperative 138T zwingend, unerlässlich
imperialist 29 Imperialist/in
impetus 55 Impuls, Anstoß
to **implement sth** 52 etw einführen, etw umsetzen, etw einsetzen
implementation 36 Umsetzung, Durchführung
implicit 66T implizit, stillschweigend

to **implore sb** *71* jdn anflehen, jdn inständig bitten
to **imply sth** *38* etw andeuten, etw nahelegen
importunity *71* Aufdringlichkeit, beharrliches Drängen
impose: to **~ sth on/upon sb** *70* jdm etw aufdrängen; *110* jdm etw auferlegen
imposition *113* Auferlegung, Verhängung
impoverished *106* verarmt
impressive *87* beeindruckend, eindrucksvoll
improvement in/to sth *76* Verbesserung bei etw
inability *69* Unfähigkeit
inaccurate *117* ungenau, unrichtig
inaction *118* Tatenlosigkeit
incarnation *31* Inkarnation, Verkörperung
incentive *64* Anreiz
incident: critical ~ *19* kritisches Ereignis, kritischer Zwischenfall
inclusion *127* Einbeziehung, Einbindung, *Inklusion*
income *57* Einkommen
inconsequential *111* unbedeutend, belanglos
inconsistent *58T* inkonsequent
increasingly *15T* zunehmend, in zunehmendem Maße
indeed *11* tatsächlich, in der Tat
in-depth *80* ausführlich
index *114V* Index, Verzeichnis, Register
to **indicate sth** *14* etw (an)zeigen, auf etw deuten, auf etw hinweisen
indication *15T* Hinweis, Anzeichen
indifference (to) *8* Gleichgültigkeit (gegenüber)
individual *109* einzeln, individuell; **High Value Individual (HVI)** *102* wichtige (feindliche) Person
individualistic *19* individualistisch
individualized *47* individualisiert
to **induce sth** *124* etw verursachen
industrious *19* fleißig, tüchtig
inefficient *93* ineffizient, unwirtschaftlich
inequality *62* Ungleichheit
inevitable *99* unausweichlich, unvermeidbar
inevitably *109* zwangsläufig
infatuation *135* Verliebtheit, Vernarrtheit
inference *58* Schlussfolgerung
infidel *135* Ungläubige/r
to **infiltrate sth** *78* etw infiltrieren
infinite *97T* unendlich, unerschöpflich
inflexible *127* unflexibel, unbeweglich
influencer *8* Einflussnehmer/in
influential *9* einflussreich
influx *140* Zustrom
information: granular ~ *89* detaillierte Informationen
infrared *100* infrarot
inhumane *97T* unmenschlich, menschenunwürdig
initially *74* anfangs, anfänglich
to **initiate sth** *35* etw einleiten, etw initiieren
to **injure sb** *126* jdn verletzen
injustice *140* Unrecht, Ungerechtigkeit
innocent *103T* unschuldig
inquiry *82V* Untersuchung, Recherche
inquisitive *121* neugierig, wissbegierig
insane *48* irrsinnig, verrückt
insecure *88* unsicher
insight (into) *114V* Einblick (in), Verständnis (von)
to **insist** *32* darauf bestehen
inspirational *35* anregend, inspirierend
to **inspire** *31* inspirieren, anregen
instance *37* Beispiel, Fall; **for ~** *8* zum Beispiel
instantaneous *106* sofort, unmittelbar
to **instigate** *33T* aufhetzen, anstacheln
to **instill** *(BE)* **/ instil** *(AE)* **sth** *135* etw vermitteln
instructions *pl* *26* Anleitung, Anweisung(en)
instrumental *24* behilflich, dienlich
insubordination *23* Gehorsamsverweigerung
insufficient *64* ungenügend, nicht ausreichend, unzureichend
to **insult sb** *29* jdn beleidigen
integral part *81* fester Bestandteil
intelligence: artificial ~ *76* künstliche Intelligenz; **~ gathering** *57V* Informationsgewinnung; **~ subcommittee** *138T* Geheimdienstunterausschuss
intelligibility *12* Verständlichkeit
to **intend** *8* beabsichtigen, vorhaben
intense *45* intensiv
intensification *97T* Intensivierung
intention *70* Absicht
intentional *66T* absichtlich, beabsichtigt
inter- *82V* zwischen-
to **interact** *24* interagieren, aufeinander eingehen
interconnectedness *114V* Vernetzung
intercultural *8* interkulturell
interference *40T* Einmischung, Beeinflussung
intergenerational *82V* zwischen den Generationen
intermediate *13* mittlere/r/s (Niveau), für fortgeschrittene Anfänger/innen
internal *37* intern; *139* inländisch, Inlands-
interruption *20* Unterbrechung
interval *36* Abstand
interwar *119* zwischen den Weltkriegen
intimidation *30* Einschüchterung
intra- *82V* -intern
introductory *15* einführend, einleitend
to **invade sth** *80* in etw eindringen
invariably *38* ausnahmslos
to **invent sth** *36* etw erfinden, sich etw ausdenken
inventor *82V* Erfinder/in
to **invest in sth** *58T* in etw investieren
to **investigate sth** *40T* etw ermitteln, etw untersuchen
investment *62* Anlage, Investition
to **invoke** *33T* zitieren, anführen
to **involve** *23* einbeziehen, beteiligen
involvement *76* Beteiligung
inward *137* nach innen
irate *48* zornig, wütend
ironic *120* ironisch
irrational *49* irrational
irrelevant *55* irrelevant
irresistible *136* unwiderstehlich
to **issue** *37* herausgeben
item *38* Artikel, Gegenstand, Punkt *(auf einer Liste)*
iteration *58T* Iteration, Wiederholung

J

to **jail sb** *118* jdn einsperren, jdn ins Gefängnis werfen
jargon *37* Fachsprache, Jargon
jarring *33T* misstönend
to **jeopardize sb/sth** *76* jdn/etw gefährden
Jew *134* Jude/Jüdin
jewellery *25V* Schmuck
jock *102* Sportler/in, Sportskanone
joint *102* gemeinsam, gemeinschaftlich
joy *70* Freude
to **judge** *14* (be)urteilen, ermessen
judgement *45* Urteilsvermögen, Urteil, Einschätzung
to **jumble sth up** *78* etw (kunterbunt) durcheinanderwerfen
justice *31* Gerechtigkeit
justification *127* Rechtfertigung
to **justify sth** *55* etw begründen, etw rechtfertigen

K

keen: to **be ~ to do sth** *20* etw unbedingt tun wollen
to **keep in mind** *22* daran denken, nicht vergessen
key team *54* Kernmannschaft
keyhole *71* Schlüsselloch
keyword *9* Schlagwort, Schlüsselwort
killing: revenge ~ *103T* Rachemord
to **kindle sth** *136* etw entzünden
kinetic power *138T* Bewegungsenergie
to **kneel** *71* knien
knowingly *78* wissentlich

L

laboratory *82V* Labor
labour *11* Arbeit, Arbeitskräfte
to **lack sth** *82V* etw nicht haben
lack (of) *9* Mangel (an)
laid-back *32* lässig, entspannt
lapse *76* Fehler, Aussetzer, Lapsus
largely *11* größtenteils, überwiegend, weitgehend
latchkey *71* Haustürschlüssel
to **launch sth** *37* etw starten
laureate *82* Preisträger/in
lawmaker *87* Abgeordnete/r
lawn *138T* Rasen(fläche)
lawsuit: to **settle a ~** *58T* einen Rechtsstreit beilegen
lawyer *79* (Rechts-)Anwalt/Anwältin
leadership *58T* Führung
leak *58T* Leck, undichte Stelle; to **~ sth** *88* etw durchsickern lassen, etw durchstechen
least: not ~ *15* nicht zuletzt
leave: parental ~ *54* Elternzeit, Erziehungsurlaub

lecture *15* Vortrag, Vorlesung
lecturer *20* Dozent/in, Hochschullehrer/in
legislation *54* Gesetzgebung
legislative *53* gesetzgebend, legislativ
legitimacy *127* Legitimität, Rechtmäßigkeit
legitimate *31* legitim, berechtigt
length: at ~ *71* schließlich
lesbian *48* Lesbe, lesbisch
to **let sb off (let, let)** *83* jdm (ein Strafe) erlassen
lethal *103T* tödlich
level: at grass-roots ~ *15T* an der Basis
to **level with sb** *138T* mit jdm offen reden
to **levy sth** *127* etw erheben
liberalization *44* Liberalisierung
to **liberalize sth** *106* etw liberalisieren
to **liberate sb** *76* jdn befreien
liberty *112* Freiheit
licensing: occupational ~ *63* Berufszulassung
lid *135* Augenlid
Lieutenant Colonel *58* Oberstleutnant
life: elixir of ~ *71* Lebenselixier; **~ expectancy** *66* Lebenserwartung
lifetime *59* Lebenszeit
lightning *135* Blitz(e) *(bei Gewitter)*
likely: to **be ~ to do sth** *8* etw wahrscheinlich tun (werden)
like-minded *116* gleichgesinnt
limelight *44* Rampenlicht *(Mittelpunkt des Interesses)*
limit *33T* Grenze, Begrenzung
to **limit sth** *64* etw begrenzen, etw einschränken
limited *24* begrenzt
limitless *82V* unbegrenzt
lined *134* gesäumt, ausgekleidet
linguistic *11* sprachlich, Sprach-, sprachwissenschaftlich
lips: parted ~ *70* geöffnete Lippen
livestock *92* Vieh
to **locate sth** *102* etw ausfindig machen
to **lock sb up** *15T* jdn wegsperren
to **loiter** *102* herumhängen, warten
lone *30* einzeln, einsam; **~ wolf** *138T* Einzelkämpfer *(einsamer Wolf)*
long: in the ~ run *14* auf lange Sicht, langfristig; **~ distance** *7* Fern-
lose: to **~ face** *21* an Prestige verlieren; to **~ out on sth** *114V* bei etw schlecht wegkommen
loss *111* Verlust; **image ~** *78* Imageverlust, Imageschaden
lover *7* Geliebte/r, Liebhaber/in
to **lower sth** *107* etw senken, etw herabsetzen
low-ranking *36* niederrangig
loyal *46* treu, loyal
loyalty *46* Treue, Loyalität
luggage *72* Gepäck
luminous *135* leuchtend
to **lure sb/sth** *64* jdn/etw locken, ködern
lust *135* Wollust, Gier
luxury hotel *103T* Luxushotel
lyrics *(pl)* *31* Liedtext

M

madness *97T* Wahnsinn
magnanimous *121* großherzig; großmütig
to **maintain** *12* aufrecht erhalten, beibehalten
major *11* Haupt-, wesentlich, größer
to **make sth up** *38* etw erfinden, sich etw ausdenken
malnutrition *96* Unterernährung, falsche Ernährung
manager: personnel ~ *33* Personalchef/in
managerial *56* Management-, Führungs-
mandatory *54* verpflichtend, vorgeschrieben, obligatorisch
to **manifest in sth** *109* sich in etw zeigen
manifestation *113* Manifestation, Erscheinungsform
manifold *121* vielfältig, mannigfaltig
to **manipulate** *8* manipulieren
manipulation *8* Manipulation
manufacturer *50* Hersteller, Produzent
manufacturing *13* Fertigung, Herstellung
margin *113* Rand, Randspalte
marginal *87* marginal, geringfügig
to **marginalize** *8* ins Abseits drängen, an den Rand drängen
marine *93* Meeres-
mark *12* (Kenn-)Zeichen, Markierung
marketer *8* Vermarkter
marketing *35* Marketing, Vermarktung
marketplace *33T* Markt
marriage: ~ counselling *90T* Eheberatung; **~ proposal** *91* Heiratsantrag
masculinity *48* Männlichkeit
mass shooter *48* Amokschütze /-schützin
to **master sth** *14* etw meistern, etw bewältigen
materialist *135* materialistisch
mathematician *77* Mathematiker/in
meaningful *23* wichtig, bedeutend, sinnstiftend
means, *pl* **means** *8* Möglichkeit, Mittel
measure *18* Maßnahme; to **~ sth** *114V* etw messen; **thrown in for good ~** *15T* obendrein
measurement *135* Abmessung, Maß
mechanism *12* Mechanismus, Mechanik
media outlet *40T* Pressekanal
medical *77* medizinisch
medicine: reproductive ~ *76* Reproduktionsmedizin
to **meet a demand** *35* eine Nachfrage befriedigen
membership *108* Mitgliedschaft
memo *87* Memo, Notiz
memory *36* Gedächtnis, Erinnerung
mental *66* geistig, psychisch, seelisch; **~ state** *90T* psychische Verfassung
merchant *90T* Händler/in
merciful *136* barmherzig
merciless *135* gnadenlos
merely *38* bloß, nur
merit *88* Verdienst, Wert, Leistung
mess: to **make a ~ of things** *82V* es vermasseln, es verpfuschen
messenger *135* Bote, Kurier
metaphor *119* Metapher
metropolitan *44* großstädtisch, Ballungs-
microbiology *12* Mikrobiologie
micromental *90T* mikromental
milky *136* milchig
mind: closed ~ *31* Engstirnigkeit; to **keep in ~** *22* daran denken, nicht vergessen
mindful: to **be ~ of sth** *79* etw berücksichtigen, an etw denken
mindless *139* hirnlos, blindwütig
mindset *64* Mentalität, Denkweise
ministry: welfare ~ *54* Sozialministerium
minor *122T* minderjährig
miscalculation *82V* Fehleinschätzung
miscommunication *22* Fehlkommunikation
misconduct *76* Fehlverhalten
misery *136* Elend
to **misinterpret** *21* fehlinterpretieren
misleading *112* irreführend
misogynist *44* frauenfeindlich
misprint *38* Druckfehler, Fehldruck
misquotation *38* falsches Zitat
missile *100* Rakete, Flugkörper
mission *88* Auftrag, Mission
missionary *35* Missionar/in
mist *136* Nebel, Dunst
mistaken *38* falsch, irrig
to **mistrust** *40T* misstrauen
misunderstanding *8* Missverständnis
misuse *79* Missbrauch
mixture *15T* Mischung
to **moan** *110* stöhnen, jammern, klagen
to **mock sb** *48* sich über jdn lustig machen
to **model sth on sth** *54* etw einer Sache zum Vorbild nehmen, etw einer Sache nachbilden
modernity *80* Moderne
modify: genetically modified *82V* genetisch verändert
molecule *82V* Molekül
momentous *109* bedeutsam, folgenreich
momentum *14* Schwung, Fahrt
to **monitor sth** *86* etw überwachen
monolingual *13* einsprachig
monotonous *26* eintönig, monoton
monstrous *70* monströs
morale *55* Moral, geistig-seelische Verfassung
morality *80* Moral *(Wertesystem)*
moreover *76* überdies, zudem
moribund *63* sterbend, todgeweiht
mortal *136* sterblich
mosque *135* Moschee
mosquito *131* Mücke
mother tongue *8* Muttersprache
motion *71* Bewegung
motionless *70* regungslos
motivational *35* motivierend, Motivations-
mould *64* Form, Gussform

to **mount** *63* *(allmählich)* wachsen; to ~ **sth** *33T* etw auf die Beine stellen
mountain range *103* Gebirge, Gebirgszug
mouthpiece *36* Mundstück
MP (Member of Parliament) *54* Parlamentsabgeordnete/r
to **mull sth** *118* etw überdenken
multifaceted *127* facettenreich
multinational *13* multinational, multinationaler Konzern
to **murmur** *135* murmeln
mute *7* Stumme/r
mutual *9* gegenseitige/r/s
mystery *71* Rätsel, Rätselhaftigkeit
myth *93* Mythos, Märchen
mythology *93* Mythologie, Sagenwelt

N

named target *102* benanntes Ziel, namentlich bekannte Zielperson
narrative *109* Erzählung, Geschichte
to **narrow** *62* sich verengen
nationalistic *19* nationalistisch
native speaker *12* Muttersprachler/in
naturalist *77* Naturforscher/in
navel stud *134* Nabelstecker
to **navigate** *66T* navigieren, den Weg finden
nearness *36* Nähe
necessarily: not ~ *50T* nicht unbedingt
necessity *23* Notwendigkeit
need *10* Bedarf, Bedürfnis, Notwendigkeit; to **be in ~ of sth** *88* etw brauchen, etw benötigen
negative *23* Verneinung, Kritik
to **neglect sb/sth** *76* jdn/etw vernachlässigen
to **negotiate** *24* verhandeln, aushandeln
negotiation *20* Verhandlung
negotiator *22* Unterhändler/in, Verhandlungsführer/in
nestled up *101* angeschmiegt
net *114V* netto, Netto-; **trawling ~** *93* Schleppnetz
net neutrality *90T* Netzneutralität
netting *101* Netz, Geflecht
nevertheless *44* trotzdem, dennoch
news: to **break the ~ to sb** *69* jdm eine Nachricht überbringen
non-governmental organization (NGO) *44* Nichtregierungsorganisation
niche *93* Nische
to **nickname** *36* *(mit Spitznamen)* nennen
to **nominate** *40* nominieren
nomination *82V* Nominierung
non-observant *134* nicht praktizierend
nor *38* auch nicht, ebenso wenig, noch
nostalgia *32* Nostalgie
nostalgic *19* nostalgisch, wehmütig
notable *94* bedeutend, bemerkenswert
notice: to **take ~ of** *8* beachten, aufmerksam werden auf
notification *88* Benachrichtigung, Mitteilung, Bescheid
notion *31* Vorstellung, Auffassung
nuanced *48* differenziert, nuanciert
nuclear fission *75* Kernspaltung
nude *25V* nackt
to **number** *9* nummerieren
numerous *121* zahlreich
nursing *55* Pflege, Krankenpflege
to **nurture sth** *140* etw entwickeln, etw pflegen, etw fördern
nutritional *99* Nahrungs-, Ernährungs-, Nähr-
nutritious *97T* nahrhaft, nährstoffreich

O

oath *82V* Eid
objectionable *127* unangenehm, bedenklich
objective *23* objektiv, zielorientiert
objectivity *82V* Objektivität
obligation *63* Pflicht, Verpflichtung
oblique *23* indirekt, versteckt
oblong *36* länglich, rechteckig
to **obscure sth** *120* verbergen, verdunkeln
to **observe sth** *50* etw beobachten
obsessed (with/by) *77* besessen (von)
obvious *78* offensichtlich, klar
occasional *72* gelegentlich
occupation *54* Beruf, Tätigkeit, Beschäftigung
occupational licensing *63* Berufszulassung
to **occur** *9* passieren, geschehen, stattfinden
odd *72* gelegentlich
odds: to **be at ~ with sth** *109* mit etw hadern
offence *29* Straftat, Vergehen
to **offend sb** *25V* jdn beleidigen, verletzen; jdm zu nahe treten
offensive *29* beleidigend, anstößig
officer: chief operating ~ *88* leitende/r Geschäftsführer/in
official *40T* Beamte/r, Funktionär/in
to **offshore sth** *109* etw ins Ausland verlagern
oftentimes *(AE)* *66T* oftmals
omniscient *36* allwissend
onboard sth *100* an Bord von etw, auf etw
once and for all *57V* ein für allemal, endgültig
one way or another *90T* so oder so, auf die eine oder andere Art
one-time *29* ehemalig
ongoing *126* laufend
onrushing *136* Heranpreschen
openness *21* Offenheit
to **operate** *15T* arbeiten, wirken, funktionieren
operating: chief ~ officer *88* leitende/r Geschäftsführer/in
operation *57V* Operation, Einsatz
operative *40T* Funktionär/in
opponent *95* Gegner/in
opportunity *9* Gelegenheit, Möglichkeit, Chance
to **oppose sth** *47* gegen etw opponieren, sich gegen etw widersetzen
opposed: as ~ to *44* im Gegensatz zu, gegenüber; to **be ~ to sth** *95* gegen etw sein
opposition *44* Widerstand
oppressed *129* unterdrückt
oppression *106* Unterdrückung
oppressive *76* unterdrückend, repressiv
to **optimize** *35* optimieren
optional *18* optional, freiwillig, freigestellt
opulent *121* superreich
orator *8* Redner/in, Rhetoriker/in
ordinary *58T* normal, gewöhnlich
organic *75* biologisch, Bio-
orientation *25V* Orientierung, Einführung
oriented: self-~ *46* selbstbezogen
orifice *36* Öffnung, Loch
to **ostracize** *8* ächten, ausschließen
otherwise *13* ansonsten, andernfalls
to **oust sth** *57V* etw verdrängen
outcome *23* Ergebnis, Resultat
outer *33T* äußere/r/s
outfit: fringe ~ *127* Randorganisation
outflow *138T* Abfluss, Abwanderung
outgrowth *58T* Folge, Konsequenz
outlet: media ~ *40T* Pressekanal
outline *64* Umriss, Entwurf
output *37* Leistung, Produktion
outraged *31* entrüstet, empört
outright *9* total, völlig, offen, direkt
outsider *23* Außenstehende/r
outskirts *(pl)* *121* Stadtrand, Randbezirk(e)
outstanding *32* hervorragend, überragend, außergewöhnlich
outstretched *136* ausgestreckt, ausgebreitet
overall *58T* allgemein, insgesamt, im Großen und Ganzen
to **overcome sth (overcame, overcome)** *53* etw bewältigen, über etw hinwegkommen
overfulfilled *38* übererfüllt
to **overload sth** *97T* etw überladen, etw überbeanspruchen
to **overlook sth** *93* etw übersehen
overpopulation *82V* Überbevölkerung
to **override sth** *66T* sich über etw hinwegsetzen, etw außer Kraft setzen
overseas *13* nach/in Übersee
to **oversee sth (oversaw, overseen)** *88* etw leiten
to **overwhelm sb** *32* jdn überwältigen, jdn überschütten
ownership *50* Besitz

P

to **package sth** *78* etw (ver)packen
pact: trade ~ *114V* Handelsabkommen
pairing *66T* Paarung
palm *97T* Palme
pamphlet *37* Broschüre
paradigm *99* Paradigma, Modell
parallel *36* Parallele
to **paralyze** *69* lähmen
parcel: part and ~ *80* fester Bestandteil
parental leave *54* Elternzeit, Erziehungsurlaub
parity *67* Gleichheit, Parität
part: integral ~ *81* fester Bestandteil; **~ and parcel** *80* fester Bestandteil
parted lips *70* geöffnete Lippen
partial *120* teilweise, Teil-

participant *53* Teilnehmer/in
to **participate (in sth)** *27* (an etw) teilnehmen, sich (an etw) beteiligen
participation (in) *48* Teilnahme, Beteiligung (an)
particular *10* bestimmt, speziell; *137* Einzelheit
particularly *56* besonders, insbesondere
particulates *(pl)* *83* Feinstaub
partnership *58T* Partnerschaft
party: third-~ *86* von dritter Seite
passionate *25V* leidenschaftlich
pastel *25V* Pastell
pasture *97T* Weide
to **pat sb/sth** *102* jdn/etw tätscheln
patch *70* Fleck, Bereich
patchy *64* fleckig, durchwachsen
patient *76* Patient/in
patriotic *19* patriotisch
payload *90T* Nutzdaten
payment *56* (Be-)Zahlung
peace *106* Frieden
pedantic *112* kleinlich, spitzfindig
peddler *69* Bettler/in
to **peer** *120* prüfend blicken
pen pal *27* Brieffreund/in
pension *63* Rente, Pension
people smuggling *117* Menschenschmuggel
per capita *114V* pro Kopf
to **perceive sth** *22* etw wahrnehmen, etw erkennen
percentage *63* Prozentsatz, Anteil
perception *66T* Wahrnehmung
periodical *37* Zeitschrift
permissible *82* zulässig
to **perpetrate sth** *134* etw begehen, etw verüben *(Verbrechen)*
to **perpetuate sth** *63* etw aufrechterhalten
persecution *106* Verfolgung
to **persist** *82V* fortbestehen
persistence *70* Beharrlichkeit, Ausdauer
personnel manager *33* Personalchef/in
persuasion *8* Überzeugung, Überzeugungskunst
persuasive *9* überzeugend
to **pervade** *30* durchdringen
pervasive *23* um sich greifend, durchdringend
perverse *63* pervers, widersinnig
pest *76* Schädling
petitioner *122T* Antragsteller/in
phenomenon, *pl* **phenomena: phenomenon,** *pl* **phenomena** *11* Phänomen, Erscheinung
philosophical *82V* philosophisch
physical *30* körperlich, physisch
physician *82V* Arzt/Ärztin
physicist *77* Physiker/in
pidgin *15T* Pidgin, Mischsprache
piercing *71* durchdringend
pigeon *29* Taube
to **pile** *70* sich häufen, sich auftürmen
to **pioneer sth** *35* etw zum ersten Mal anwenden, etw entwickeln
pipe bomb *122T* Rohrbombe
pitfall *19* (Stolper-)Falle, Schwierigkeit
placatory *126* beschwichtigend
placement *26* Praktikum
plantation *94* Anpflanzung, Plantage
plausible *93* plausibel, glaubwürdig
plea *126* Bitte
pleasant *119* angenehm
pleasure *25V* Vergnügen, Freude
plenty *37* Überfluss
plenty of *40T* eine Menge, viel
plight *63* Notlage
to **plot to do sth** *103T* (heimlich) planen, etw zu tun
pneumatic tube *36* Rohrpost
poetry *8* Dichtung, Lyrik
point: to **~ at sb/sth** *7* auf jdn/etw zeigen; to **~ to sth** *11* auf etw hindeuten; **tipping ~** *108* Kipppunkt, kritischer Punkt, Wendepunkt
polarization *40T* Polarisierung
to **polish sth** *113* etw (auf)polieren
poll *127* Umfrage, Wahl; to **~** *127* abschneiden *(in einer Umfrage/Wahl)*
to **pollinate sth** *97T* etw bestäuben
pollinator *97T* Bestäuber
pollution *82V* (Umwelt-)Verschmutzung
populism *44* Populismus
populist *44* populistisch
portable *58T* tragbar, übertragbar
to **portray sb** *134* jdn porträtieren, jdn darstellen
to **pose sth** *76* etw darstellen
position: to **~ sb/sth** *58T* jdn/etw platzieren, jdn/etw positionieren; **senior ~** *58T* leitende Position
positive *23* Bejahung, Zustimmung
to **possess sth** *70* etw besitzen
possession *71* Besitz, Besitztum
postgraduate diploma *25V* Aufbaustudium
to **postulate sth** *77* etw annehmen *(These)*, etw postulieren
posture *8* (Körper-)Haltung
posturing *48* Getue
poultry *92* Geflügel
to **pour** *135* strömen
poverty *44* Armut
power: kinetic ~ *138T* Bewegungsenergie
powerhouse *92* treibende Kraft
powerless *70* machtlos, unfähig
practitioner *77* Fachmann/frau, Praktizierende/r
to **pray** *135* beten
prayer *71* Gebet
to **preach sth** *136* etw predigen
predecessor *44* Vorgänger/in, Vorläufer/in
predicament *121* Notlage
predicated: to **be ~ on sth** *97T* auf etw basieren
predictor *48* Prädiktor, Anzeichen (für)
predominantly *21* überwiegend
preference *50T* Präferenz, Vorliebe
premise *127* Prämisse, Voraussetzung
premised *82V* vorausgesetzt
prerequisite *82V* erforderlich, notwendig
to **prescribe sth** *94* etw verschreiben
preselection *61* Vorauswahl
present: at ~ *96* momentan, derzeit, zurzeit
to **preserve sth** *14* etw bewahren, etw erhalten
presidential election *40T* Präsidentschaftswahl
presumably *97T* vermutlich
prevailing *22* herrschend, allgemein geltend
prevalent *76* (weit) verbreitet, vorherrschend
to **prevent sb from doing sth** *36* jdn davon abhalten, etw zu tun
prevention *138* Prävention, Vorbeugung
previous *30* vorherig, früher
primacy of sth *90T* Primat von etw
primarily *90T* vorrangig, hauptsächlich
primary school *12* Grundschule
principle *12* Grundsatz, Prinzip
principles: guiding ethical principle *82V* ethische Leitlinie
print: hoof ~ *135* Hufabdruck
prior *103T* vorrangig
to **prioritise sth** *23* etw priorisieren
priority *23* Priorität, Vorrang
privacy *58T* Privatsphäre
to **privatize sth** *106* etw privatisieren
problem: to **tackle a ~** *52* ein Problem angehen
problematic *33T* problematisch
to **process sth** *66T* etw (weiter)verarbeiten
procession *70* Prozession
to **proclaim sth** *136* etw verkündigen
producer *81* Produzent/in
profession *79* Beruf
proficiency *122T* Können, Kenntnisse, Fähigkeiten
profound *117* tief greifend, tief gehend, fundiert
to **programme sth** *66* etw programmieren
to **progress** *82V* vorankommen, weiterkommen
prolonged *30* anhaltend, andauernd
prominent *111* bekannt, bedeutend
to **promote sth** *14* etw fördern, etw unterstützen
prompt *69* Stichwort, Vorgabe
prone to *46* anfällig für
prop *134* Requisite
to **propel sth** *106* etw (an)treiben
proper *22* ordentlich, angemessen
prophecy *38* Prophezeiung
prophet *135* Prophet/in
proponent *122T* Befürworter/in
proportion *55* Anteil
proposal *125* Vorschlag; **marriage ~** *91* Heiratsantrag
to **propose sth** *93* etw vorschlagen, etw unterbreiten, etw darlegen
to **prosecute sb** *78* jdn strafrechtlich verfolgen
prospect *26* Aussicht, Perspektive
prosperity *82V* Wohlstand
prosperous *63* florierend, wohlhabend
protection *29* Schutz, Schutzvorkehrung
protectionist *106* protektionistisch
protester *49* Demonstrant/in
to **prove** *13* sich erweisen (als)
proverb *25V* Sprichwort

to **provide sth** *8* etw (an)bieten, etw zur Verfügung stellen
provided (that) *12* vorausgesetzt, (dass)
provision *109* Bereitstellung, Versorgung
provocateur *33T* Provokateur/in
to **provoke** *31* provozieren
psychological *88* psychologisch
psychologist *8* Psychologe/-in
public health *97T* öffentliches Gesundheitswesen
puffy *135* geschwollen, aufgedunsen
pugnacious *126* kampflustig, streitsüchtig
pull-to-refresh *88* Pull to Refresh *(Ziehen zum Aktualisieren)*
pulse *70* Puls
punctuality *25V* Pünktlichkeit
to **punish sb** *63* jdn bestrafen
punishment *140* Strafe, Bestrafung
to **purchase sth** *50T* etw kaufen
pure *33T* rein, schier
purpose *8* Absicht, Zweck; to **serve a ~** *8* einem Zweck dienen
purposeful *101* zielgerichtet, zielstrebig
to **pursue sth** *24* einer Sache nachgehen, etw verfolgen
to **put sth forward** *82V* (Argument/Vorschlag) vorbringen, etw zur Diskussion stellen

Q

quantity *94* Menge, Quantität
quarter *38* Quartal
to **question sth** *82V* etw infrage stellen
questionable *76* fragwürdig, bedenklich
to **queue** *13* sich *(in einer Warteschlage)* anstellen, Schlange stehen
quota *38* Kontingent, Quote

R

race: arms ~ *88* Wettrüsten
racial *32* rassisch, Rassen-
radiation *76* Strahlung
radicalization *134* Radikalisierung
to **radicalize** *122T* sich radikalisieren
railroad *(AE)* *69* Eisenbahn
to **raise the stakes** *88* den Einsatz erhöhen
rallying cry *124* Parole, Schlachtruf
ramification *76* Auswirkung, Effekt
range *27* Bereich, Bandbreite, Palette; **free ~** *97T* Freiland(haltung); **mountain ~** *103* Gebirge, Gebirgszug
rank *57V* Dienstgrad; to **~ sb/sth** *114* jdn/etw einstufen, jdn/etw (ein-)ordnen
ranking (list) *30* Rangfolge, Rangliste
to **rankle sb** *33T* jdm zu schaffen machen
rape *48* Vergewaltigung
to **rate** *54* bewerten, beurteilen
rather than *15T* anstatt
ration *37* Ration, Zuteilung
rational *76* vernünftig, vernunftbegabt
ravaged *106* verwüstet
to **raze sth** *94* etw zerstören
to **readmit sb** *120* jdn wieder aufnehmen
realisation *27* Erkenntnis
reality *136* Gegebenheit
realm *76* Bereich
to **rear sb/sth** *92* jdn/etw aufziehen
reason: for this ~ *8* aus diesem Grund
reasonable *82V* vernünftig
rebellion *36* Rebellion, Aufstand
rebellious *36* aufsässig, rebellisch
to **recall sth** *22* sich an etw erinnern; *38* etw zurückrufen
recess *36* Nische, Winkel
recipient *9* Empfänger/in
reciprocal *63* reziprok, gegenseitig
to **recircuit sth** *66T* etw neu verdrahten, etw neu verschalten
to **recite** *136* etw vortragen
to **reclaim** *47* zurückfordern, zurückerobern
recognition *63* (An-)Erkennung, (Wieder-)Erkennen
record: on ~ *38* aktenkundig, dokumentiert; to **speak on the ~** *30* sich offiziell äußern
recorded *38* dokumentiert, erfasst
recording *122* Aufnahme, Aufzeichnung
to **recreate** *33* wiederherstellen, nachbauen
recruit *57V* Rekrut/in
to **rectify** *37* berichtigen, richtigstellen
to **redefine sth** *50T* etwas neu umbenennen, etw neu definieren
to **redesign sth** *80* etw überarbeiten, etw umgestalten
to **redraft sth** *80* etw neu entwerfen
reduction *37* Verringerung, Senkung
reductionist *80* reduktionistisch
refer: to **~ to sb/sth** *30* jdn/etw erwähnen, sich auf jdn/etw beziehen; to **~ to sb/sth as** *11* jdn/etw bezeichnen als
to **reflect sth** *7* etw reflektieren, etw widerspiegeln
reflection *70* Reflexion, Nachdenken
reflective *32* nachdenklich, reflektierend
reform *64* Reform
refresh: pull-to-~ *88* Pull to Refresh *(Ziehen zum Aktualisieren)*
refusal *120* Ablehnung, Verweigerung
to **refuse sth** *25V* etw verweigern, etw ablehnen
to **regard** *25V* schätzen, würdigen
regardless of sth *24* ungeachtet einer Sache
regeneration *94* Wiederherstellung, Erneuerung
regenerative *94* regenerativ, erneuerbar
regime *44* Regime
regulation *131* Vorschrift; **safety ~s** *(pl)* *76* Sicherheitsvorschriften, Arbeitsschutzvorschriften
regulatory agency *86* Aufsichtsbehörde, Regulierungsagentur
to **reissue** *38* neu auflegen
to **reject** *32* ablehnen, zurückweisen
rejection *108* Ablehnung
to **rejig** *(BE)* / **rejigger** *(AE)* **sth** *66T* etw ändern
to **relapse into sth** *119* wieder in etw zurückfallen
to **relate to sb/sth** *139* einen Bezug zu jdm/etw haben, mit jdm/etw in Zusammenhang stehen
related: to **be ~ to sth** *78* mit etw in Zusammenhang setzen
relation *29* Beziehung, Verhältnis
release: weapon ~ *100* Waffenfreigabe, -abwurf
to **relent** *136* einlenken, nachgeben
relevance: to **have ~** *74* von Bedeutung sein
reliability *82V* Zuverlässigkeit, Verlässlichkeit
relief *135* Erleichterung, Entlastung, Linderung
to **rely on sb/sth** *95* sich auf jdn/etw verlassen
to **remain** *10* bleiben
to **remake (remade, remade)** *62* erneuern
remedy *62* Heilmittel; to **~ sth** *82V* etw abhelfen
reminder *102* Erinnerung, Mahnung
remorse *136* Reue
remotely *100* aus der Ferne
removal *31* Entfernung
remove: to **~ sth** *29* etw entfernen, etw beseitigen; **at a ~** *80* mit Abstand
to **render** *106* machen
to **renege on sth** *118* etw nicht einhalten
to **renounce sth** *76* etw widerrufen
to **repel sb** *126* jdn abstoßen
repetition *26* Wiederholung
repetitive *16* sich ständig wiederholend, *(z.B. Arbeit)* monoton
reportedly *40T* Berichten zufolge
to **represent sth** *15T* etw ausmachen, etw repräsentieren
representative *25V* Vertreter/in, Beauftragte/r; **sales ~** *20* Handelsvertreter/in
repression *70* Verdrängung, Zurückdrängung
to **reprint** *37* nachdrucken, neu auflegen
reprise *33T* Reprise, Wiederholung
reproach *24* Vorwurf, Anschuldigung
reproductive medicine *76* Reproduktionsmedizin
repulsed *137* angewidert
reputation *119* Ansehen, Ruf
researcher *20* Forscher/in, Wissenschaftler/in
resentment *48* Unmut, Groll, Ressentiment
to **reserve** *30* reservieren, sich vorbehalten
to **reside** *122T* residieren, ansässig sein
resignation *20* Kündigung
to **resist sth** *31* einer Sache widerstehen
resistance *106* Widerstand
resistant (to sth) *94* resistent (gegen etw)
resolution *110* Vorsatz, Entschluss

to **resolve sth** *33T* etw (auf)lösen
to **resonate** *62* widerhallen, mitschwingen
resourced *30* ausgestattet
respective *58* jeweilig
respectively *92* beziehungsweise
to **respond** *7* antworten, reagieren
respondent *42* Befragte/r
responsibility: to **abdicate ~** *118* sich aus der Verantwortung ziehen
responsible: to **hold sb ~** *79* jdn zur Verantwortung ziehen
to **restore sth** *97T* etw restaurieren, etw wieder aufbauen
to **restrict** *58T* einschränken, beschränken
restriction *30* Beschränkung, Einschränkung
restrictionist *122T* Restriktionist *(Befürworter der Beschränkung)*
restructuring *45* Umstrukturierung
to **result in sth** *22* zu etw führen
retailer *64* Einzelhändler/in
to **retain sb/sth** *39* jdn/etw behalten, etw beibehalten, etw bewahren
to **rethink (rethought, rethought)** *44* überdenken
to **retire** *72* sich zurückziehen
to **retrain** *66T* umlernen, umschulen
retreat *44* Rückzug, Rückgang
return *63* Ertrag, Rendite
reunification *82V* Wiedervereinigung
to **revel** *135* feiern, schwelgen, ausgelassen sein
revelation *58T* Enthüllung
revenge killing *103T* Rachemord
revenue *90T* Einkünfte, Einnahmen
to **revere sb** *87* jdn verehren
reverence *33T* Verehrung
to **reverse sth** *96* etw rückgängig machen
to **review sth** *114V* etw bewerten, etw prüfen
to **revisit sth** *126* nochmals zurückkommen auf etw
to **revolve** *76* rotieren, sich drehen
reward *88* Belohnung; to **~ sb** *87* jdn belohnen
rhetoric *114V* Redekunst, Phrasendrescherei
rhetorical *48* rhetorisch
rhetorical device *8* Stilmittel
ride-hailing *50T* einen Fahrdienst in Anspruch nehmen
to **ridicule sb** *49* jdn lächerlich machen
ridiculous *20* lächerlich, unglaublich
right: sovereign ~ *130* Hoheitsrecht
righteous *134* rechtschaffen, gerecht
rightfully *80* rechtmäßig, zu Recht
right-hand *36* rechte/r/s, auf der rechten Seite
rightly *8* mit/zu Recht
right-wing *33* *(politisch)* rechts
rigorous *122T* streng, drastisch, rigoros
to **ring out (rang, rung)** *135* erschallen
riot: to **run ~** *71* randalieren, toben
to **rip sth up** *118* etw zerreißen
ripple *126* Welle
rogue: to **go ~** *87* abtrünnig werden
roomy *69* geräumig
root *11* Wurzel
rotational grazing *94* Rotationsweiden
roughly *46* ungefähr, etwa
route: en ~ *102* auf dem Weg
routed *82V* verwurzelt
row *77* Reihe, Zeile
to **rule out sth** *76* etw ausschließen
ruling *33* Entscheidung
run: to **~ riot** *71* randalieren, toben; **in the long ~** *14* auf lange Sicht, langfristig

S

sacred *135* heilig
to **sacrifice sth** *112* etw opfern
safeguard *82V* Schutzmaßnahme
safety regulations *(pl)* *76* Sicherheitsvorschriften, Arbeitsschutzvorschriften
sake: for heaven's ~ *69* um Himmels willen; **for the ~ of sth** *67* einer Sache zuliebe, einer Sache wegen
sales representative *20* Handelsvertreter/in
sandwiched between sth *23* zwischen etw gelegt, eingeklemmt von etw
to **sanitize sth** *119* etw säubern, etw zensieren
to **sap** *64* schwächen, untergraben
satanic *135* satanisch, unmoralisch
satisfaction *55* Zufriedenheit
to **saunter** *134* schlendern
savannah *82V* Savanne
save *70* außer
savvy *48* versiert, gewieft, erfahren
scale *62* Ausmaß, Umfang
scarce *93* knapp, rar
scarcity *63* Mangel, Knappheit
to **scare sb** *50T* jdn erschrecken, jdm Angst machen
scent *70* Duft
schedule: tight ~ *20* enger Zeitplan
schema *66T* Schema
scheme *27* Programm, Projekt
scholar *33T* Gelehrte/r
scientific *15T* wissenschaftlich
to **scoff at sb/sth** *33T* über jdn/etw spotten
to **scoop up sth** *94* etw an Bord holen
scope *79* Rahmen, Umfang
scorching *136* Brennen
scornful *134* spöttisch, verächtlich
scramble (for sth) *64* Gerangel (um etw)
scrap *36* Stück, Fragment
to **scrape sth** *136* sich an etw kratzen, schrammen
to **screen sb from sth** *71* jdn von etw abschirmen
screenplay *134* Drehbuch
to **scuttle** *135* trippeln
seamless *22* nahtlos
secessionist *126* Abtrünnige/r
secondary *139* sekundär, zweitrangig; **~ school** *13* weiterführende Schule
to **secure sth** *22* (sich) etw sichern, etw sicherstellen
Securities and Exchange Commission *90T* Börsenaufsichtsbehörde *(USA)*
security *138T* Sicherheit
security blanket *47* Rettungsdecke
sedentary *65* sitzend
seductive *88* verführerisch
seed *131* Samen, Saat(gut), Keim
to **seek out sth (sought, sought)** *82V* etw ausfindig machen
seemingly *36* scheinbar, anscheinend
to **seize on sth** *55* etw aufgreifen, etw ergreifen
to **select sb/sth** *78* jdn/etw (aus) wählen
selection *18* Auswahl
self-confident *19* selbstsicher
self-defence *40* Selbstverteidigung
self-determination *126* Selbstbestimmung
self-evidently *110* selbstverständlich
self-indulgent *135* ausschweifend, maßlos
selfishness *82V* Egoismus, Selbstsucht
self-restraint *134* Selbstbeherrschung
self-subsistent *136* selbsterhaltend
senior *8* leitend, älter, ranghöher; *83* Vorgesetzte/r; **~ position** *58T* leitende Position
sensation *103T* Gefühl, Empfinden
sensational *112* reißerisch, effekthascherisch
sense: common ~ *91* gesunder Menschenverstand; **~ (of)** *25* Sinn (für)
sensible *45* vernünftig, sinnvoll
sensitive *21* empfindlich, sensibel
sentiment *82V* Geisteshaltung
separately *20* einzeln
separation *136* Trennung
separatism *105* Separatismus, Loslösungsbestreben
seriousness *21* Seriosität, Ernsthaftigkeit
to **serve a purpose** *8* einem Zweck dienen
service *13* Dienst, Dienstleistung
session *26* Sitzung, Termin, Treffen
to **set off sth** *64* etw in Gang setzen
to **set up (set, set)** *40T* planen, arrangieren
setback *131* Rückschlag
to **settle a lawsuit** *58T* einen Rechtsstreit beilegen
settlement *11* Siedlung, Kolonie
sexist *8* sexistisch
sexual harassment *21* sexuelle Belästigung
shameful *126* schändlich
to **shape sth** *15T* etw formen
sharp *135* scharf
shell *135* Muschel, Gehäuse
shift *63* Verschiebung, Verlagerung, Wandel; to **~** *44* (sich) verlagern, (sich) verändern
shifty eyes *134* unsteter Blick
shiny *109* glänzend
shooter: mass ~ *48* Amokschütze /-schützin
shooting *47* Schießerei
to **shorten sth** *90* etw (ver)kürzen
shortly *37* bald, in Kürze
to **shrink** *55* schrumpfen
shrouded *93* verschleiert, eingehüllt
shudder *71* Schauder, Zittern
to **shut down (shut, shut)** *78* schließen
sibling *82V* Geschwister

to **signal** *21* signalisieren
significance *37* Bedeutung, Stellenwert
to **silence sb** *30* jdn zum Schweigen bringen
similarity *15T* Ähnlichkeit
to **simmer** *114V* köcheln
simultaneous *12* gleichzeitig
sin *136* Sünde
sinful *135* sündig
situation: dire ~ *118* bedrohliche Lage
skilled *12* erfahren, geübt
to **skip sth** *138* etw überspringen, etw auslassen
to **slash sth** *122T* etw *(drastisch)* reduzieren, etw senken
Slavic *21* slawisch
slender *70* schmal, feingliedrig
to **slide (slid, slid)** *39* rutschen, gleiten
slight *15T* gering
slim *61* schlank
slime *135* Schleim
slip *38* Versehen, Irrtum
slit *36* Schlitz
slur *33T* Verleumdung
snail *135* Schnecke (mit Schneckenhaus)
snap streak *88* Schnappschuss-Serie, „Flamme" *(Snapchat)*
to **snatch sth up** *137* etw ergreifen
to **sneak** *135* schleichen
to **sneer** *134* grinsen
to **soar** *63* steigen
sob *70* Schluchzer; to ~ *70* schluchzen
sobering *62* ernüchternd
socialization *90T* Sozialisierung
society: civil ~ *94* Zivilgesellschaft; **consumerist ~** *44* Konsumgesellschaft
sociologist *82V* Soziologe/-in
to **soften** *23* mildern, abmildern
softness *136* Sanftheit, Schwäche
soil *94* Erde, Boden; **~ erosion** *93* Bodenerosion
sole (of your shoes) *22* (Schuh-)Sohle
solidarity *8* Solidarität
sophisticated *77* raffiniert, anspruchsvoll
of sorts *87* so etwas wie
soul *69* Seele
sound *129* solide, vernünftig
source *13* Quelle, Herkunft
sovereign right *130* Hoheitsrecht
soya *97T* Soja
soybean *(AE) 93* Sojabohne
span *47* Spanne
to **spark** *66T* zünden, Feuer fangen
sparrow *69* Spatz, Sperling
species, *pl* **species** *94* Art *(Biologie)*
specific *12* bestimmt, speziell, spezifisch
speckled: trash-~ *135* mit Müll gesprenkelt
spectacles *(pl) 36* Brille
spectacular *35* sensationell, spektakulär
to **speculate on/about sth** *125* sich über etw Gedanken machen
to **spin around (spun, spun)** *101* sich drehen, herumwirbeln
spiral *135* Spirale; to ~ *137* sich schrauben, sich winden
to **split (up)** *15* sich trennen, sich aufteilen
spoke *66T* Speiche
spokesperson *30* Sprecher/in
spouse *122T* Ehepartner/in
square *102* Planquadrat
to **squint** *102* schielen, spähen
stabbing *106* Messerstecherei
staffed *100* (mit Personal) besetzt
to **stage sth** *15* etw inszenieren, etw veranstalten, etw aufführen
to **stagger** *54* staffeln; to ~ **sb** *97T* jdn überwältigen
staggering *97T* niederschmetternd
stained: travel-~ *71* schmutzig von der Reise
stake: to **be at ~** *44* auf dem Spiel stehen
stakes: to **raise the ~** *88* den Einsatz erhöhen
stance *82V* Haltung, Einstellung
to **stand out** *47* auffallen, herausstechen
standard-bearer *33T* Bannerträger/in, Vorkämpfer/in
standpoint *22* Standpunkt
stare *70* starrer Blick
startling *118* alarmierend, erschreckend, erstaunlich
to **starve** *94* verhungern
to **state** *38* erklären, feststellen; **mental ~** *90T* psychische Verfassung
statistical *32* statistisch
to **stay in touch** *12* in Verbindung/ Kontakt bleiben
stead: in its ~ *37* an seiner/ihrer Stelle
steadfast *48* standhaft
steamboat *131* Dampfer
steed *136* Ross
steel *110* Stahl
to **steer sth** *80* etw steuern, etw lenken
to **stem from sth** *47* sich ableiten von etw
to **stick to sth (stuck, stuck)** *46* bei etw bleiben, sich an etw halten
stillness *72* Stille
to **stir sth** *135* etw rühren, etw mischen
stock: ~ exchange *63* (Wertpapier-) Börse; to **take ~** *33T* Bestand aufnehmen, Bilanz ziehen
to **stockpile** *47* horten
stocky *101* untersetzt
to **stoke sth** *135* etw schüren, etw anfachen
storm in a teapot *31* Sturm im Wasserglas
to **strain to do sth** *136* sich anstrengen etw zu tun
stranded: to **be ~** *120* festsitzen, gestrandet sein
stranglehold *134* Würgegriff
to **strap on sth** *138T* sich etw umschnallen
streak: snap ~ *88* Schnappschuss-Serie, „Flamme" *(Snapchat)*
to **strengthen** *8* kräftigen, stärken
to **stress sth** *103* etw betonen, etw hervorheben
to **strike a chord with sb (struck, struck)** *87* bei jdm auf Anklang stoßen
to **strike sb** *15T* jdn treffen, jdm auffallen
to **strip sth away** *94* etw wegräumen
to **strive** *70* streben, bemüht sein
structural *64* Struktur-, strukturell
to **strut** *134* stolzieren
stubborn *50* störrisch
studs: navel stud *134* Nabelstecker
to **stumble across sth** *88* zufällig über etw stolpern
to **stump sb** *48* jdn verwirren, jdn aus der Fassung bringen
stylistic *57* stilistisch
sublime *137* unvergleichlich, erhaben
to **submit** *19* einreichen, vorlegen, zusenden
to **subscribe to sth** *58T* etw abonnieren
subscription *90T* Abonnement
subsequent *55* nachfolgend, anschließend
to **subside** *13* zurückgehen, verebben, zurückgehen
subsidiary *20* Tochterunternehmen, Filiale
subsidy *64* Subvention
to **substitute for sb/sth** *37* jdn/etw ersetzen
substitution *38* Austausch, Auswechslung
subtle *70* subtil, fein
to **succeed** *48* erfolgreich sein, Erfolg haben
such as *13* wie (zum Beispiel)
to **sue** *33T* verklagen
sufficient *11* ausreichend, hinreichend
suicide *72* Selbstmord
to **suit sb/sth** *15T* zu jdm/etw passen
summit *106* Gipfel(treffen)
superbugs *94* Superkeime
superficial *113* oberflächlich, vordergründig
superiority *120* Überlegenheit
to **supervise sb** *108* jdn beaufsichtigen
to **supply sth** *103* etw liefern, etw bieten, etw bereitstellen
supporter *40T* Anhänger/in
to **suppose** *15T* annehmen
supposedly *44* vermeintlich, angeblich
suppression *126* Unterdrückung
supranational *106* länderübergreifend
supremacist *29* Rassist/in, Verfechter/ in der Rassentrennung
surface *93* Oberfläche; to ~ **sth** *138T* etw aufgreifen
surgery *45* Operation
to **surround sth** *30* etw umgeben
surrounding *25V* Umgebung
to **surveil sb/sth** *78* jdn/etw überwachen
surveillance *78* Überwachung
susceptibility *88* Empfänglichkeit, Anfälligkeit
suspected *140* mutmaßlich
suspension *70* Aussetzung
to **sustain sth** *86* etw (aufrecht)erhalten, etw (unter)stützen
sustainability *94* Nachhaltigkeit

to **sway** *134* sich wiegen
sweatshop *119* Ausbeutungsbetrieb
to **swell sth** *135* etw anschwellen lassen
swiftly *121* rasch, flugs
to **swipe** *88* wischen *(auf dem Touchscreen)*
syllabus *30* Lehrplan
sympathy *45* Sympathie, Mitgefühl
symposium *53* Fachkonferenz
to **synthesize sth** *82V* etw synthetisieren, etw künstlich herstellen
system: feeder ~ *138T* Zuführungssystem

T

tabloid (newspaper) *31* Boulevardzeitung
to **tackle a problem** *52* ein Problem angehen
tactile *19* taktil *(berührt gerne Menschen)*
tailored *88* maßgeschneidert
take: to **~ advantage of sth** *106* sich etw zunutze machen, etw ausnutzen; to **~ care of sb** *57* sich um jdn kümmern; to **~ into account** *33* berücksichtigen
tale: cautionary ~ *90T* abschreckendes Beispiel
talented *63* begabt, talentiert
tank: think ~ *109* Expertenkommission, Denkfabrik
tar *135* Teer
target: named ~ *102* benanntes Ziel, namentlich bekannte Zielperson
tariff *107* Tarif; *110* Handelszoll
tarp: camo ~ *101* Tarnplane
tax *45* Steuer
teapot: storm in a ~ *31* Sturm im Wasserglas
to **tear apart (tore, torn)** *118* auseinanderreißen
technical *76* technisch
telescreen *36* Televisor
tell *101* verräterisches Zeichen, Hinweis
tempted *126* versucht
to **tend to do sth** *12* dazu neigen, etw zu tun
tendency *82V* Neigung, Tendenz
tender *69* zart
tenet *138T* Grundsatz, Lehre
tense *20* angespannt, verkrampft
tension *30* Spannung
terms: in ~ of … *58T* was … betrifft/angeht
to **testify** *75* aussagen
the likes of sth *94* solche wie etw
thee *136* dich, dir *(veraltet oder auf Gott bezogen)*
theft *78* Diebstahl
thereby *44* dabei, dadurch
therefore *16* daher, deshalb, demzufolge
think tank *109* Expertenkommission, Denkfabrik
third party *86* von dritter Seite
thought *23* Gedanke
thread *135* Faden, Strang
threat *29* Bedrohung
thrilled *50T* begeistert
thrilling *139* aufregend, erregend
thriving *63* florierend, blühend, gedeihend
throughout … *13* der/die/das ganze … (hindurch), überall in …
thus *8* daher, deshalb, somit
to **thwart sth** *138T* etw verhindern, etw vereiteln
tight schedule *20* enger Zeitplan
to **tighten sth** *140* etw anziehen, etw verschärfen
time frame *46* Zeitrahmen
to **tinge sth** *136* etw färben
tipping point *108* Kipppunkt, kritischer Punkt, Wendepunkt
titled *16* betitelt
to **be to do sth** *24* etw tun sollen
tobacco *88* Tabak
tolerance *12* Toleranz, Verständnis
tons of *50T* jede Menge
toolbox *55* Werkzeugkasten
topless *31* oben ohne
to **topple** *119* stürzen
torment *136* Folter, Qual
towering *136* emporragend, gewaltig
toxic *55* toxisch, giftig, Gift-
to **trace sth** *23* etw (zurück)verfolgen
trade *63* Handel; **~ pact** *114V* Handelsabkommen; **~ union** *55* Gewerkschaft
trade-off *138T* Ausgleich, Abwägung, Kompromiss
traditionalist *25* traditionell, traditionalistisch
tragic *120* tragisch
trait *22* Wesenszug, Eigenschaft
transition *44* Übergang, Umstellung
to **translate** *9* übersetzen, (sich) übertragen (lassen)
transnational *109* transnational, grenzübergreifend
transparency *40T* Transparenz
trash: to **~ sth** *97T* etw demolieren; **~-speckled** *135* mit Müll gesprenkelt
travel-stained *71* schmutzig von der Reise
trawling net *93* Schleppnetz
to **treat** *21* behandeln
treatable *94* behandelbar
trial *82V* Untersuchung, Studie; **clinical ~** *76* klinische Prüfung, klinische Studie
trickle-down economics *108* Trickle-Down-Wirtschaft *(Theorie, dass Wirtschaftswachstum allen zugute kommt)*
to **trigger sth** *30* etw auslösen
triumph *71* Triumph
trivial *70* belanglos
trouble *63* Ärger, Problem(e)
truly *136* in Wahrheit
tumultuous *70* tumultartig, ungestüm
to **turn out to be …** *14* sich erweisen/herausstellen als …
to **twitter** *69* zwitschern
typeface *8* Schrift(art)

U

ubiquitous *87* allgegenwärtig
ultimate *58T* ultimativ, letzte/r/s
ultimately *106* letztlich, letztendlich
umbilical cord *58* Nabelschnur
unaccustomed *23* ungewohnt, nicht gewöhnt
unambiguously *79* eindeutig
unaware: to **be ~ of sth** *87* sich einer Sache nicht bewusst sein
uncertain *38* unsicher
unclean *135* unrein
unconscious *66T* unbewusst, unterbewusst
unconstitutional *129* verfassungswidrig
unconvincing *136* nicht überzeugend
under her breath *70* flüsternd
to **undercut** *33T* untergraben
to **underestimate sb/sth** *25* jdn/etw unterschätzen
to **undergo sth** *44* sich einer Sache unterziehen
to **underpin sth** *110* etw (ab)stützen, etw untermauern
understandable *16* verständlich
undertone *136* Unterton, Grundstimmung
underway *31* im Gange, angelaufen
undeserved *120* unverdient
undoubtedly *13* zweifellos
uneasy *20* besorgt, unbehaglich, mulmig
unemployment *58T* Arbeitslosigkeit
unethical *100* unethisch
unexpected *136* unerwartet
to **unfold** *138T* sich entwickeln, sich abspielen
unforgiving *136* gnadenlos, unerbittlich
to **unify** *15T* vereinigen, vereinheitlichen
unilateral *126* einseitig
unimaginable *76* unvorstellbar
unimpressed *46* unbeeindruckt
unintelligible *11* unverständlich
unintended *80* unbeabsichtigt
unintentional *63* unbeabsichtigt
union *29* Gewerkschaft; **trade ~** *55* Gewerkschaft
unique *97T* einzigartig
uniqueness *106* Einzigartigkeit
to **unite** *105* etw vereinen, etw vereinigen
unity *106* Einheit
universal *11* universell, allgemein, weltweit
unjust *53* ungerecht
to **unleash sth** *100* etw auslösen, etw entfesseln
unofficial *40T* inoffiziell
unpleasant *80* unangenehm, unschön
unpopular *20* unbeliebt, unpopulär
unprecedented *13* beispiellos, einmalig, noch nie da gewesen
to **unravel sth** *118* etw entwirren, etw enträtseln
unreasonable *32* unvernünftig, unangemessen
unregulated *94* ungeregelt
unrepeatable *13* nicht wiederholbar, einmalig
to **unroll** *36* ausrollen
unscathed *135* unversehrt
to **unscramble sth** *97T* etw entflechten
unsolved *71* ungelöst

BILDQUELLENVERZEICHNIS

S. 7/1: Shutterstock / Shelly Still; **S. 7/2:** Shutterstock / Akuma-Photo; **S. 7/3:** Shutterstock / VovanIvanovich; **S. 9:** Shutterstock / Lightspring; **S. 12:** Shutterstock / pathdoc; **S. 13:** Shutterstock / Good Mood; **S. 16:** Shutterstock / Ditty_about_summer; **S. 17:** Prof. Dr. Ulrich Ammon, Universität Duisburg-Essen / Geisteswissenschaft; **S. 18/1:** Shutterstock / Cienpies Design; **S. 18/2:** Shutterstock / Cienpies Design; **S. 22:** Shutterstock / TierneyMJ; **S. 25/1–4:** CapitalRose; **S. 27/1:** Shutterstock / Monkey Business Images; **S. 27/2:** Shutterstock / Robert Davies; **S. 30:** ddp images / intertopics; **S. 31:** ddp images / intertopics / Evening Standard; **S. 36:** Shutterstock / Anita Ponne; **S. 37:** Shutterstock / Monster Ztudio; **S. 38/1:** Bridgeman Images / Granger; **S. 38/2:** Shutterstock / aodaodaodaod; **S. 40:** Shutterstock / BigNazik; **S. 42:** dpa Picture-Alliance / Uwe Zucchi; **S. 43/1:** Shutterstock / Rob Crandall; **S. 43/2:** Shutterstock / Ing. Andrej Kaprinay; **S. 43/3:** Shutterstock / Artisticco; **S. 45:** Shutterstock / MR.Yanukit; **S. 47:** Laif / REPORT DIGITAL-REA / Jim WEST; **S. 51:** Shutterstock / LStockStudio; **S. 53/1:** FPI Fair Pay Innovation Lab gGmbH Berlin; **S. 53/2:** Shutterstock / Ollyy; **S. 55:** Shutterstock / kondrukhov; **S. 59:** Cartoonstock / Baloo-Rex May; **S. 61/1:** Shutterstock / ESB Professional; **S. 61/2:** Shutterstock / J Dennis; **S. 61/3:** Shutterstock / Sangoiri; **S. 62/1:** Shutterstock / Patricia Hofmeester; **S. 62/2:** Shutterstock / Stripped Pixel; **S. 63:** Shutterstock / Elnur; **S. 64:** Shutterstock / Hyejin Kang; **S. 67/1:** Cartoonstock / Larry Lambert; **S. 67/2:** Statista / Brookings Institute; **S. 70:** Shutterstock / lzf; **S. 71:** Shutterstock / Eugene Zagatin; **S. 74/1:** The Curious Incident of the Night-Time, Shutterstock / Alexey Fedorenko; **S. 74/2:** The Secret Life of Bees, Shutterstock / bananadd13; **S. 74/3:** Brave New World, Shutterstock / Romolo Tavani; **S. 74/4:** Never Let Me Go, Shutterstock / Barbara Delgado; **S. 74/5:** Buckingham Palace, District Six, Shutterstock / littlewormy; **S. 75/1:** Shutterstock / Pixelbliss; **S. 75/2:** Shutterstock / Natchapon Srihon; **S. 75/3:** Shutterstock / Paul Fleet; **S. 75/4:** Shutterstock / gualtiero boffi; **S. 75/5:** dpa Picture-Alliance / Con / Ron Sachs; **S. 75/6:** Shutterstock / Rawpixel.com; **S. 75/7:** Imago stock&people / Leemage; **S. 75/8:** ddp images / United Archives; **S. 77/1:** Bridgeman Images / SZ Photo / Gerhard Blank; **S. 77/2:** Mauritius images / alamy / Art Directors & TRIP; **S. 77/3:** Süddeutsche Zeitung Photo / TopFoto / United Archives; **S. 77/4:** Bridgeman Images / Granger; **S. 77/5:** Shutterstock / Everett Historical; **S. 77/6:** Shutterstock / Everett Historical; **S. 79:** Shutterstock / Gorodenkoff; **S. 82:** Lennart-Berna-dotte-Haus in Lindau; **S. 84:** Shutterstock / Triff; **S. 85:** Shutterstock / Lukasz Z; **S. 87/1:** Shutterstock / DisobeyArt; **S. 87/2:** Shutterstock / BLACKDAY; **S. 91:** Cartoonstock / Daniel Beyer; **S. 93/1:** Shutterstock / FR.Agro; **S. 93/2:** Shutterstock / Dimitrios Vlassis; **S. 99:** dpa Picture-Alliance / dpa Infografik; **S. 101:** Shutterstock / Gorodenkoff; **S. 104:** Cartoonstock / Harley Schwadron; **S. 105/1:** Cartoonstock / Mike Baldwin; **S. 105/2:** Shutterstock / Michael Wick; **S. 105/3:** shutterstock / AlexLMX; **S. 105/4:** Cartoonstock / Chris Madden; **S. 105/5:** Cartoonstock / BART; **S. 105/6:** Shutterstock / Tashatuvango; **S. 105/7:** Shutterstock / Artem Oleshko; **S. 105/8:** Shutterstock / Seita; **S. 105/9:** Cartoonstock / Dan Collins; **S. 105/10:** Shutterstock / JMiks; **S. 105/11:** Shutterstock / WindVector; **S. 105/12:** Shutterstock / oneinchpunch; **S. 105/13:** Shutterstock / Hi-Vector; **S. 105/14:** akg-images / Jason Hook; **S. 105/15:** Shutterstock / one photo; **S. 105/16:** Shutterstock / Uniyok; **S. 107:** Shutterstock / Rawpixel.com; **S. 108/1:** Shutterstock / Nerthuz; **S. 108/2:** ddp images / Alex Milan Tracy / Sipa USA; **S. 108/3:** ddp images / CrowdSpark / Brais G. Rouco; **S. 109:** Shutterstock / NORRIE3699; **S. 110:** Shutterstock / M-SUR; **S. 116:** Cagle Cartoons Inc., Santa Barbara; **S. 117/1:** Laif / contrasto / Giulio Piscitelli; **S. 117/2:** Laif / eyevine / Alicia Canter; **S. 117/3:** Visum / Panos Pictures / PANOS / Tristan Vickers; **S. 117/4:** Shutterstock / Savvapanf Photo; **S. 118:** Shutterstock / Maren Winter; **S. 119:** Shutterstock / Photomarine; **S. 126:** Mauritius images / age fotostock / Rafael Campillo; **S. 132:** Shutterstock / canadastock; **S. 133:** Shutterstock / areporter; **S. 134:** Shutterstock / ildintorlak; **S. 136:** Shutterstock / Prachaya Roekdeethaweesab; **S. 140/1:** Shutterstock / Wilm Ihlenfeld; **S. 140/2:** Shutterstock / ANURAKE SINGTO-ON; **S. 140/3:** Shutterstock / KAE CH; **S. 140/4:** Shutterstock / Rawpixel.com; **S. 140/5:** Shutterstock / John Kehly; **S. 142/1:** Shutterstock / Creativa Images; **S. 142/2:** Shutterstock / Eiko Tsuchiya; **S. 142/3:** Shutterstock / Monkey Business Images; **S. 142/4:** Shutterstock / Konstantin Chagin; **S. 142/5:** Shutterstock / BrAt82; **S. 143/1:** Shutterstock / michaeljung; **S. 143/2:** Shutterstock / Monkey Business Images; **S. 143/3:** Shutterstock / Patricia Soon; **S. 143/4:** Shutterstock / aerogondo2; **S. 143/5:** Shutterstock / My Life Graphic; **S. 144/1:** Shutterstock / hafakot; **S. 144/2:** Shutterstock / whiteMocca; **S. 144/3:** Shutterstock / Dan Race; **S. 144/4:** Shutterstock / Natali_ Mis; **S. 144/5:** Shutterstock / stoatphoto; **S. 146/1:** Shutterstock / Peteri; **S. 146/2:** Shutterstock / Merla; **S. 146/3:** Shutterstock / maradon 333; **S. 146/4:** Shutterstock / Ints Vikmanis; **S. 146/5:** Shutterstock / Georgios Alexandris

Canada & United States of America

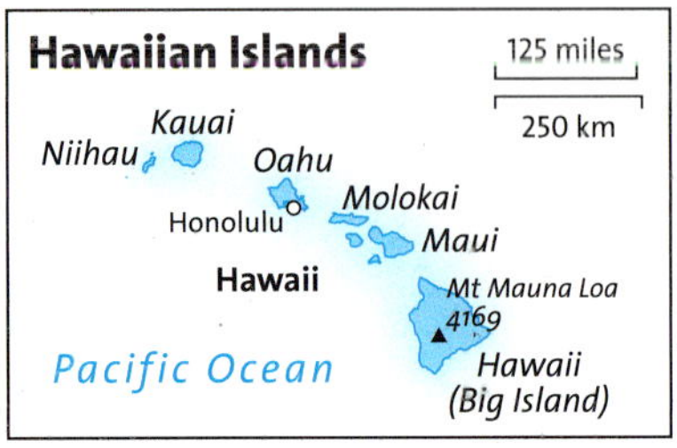

Abbreviations CANADA:
NB = New Brunswick
P.E.I. = Prince Edward Island

Abbreviations UNITED STATES:
CT = Connecticut
DE = Delaware
NH = New Hampshire
NJ = New Jersey
MA = Massachusetts
MD = Maryland
PA = Pennsylvania
RI = Rhode Island
VT = Vermont